Microsoft® XNA™ Game Studio Creator's Guide

An Introduction to XNA Game Programming

Contents at a Glance

Contents

20   Lighting   **309**

Lighting Methods,   310

> *Source Lights,   310*
>
> *Reflective Lighting Properties of Materials,   310*
>
> *Reflective Normals,   311*

Implementing Directional Lighting Using XNA's
BasicEffect Class,   312

> *BasicEffect Default Lighting,   312*
>
> *Directional Lighting Example,   313*

Implementing Point Light Using the Phong Reflection Model,   318

> *Calculating Point Light,   320*
>
> *Point Light in the Pixel Shader Example,   320*
>
> *Point Light in the Vertex Shader Example,   329*

Chapter 20 Review Exercises,   330

21   Input Devices   **333**

Handling Keyboard Input,   334

Handling Mouse Input,   335

Handling Controller Input,   335

> *Game Pad States,   335*
>
> *Handling Pressed and Released States,   336*
>
> *Thumbsticks,   337*
>
> *Triggers,   337*
>
> *Adjusting the Input Device Responsiveness,   337*
>
> *Adding a Rumble,   338*
>
> *Input Example,   338*

Chapter 21 Review Exercises,   352

22   Content Pipeline Processors   **353**

Content Processors,   354

> *ContentImporter,   355*
>
> *ContentTypeWriter,   355*
>
> *ContentTypeReader,   355*

Custom Content Processor Example,   356

> *Building a Custom Content Processor in Windows,   356*
>
> *Implementing Your Custom Content Processor
> on the Xbox 360,   363*

Chapter 22 Review Exercises,   364

Acknowledgments

Stephen Thanks again to Patrick Chin, who has helped me with many book projects and has also taught me a few lessons in humility while playing *Halo 2* no-scope sniper games. I'd also like to thank Christa for helping me keep my priorities straight.

Pat Thank you to the people who have taken time out to help me get here and complete this project. For very generous contributions of time and assistance, thank you to my mother-in-law, Masa Ohashi, and to my parents, Jack and Donna McGee. I also want to thank my guides and mentors: the late Brian Anderson, John Blackwell, Kevin Cudihee, Medhat Elmasry, Jason Harrison, Bill Howorth, and Dr. Benjamin Yu, PhD. From the game industry, thank you to Cathy Marshall and Wes Gale from Magellan Interactive for helping to set me on this path, and thanks to Tybon Wu from Electronic Arts for the technical consulting.

Together we would like to acknowledge the following people, whose contributions can be found in the examples in this book.

Thank you to the artists Eric Bancroft, Sheila Nash, and Phillip T. Wheeler for bringing the media of this text to life.

Eric Bancroft, freelance artist and instructor, contributed the CF-18 Hornet fighter jet model. Eric can be found on the web at www.abandonedrebel.com and eric@abandonedrebel.com.

Sheila Nash (http://sheilanash.com) has been a video game artist for 15 years on a variety of game platforms. She spends most of her time as a senior technical artist, optimizing the art process of game production. Sheila provided the hot rod model; brick wall and stone floor; back wall, side wall, and ground; tiled grass; tree; danger sign; and warning light.

Thank you to Phillip T. Wheeler, 3D modeler/animator, for the Zarlag *Quake II* model.

We are grateful for industry support from Mete Ciragan of chUmbaLum sOft, Todd Hollenshead of id Software, John McLusky of Planetside, and Microsoft.

Thank you, Mete, for providing the game world with a powerful 3D modeling and animation program to create models for our games. Visit Mete's site at www.milkshape3d.com to obtain a 30-day trial edition of MilkShape. We use MilkShape because it creates great models and animations, is intuitive, and is affordable for the average developer on a budget. Watch the website for the latest updates.

The *Quake II* loader code is based in id Software's design and is available under the terms of the GNU public license as stated by id Software. We are grateful to id Software for innovative products and for their positive community spirit.

Planetside provides a great utility, Terragen, for generating photorealistic scenery, which we use in our game world. Planetside provides a noncommercial edition and also a commercial edition with support and access to even larger image sizes. Watch their site (www.planetside.co.uk) for the latest updates.

Thank you, Microsoft, for the XNA game development platform. Thank you for amazing freeware XNA development tools and for opening up the Xbox 360, a world-class game console, to everyday and independent developers.

For game community support, thank you to Dennis Medema and Jorrit Rouwe for helping us locate resources for this project.

Introduction

This book shows you how to write complete 3D games from scratch. It will teach you the math, graphics, audio effects, and algorithms for all the features you would expect in a quality 3D game. This text explains how to set up your environment to write your XNA and shader code. It also explains how to create 3D models on a budget and how to use commercial standard models that are created by professional game artists. When you finish reading this book, you will have the ability to write a graphics engine and a full game that contains realistic scenery, fiery effects, 3D models, terrain, animations, collision detection, 3D audio, score tracking, and more.

This material is intended for beginning to intermediate programmers. You may be a beginning programmer who knows how to write an if-else statement and for loop using C, C++, C#, Java, JavaScript, PHP, or other C-style languages—or you may even be a computer-science student or graduate who wants to learn game programming and needs a book with substance. Whatever your level of experience, this book rapidly delivers the material you need in an easy-to-learn format:

❭ Step-by-step examples get to the point without any unwanted clutter.

❭ We avoid deeply nested structures and bloated game projects that would complicate the learning process.

❭ Examples in each chapter of the book can be built independently of each other and thus easily mixed and matched in your own projects.

❭ All examples are compatible with each other.

❭ Every chapter is designed so you can learn the topics quickly and thoroughly.

This book is written by authors who are experienced in game programming and know how to teach it to a wide audience. The material in this book and the methods of delivery have been successfully tested in the classroom with students of varying levels of experience. Pat has been developing courses in game programming and has taught game programming at one of Western Canada's largest post-secondary institutions, the British Columbia Institute of Technology, since 2001. He quickly discovered that about half of the people in his classes were very new to programming and the other half were computer science students or college and university computer science graduates. Right away, Pat developed a formula for fast learning that was simple enough for anyone with basic programming experience to understand, but substantial enough to satisfy the seasoned programmer. Term after term, Pat receives rave reviews from students of all levels of experience for showing them how to build complete games from scratch.

Stephen also brings relevant experience, having recently coauthored a book on applying 3D graphics for augmented reality. Stephen and Pat package their experience to deliver you the *Microsoft XNA Game Studio Creator's Guide*.

ABOUT THE DOWNLOAD

The base code, media files, and solutions for all examples presented in this book are available in the downloads section of this book's catalog page at www.mhprofessional.com/product.php?isbn=007149071X. Links to utilities used for model creation and scenery generation can also be found at this location.

Additional information and discussion relevant for this text can be found at www.GameDeveloperOnline.com.

All code examples explained in the pages of this book can be built using either the Windows base code project or Xbox 360 base code project. All code examples can run on either platform, so you can use the same base code project for every example in the book. You can check your work by examining the complete solution, or you can start with the solution if you need to modify it or use it as a basis for another project.

Each chapter ends with a set of optional exercises. We recommend you try them to practice and actively focus on the most relevant points discussed in each chapter.

DOWNLOAD THE EXAMPLES FOR THIS BOOK

You will find all of the resources for the examples in this book available for download from the book's catalog page at www.mhprofessional.com (see the Introduction for more details).

XNA AND YOUR PC VIDEO CARD

Before you start installing the software required for XNA development, you should ensure that your PC meets the basic requirements for GSE. The tricky consideration is your video card; if your card does not meet the requirements, you will not be able to run GSE projects on your PC.

Of course, this is all academic if you plan on developing solely for the Xbox 360; if that's the case, you don't need to worry about your video card. If you have encountered the following GSE error, you may have already discovered that your card has an issue:

"Could not find a Direct3D device that has a Direct3D9-level driver and supports pixel shader 1.1 or greater."

If you see this error, you should go to the GSE documentation FAQ (Microsoft XNA Game Studio Express | XNA Game Studio Express Documentation) and find the following topic:

"What do I do to fix the error message 'NoSuitableGraphicsDeviceException was unhandled'?"

This page provides instructions for determining the version of DirectX installed on the computer, gives instructions for how to set hardware acceleration to full, and explains how to determine which shader models are supported by your video card.

GSE requires your PC's video card to support shader model 1.1 or greater. However, Microsoft recommends that you have a graphics card that supports shader model 2.0 or greater. If you would like to programmatically check which version your card supports, refer to Microsoft XNA Game Studio Express | XNA Game Studio Express Documentation | How to: Check for Shader Model 2.0 Support. This page (found at http://msdn2.microsoft.com/en-us/library/bb195248.aspx) provides the following code, which uses the static property GraphicsAdapter.Adapters to query the adapters on the system to display their capabilities (in this case, checking for pixel shader 2.0 support):

```
// check all available adapters on the system
foreach (GraphicsAdapter adapter in GraphicsAdapter.Adapters)
{
```

```
// get the capabilities of the hardware device
GraphicsDeviceCapabilities caps =
adapter.GetCapabilities(DeviceType.Hardware);

if (caps.MaxPixelShaderProfile < ShaderProfile.PS_2_0)
{
    // this adapter does not support Shader Model 2.0
    System.Diagnostics.Debug.WriteLine
    ("This adapter does not support Shader Model 2.0.");
}
}
```

Now that you have your development environment ready to go, the next chapter
will walk you through some of the most important features of the GSE IDE.

CHAPTER 2

Developer Basics

IF you are itching to get coding, but are not familiar with Microsoft's integrated development environments, this chapter will help you use Microsoft XNA Game Studio Express (GSE) to program, debug, and deploy your game projects. Once your PC and Xbox 360 have been prepared as outlined in Chapter 1, "Set Up an XNA Development Environment," you are ready to code with GSE.

MANAGING THE CODE PROJECT

GSE is a first-class integrated development environment (IDE) that leverages Microsoft Visual C# Express. This free coding studio is very similar to Microsoft Visual C# .NET; it enables you to program, edit, debug, and deploy your C# applications. Compared to other freeware developer tools, GSE is a Rolls Royce. Using this software, you can code in comfort and allow the IDE to improve your efficiency.

Opening Microsoft XNA Game Studio Express

To launch GSE, from the Start menu select Programs and choose Microsoft XNA Game Studio Express | XNA Game Studio Express. GSE will open the Start Page, which presents your recent projects, links to tutorials, and links to online articles, discussions, and events related to C# development (see Figure 2-1).

Creating a Game Studio Project

A GSE project will store references to all of your code files and resources that are used by your game application. There are currently two types of XNA game projects: the Windows Game project and the Xbox 360 Game project.

Each type of project references a slightly different instruction set. The Windows Game project can be run on a PC, but the Xbox 360 Game project cannot because it uses a reduced instruction set that is required by the Xbox 360 console.

Coding Differences Between Windows and the Xbox 360

The base code that is automatically generated by GSE for the Xbox 360 Game project is identical to the code generated for a Windows Game project. Some slight differences exist between the two instruction sets available, such as mouse support, which is only available in Windows. However, in the majority of cases, you can write your code in one project type and then copy your source files and resources to the other project type and you will still be able to run your project. The Xbox 360 is slightly stricter in enforcing variable default declarations, but even if you forget the differences, GSE provides excellent debug information to inform you of any issues and how to resolve them when testing your code in one environment or the other.

FIGURE 2-1

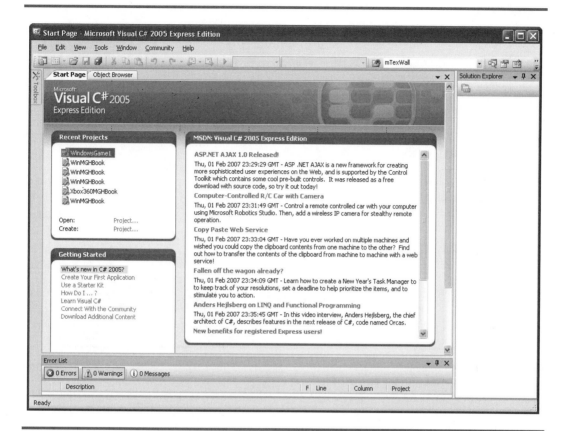

Microsoft Visual C# Express Start Page

You can have confidence that almost all the code you write for a Windows Game project is going to work in an Xbox 360 Game project, and vice versa. In most cases, platform compatibility will not be an issue because XNA is designed to work in both environments. Of course, you still need to test in both environments, but plan for an excellent level of compatibility between platforms.

Creating a Windows Game Project

You can create a project by selecting File and then New Project. At this point, several options are available to you. If you want your project to run on Windows, then choose the *Windows Game* icon that appears in the *New Project* dialog (see Figure 2-2). To proceed, you need to fill in each of the text boxes at the bottom of the *New*

FIGURE 2-2

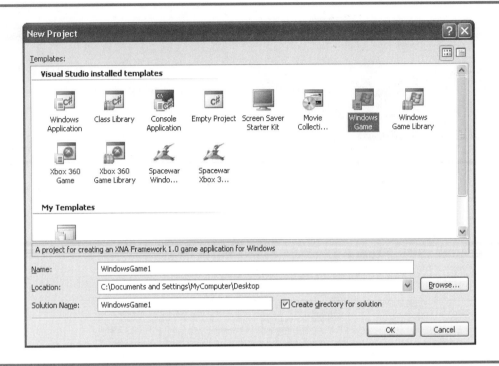

Entering the file path and project name

Project dialog. These values include the name of the project and the file path for the directory where you would like your project to be created.

When you first create a project, a code-editing window will open on the left (see Figure 2-3). The *Solution Explorer* in the right panel shows a listing of code files and may display resources such as a project icon and other items you have selected. The *Error List* at the bottom of the page displays error messages for lines of code that will not compile, warning messages such as information about variables that are not used, and instructions that are deprecated but have been allowed to compile.

If the code editor, *Solution Explorer*, or *Error List* do not appear, these options can be enabled from the View menu.

Creating an Xbox 360 Game Project

The creation of an Xbox 360 Game project is similar to creating a Windows Game project. But before you can actually run an Xbox 360 game project, you will need to sign into Xbox Live and download the XNA Game Launcher, as outlined in Chapter 1,

FIGURE 2-3

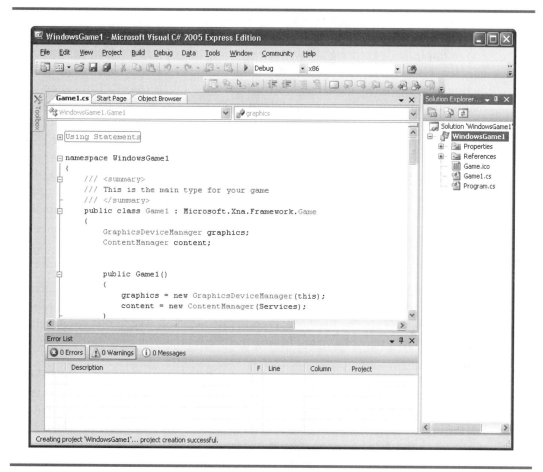

GSE project with code window, *Error List,* and *Solution Explorer*

"Set Up an XNA Development Environment." Once you have this installed, you will have to connect your PC to your Xbox 360. Connecting your PC to your Xbox 360 will be explained later in this chapter.

Once you have a connection from your PC to your Xbox 360, you will be able to compile an Xbox 360 Game project. Creating an Xbox 360 Game project is similar to creating a Windows Game project. The only difference is that you select the *Xbox 360 Game* icon in the *New Project* dialog. When you create the project, GSE will generate the base code needed to build a game that runs on the Xbox 360. The development environment will look like the Windows Game project shown in Figure 2-3.

Editing Your Code

The GSE code window offers a friendly environment for writing and editing your code. The latest IDE editing features enable you to write code quickly and accurately. For example, code coloring allows for easy readability by distinguishing comments in green, C# structures and functions in blue, and user-defined code in black. Also, incomplete lines of code are marked with red lines. Furthermore, AutoComplete is readily available to assist you in completing your instructions with methods and variables for your classes. ToolTips, which display descriptive summaries, appear when you hover the mouse over variables and instructions that are referenced from Microsoft's code libraries.

The other windows also provide features that will make your programming experience more enjoyable. For example, the *Solution Explorer* enables you to quickly navigate from page to page. In short, GSE is rich with editing features that are waiting for you to discover them.

Adding and Removing Code Files to and from the Project

By default, when you create a new game project, GSE will generate a Game1.cs file, a Program.cs file, and a Game.ico file (for a Windows Game project). You'll see these files listed in the *Solution Explorer*. Options are available to add files to (or remove them from) the project by right-clicking the project name in the *Solution Explorer* (see Figure 2-4).

To add new source files to the project, right-click the project name in the *Solution Explorer,* choose Add, and then select New Item. In the *New Item* dialog that appears, a C# file can be created by selecting *Code File.* You must specify a name for the C# file in the *Name* box before the file can be added. Once you have provided a file-name, click the *Add* button to have the file added to the project.

To add existing source files to the project, right-click the project name in the *Solution Explorer,* choose Add, and then select Existing Item; an *Add Existing Item* dialog will appear. By default, the *Add Existing Item* dialog displays all files listed in the source folder of the current project. When you left-click the source files to be added and click Add, GSE will load the files into the project; after they have been added, they will be listed in the *Solution Explorer.*

Compiling and Running Game Studio Projects

You can use the *Start Debugging* action to compile your code, generate debugging information, and run the project in one step. In the case of an Xbox 360 Game project, this will also deploy the project to your Xbox 360. You can access the *Start Debugging* action from the Debug menu or by pressing the F5 key.

FIGURE 2-4

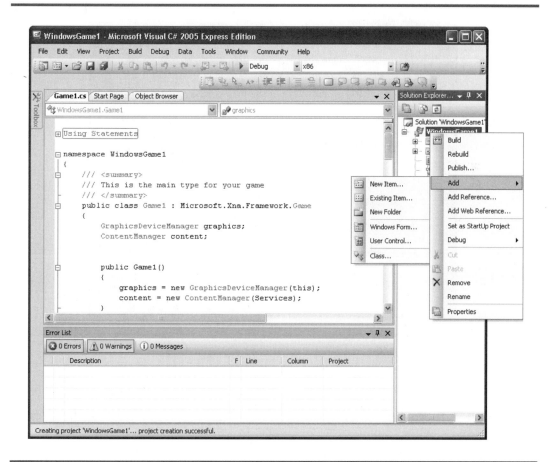

Project file Add options available in the *Solution Explorer*

By default, both newly created Windows Game projects and Xbox 360 Game projects are generated with the source code needed to build a basic window. The output from compiling a brand-new project will be a game window as shown in Figure 2-5.

Saving the Game Studio Project

When compiling, GSE will automatically save all edits to the game project. Between builds, you can manually save changes to the *.cs file that is currently showing in the code editor, or you can save changes to the entire project. Under the File menu,

FIGURE 2-5

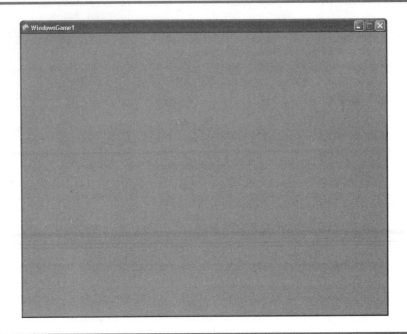

Newly built game window

three different options are available for saving the project: Save *.cs, Save *.cs As, and Save All.

Deploying an Xbox 360 Game Project

When you have a project that is ready to run on your Xbox 360, you can use GSE to deploy it to your Xbox. The first step of deployment requires that you go to your Xbox 360 and configure it to connect it to your PC. On the Games blade of the Xbox 360 Dashboard (under Demos and More), launching XNA Game Launcher will display the *XNA Game Launcher* main page (see Figure 2-6).

The *Connect to Computer* option is disabled the first time you run XNA Game Launcher. To enable it, you must go to *Settings* and select *Generate Connection Key*. After you generate the key, but before you accept it, you must enter the key number into GSE on your PC. From GSE, under Options | Tools, select XNA Game Studio Xbox 360 and click Add to launch the *Add Xbox 360 Name and Connection Key* dialog. In this dialog, you must enter a computer name so you can identify your PC con-

FIGURE 2-6

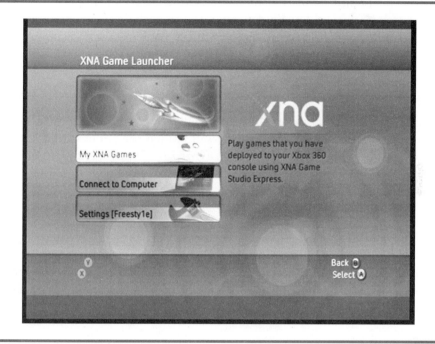

XNA Game Launcher main page

nection and the connection key that was just generated. Once you complete this task, select *Accept New Key* from the *Connection Key* dialog on your Xbox 360 to finalize the process. After you have accepted the key, you will be brought back to the *Settings* dialog, which will now report *[key set]* to notify you that you were successful in applying the key on your Xbox 360. You can now select the *Back* button to return to the *XNA Game Launcher* page.

On the *XNA Game Launcher* page, select the *Connect to Computer* option and press the *A* controller button to make the connection.

If you want to test your Xbox 360 Game project, select *Start Debugging* under the *Debug* menu (or press F5) to deploy and run your game on the Xbox 360.

Alternatively, if you just want to deploy your game to the Xbox 360, from GSE, right-click the project name in the *Solution Explorer* and choose Deploy. This will enable you to play the game on your Xbox 360. The progress of your deployment will be displayed in the *Output* window of GSE. The *Connect to Computer* screen will also show the progress of deployment along with a listing of files that have been transferred to your Xbox 360. When the deployment is complete, select the *B* button to back out of the *Connect to Computer* page. When the project has been loaded onto the Xbox 360, select *My XNA Games* and press the *A* controller button from the *XNA Game Launcher* page to display your XNA projects (see Figure 2-7). You can select and run any that are listed.

Opening an Existing Game Studio Project

A GSE project can be opened by double-clicking the solution file. Solution files have an .sln extension. The project will launch the game studio and show the code editor, *Solution Explorer*, and *Error List*. If any of these items do not appear when the game studio is open, they can be opened individually from the View menu.

DEBUGGING

There is no silver bullet when it comes to debugging techniques. However, having many techniques in your arsenal will aid your ability to examine (or trace) code, and it will help you write robust code quickly and efficiently.

FIGURE 2-7

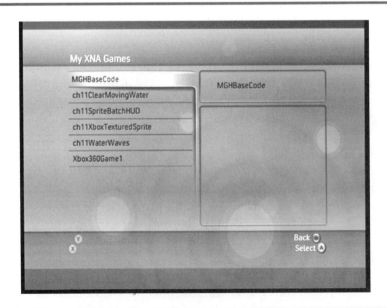

My XNA Games page showing a listing of games

FIGURE 2-11

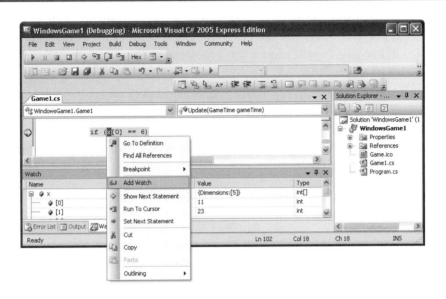

Adding a variable to a watch list

CHAPTER 2 REVIEW EXERCISES

To get the most from this chapter, try out these chapter review exercises.

1. Create a Windows Game project using the template that is available in the *New Project* dialog. Inside the Update() method, add this code:

```
int x = 5;
System.IO.StreamWriter sw
= new System.IO.StreamWriter(@"..\..\..\DebugLog.txt", true);
sw.Write("X = ");
sw.WriteLine(x);
sw.Close();
```

Create a breakpoint by clicking the left margin next to the instruction sw.Close(). A red dot should appear beside it when the breakpoint is set. Then, compile and run your program. When the program halts at the instruction beside the breakpoint, move the cursor over the variable *x* and note the ToolTip displays the value stored in this variable. While the program is running, right-click *x* and choose *Add Watch* to monitor the variable in the Watch window.

Next, press F5 to resume the program. It will run and halt again at the breakpoint. You can then click the breakpoint in the left margin to remove it. Pressing F5 will resume the program until you stop the debugger by pressing SHIFT+F5.

When you have finished running the program, you can view text output in the DebugLog.txt file that is located in your source folder.

2. Create an Xbox 360 Game project using the template that is available in the *New Project* dialog. Using the Xbox 360 project, repeat the steps requested in Exercise 1.

Introduction to XNA Graphics Programming

THIS chapter discusses the most basic elements for all game graphics by introducing the structures needed to begin graphics programming. Namely, it shows how to create a game window and explains the methods behind it. Then, the methods and objects for drawing points, lines, and triangles are introduced and applied. By the end of this chapter, you could use this logic to build a basic village in a 3D world. Learning how to draw basic shapes in a game window might not grab you at first, but all great graphics effects and even 3D models are rendered with the same logic presented in this chapter.

The XNA platform offers a simple process for creating, drawing, and updating a game window. The flowchart shown here summarizes the steps required to build, update, and draw graphics within a game window.

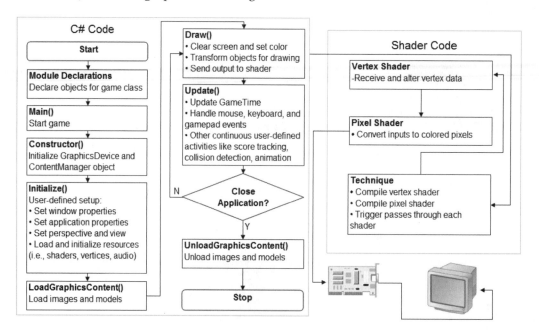

CREATING THE XNA GAME WINDOW

Hardly any C# code is needed to generate and display a basic XNA game window like the one shown in Figure 3-1.

Chapter 2, "Developer Basics," explained how to create a game studio project for either a Windows PC or the Xbox 360 platform. These projects can be created using the Xbox 360 and Windows Game project templates—they generate practically identical code. The only difference in code is the namespace for the game class. The Windows template assigns the name WindowsGame1 by default and the Xbox 360 assigns the namespace Xbox360Game1 by default—that's it. These templates

FIGURE 3-1

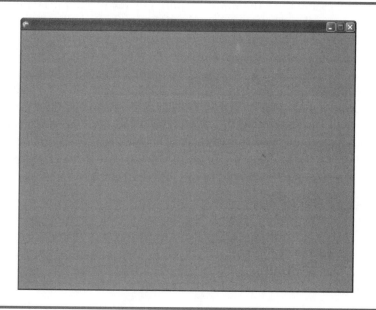

Basic XNA game window

provide the basic foundation you need to create an XNA game window. The XNA code in these templates is basically the same, but the XNA framework references for the Windows and Xbox 360 projects are different. You can write all of your code in one environment and then reference it in either an Xbox 360 or a Windows project to run it. Microsoft has intentionally made window creation and portability between projects simple so you can run with it. Obviously, Microsoft wants you to take the platform beyond the outer limits.

Initializing the Game Application

When you want to create a new XNA game project, the easiest method is to use the project templates that come with GSE. To begin a new project, follow these steps:

1. Open GSE by choosing Start | Programs | Microsoft XNA Game Studio Express | XNA Game Studio Express.

2. From the main GSE window, choose File | New Project.

3. Choose either the Windows Game or Xbox 360 Game template.

You may want to create your own XNA application from scratch, or you may be curious to know what's happening under the hood when you choose one of these templates. Like any other C# application, an XNA application begins by referencing the assemblies and the namespaces required by the program. To plug into the XNA platform you will need references to the XNA framework along with namespaces for the XNA framework's Audio, Content, Graphics, Input, and Storage components. When you use an Xbox 360 or Windows Game project template, these namespaces are automatically added for you in the default Game1.cs file that is generated.

To avoid potential naming conflicts for this class (with any identically named classes), a namespace is needed for the game class. The Xbox 360 Game project template generates the namespace Xbox360Game1. The Windows Game project template generates the namespace WindowsGame1. The namespace is followed by a class declaration for the game application class, which both project templates declare as Game1. The templates also add the required assembly references for you.

GraphicsDeviceManager

Every XNA application requires a GraphicsDeviceManager object to handle the configuration and management of the graphics device. The GraphicsDevice class is used for drawing primitive-based objects. The GraphicsDeviceManager object is declared at the module level:

```
GraphicsDeviceManager    graphics;
```

The GraphicsDeviceManager object is initialized in the game class constructor, Game1():

```
graphics = new GraphicsDeviceManager(this);
```

ContentManager

The ContentManager is used to load, manage, and dispose of binary media content through the *content pipeline*. Graphics and media content can be loaded with this object when it is referenced in the game project. The ContentManager object is declared at the top of the game class:

```
ContentManager    content;
```

The ContentManager object is initialized in the constructor Game1():

```
content = new ContentManager(Services);
```

Initialize()

After the GraphicsDeviceManager and ContentManager objects have been created, you can use the Initialize() override method to trap the one-time game startup event. Initialize() is a natural place to trigger basic setup activities such as the following:

❯ Setting window properties such as the title or full screen options

❯ Setting the perspective and view to define how a user sees the 3D game

❯ Initializing image objects for displaying textures

❯ Initializing vertices for storing color, and image coordinates to be used throughout the program

❯ Initializing vertex shaders to convert your primitive objects to pixel output

❯ Initializing audio objects

❯ Setting up other game objects

LoadGraphicsContent()

The LoadGraphicsContent() override method is generated by the Xbox 360 and Windows Game project templates for loading binary image and model content through the graphics pipeline. You could actually load your binary graphics content from the Initialize() method or from your own methods. Chapter 7, "Texturing Your Game World," will explain how to do this. However, loading your binary graphics content from LoadGraphicsContent() ensures that your managed graphics content is always loaded in the same place.

Drawing and Updating the Game Application

Once an XNA application is initialized, it enters a continuous loop that alternates between drawing and updating the application. The sequence is generally consistent but sometimes the Draw() method will be called twice, or more, before the Update() method is called, and vice versa. Consequently, your routines for updating and drawing your objects must account for this variation in timing. All code for drawing graphics objects in the window is triggered from the Draw() method. The Update() method handles code for updating objects, handling events within the application, and your own defined events—such as checking for game object collisions, handling keyboard or game pad events, tracking the score, and tending to other game features that require maintenance every frame. Both of these functions are performed for every frame that is displayed to the player.

Draw()

The Draw() method is an override that handles the drawing (also known as *rendering*) for the game program. Throughout this book, the Draw() routine is basically the same in every example. Draw() starts by clearing the screen background, setting the screen color, and then drawing the graphics onto the screen.

Update()

The Update() method is where you check and handle game-time events. The Xbox 360 and Windows Game project templates automatically add this override method. Events typically handled here include mouse clicks, keyboard presses, game-pad control events, and timers. Update() is also a place for many other activities that require continuous checks or updates. Update() activities might include advancing animations, detecting collisions, and tracking and modifying game scores.

Closing the Game Application

The Xbox 360 and Windows Game project templates automatically add an override for the UnloadGraphicsContent() method. This method will dispose of your managed graphics media when the game program shuts down. The UnloadGraphicsContent() method also conveniently frees your memory resources even when the game application is closed unintentionally.

Basic XNA Game Window Example

This example shows all of the C# code that is generated by the Xbox 360 and Windows Game project templates. When the GSE wizard is used to create a game project, two source files are generated for your project. One of these is the Program1.cs file, which begins and launches the game application:

```csharp
using System;

namespace WindowsGame1 // namespace is Xbox360Game1 for Xbox 360 game
{
    static class Program
    {
        static void Main(string[] args)
        {   // application entry point
            using (Game1 game = new Game1())
            {
                game.Run();
            }
        }
    }
}
```

The second default file is the Game1.cs file. This file is generated to house the game class that initializes, updates, and closes the game application:

```csharp
// framework references
#region Using Statements
```

Introduction to XNA Graphics Programming

```csharp
using System;
using System.Collections.Generic;
using Microsoft.Xna.Framework;
using Microsoft.Xna.Framework.Audio;
using Microsoft.Xna.Framework.Content;
using Microsoft.Xna.Framework.Graphics;
using Microsoft.Xna.Framework.Input;
using Microsoft.Xna.Framework.Storage;
#endregion

namespace WindowsGame1
{
public class Game1 : Microsoft.Xna.Framework.Game
{
    GraphicsDeviceManager graphics; // handles drawing
    ContentManager content;         // loads, manages, & disposes gfx media

    public Game1()
    {   // initialize graphics and content objects
        graphics      = new GraphicsDeviceManager(this);
        content       = new ContentManager(Services);
    }

    protected override void Initialize()
    {
        // initialize window, application, starting setup
        base.Initialize();
    }

    // load graphics content
    protected override void LoadGraphicsContent(bool loadAllContent)
    {
        if (loadAllContent)
        { } // managed graphics content from graphics pipeline
        else
        { } // unmanaged graphics content
    }

    protected override void UnloadGraphicsContent(bool unloadAllContent)
    {   // dispose of graphics content
        if (unloadAllContent == true)
        {
```

```
        content.Unload();
    }
}


protected override void Update(GameTime gameTime)
{   // animations, collision checking, event handling

    // allows the default game to exit on Xbox 360 and Windows
    if(GamePad.GetState(PlayerIndex.One).Buttons.Back
        ==ButtonState.Pressed)
        this.Exit();

    base.Update(gameTime);
}


protected override void Draw(GameTime gameTime)
{   // draw to window
    graphics.GraphicsDevice.Clear(Color.CornflowerBlue);

    // call shader code here

    base.Draw(gameTime);
}
}
}
```

That's all of the C# code needed to draw an XNA game window, as shown previously in Figure 3-1. As you can see, creating and displaying a window is fairly simple. This code is generated by the GSE project template and will run on either the Xbox 360 or on your Window PC.

Drawing Graphics in the XNA Game Window

At this point, your XNA game window will only display 2D graphics—you will need a shader to draw 3D graphics. Shaders are explained in more detail in Chapter 4, "Shaders." In a nutshell, shaders receive vertex data from the C# application, apply filters, and then perform other user-defined operations such as texturing, coloring, and lighting. The output from the shader is pixel output in your game window.

DRAWING SHAPES

Graphics start with basic shapes that are created from points, lines, or triangles. These basic elements are referred to as *primitive objects*. Primitive objects are drawn

FIGURE 3-2

Cartesian coordinate system for drawing in 3D

in 3D space using a Cartesian coordinate system where position is mapped in the X, Y, and Z planes (see Figure 3-2).

Even complex shapes are built with a series of points, lines, or triangles. A static 3D model is basically made from a file containing vertex information that includes X, Y, Z position, color, image coordinates, and possibly other data. The vertices can be rendered by outputting points for each vertex, with a grid of lines that connects the vertices, or as a solid object that is built with a series of triangles—which are linked by the vertices.

Primitive Objects

Complex shapes are created with primitive objects that regulate how the vertices are displayed. The vertex data could be rendered as points, linear grids, or solid triangles.

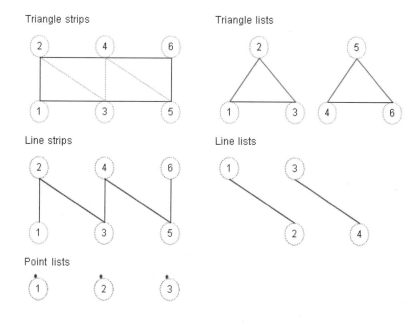

Drawing Syntax

XNA delivers simple syntax for drawing shapes from primitive objects.

Primitive Object Types

Table 3-1 details the five common primitive object types. You will notice that triangles and lines can be drawn in strips or in lists. Lists are required for drawing separate points, lines, or triangles. Strips, on the other hand, are more efficient where the lines or triangles are combined to create one complex shape like a 3D model.

Strips are also more efficient than lists for saving memory and, as a result, enable faster drawing. When you're drawing a triangle strip, adding one more vertex to the strip generates one more triangle. A strip practically cuts the memory requirements for vertex data in half when compared to a list:

$$\text{Total triangle list vertices} = N_{triangles} * 3 \text{ vertices}$$
$$\text{Total triangle strip vertices} = N_{triangles} + 2 \text{ vertices}$$

The same logic applies for drawing lines. The line strip is more efficient for complex grids:

$$\text{Total line list vertices} = N_{lines} * 2 \text{ vertices}$$
$$\text{Total line strip vertices} = N_{lines} + 1 \text{ vertex}$$

Vertex Types

A vertex object stores vertex information, which could include X, Y, and Z positions, image coordinates, a normal vector, and color. The XNA platform offers four predefined vertex formats that are fairly self-explanatory (see Table 3-2).

TABLE 3-1

Primitive Type	Function
TriangleStrip	Enables linking of triangles to create complex solid shapes
TriangleList	Enables groups of separate triangles
LineStrip	Enables linking of lines to create wire grids
LineList	Enables groups of separate lines
PointList	Enables groups of separate points

Common Primitive Types

TABLE 3-2

Vertex Storage Format	Function
VertexPositionColor	Stores X, Y, Z and color coordinates
VertexPositionTexture	Stores X, Y, Z and image coordinates
VertexPositionNormal	Stores X, Y, Z and a normal vector
VertexPositionNormalTexture	Stores X, Y, Z, a normal vector, and image coordinates

Storage Formats for Vertex Buffers

VertexDeclaration

A VertexDeclaration object stores the vertex format for the data contained in each vertex of the shape or model. Before drawing the object, the graphics device must be set to use the correct format to allow for proper retrieval of vertex data from each vertex array. Here is the syntax required to declare and initialize the VertexDeclaration object:

```
VertexDeclaration  vertexDeclaration
= new VertexDeclaration( GraphicsDevice   gfx.GraphicsDevice,
                         VertexElement[]  elements);
```

Before an object is drawn, the graphics device's VertexDeclaration property is assigned so that it can retrieve the vertex data and render it properly:

```
gfx.GraphicsDevice.VertexDeclaration = vertexDeclaration;
```

DrawUserPrimitives

When an object is drawn using primitive types, five items are set just before it is rendered:

1. The vertex type is declared.

2. The primitive type is set so drawings can be rendered using points, lines, or triangles.

3. The vertex array that stores the X, Y, Z, color, texture, and normal data used for drawing is assigned.

4. The starting element in the vertex array is set.

5. The total count for the primitives to be drawn is assigned.

This information is passed to the DrawUserPrimitives() method:

```
gfx.GraphicsDevice.DrawUserPrimitives<struct customVertex>(
                enum     PrimitiveType,
                struct   customVertex vertices,
                int      startingVertex,
                int      primitiveCount);
```

Drawing Primitive Objects Example

This demonstration shows how to draw the five common primitive shapes with vertex data. When the steps are complete, the game window will show two triangles in a strip, two triangles in a list, two lines in a strip, two lines in a list, and two points in a list (see Figure 3-3). At first glance, the output from this demonstration might seem dull, but keep in mind this is the foundation of any 3D world, so understanding it is worthwhile.

This example begins with either the WinMGHBook project or the Xbox360MGHBook project in the BaseCode directory in the download from the website. The basic code for these projects is identical. The framework differences between the two allow the WinMGHBook project to run on your PC and the Xbox360MGHBook project to run on the Xbox 360.

FIGURE 3-3

Final output for the drawing primitive objects example

With this base code, you can move through the 3D world either by moving the left thumbstick on the game controller up or down or by pressing the UP or DOWN ARROW on the keyboard. Moving the left thumbstick to the left or right allows you to strafe—as do the LEFT and RIGHT ARROW keys on the keyboard. Moving the right thumbstick, or the mouse, allows you to adjust the view. Before you start this example, you may want to run the project and experiment in the basic 3D world.

For this example, the first required addition to the base code is setting up a VertexDeclaration. The VertexDeclaration will later be used to set the vertex format for your GraphicsDevice. The GraphicsDevice must be assigned so it can retrieve data from the vertex array in the correct format and draw primitive shapes with it. In the module level of your game class (in Game1.cs) add this VertexDeclaration:

```
private VertexDeclaration mVertexDeclaration;
```

This vertex type object, mVertexDeclaration, defines the data for each vertex. You should choose the VertexPositionColor format so that you can store the position and color of all the objects that will be drawn in the example. At the end of Initialize(), add this code to define the vertex type:

```
mVertexDeclaration = new VertexDeclaration(gfx.GraphicsDevice,
VertexPositionColor.VertexElements);
```

Triangle Strip

When you work through the next portion of this example, and you run your project, two triangles will appear together in the right side of the game window.

You must declare a vertex array in your game class to store four vertices containing position and color information for the two triangles that will be drawn in the strip. To do so, add this code:

```
private VertexPositionColor[] mVtTriStrip = new VertexPositionColor[4];
```

Next, a method containing code to initialize the positions and colors for each vertex in the triangle strip can be added to the game class:

```
private void init_tri_strip()
{
    mVtTriStrip[0]=new VertexPositionColor(new Vector3(-1.5f, 0.0f, 3.0f),
                Color.Orange);
    mVtTriStrip[1]=new VertexPositionColor(new Vector3(-1.0f, 0.5f, 3.0f),
                Color.Orange);
    mVtTriStrip[2]=new VertexPositionColor(new Vector3(-0.5f, 0.0f, 3.0f),
                Color.Orange);
```

```
mVtTriStrip[3]=new VertexPositionColor(new Vector3( 0.0f, 0.5f, 3.0f),
                 Color.Orange);
}
```

The method init_tri_strip() should be called at the end of Initialize() to set up the array of vertices for the triangle strip when the program begins:

```
init_tri_strip();
```

Next, you need a method in the game class for drawing the primitive object from the vertex array. For most examples throughout this book, the drawing of primitive shapes is done in five simple steps:

1. Declare transformation matrices for scaling, moving, and rotating your graphics.

2. Initialize the transformation matrices.

3. Build the cumulative transformation by multiplying the matrices.

4. Pass the cumulative transformation to the shader.

5. Select the vertex type, primitive type, and number of vertices, and then draw the object.

The first three steps involve setting up a cumulative matrix to transform the object through scaling, translations, and rotations. Transformations are covered in Chapter 5, "Animation Introduction." More detail is presented in Chapter 4, "Shaders," to explain step 4 (where the shader variables are set). For the purpose of introducing vertices and primitive shapes in this chapter, we'll focus on step 5.

You are going to draw the triangle at the position where the vertices were defined earlier. To do this, you add the draw_objects() method to the game class. draw_objects() uses the vertex data declared earlier to draw two triangles together in a strip.

```
void draw_objects()
{
    // 1: declare matrices
    Matrix matIdentity;

    // 2: initialize matrices
    matIdentity = Matrix.Identity; // always start with identity matrix

    // 3: build cumulative world matrix using I.S.R.O.T. sequence
    // identity, scale, rotate, orbit(translate & rotate), translate
    mMatWorld = matIdentity;
```

```
// 4: pass wvp matrix to shader
worldViewProjParam.SetValue(mMatWorld * mMatView * mMatProj);
mfx.CommitChanges();

// 5: draw object - select vertex type, primitive type, # of primitives
gfx.GraphicsDevice.VertexDeclaration = mVertexDeclaration;
gfx.GraphicsDevice.DrawUserPrimitives<VertexPositionColor>(
    PrimitiveType.TriangleStrip, mVtTriStrip, 0, 2 );
}
```

Note the two last instructions in the draw_objects() method. The GraphicsDevice is assigned the same VertexDeclaration format defined earlier for each vertex. This property allows the GraphicsDevice to retrieve the data in the correct format, which in this case contains color and position data. The DrawUserPrimitives() method is assigned the <VertexPositionColor> format, the primitive type TriangleStrip is selected for output, and the vertex array mVtTriStrip is selected as the source of vertices with color and position data. The last two parameters of the DrawUserPrimitives() method select the offset of the vertex array and the total primitives to be drawn.

draw_objects() must be called while the BasicShader.fx file is referenced in the Draw() method. Inside the Draw() method, the call to draw_objects() must be nested between the Begin() and End() methods for the pass to the BasicShader.fx shader. (As mentioned earlier, more explanation will be provided for this section in Chapter 4, "Shaders.") To help show where draw_objects() needs to be called, some extra code that already exists in the project is included here in italics:

```
// begin shader - BasicShader.fx
// draws objects with color and position
mfx.Begin();
mfx.Techniques[0].Passes[0].Begin();
    draw_objects();
mfx.Techniques[0].Passes[0].End();
mfx.End();
```

Try running this version of the program, and you'll find that the graphics output is displayed in the game window. More specifically, two triangles in a strip will appear in the right side of the window.

Triangle List

When you need to draw separate triangles, the triangle list is handy. To continue with this example, you will display two triangles in a list in the left side of the window.

A vertex array with room for six vertices for two triangles is needed to store the position and color data that will be used to draw the triangles. To set up this array, add the following declaration to the top of the game class:

```
private VertexPositionColor[] mVtTriList = new VertexPositionColor[6];
```

A method for initializing each vertex in the triangle list, init_tri_list(), is needed in the game class:

```
private void init_tri_list()
{
    mVtTriList[0] = new VertexPositionColor(new Vector3( 0.5f, 0.0f, 3.0f),
                Color.LightGray);
    mVtTriList[1] = new VertexPositionColor(new Vector3( 0.7f, 0.5f, 3.0f),
                Color.LightGray);
    mVtTriList[2] = new VertexPositionColor(new Vector3( 0.9f, 0.0f, 3.0f),
                Color.LightGray);
    mVtTriList[3] = new VertexPositionColor(new Vector3( 1.1f, 0.0f, 3.0f),
                Color.LightGray);
    mVtTriList[4] = new VertexPositionColor(new Vector3( 1.3f, 0.5f, 3.0f),
                Color.LightGray);
    mVtTriList[5] = new VertexPositionColor(new Vector3( 1.5f, 0.0f, 3.0f),
                Color.LightGray);
}
```

Call init_tri_list() from Initialize() to fill the vertex array with data that can be used to draw the two triangles in the list:

```
init_tri_list();
```

At the end of draw_objects(), after the triangle strip is drawn, the triangle list can be rendered with an additional DrawUserPrimitives instruction. Drawing more than one primitive object from the same method is possible because both primitive objects use the same vertex format, VertexPositionColor. Notice that the PrimitiveType specified for this new addition is TriangleList. The total number of primitives rendered in the list is two. The data in our vertex array for the triangle list, mVtTriList, is being referenced when drawing the triangle list. The default vertex array offset of 0 is set:

```
gfx.GraphicsDevice.DrawUserPrimitives<VertexPositionColor>(
    PrimitiveType.TriangleList, mVtTriList, 0, 2);
```

When you run the new version of the program, it will show the two triangles in the strip and the two triangles in the list.

Introduction to XNA Graphics Programming

Drawing a Line Strip

You have seen how triangles can be created and drawn using strips and lists. The same logic applies for drawing lines. For this next portion of the example, a line strip will be used to draw two joined lines on the right. The line strip might be useful for you if you ever want to show a wire grid between the vertices that make the 3D object. You undoubtedly have seen this effect used when rendering 3D models or terrain with line strips instead of triangle strips.

A vertex array must be declared with the position and color data that build the line strip. For this example, enough room will be given to store two lines in the strip. In other words, three vertices are required. To declare the vertex array, add this code to the module declarations section:

```
private VertexPositionColor[] mVtLineStrip = new VertexPositionColor[3];
```

Next, add a method to store the vertex information for each of the vertices in the line strip. For each vertex, the X, Y, and Z position is specified and the color is assigned.

```
private void init_line_strip()
{
    mVtLineStrip[0]=new VertexPositionColor(new Vector3(1.3f, 0.8f, 3.0f),
    Color.Gray);
    mVtLineStrip[1]=new VertexPositionColor(new Vector3(1.0f, 0.13f, 3.0f),
    Color.Gray);
    mVtLineStrip[2]=new VertexPositionColor(new Vector3(0.7f, 0.8f, 3.0f),
    Color.Gray);
}
```

To initialize the line strip when the program begins, add the call statement for init_line_strip() to the end of the Initialize() method:

```
init_line_strip();
```

Finally, code for drawing our line strip is added as the last line in the draw_objects() method after the setup for the rendering has been completed. This instruction tells the GraphicsDevice to draw two lines in a strip using position and color data and to extract the vertex data from the mVtLineStrip array.

```
gfx.GraphicsDevice.DrawUserPrimitives
<VertexPositionColor>(PrimitiveType.LineStrip, mVtLineStrip, 0, 2);
```

When you run the game application, the output will show the line strip in the left side of the window.

Adding a Line List

Now that drawing lines using strips has been demonstrated, this next section of code will show how to add two lines that are drawn using a list.

Each line in the list requires two separate vertices. This part of the demonstration begins by showing how to draw one line in a list.

The vertex array needed to store each vertex in the line list is declared in the module declarations section of the game class.

```
private VertexPositionColor[] mVtLineList = new VertexPositionColor[4];
```

A method, init_line_list(), for initializing each vertex in the line list with X, Y, Z, and color data is added to the methods section:

```
private void init_line_list()
{
    mVtLineList[0]=new VertexPositionColor(new Vector3( 0.0f, 0.7f, 3.0f),
                   Color.Black);
    mVtLineList[1]=new VertexPositionColor(new Vector3(-1.0f, 0.7f, 3.0f),
                   Color.Black);
    mVtLineList[2]=new VertexPositionColor(new Vector3( 0.0f, 0.8f, 3.0f),
                   Color.Black);
    mVtLineList[3]=new VertexPositionColor(new Vector3(-1.0f, 0.8f, 3.0f),
                   Color.Black);
}
```

init_line_list() is called from Initialize() to set up the line list when the program begins:

```
init_line_list();
```

Finally, a new instruction should be added to the very end of the draw_objects() method to render the line list. The first parameter of the DrawUserPrimitives() method sets the LineList type, the second parameter selects the mVtLineList array as the source of vertex data for the primitive object being drawn, the third parameter sets the default array offset of 0, and the last parameter sets the total number of lines that are rendered.

```
gfx.GraphicsDevice.DrawUserPrimitives
<VertexPositionColor>(PrimitiveType.LineList, mVtLineList, 0 , 2);
```

Introduction to XNA Graphics Programming

When you run the program, two separate lines will appear in the right side of the window.

Adding a Point List

Now for our final primitive object—the point list. In this portion of the demonstration, two points from a list will be added to the window.

First, a class declaration for a vertex array is used to store each point in the list using the position and color format:

```
private VertexPositionColor[] mVtPointList = new VertexPositionColor[2];
```

Next, a method is required to initialize each vertex in the point list with X, Y, Z position data and color information. To do this, add the following method to the game class:

```
private void init_pointList()
{
    mVtPointList[0]=new VertexPositionColor(new Vector3(0.25f, 0.8f, 3.0f),
                   Color.Black);
    mVtPointList[1]=new VertexPositionColor(new Vector3(0.25f, 0.0f, 3.0f),
                   Color.Black);
}
```

The point list should be initialized when the program starts. A call to init_pointList() from the Initialize() method will do this:

```
init_pointList();
```

Now the point list can be drawn. Add the following DrawUserPrimitives() instruction to the draw_objects() method. The parameters indicate that a PointList is being rendered, two points are being drawn, and the vertex data should be read from the mVtPointList vertex array.

```
gfx.GraphicsDevice.DrawUserPrimitives
<VertexPositionColor>(PrimitiveType.PointList, mVtPointList, 0, 2);
```

When you run the program, two points will appear in the middle of the window.

This chapter has shown how a typical XNA game window is generated, displayed, and updated with graphics. The vertices and primitive surfaces drawn with them are the foundation for all XNA game graphics. Even fiery effects and 3D models begin with vertices and primitive surfaces.

CHAPTER 3 REVIEW EXERCISES

To get the most from this chapter, try out these chapter review exercises:

1. Implement the step-by-step examples presented in this chapter.

2. After obtaining the completed solution for Exercise 1, which modifications must be made to make the output appear as shown here?

3. Use line and triangle primitives to create a small house with a roof and fence around it. You can use triangle strips, triangle lists, line strips, and line lists.

CHAPTER 4

Shaders

XNA

XNA uses shader-based rendering to convert vertex data into pixel output. This method achieves higher performance because shaders offload graphics processing onto the graphics card. Whether you use your own shader or XNA's BasicEffect shader, you have to use a shader to draw 3D graphics from your XNA code. The shader also gives you the power to customize the way your vertices are displayed. Shaders can be used to manipulate all vertex properties (e.g., color, position, and texture). The ability to provide additional vertex processing through the shader makes it possible to use shaders for implementing lighting, blending effects such as transparency, and multitexturing. For some effects—such as point sprites for fire, multitexturing, and custom lighting—you will need to write your own shader to implement the effect.

GRAPHICS PIPELINE

In discussions about shaders, you will often hear references to the graphics pipeline. The graphics pipeline describes the process of converting vertex and primitive inputs into pixel output. Vertex and pixel shaders, of course, play a key role in this processing. The vertex shader applies transformations to the vertex inputs. When the transformed vertices are passed to the shader, the output that will not be visible to the viewer is clipped and the back faces are removed (this is called culling). Rasterization is performed to convert the vector data to an output image. Interpolation is performed between vertices to uniformly distribute vertex data between coordinates. In the pixel shader, coloration and texturing are applied before outputting pixels to the screen. Figure 4-1 provides a high-level summary of graphics pipeline operations.

FIGURE 4-1

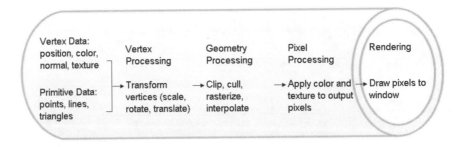

Graphics pipeline summary

HADERS

Shaders offer you some control over how the processing is done in the graphics pipeline. In most cases, you will want to write your own shader code. This section explains why and shows you how to do it.

Shader Structure

The shader shown here does nothing more than receive vertices that contain color and position data. The vertex shader receives this data, and then outputs the position data to the graphics pipeline. The vertex shader output (that can be modified by the pixel shader) is interpolated before it reaches the pixel shader. The pixel shader receives the color data and outputs it one pixel at a time:

```
float4x4 fx_matWorldViewProj : WORLDVIEWPROJ;

struct VS_INPUT{
    float4 f4Position    : POSITION0;
    float4 f4Color       : COLOR0;
};

struct VS_OUTPUT{
    float4 f4Position    : POSITION0;
    float4 f4Color       : COLOR0;
};

struct PS_OUTPUT{
    float4 f4Color       : COLOR0;
};

// alter vertex inputs
void vertex_shader(in VS_INPUT IN, out VS_OUTPUT OUT){
    OUT.f4Position      = mul(IN.f4Position, fx_matWorldViewProj);
    OUT.f4Color         = IN.f4Color;
}

// alter vs output and send to hardware one pixel at a time
void pixel_shader(in VS_OUTPUT IN, out PS_OUTPUT OUT){
    float4 fColor       = IN.f4Color;
    OUT.f4Color         = clamp(fColor, 0, 1);
}
```

```
// define vertex shader and pixel shader for each pass
technique simple{
    pass p0{
        // define vertex shader and pixel shader
        vertexshader    = compile vs_1_1 vertex_shader();
        pixelshader     = compile ps_2_0 pixel_shader();
    }
}
```

Vertex Shaders

A vertex shader is the portion of the shader that performs operations on each vertex received from your XNA code. You can use the vertex shader to alter and draw any vertex property. It can be used for per-vertex lighting, modifying the position, changing the color, or adjusting image coordinates. For example, the vertex shader may alter this information using other inputs such as transformations and filtering. When alterations to each vertex are complete, the color and texture output is sent to a pixel shader for further processing (if desired). Position and normal data may also be passed to the pixel shader if any calculations require this information. However, the position and normal data cannot be altered once it leaves the vertex shader.

At the very least, the vertex shader must output position data. Elements that are passed to the pixel shader are interpolated across the polygon before they are sent to the pixel shader.

Pixel Shaders

Pixel shaders convert vertex data from the vertex shader into colored pixel data. The pixel shader cannot manipulate the position or normal vector information but it can perform per-pixel operations to implement lighting, coloration, texture sampling, and blending. In terms of volume, per-pixel operations are more expensive than per-vertex operations. However, effects such as lighting are noticeably richer when you do them in the pixel shader—sometimes the performance hit is worth it. When processing in the pixel shader is complete, the pixel shader outputs colored pixels to the graphics card one pixel at a time.

Technique and Passes

A *technique* defines the vertex shaders and pixel shaders used during each *pass* through the pixel-rendering process. In most cases, drawing is done in one pass. However, you might want to specify more than one pass if you have to implement blended textures (through multitexturing). Chapter 10, "Combining Images for Better Visual Effects," shows an example of a multipass technique used to create running water.

Shaders

High Level Shader Language

For XNA games, most shaders are written in Microsoft's High Level Shader Language (HLSL). HLSL resembles C syntax, and because C# is also a member of the C family, the data types, conditional structures, loops, functions, and other syntax used in HLSL code are an easy transition for an XNA coder. You could write your shaders in assembly language, but assembly syntax is more difficult to read and is more prone to incompatibilities between graphics cards. Also, because HLSL and XNA were designed for implementation on the Xbox 360, and they were both created by Microsoft, you are certainly going to want to write most (if not all) of your shader code in HLSL.

Initially, game programmers only wrote shaders in assembly language, but assembly code is specific to video card hardware and this caused issues. Graphics card manufacturers such as NVIDIA, AMD (formerly ATI), and others have similar assembly code instruction sets, but differences between video cards sometimes cause shader incompatibilities. Because of this, games that use cutting-edge shader code, or shader code that is unique to a graphics card vendor, may not port well to machines that use other types of graphics cards. If you are only developing for the Xbox 360, you could use the latest HLSL features as long as they run on your Xbox 360. If you are writing code to run on PCs, you should consider potential differences in graphics cards when writing your shaders.

For the XNA platform, Microsoft requires that your PC graphics card support at least shader model 2.0. However, shaders that are written using shader model 1.1 will also run on the Xbox 360.

Shader Inputs and Outputs

Parameters that are received and returned from the vertex and pixel shaders can be passed either through parameter lists in the shader headers or through structs. Either way, the data fields are denoted with *semantics* to bind the inputs and outputs passed between shaders and to bind the data from the shader to the graphics pipeline.

Shader Semantics

A shader semantic binds shader inputs to vertex data that is output from your XNA code. Shader semantics are also used to bind inputs and outputs together for passing data between shaders. In other words, a semantic is a syntactical element that denotes a piece of data that is passed between your XNA code, shaders, and the graphics pipeline. You can specify shader semantics for color, texture coordinates, normal vectors, position data, and more. Because it is possible to input more than one instance of a specific data type, you must use a numeric suffix to define the data type instance when referencing it more than once.

Common Vertex Shader Input Semantics   Here are some common vertex shader inputs that allow you to pass vertex properties from your XNA code to the vertex shader:

```
COLOR[n]     // color
NORMAL[n]    // normal vector
POSITION[n]  // vertex position
PSIZE[n]     // point size for point sprites
TEXCOORD[n]  // texture coordinates
```

The number, denoted by [n], specifies the instance of the data type since you can have more than one field storing data of the same type.

Common Vertex Shader Output Semantics   Vertex shader output semantics denote the data that is passed from a vertex shader to the pixel shader, where more processing can be performed on the vertex inputs, or to the graphics pipeline, where the vertex data is channeled for display in the window. You use semantics to bind the data that is passed between the vertex shader and the pixel shader. The outputs from the vertex shader use these semantics:

```
COLOR[n]     // color
POSITION[n]  // position
PSIZE        // size for point sprites
TEXCOORD[n]  // texture coordinates
```

Common Pixel Shader Input Semantics   The pixel shader can modify the color and texture data; it receives this information through the semantics shown here. You will notice that the position semantic is absent. The pixel shader can receive position information to implement calculations for effects such as lighting. However, the pixel shader cannot alter the position information because it is sent to the graphics pipeline from the vertex shader.

```
COLOR[n]     // color
TEXCOORD[n]  // texture coordinates
```

Common Pixel Shader Output Semantics   In most cases, and throughout this book, the only output returned from the pixel shader is the color of a pixel. Fittingly, the main output semantic for the pixel shader is the COLOR semantic:

```
COLOR[n]     // output color.
```

Shader Data Types

When looking at HLSL code, you will notice the shader data types are very similar in syntax to XNA data types. Table 4-1 compares the XNA data types with the HLSL data types used in this book.

TABLE 4-1

XNA Data Type	HLSL Data Type
Matrix	float4x4
Texture2D	Texture
struct MyStruct { public MyStruct(int i) { } };	Struct
Int	int
Float	float
Vector2	float2 // array with two elements
Vector3	float3 // array with three elements
Vector4	float4 // array with four elements
Color	float3 (with no alpha blending) or float4 (with alpha blending)

Comparison of XNA Data Types with Shader Data Types

HLSL Intrinsic Functions

HLSL provides several functions, and they are fully documented on Microsoft's MSDN site. Table 4-2 is a reference for the intrinsic functions used in this book. They are explained in more detail as they are used in each chapter.

Flow Control Syntax

Shaders implement C-like syntax for loops and conditional structures. Loop structures include for-loops, do-while loops, and while-loops. HLSL if-else syntax is the same used for any C-style language.

Referencing the Shader in Your XNA Project

To use shaders, your XNA application needs to load and reference them. The XNA platform makes this task easy by providing an Effect class with methods for loading and compiling the shader. Your XNA code can modify global shader variables through the EffectParameter class.

Referencing the Shader File in Your XNA Project

To create a new shader in your project, right-click the Shaders folder in the Solution Explorer. Then, select Add | New Item. In the *Add New Item* dialog that appears, you can enter the shader name. Note that the *.fx extension is the required extension for your shader file. Once the name is entered, click *Add* to add this file to your project.

TABLE 4-2

HLSL Intrinsic Functions	Inputs	Component Type	Outputs
abs(a)	**a** is a scalar, vector, or matrix.	float, int	Absolute value of **a**
clamp(a, min, max)	clamp(**a**, min, max)	float, int	Clamped value for **a**
cos(a)	**a** is a scalar, vector, or matrix.	float	Same dimension as **a**
dot(a, b)	**a** and **b** are vectors.	float	A scalar vector (dot product)
mul(a, b)	**a** and **b** can be vectors or matrices, but the **a** columns must match the **b** rows.	float	Matrix or vector, depending on the inputs
normalize(a)	**a** is a vector.	float	Unit vector
pow(a, b)	**a** is a scalar, vector, or matrix. **b** is the specified power.	**a** is a float. **b** is an integer.	a^b
Saturate(a)	**a** is a scalar, vector, or matrix.	**a** is a float.	**a** clamped between 0 and 1
sin(a)	**a** is a scalar, vector, or matrix.	float	Same dimension as **a**
tan(a)	**a** is a scalar, vector, or matrix.	float	Same dimension as **a**
tex2D(a,b)	**a** is a sampler2D. **b** is a vector.	**a** is a sampler2D. **b** is a two-dimensional float.	Vector

HLSL Intrinsic Functions

GSE will add code to generate a class shell, so you will need to manually delete this code before entering the code for your shader.

Alternatively, you can add a prewritten shader to your project from the Solution Explorer by right-clicking your project or shaders folder and selecting Add | Existing Item. From there, you can select the *.fx file from the *Add Existing Item* dialog that appears.

Effect

An Effect object allows you to load and compile the shader code, to finalize any variable changes that you made to the shader, and, of course, to send vertex data from your XNA code to the shader. The Effect class is used for declaring the Effect object:

```
private Effect                    effect;
```

When the shader is referenced in your project from the Solution Explorer, it can be read using the Load() method. HLSL shader files traditionally are named with an .fx extension. However, when the shader is referenced in the Solution Explorer, the .fx extension is dropped from the filename in the load statement from the code:

```
effect = content.Load<Effect>(@"DirectoryPath\ShaderName");
```

EffectParameter

EffectParameter objects allow you to set global variables in the shader from your XNA code. The EffectParameter class is used when declaring this object:

```
private EffectParameter          effectParameter;
```

When you have defined the EffectParameter object in your XNA code, you can then use it to reference global shader variables. An Effect object's Parameters collection stores references to all the global shader variables. The collection is indexed by the global variable name. Thus, the following stores a reference to a global shader variable:

```
effectParameter = effect.Parameters["globalVariableName"];
```

Once the EffectParameter objects have been declared and initialized, setting the variable in the shader is a two-step process. First, you assign the value using the SetValue() method:

```
effectParameter.SetValue(DataValue);
```

The parameter used in SetValue() must match the data type of the variable being set. Once the value has been set, you must finalize the change in the shader's state using the CommitChanges() method:

```
effect.CommitChanges();
```

Basic XNA Shader Example

This example demonstrates one of the most basic shaders, which does nothing more than output a primitive surface that uses a set of vertices for storing color and position. You will make adjustments to the shader so you can use your XNA code to change the color and position of the vertices that are drawn from the shader. In this case, the blue component of the rectangular surface will be set to automatically increment and decrement between 0 (for no blue) and 1 (for full blue) to create a flashing effect. The rectangular surface's position on the X axis will also be automatically incremented and decremented from the shader using a timescale to make it slide back and forth.

In Chapter 3, "Introduction to XNA Graphics Programming," we covered graphics basics for drawing primitive surfaces that use vertices that store position and color. The example in this chapter takes the material discussed in Chapter 3 a little further by showing how to control the vertex data output from the shader. On the surface, this example may not appear to offer anything remotely useful for a video game implementation. It has been kept simple to introduce the topic. Shaders will be discussed again in this book, and you will definitely find your efforts to understand this example worthy of your time. Chapter 7, "Texturing Your Game World," shows how to use the shader to texture your primitive surface with images; Chapter 10, "Combining Images for Better Visual Effects," shows how to create multitexturing effects using shaders; Chapter 18, "Particle Effects," explains how shaders can be implemented for fiery effects; and Chapter 20, "Lighting," demonstrates how to create advanced lighting using shaders.

This example begins with either the WinMGHBook base code or the Xbox360MGHBook base code—both can be found in the BaseCode folder in the download from the book's website.

First, a new shader, IntroShader.fx, must be referenced in your project from the Solution Explorer. The code for this shader is identical to the code discussed earlier in this chapter. It does nothing more than receive color and position data from your XNA code and display it. You can find this code under the Shaders directory in IntroShader.fx:

```
float4x4 fx_WVP : WORLDVIEWPROJ;

// vertex shader input
struct VS_INPUT{           // vertex data received from XNA code
    float4 f4Position    : POSITION0;
    float4 f4Color       : COLOR0;
};

struct VS_OUTPUT{          // output from vertex shader to pixel shader
    float4 f4Position    : POSITION0; // also goes to gfx pipeline
    float4 f4Color       : COLOR0;    // processed further in pixel shader
};

struct PS_OUTPUT{          // output to window is a colored pixel
    float4 f4Color       : COLOR0;
};

// alter vertex inputs
void vertex_shader(in VS_INPUT IN, out VS_OUTPUT OUT){
    float4  f4Pos  = IN.f4Position;
    OUT.f4Position = mul(f4Pos, fx_WVP);
    OUT.f4Color    = IN.f4Color;
}
```

```
// alter vs output and send to hardware one pixel at a time
void pixel_shader(in VS_OUTPUT IN, out PS_OUTPUT OUT){
    OUT.f4Color    = IN.f4Color;
}


// the shaders are defined here
technique simple{
    pass p0{
        vertexshader = compile vs_1_1 vertex_shader();
        pixelshader  = compile ps_1_1 pixel_shader();
    }
}
```

Basic XNA Shader Example Continued: Referencing the Shader from XNA

To reference your shader in code, you need an Effect object. Also, when drawing your object with this shader, you need an EffectParameter object to set the WVP matrix (to position your object), so it can be viewed properly in your window. The WVP matrix is explained in Chapter 15, "Building a Graphics Engine Camera." The Effect and EffectParameter objects should be added at the top of the game class so they can be used in your project:

```
private Effect             mfxEffect;      // shader object
private EffectParameter    mfxEffectWVP;   // cumulative matrix w*v*p
```

After your shader has been referenced in the Solution Explorer, you need to add code to load and initialize it from the Initialize() method. This allows you to compile and reference your shader when the program begins. Also, the EffectParameter object, mfxEffectWVP (declared earlier), is initialized to reference the fx_WVP global variable in the shader. Note that the file path is hard-coded to the IntroShader.fx file in the Shaders folder:

```
mfxEffect      = content.Load<Effect>(@"shaders\IntroShader");
mfxEffectWVP   = mfxEffect.Parameters["fx_WVP"];
```

The shader is now referenced and defined in your code. Next, you need to declare a set of vertices that can use this shader. Because the shader is designed to modify only position and color, it makes sense that the vertex definition is also set to store only color and position. This declaration in the game class at the module level will enable its use throughout the class:

```
private VertexPositionColor[]    mVertices = new VertexPositionColor[4];
```

A method is required to initialize the vertices that you will use to build the rectangular surface. Therefore, you'll add the initVertices() method to the game class to define each corner vertex of this rectangle:

```
private void initVertices(){
    Vector3 pos = new Vector3(0.0f, 0.0f, 0.0f);
    Color color = Color.White;

    // set for vertices of surface with pos and color data
    pos.X = -3.0f;   pos.Y = 3.0f; pos.Z = 15.0f;
    mVertices[0] = new VertexPositionColor(pos, color); // top right
    pos.X = -3.0f;   pos.Y = -3.0f; pos.Z = 15.0f;
    mVertices[1] = new VertexPositionColor(pos, color); // bottom right
    pos.X = 3.0f;    pos.Y = 3.0f; pos.Z = 15.0f;
    mVertices[2] = new VertexPositionColor(pos, color); // top left
    pos.X = 3.0f;    pos.Y = -3.0f; pos.Z = 15.0f;
    mVertices[3] = new VertexPositionColor(pos, color); // bottom left
}
```

To initialize the vertices that will be used to build the rectangle when the program starts, initVertices() is called from the Initialize() method:

```
initVertices();
```

The code used to draw the rectangle from the vertices that have been declared follows the same five steps described in the preceding chapter. Step 4 of this method makes use of the new EffectParameter by setting the matrix in the new shader for positioning the rectangle properly relative to the camera. The new Effect object, mfxEffect, is then used to commit the changes to the shader:

```
private void drawRectangle(){
    // 1: declare matrices
    Matrix matIdentity, matTransl;

    // 2: initialize matrices
    matIdentity = Matrix.Identity; // always start with identity matrix
    matTransl   = Matrix.CreateTranslation(0.0f, -0.9f, 0.0f);

    // 3: build cumulative world matrix using I.S.R.O.T. sequence
    // identity, scale, rotate, orbit(translate & rotate), translate
    mMatWorld = matIdentity * matTransl;

    // 4: pass wvp matrix to shader
```

```
mfxEffectWVP.SetValue(mMatWorld * mMatView * mMatProj);
mfxEffect.CommitChanges();

// 5: draw object - select vertex type, primitive type, # of primitives
gfx.GraphicsDevice.VertexDeclaration = mVertPosColor;
gfx.GraphicsDevice.DrawUserPrimitives<VertexPositionColor>(
                   PrimitiveType.TriangleStrip, mVertices, 0, 2);
}
```

When drawing the rectangle, you will use a new version of the Draw() method to reference the new shader. All drawing that uses this new shader must be triggered between the Begin() and End() statements for the Effect object mfxEffect. The vertex shaders and pixel shaders that you will use are set inside each pass. But, in this case, only one pass is used in the shader. All drawing is done from within the Begin() and End() methods for the pass. To draw the new rectangular surface, replace the existing Draw() method with this revision:

```
protected override void Draw(GameTime gameTime){
    // clear screen, set background, start drawing
    gfx.GraphicsDevice.Clear(Color.Black);

    // begin shader - IntroShader.fx
    mfxEffect.Begin();
    mfxEffect.Techniques[0].Passes[0].Begin();

        // draw objects
        drawRectangle();

    // end shader - IntroShader.fx
    mfxEffect.Techniques[0].Passes[0].End();
    mfxEffect.End();

    // stop drawing and present offscreen buffer
    base.Draw(gameTime);
}
```

If you ran the project with the current modifications, it would show a white stationary rectangle with a black background.

One of the first modifications you will make is to modify the blue component of the RGB colors that are rendered. In the shader, you can do this by creating a global variable at the top of the IntroShader.fx file:

```
float     fx_Blue;
```

Next, you need a function inside the IntroShader.fx file to change the blue component of the RGB color that is drawn from the shader. Note that you use the color vector's b component to adjust the blue intensity by assigning to it the global value fx_Blue:

```
float4 changeBlueValue(){
    float4 f4col;
    f4col.r=0.0f; f4col.g=0.0f; f4col.b=fx_Blue; f4col.a=1.0f;
    return f4col;
}
```

NOTE Shader functions must be declared before they are used in the shader; otherwise, the shader file will not compile. This requirement, of course, applies when placing changeBlueValue() in the shader, and the same logic applies for the changePosition() function that follows.

The code that outputs the color from the vertex shader to the pixel shader must now change to handle the modifications to the blue component. Note that when you are multiplying vectors in HLSL, the product becomes $(a_1*b_1, a_2*b_2, a_3*b_3, a_4*b_4)$. Replace the existing color assignment in the vertex shader with this version to alter the blue component:

```
OUT.f4Color    = IN.f4Color * changeBlueValue();
```

To reference the fx_Blue shader variable used to adjust the blue component from your XNA code, you declare the EffectParameter mfxEffectBlue. In the Game1.cs file, add a module declaration for it:

```
private EffectParameter mfxEffectBlue;    // blue color (range is 0 to 1)
```

Next, to initialize this object, add the following line to the Initialize() method of your game class after the code where the Effect object, mfxEffect, has been loaded and initialized:

```
mfxEffectBlue = mfxEffect.Parameters["fx_Blue"];
```

Class-level variables are used to adjust the blue component of the color that is output every frame. A Boolean value is used to track whether the floating point is increasing or decreasing, and a float is used to track the actual value:

```
private float    mfBlue        = 0.0f;
private bool     mbBlueIncrease = true;
```

A method is used to increase or decrease the value of the blue component each frame. The blue portion of the RGB color ranges between 0 and 1, where 0 is no color and 1 is full blue. Each frame, this value is incremented or decremented by a scaled amount based on the time difference between frames. This time scalar ensures the color change is at the same rate regardless of the system that shows the animation. Add the setBlueColor() method to your game class to implement this routine:

```
void setBlueColor(GameTime gameTime){
    // use elapsed time between frames to increment
    // this ensures a smooth animation which takes the same time to
    // complete on any system
    if(mbBlueIncrease)
        mfBlue += (float)gameTime.ElapsedGameTime.Milliseconds/1000.0f;
    else
        mfBlue -= (float)gameTime.ElapsedGameTime.Milliseconds/1000.0f;

    if (mfBlue <= 0.0f)             // decrement as long as greater than 0
        mbBlueIncrease = true;
    else if (mfBlue >= 1.0f)    // increment as long as less than 1
        mbBlueIncrease = false;

    mfxEffectBlue.SetValue(mfBlue); // set new blue value in shader
    mfxEffect.CommitChanges();      // commit new state to shader
}
```

To update the blue color each frame, you call setBlueColor() from the Update() method:

```
setBlueColor(gameTime);
```

If you run the code now, you will notice that the blue color component changes, ranging from between 0 and 1. Because the red and green colors are set at 0, the color range for the rectangle is between black and dark blue.

Next, you will make another change to automatically adjust the position of the rectangle—to move it side to side on the X axis. To enable this, in the global variable section of the shader, you declare a variable to store the value of the position on the X plane:

```
float fx_PosX;
```

This function, added to the shader, changes the value of the X position:

```
float4 changePosition(float4 f4Position){
    float4 f4Pos = f4Position;
    f4Pos.x      += fx_PosX;
```

```
    return f4Pos;
}
```

To implement the change in the vertex shader, replace the definition for f4Pos with the definition that follows. This takes the current position and shifts it on the X axis by the amount stored in the fx_PosX global variable:

```
float4  f4Pos =  changePosition(IN.f4Position);
```

Back in your XNA code, an EffectParameter is required to reference the fx_PosX global variable in the shader:

```
private EffectParameter mfxEffectPosX;     // position
```

To initialize this effect parameter inside Initialize(), after the Effect object is set up, add the following instruction to reference the fx_PosX shader variable from the Effect's collection:

```
mfxEffectPosX = mfxEffect.Parameters["fx_PosX"];
```

With a reference to a shader variable that is used to modify the position of the rectangle, some XNA code can be added to actually track the X value and reset it. Add the float mfXpos declaration to store the current X increment for the rectangle. Also, add the mbXIncrease Boolean variable to track whether the variable is to be incremented or decremented:

```
private float    mfXpos     = 0.0f;
private bool     mbXIncrease = true;
```

The code for updating the X increment is added to the game class:

```
void setPositionX(GameTime gameTime){
    // use elapsed time between frames to increment
    // this ensures a smooth animation which takes the same time to
    // complete on any system
    if (mbXIncrease)
        mfXpos += (float)gameTime.ElapsedGameTime.Milliseconds/1000.0f;
    else
        mfXpos -= (float)gameTime.ElapsedGameTime.Milliseconds/1000.0f;

    if (mfXpos <= -1.0f)          // decrement as long as greater than -1
        mbXIncrease = true;
    else if (mfXpos >= 1.0f)    // increment as long as less than 1
        mbXIncrease = false;
```

```
    mfxEffectPosX.SetValue(mfXpos); // set new X value in shader
    mfxEffect.CommitChanges();      // commit new state to shader
}
```

Updates to the X increment for the rectangle are triggered from the Update() method every frame:

```
setPositionX(gameTime);
```

When you run this version of the code, you will see a flashing blue rectangle that moves from side to side.

XNA'S BASICEFFECT CLASS

XNA offers the BasicEffect class, which actually is a built-in shader that you can use to render your 3D graphics. On one hand, compared to writing your own HLSL, the BasicEffect class does not offer you as much flexibility to customize the way your vertex data is filtered, blended, and displayed as pixel output. However, you can rely on the BasicEffect class to quickly and simply implement lighting, and it is especially useful for rendering 3D models. Chapter 12, "3D Models," demonstrates the use of the BasicEffect shader to render and light 3D models. The BasicEffect class lighting properties are explained and implemented in Chapter 20, "Lighting."

A BasicEffect object is instantiated with the BasicEffect class:

```
BasicEffect    basicEffect
= new BasicEffect(GraphicsDevice device, EffectPool effectPool);
```

Setting Properties Within the BasicEffect Class

When drawing objects using the BasicEffect class, you will need to set the World, View, and Projection matrices to implement object movement, scaling, and rotations and to position your objects in the window so they can be seen properly as you view the 3D world. These matrices are explained in more detail in Chapter 15, "Building a Graphics Engine Camera." When implementing a custom shader (as demonstrated earlier in the chapter), an EffectParameter is used to set these matrix values. With the BasicEffect class, you don't have to create an EffectParameter object for each variable you want to set. Instead, you can assign these values to the BasicEffect's World, View, and Projection properties:

```
Matrix  basicEffect.World      = Matrix  worldMatrix;
Matrix  basicEffect.View       = Matrix  viewMatrix;
Matrix  basicEffect.Projection = Matrix  projectionMatrix;
```

Similar to the custom shader, whenever you change the state of the BasicEffect shader—by assigning a value to one of the BasicEffect's attributes—you have to finalize the change by calling the CommitChanges() method:

```
basicEffect.CommitChanges();
```

Techniques and Passes Within the BasicEffect Class

Similar to a custom shader that you would write on your own, the BasicEffect class uses a technique to define the vertex and pixel shaders and to set the total number of passes used to render an object each frame. To use the BasicEffect shader when drawing your objects, you use the following construct to select the technique and pass(es) within it. All drawing is performed between the Begin() and End() methods for the BasicEffect object:

```
basicEffect.Begin();
foreach (EffectPass pass in basicEffect.CurrentTechnique.Passes){
    pass.Begin();
        // rendering is done here
    pass.End();
}
basicEffect.End();
```

BasicEffect Class Example

This demonstration shows how to convert the existing base code to use the BasicEffect class to draw the ground with a grass texture. Currently, the base code uses the shader TextureShader.fx. Note that this demonstration uses texturing to apply images to the surfaces you draw before a proper explanation is given. Chapter 7, "Texturing Your Game World," provides a more detailed explanation of how the texturing works.

This example begins with either the WinMGHBook or the Xbox360MGHBook base code from the BaseCode folder in this book's download. Converting it to use the BasicEffect class to draw the textured ground can be done in two steps.

First, you will need to declare an instance of the BasicEffect at the top of the game class so it you can use it throughout the class:

```
BasicEffect basicEffect;
```

The BasicEffect instance should be initialized when the program begins in Initialize(). Regenerating this BasicEffect instance locally anywhere else on a continuous basis will slow down your program considerably, so you should only do it when the program starts:

```
basicEffect    = new BasicEffect(gfx.GraphicsDevice, null);
```

Next, replace the existing draw_ground() method in the game class with this new version, which uses a BasicEffect object to do the rendering. Most of the routine remains the same. However, in step 4, the World, View, and Projection properties for the BasicEffect class are set to provide it with information about the camera. This way, it can render the ground and be seen properly by the camera. Also in step 4, the texture is set to the grass texture. These changes are then committed to the shader. In step 5, the BasicEffect technique is selected and the rendering is done in the passes that have been automatically selected by the technique.

Replace the existing version of draw_ground() with this routine to draw the ground with the BasicEffect shader:

```
private void draw_ground(){
    // 1: declare matrices
    Matrix matIdentity, matTransl;

    // 2: initialize matrices
    matIdentity = Matrix.Identity; // always start with identity matrix
    matTransl = Matrix.CreateTranslation(0.0f, -0.9f, 0.0f);

    // 3: build cumulative world matrix using I.S.R.O.T. sequence
    // identity, scale, rotate, orbit(translate & rotate), translate
    mMatWorld = matIdentity * matTransl;

    // 4: pass matrix values to shader and commit them
    basicEffect.World         = mMatWorld;
    basicEffect.View          = mMatView;
    basicEffect.Projection     = mMatProj;
    basicEffect.TextureEnabled = true;
    basicEffect.Texture       = mTexGrass;
    basicEffect.CommitChanges();

    // 5: draw object - select vertex type, primitive type, # of primitives
    basicEffect.Begin();
    foreach (EffectPass pass in basicEffect.CurrentTechnique.Passes){
    pass.Begin();
        gfx.GraphicsDevice.VertexDeclaration = mVertPosColorTex;
        gfx.GraphicsDevice.DrawUserPrimitives<VertexPositionColorTexture>(
                    PrimitiveType.TriangleStrip, mVertGround, 0, 2);
    pass.End();
    }
    basicEffect.End();
}
```

Because no external shader is referenced, draw_ground() would already use the BasicEffect shader to draw the ground, so you do not need to reference any other shaders in the draw method. If you wanted, you could replace the existing Draw() routine with this version to draw the ground without referencing any other shaders:

```
protected override void Draw(GameTime gameTime) {
    // clear screen, set background, start drawing
    gfx.GraphicsDevice.Clear(Color.CornflowerBlue);
    draw_ground();
    base.Draw(gameTime);
}
```

When you run the code now, the textured ground will appear as before, but this time it will be rendered using the BasicEffect class.

If you have ever seen the NVIDIA or AMD shader demos, you would agree that shaders can be used for some incredibly slick and even crazy graphics effects. The examples in this chapter have intentionally been kept simple by comparison but will gradually become more complex as the chapters progress.

CHAPTER 4 REVIEW EXERCISES

1. Implement the step-by-step examples in this chapter.

2. In the first example, try adding a field with a POSITION semantic to the pixel shader output and notice that it can't be done. Why is this the case?

3. In the first example, replace the instruction in the vertex shader that defines the color output with the following:

    ```
    OUT.f4Color    = IN.f4Color;
    ```

    In the pixel shader, replace the instruction that defines the color output with this:

    ```
    OUT.f4Color    = IN.f4Color * changeBlueValue();
    ```

    When you run the code after this change, the output will be the same as before, but the color transformation will be performed on a per-pixel basis rather than a per-vertex basis.

CHAPTER 5

Animation Introduction

AFTER working through Chapter 3, "Introduction to XNA Graphics Programming," you should now be comfortable building structures with lines and triangles. If you create a butterfly, a bird, a car, an airplane, or even a monster out of lines and triangles, you will surely want to animate your 3D object. Animation is the vital ingredient that brings life to your creation when you flick the switch.

Animating an object requires that you have the ability to rotate, move, or even resize the object. The process of scaling and moving objects is referred to as a *transformation*. Transformations include:

❭ Setting the *identity* as a default for the World matrix if no transformations are specified.

❭ *Scaling* to resize the object.

❭ Using *translations* for horizontal, vertical, up, down, and diagonal movements on the X, Y, and Z planes.

❭ *Rotating* an object about its own axis. This is referred to as a *revolution*.

❭ *Rotating* an object about an external fixed point. This is referred to as the object's *orbit*.

XNA offers several methods for performing transformations. Familiarity with these methods is crucial since they greatly reduce the amount of code you have to write to bring movement to your 3D environment.

While this chapter may seem to be somewhat trivial, the topic of transformations is extremely important. For new graphics programmers, understanding this chapter and Chapter 6, "Character Movement," is essential to harness XNA and take control of your 3D animations.

RIGHT HAND RULE

Like all 3D graphics libraries, XNA allows you to create 3D worlds on a Cartesian graph with X, Y, and Z axes. The orientation of each axis on the graph, with respect to the other axes, defines the direction for positive and negative translations and rotations. With an upright Y axis, it is possible to have an X axis that runs either outward to the left or to the right, and a Z axis that increases either in a forwards or backward direction. The XNA developer team has implemented the Cartesian coordinate system from a Right Hand Rule perspective. Figure 5-1 shows two possible scenarios under the Right Hand Rule where positive movement in the X, Y, and Z planes depends on the direction along the Z plane from the viewer (known as the camera) to the target being looked at (known as the view). The graphics engine used in this book implements a camera where the direction along Z from the camera to the

FIGURE 5-1

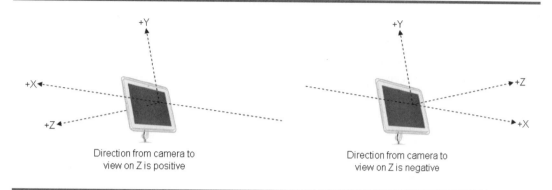

Direction from camera to
view on Z is positive

Direction from camera to
view on Z is negative

Applying the Right Hand Rule

view is positive. See Chapter 15, "Building a Graphics Engine Camera," for more detail on this camera implementation. This scenario is illustrated on the left side of Figure 5-1.

When you use the graphics engine for this book, which is summarized in the scenario on the left of Figure 5-1, keep the following points in mind:

❯ Positive translations on the X axis are toward the left.

❯ Positive translations on the Y axis are upward.

❯ Positive translations on the Z axis are away from the viewer.

In any case, there is a common mnemonic device to remember how the Right Hand Rule affects the direction of rotation in the X, Y, and Z planes. To determine the positive direction for a rotation about X, Y, and Z, with your right hand imagine gripping the axis with your thumb extended in the direction of the arrow. When you curl your fingers about the axis in a counter-clockwise direction, this is the positive rotation.

MATRIX LOGIC

3D transformations are performed using matrix algebra. With this in mind, XNA provides several methods to automate the process of building and applying matrices to resize, rotate, and translate objects in 3D space. More detail about the underlying linear algebra is provided in Chapter 14, "Matrices." However, even after the math behind the matrices is explained, the XNA methods for applying matrix transformations will remain crucial as a fast and efficient way to perform transformations.

Each type of transformation is implemented with a separate matrix. Scaling an object, rotating an object about X, Y, and Z, and translating an object all require separate transformation matrices. Once each individual transformation matrix has been defined, they are combined using multiplication to build one cumulative transformation matrix. This cumulative matrix is referred to as the *World matrix*.

Transformation Order

The order that the matrices for scaling, rotating, and translating are combined is significant. For successful transformations, it is essential that you combine individual transformations in the following order:

1. Set the **Identity**.

2. **Scale** the object.

3. **Revolve** the object about its axis.

4. **Orbit** the object about an external point. (This involves a translation followed by a rotation.)

5. **Translate** the object.

> **TIP** To remember the order of transformations for the Right Hand Rule, use the I.S.R.O.T. sequence. I.S.R.O.T. stands for Identity, Scale, Revolve, Orbit, Translate.

NA MATRIX SYNTAX

XNA stores matrices in the Matrix object. The Matrix object stores data used to calculate transformations. Most of the time, XNA will automate your use of matrices, so you do not have to fuss about the data or structure of your matrices. Occasionally, you will want to work with matrices more closely to perform complex transformations. Chapter 14, "Matrices," explains their structure in more detail.

Identity Matrix

You cannot actually transform an object with the identity matrix. The identity matrix is only used as a default matrix to initialize the cumulative transformation matrix, known as the World matrix, in the shader when no other transformations are assigned. If the identity matrix is the only matrix used in the World transformation, the primitive surface or 3D model will be drawn wherever the X, Y, and Z coordinates for this object are defined.

Multiplying a data matrix by the identity matrix gives the data matrix as a product. Whenever there are transformations, you can omit the identity matrix from your calculation and still end up with the same transformation. XNA provides an instance for you that can be obtained with the reference Matrix.Identity:

```
Matrix matrix = Matrix.Identity;
```

Scaling Matrix

The scaling matrix is used to resize objects drawn using primitives or 3D models. The Matrix.Scale() method can be used to generate a scaling matrix based on the amount of resizing needed on X, Y, and Z. The Matrix.Scale() method accepts three float parameters to set the amount of sizing on the X, Y, and Z planes.

```
Matrix matrix = Matrix.Scale(float X, float Y, float Z);
```

Here are some examples of scaling:

```
// half size on X, Y, and Z
Matrix matrix = Matrix.CreateScale(0.5f, 0.5f, 0.5f);
// double size on X, Y, and Z
Matrix matrix = Matrix.CreateScale(2.0f, 2.0f, 2.0f);
// double Y. X and Z stay same
Matrix matrix = Matrix.CreateScale(1.0f, 2.0f, 1.0f);
```

Rotation Matrices

Rotations about each of the X, Y, and Z axes are implemented with another matrix. XNA provides a separate method for generating each of these rotation matrices. The input parameter for each method requires an angle in radians. Remember that 2π radians = 360 degrees.

```
Matrix matrix =  Matrix.CreateRotationX(float radians);
Matrix matrix =  Matrix.CreateRotationY(float radians);
Matrix matrix =  Matrix.CreateRotationZ(float radians);
```

Translation Matrices

XNA provides a one-step, user-friendly method to build a simultaneous translation along the X, Y, and Z planes. Here is the syntax:

```
Matrix matrix = Matrix.CreateTranslation(float X, float Y, float Z);
```

STEPS FOR DRAWING A PRIMITIVE OBJECT OR A 3D MODEL

The routine used to draw an object using primitives or a 3D model can be implemented in many ways. For consistency and clarity, most examples in this book follow this routine for drawing objects that use primitives:

1. Declare the transformation matrices.

2. Initialize the transformation matrices.

3. Build the total cumulative transformation matrix, known as the World matrix, using the I.S.R.O.T. sequence.

4. Set the shader variables.

5. Draw the object.

CAUTION For effective transformations, center the vertices that define your objects at the origin. Failing to do this can create unwanted translations that are difficult to handle and debug.

Declaring and Initializing Individual Matrices

Steps 1 and 2 of this recommended drawing routine require the declaration and initialization of each individual transformation matrix. As a minimum, the identity matrix is created to initialize the World matrix in the shader if no transformations are set.

Building the Cumulative World Matrix

In step 3 of this drawing routine, the cumulative World matrix is built by multiplying the individual matrices together. The I.S.R.O.T. sequence must be used to build this matrix. However, if a scale, rotation, orbit, or translation is performed, you can omit the identity matrix.

Setting the Shader Values

In step 4 of the drawing routine, the product of the transformation matrices, also known as the World matrix, is set in the shader. You may also set other variables in the shader, such as textures or colors, if you need to modify these values when rendering. Once the variable states in the shader have been changed from your XNA code, the CommitChanges() method is called to finalize the changes in the shader.

Drawing the Object

Step 5 of this recommended routine involves drawing the output. In the preceding chapter, steps for selecting the vertex type and drawing surfaces using primitive objects were explained in detail. However, this last step could be modified to draw 3D models. Either way, the steps taken to apply the transformations remain the same.

APPLYING TRANSFORMATIONS: EARTH AND MOON EXAMPLE

This example demonstrates transformations by drawing simple Earth and Moon objects. Both the Earth and Moon objects are actually just triangles. The Earth is shown revolving about its own axis. The Moon is shown with its own revolution as it also orbits around the Earth (see Figure 5-2).

This example begins with either the WinMGHBook project or the Xbox360MGHBook project found in the BaseCode folder in the download.

A vertex array to store the position and color elements for each of the three vertices in the triangle is required. To create an array that can store this vertex information (which can be used throughout the game class) in your Game1.cs file, add the following class-level declaration:

```
private VertexPositionColor[]   mVertTriangle   = new
VertexPositionColor[3];
```

To implement a continuous rotation for both the Earth and Moon, module-level variables are used in the game class. These variables store the current rotation about the Y axis.

```
float mfEarthY, mfMoonY;
```

Adding the init_triangle() method to your game class initializes the vertices used by both the Earth and Moon. To ensure a smooth animation, the vertices are centered about the origin when they are initialized:

```
private void init_triangle()
{
    Vector3 pos = new Vector3(0.0f, 0.0f, 0.0f);
    pos.X = 0.5f; pos.Y = 0.0f; pos.Z = 0.0f;
    mVertTriangle[0] = new VertexPositionColor(pos, Color.Orange);
    pos.X = 0.0f; pos.Y = 0.5f; pos.Z = 0.0f;
    mVertTriangle[1] = new VertexPositionColor(pos, Color.OrangeRed);
    pos.X =-0.5f; pos.Y = 0.0f; pos.Z = 0.0f;
    mVertTriangle[2] = new VertexPositionColor(pos, Color.OrangeRed);
}
```

FIGURE 5-2

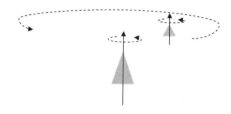

Earth and Moon example

The vertices for the Earth and Moon are set when the program begins, so init_triangle() is called from the Initialize() method:

```
init_triangle();
```

Here are the five recommended steps for drawing the revolving Earth object:

1. Declare the matrices.

2. Initialize the matrices. The identity matrix is initialized as a default matrix in the event of no transformations. (Try leaving it out of the transformation, and notice you still get the same result.) A matrix that generates the Earth's revolution on the Y axis is computed based on a constantly changing angle in radians. Every frame, the angle is incremented with a value based on the time lapse between frames. This time-scaled increment to the rotation angle ensures that the animation appears smoothly while maintaining a constant rate of change. Scaling the increment based on time is necessary because durations between frames can vary depending on other tasks being performed by the operating system. Finally, a translation is created to move the Earth 0.5 units upward on the Y axis and 3.0 units inward on the Z axis.

3. The World matrix is built by multiplying each of the matrices in the transformation using the I.S.R.O.T. sequence.

4. The World matrix used to transform the Earth is passed to the shader as part of the World*View*Projection matrix.

5. The triangle is rendered by drawing vertices with a triangle strip.

Adding draw_earth() to the game class provides the code needed for transforming and drawing the Earth:

```
private void draw_earth()
{
    // 1: declare matrices
    Matrix matIdentity, matTransl, matRotationY;

    // 2: initialize matrices
    matIdentity     = Matrix.Identity;

    // calculate rotation about the Y axis
    matRotationY    = Matrix.CreateRotationY(mfEarthY);
    mfEarthY        += (float)TargetElapsedTime.Milliseconds / 1000.0f;
    mfEarthY        = mfEarthY % (float)(2 * Math.PI);  // prevent overflow
```

```
// translation
matTransl          = Matrix.CreateTranslation(0.0f, 0.5f, 3.0f);


// 3: build cumulative World matrix using I.S.R.O.T. sequence
// identity, scale, rotate, orbit(translate & rotate), translate
mMatWorld = matIdentity * matRotationY * matTransl;


// 4: pass World matrix to shader
worldViewProjParam.SetValue(mMatWorld * mMatView * mMatProj);
mfx.CommitChanges();


// 5: draw object - select vertex type, primitive type, # of primitives
gfx.GraphicsDevice.VertexDeclaration = mVertPosColor;
gfx.GraphicsDevice.DrawUserPrimitives<VertexPositionColor>
(PrimitiveType.TriangleStrip,
 mVertTriangle, 0, 1);
}
```

Next, the draw_moon() method implements the same five-step drawing routine to transform and render the same vertices as a Moon object. The Moon has its own revolution about the Y axis, and it also orbits around the Earth. In addition, the Moon is scaled to one fifth the size of the Earth.

The draw_moon() method performs all of the same transformations as the draw_earth() method. Plus, draw_moon() implements scaling and an orbit. All of the matrices declared in the draw_earth() method are declared in draw_moon() to perform the same transformations. Also, additional matrices are declared and set in this method to handle the scaling and orbit. The scale is set to draw the object at one fifth the size of the Earth by assigning the scale matrix the following value:

```
Matrix.CreateScale(0.2f, 0.2f, 0.2f);
```

Remember that the orbit is a two-step process that involves a translation followed by a rotation. When the World matrix is built, the crucial I.S.R.O.T. sequence is used to ensure that the matrices are multiplied in the proper order:

mMatWorld = matIdentity * matScale * matRotationY
* matOrbTranslation * matOrbRotation * matTransl;

Since the same vertices are used for drawing the Moon and the Earth, steps 4 and 5 of draw_moon() are identical to those in draw_earth().

```
private void draw_moon()
{
```

```
// 1: declare matrices
Matrix matIdentity, matScale, matRotationY, matTransl;
Matrix matOrbTranslation, matOrbRotation;

// 2: initialize matrices
matIdentity       = Matrix.Identity; // default
matScale          = Matrix.CreateScale(0.2f, 0.2f, 0.2f);

mfMoonY           = mfMoonY % (float)(2 * Math.PI);
mfMoonY           +=1.5f*(float)TargetElapsedTime.Milliseconds/1000.0f;
matRotationY      = Matrix.CreateRotationY(mfMoonY);

matOrbTranslation = Matrix.CreateTranslation(0.0f, 0.5f, 1.0f);
matOrbRotation    = Matrix.CreateRotationY(mfMoonY);
matTransl         = Matrix.CreateTranslation(0.0f, 0.5f, 3.0f);

// 3: build cumulative World matrix using I.S.R.O.T. sequence
// identity, scale, rotate, orbit(translate & rotate), translate
mMatWorld = matIdentity * matScale * matRotationY * matOrbTranslation
            * matOrbRotation * matTransl;

// 4: pass World matrix to shader
worldViewProjParam.SetValue(mMatWorld * mMatView * mMatProj);
mfx.CommitChanges();

// 5: draw object - select vertex type, primitive type, # of primitives
gfx.GraphicsDevice.VertexDeclaration = mVertPosColor;

gfx.GraphicsDevice.DrawUserPrimitives<VertexPositionColor>
(PrimitiveType.TriangleStrip, mVertTriangle, 0, 1);
}
```

Both the draw_earth() and draw_moon() methods are called from the Draw()
method in the game class. Since the triangle stores vertices that are compatible with
those defined in the BasicShader.fx file, you should call these draw methods between
the Begin() and End() statements for the mfx object:

```
draw_earth();
draw_moon();
```

When you compile and run this code, it will show the Earth as a revolving triangle
being orbited by a revolving Moon (refer to Figure 5-2).

Spend the time you need to ensure that you understand transformations. It is not an overly complex topic, but it can be challenging for beginner graphics programmers who do not give transformations the learning time the topic deserves. You will enjoy the rest of the book more when you have mastered this introduction to animation.

Be fearless when experimenting with your transformations. When you test and run your projects, you will probably know right away if your transformations are working properly. Of course, use the documentation presented in this section as a guide to understanding the topic. The real learning will happen when you try to create your own transformations.

CHAPTER 5 REVIEW EXERCISES

1. Implement the step-by-step example presented in this chapter.

2. Using primitives, create a stationary airplane with a rotating propeller that is made from triangles, as in the following illustration. When initializing the vertices that store the propeller, be sure to center the X, Y, and Z coordinates around the origin. Failure to center the X, Y, and Z coordinates of your surface about the origin will offset your rotations and will lead to strange results when unbalanced objects are transformed.

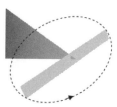

3. When you finish Exercise 2, transform your propeller so it serves as a rotor for a helicopter. Using the same set of vertices, write another procedure to transform and render the same rectangle used for the main rotor as a back rotor, as shown here.

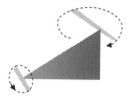

CHAPTER 6

Character Movement

AFTER reading and applying the material covered in Chapter 5, "Animation Introduction," you should be comfortable performing simple animations with translations and rotations. For most gamers, it is not enough just to make a bird flap its wings or make the propeller of an airplane spin; anybody with half an ounce of curiosity wants to see these objects actually fly. This chapter introduces a simple animation method that allows moving objects to travel independently within your 3D world.

 **NOTE** — Additional methods for enabling the movement of objects are covered in Chapter 19, "Keyframe Animations."

Regardless of the method used to move objects and characters, basic movement is generated by updating the X, Y, and Z position coordinates, as well as the rotation angles of the moving object rendered at every frame.

DIRECTION

When you animate vehicles that fly, drive, sail, or glide, you would most likely expect them to point in the direction they are traveling. Calculating the angle of direction can be done using several methods. Without this calculation, your vehicles could look like they are flying backward or even sideways. Trigonometry offers a simple intuitive approach to calculate the angle of direction that is used often throughout this book. However, vectors can also be used to compute direction. Using vectors to calculate direction is actually a more powerful method for implementing rotations of direction because they offer a simpler means to implement complex transformations.

Calculating Direction Using Trigonometry

The trigonometry applied in this chapter is actually very simple and only involves using the arctangent function. The arctangent function enables calculations of direction about the Y axis when the X and Z coordinates of the object are known.

When the Right Hand Rule is used, all positive rotations are counterclockwise. To calculate an object's angle about the Y axis, draw a line from the object's position to the preceding axis in the rotation to create a right-angle triangle. The tangent of the angle between the hypotenuse and the axis can be calculated with the following equation:

$\tan \theta$ = opposite side length / adjacent side length (where θ is the angle)

This equation can be rearranged to isolate the angle:

$\theta = \tan^{-1}$ (opposite / adjacent)
$\theta =$ atan (opposite / adjacent)

Figure 6-1 shows the angle about the Y axis in relation to the hypotenuse, opposite, and adjacent sides of the right-angle triangle.

Calculating Direction Using Speed

When Y is constant, the change in X and Z during each frame measures speed. On a three-dimensional graph, the X and Z speed combination will always fall in one of four quadrants, depending on whether each of the X and Z speeds is positive or negative.

Calculating Direction Using the Math.Atan() Function To calculate the angle of direction about the Y axis, create an imaginary right-angle triangle by drawing a line from the X, Z coordinate to the preceding X or Z axis. This line must be perpendicular to the X or Z axis. You can use XNA's Math.Atan() function to compute the angle of rotation about the Y axis using the corresponding X and Z values as opposite and adjacent parameters:

```
double radians = Math.Atan( (double) opposite / (double) adjacent );
```

The Math.Atan() function then returns the angle of rotation about Y for the immediate quadrant. An offset that equals the total rotation for the preceding quadrants is added to this angle to give the total rotation in radians. Figure 6-2 illustrates the relationship between the X and Z speeds for each quadrant and their offsets.

FIGURE 6-1

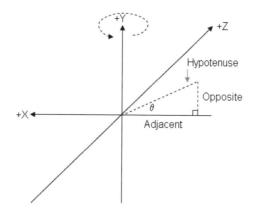

Hypotenuse, opposite, and adjacent sides of a right-angle triangle

FIGURE 6-2

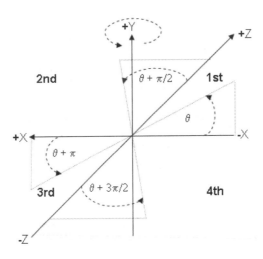

Calculating angle of direction about the Y axis using speed quadrants

When the Math.Atan() function is used, each quadrant uses a slightly different equation to generate the rotation about the Y axis. These individual quadrant equations are summarized in Table 6-1.

Understanding this basic trigonometry can help you develop algorithms to generate your own direction angles.

Calculating Direction Using the Math.Atan2() Function   Thankfully, there is an easier way to employ trigonometry to calculate the angle of direction about the Y axis. The Math.Atan2() function eliminates the need to factor quadrant differences into the

TABLE 6-1

Quadrant	Offset	Equation
I	0	Math.Atan $(z/-x)$
2	$\pi/2$	Math.Atan (x/z) + $\pi/2$
3	π	Math.Atan $(-z/x)$ + π
4	$3\pi/2$	Math.Atan $(-x/-z)$ + $3\pi/2$

Quadrant Equations to Calculate the Angle of Direction About the Y Axis

calculations. To compute the angle of rotation about the Y axis with the Math.Atan2() function, the calculation becomes this:

```
double radians = Math.Atan2((double) X / (double) Z)
```

This equation can be used to calculate the angle of direction about the Y axis for all quadrants.

Both the Math.Atan() and Math.Atan2() functions will be demonstrated in the example presented in this chapter.

Calculating Direction Using Vectors

Calculating direction using vectors is the more powerful method. The math behind implementing vectors of direction is explained in more detail later in Chapter 13, "Vectors," Chapter 14, "Matrices," and Chapter 15, "Building a Graphics Engine Camera," so you may choose to read these chapters first for a better understanding of how the vectors work. The vector logic for calculating direction is being presented ahead of these chapters to ensure you have a better way to move your vehicles, vessels, and aircraft through your 3D world.

The vectors that describe the orientation of a moving object can be summarized using the Look, Up, and Right vectors. These vectors describe the moving object's direction and uprightness (see Figure 6-3).

The Look vector is calculated from the difference in the view position and the position of the object. When you are animating objects, the Look vector could also be the same as the object's speed vector. The Up vector describes the upright direction. For most objects that are animated in this book, the starting upright direction is 0, 1, 0. When we stand on our own two feet we have an Up vector of 0, 1, 0. The Right vector describes the perpendicular from the surface created by the Up and Look vectors. The Right vector can be used for a strafe in addition to assisting with the computation of angles of direction.

If the Up vector is known, the Right vector can be calculated using the cross product of the Look and Up vectors. The Right vector equals the cross product of the Up and Look vectors.

FIGURE 6-3

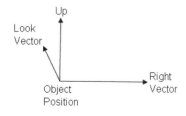

Direction vectors

When these vectors are normalized, or scaled so their length is 1, they can be used in a matrix that calculates the angle of direction. The cells of the matrix are defined with the data from the three direction vectors:

```
mat.M11 = v3R.X; mat.M12 = v3R.Y; mat.M13 = v3R.Z; mat.M14 =0.0f;//Right
mat.M21 = v3U.X; mat.M22 = v3U.Y; mat.M23 = v3U.Z; mat.M24 =0.0f;//Up
mat.M31 = v3L.X; mat.M32 = v3L.Y; mat.M33 = v3L.Z; mat.M34 =0.0f;//Look
mat.M41 = 0.0f;  mat.M42 = 0.0f;  mat.M43 = 0.0f;  mat.M44 =1.0f;
```

An example showing how to implement this structure is presented later in the chapter.

Scaling Animations with Time Lapse Between Frames

When animating objects, it is essential you ensure your animations run at the same speed regardless of the processing power of the system that runs them. If you are a starving student, you might only be able to afford a slow PC—maybe with an older graphics card—but the computers in the labs at your college or university might be faster, or vice versa. If you develop your games on a slow PC, and you don't regulate the timing of your animations, they will look like they are playing in fast forward when you run them on a faster PC. The reverse is true if you develop your games on a super-charged PC and then run them on a slower machine. Also, when you port your games over to the Xbox 360, you are almost certain to experience a difference in processing power compared to your development PC. To compound this issue, every frame of your game will exert different demands on the processor, and you might be running other programs in the background that are stealing valuable processor cycles. With all of these varying system and performance factors to consider, a mechanism to control the speed of your animations is a must-have item.

The trick to controlling animation speed is simple. The equation used to control the translation speed looks like this:

```
Vector3 Position +=  Increment.XYZ * TimeBetweenFrames / ConstantScale;
```

Controlling rotation speed is similar:

```
float radians += Increment * TimeBetweenFrames / ConstantScale;
```

These equations offer a self-adjusting mechanism to account for varying frame rates. For example, a faster machine will produce more frames, but the animation won't run faster because the time scale will reduce the increment for each frame. In the end, you will have more frames and a smoother animation, but the animation speed will be the same as an animation that runs on a slower machine. If you do not factor in the time difference between frames, your animations will run at uncontrollable speeds.

Character Movement Example

In this example, you animate a single prop aircraft so that it flies within the boundaries of your virtual world. Of course, you will also ensure that the plane is pointing in the direction it's supposed to fly; first with methods that use trigonometry and then with methods that use direction vectors. This example demonstrates how to use animations that involve translations and rotations, how to animate an object at a constant speed, and how to calculate the angle of direction using a constant speed.

FIGURE 6-4

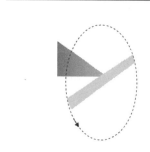

To keep this example simple, the airplane is built with nothing more than a triangle for the body and a spinning rectangle for the propeller (see Figure 6-4).

If you want, you can easily swap these primitive objects with 3D models; the sequence of instructions to create the transformation for the animation would remain identical.

Airplane animation

This example begins with either the files in the WinMGHBook project or the Xbox360MGHBook project from the BaseCode folder in the book's download.

A Stationary Airplane with a Spinning Propeller

This first part of the demonstration explains how to create an airplane using a stationary triangle and a rotating rectangle that is perpendicular to the front tip of the triangle. Two separate objects for storing vertices are needed: the body of the airplane and the propeller. Their declarations are required in the module-level area of the game class:

```
private VertexPositionColor[] mVertAirplane   = new VertexPositionColor[3];
private VertexPositionColor[] mVertProp       = new VertexPositionColor[4];
```

Code to initialize each vertex—in both the airplane and the propeller—sets the position and color values for each coordinate. Note that the joining point for both objects is centered at the origin (see Figure 6-5).

 **NOTE** Centering the joining points for separate objects that are animated together about the origin will prevent unwanted translations. These can be difficult to debug.

FIGURE 6-5

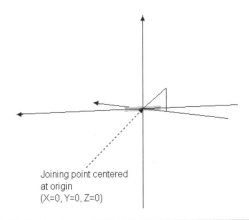

Joining point centered
at origin
(X=0, Y=0, Z=0)

Connection points centered at the origin

The methods init_airplane_body() and init_prop() are added to the game class to initialize each array of vertices:

```
private void init_airplane_body(){
    Vector3 pos = new Vector3();
    pos.X = 0.0f; pos.Y = 0.0f; pos.Z = 0.0f;          // front bottom
    mVertAirplane[0] = new VertexPositionColor(pos, Color.Orange);
    pos.X = 0.0f; pos.Y = 0.5f; pos.Z =-1.0f;          // back top
    mVertAirplane[1] = new VertexPositionColor(pos, Color.OrangeRed);
    pos.X = 0.0f; pos.Y = 0.0f; pos.Z =-1.0f;          // back
    mVertAirplane[2] = new VertexPositionColor(pos, Color.OrangeRed);
}
private void init_prop(){
    Vector3 pos = new Vector3();
    pos.X = -0.5f; pos.Y = 0.05f; pos.Z = 0.0f;        // top right
    mVertProp[0] = new VertexPositionColor(pos, Color.LightBlue);
    pos.X = -0.5f; pos.Y = -0.05f; pos.Z = 0.0f;       // bottom right
    mVertProp[1] = new VertexPositionColor(pos, Color.LightBlue);
    pos.X = 0.5f; pos.Y = 0.05f; pos.Z = 0.0f;         // top left
    mVertProp[2] = new VertexPositionColor(pos, Color.LightBlue);
    pos.X = 0.5f; pos.Y = -0.05f; pos.Z = 0.0f;        // bottom left
    mVertProp[3] = new VertexPositionColor(pos, Color.LightBlue);
}
```

To initialize the propeller and airplane body when the program begins, call init_airplane_body() and init_prop() from Initialize():

```
init_airplane_body();
init_prop();
```

In the beginning of this demonstration, the airplane is drawn as a stationary object. A translation matrix generated by the instruction

```
Matrix.CreateTranslation(0.0f, 0.5f, 2.0f)
```

moves the plane in a one-time translation 0.5 units up the Y axis and 2.0 units inward along the Z axis. A slight rotation is generated with this instruction:

```
Matrix.CreateRotationY((float)Math.PI / 8.0f)
```

This makes it easier to view the airplane from the camera's starting position. When the identity, rotation, and translation are combined, the I.S.R.O.T. (Identity, Scale, Revolve, Orbit, Translate) sequence is used to build the cumulative transformation:

```
mMatWorld = matIdentity * matRotY * matTransl;
```

draw_airplane_body() declares and initializes the transformation matrices in the first two steps. Then, the cumulative World matrix is built in the third step. In the fourth step, the cumulative transformation stored in the World matrix is sent to the shader. Finally, in the fifth step, the triangle is drawn from the transformed vertices. draw_airplane_body() is added to the game class to transform and render the vertices for the triangle.

```
private void draw_airplane_body(){
    // 1: declare matrices
    Matrix matIdentity, matTransl, matRotY;

    // 2: initialize matrices
    matIdentity = Matrix.Identity; // always start with identity matrix
    matTransl   = Matrix.CreateTranslation(0.0f, 0.5f, 2.0f);

    // need to rotate slightly about Y so you can see it
    matRotY     = Matrix.CreateRotationY((float)Math.PI/8.0f);

    // 3: build cumulative world matrix using I.S.R.O.T. sequence
    // identity, scale, rotate, orbit(translate & rotate), translate
    mMatWorld = matIdentity * matRotY * matTransl;

    // 4: pass world matrix to shader
    worldViewProjParam.SetValue(mMatWorld * mMatView * mMatProj);
    mfx.CommitChanges();
```

```
    // 5: draw object - select vertex type, primitive type, # of primitives
    gfx.GraphicsDevice.VertexDeclaration = mVertPosColor;
    gfx.GraphicsDevice.DrawUserPrimitives<VertexPositionColor>(
        PrimitiveType.TriangleStrip, mVertAirplane, 0, 1);
}
```

Instructions for rendering the propeller are similar to steps taken to position and draw the airplane. The main difference in draw_propeller() is the inclusion of a continuous rotation about the Z axis. Adding a variable to store rotation on the Z axis will permit updates to this variable with each frame. This data can be used to generate the continuous rotation.

```
float mfRotZ;
```

In this example, the propeller is assumed to be rotating counterclockwise, so the calculation that generates the value for mfRotZ is always greater than or equal to 0. If you need to reverse the rotation so it is negative, negating mfRotZ will generate clockwise rotation. The draw_propeller() method is added to the game class to transform and draw the vertices; this creates a spinning rectangle. A time lapse between frames is obtained with the TargetElapsedTime.Milliseconds attribute.

```
private void draw_propeller(){
    // 1: declare matrices
    Matrix matIdentity, matTransl, matRotY, matRotZ;

    // 2: initialize matrices
    matIdentity = Matrix.Identity; // always start with identity matrix
    matRotY     = Matrix.CreateRotationY((float)Math.PI / 8.0f);
    matTransl   = Matrix.CreateTranslation(0.0f, 0.5f, 2.0f);

    // create continuous rotation based on time between frames
    mfRotZ += (float)TargetElapsedTime.Milliseconds / 50.0f;
    mfRotZ = mfRotZ % ((float)Math.PI * 2.0f); // stop variable overflow
    matRotZ = Matrix.CreateRotationZ(mfRotZ);   // create Z rotation

    // 3: build cumulative world matrix using I.S.R.O.T. sequence
    // identity, scale, rotate, orbit(translate & rotate), translate
    mMatWorld = matIdentity * matRotZ * matRotY *  matTransl;

    // 4: pass world matrix to shader
    worldViewProjParam.SetValue(mMatWorld * mMatView * mMatProj);
    mfx.CommitChanges();
```

```
// 5: draw object - select vertex type, primitive type, # of primitives
gfx.GraphicsDevice.VertexDeclaration = mVertPosColor;
gfx.GraphicsDevice.DrawUserPrimitives<VertexPositionColor>(
    PrimitiveType.TriangleStrip, mVertProp, 0, 2);
}
```

To draw these objects with a shader that renders color and vertices, both draw_airplane_body() and draw_propeller() are called from the Draw() method between the Begin() and End() statements for the BasicShader.fx shader object:

```
draw_airplane_body();
draw_propeller();
```

When you run this code, a stationary airplane body and a propeller that rotates on the Z axis will appear (refer to Figure 6-4).

A Flying Airplane with a Spinning Propeller

To move your airplane, it needs speed. And to calculate the speed, the current position must be tracked at every frame. Add the Vector3 variables, *mv3Speed* and *mv3AirplanePos*, to the game class to enable speed and position tracking for the airplane:

```
Vector3 mv3Speed;
Vector3 mv3AirplanePos;
```

When the speeds are initialized, they can be randomized. Using the init_speed() method in your game class randomizes the airplane's speed when the program starts. This helps to ensure that the airplane's route varies each time the game is run:

```
void init_speed(){
    Random randomNumber = new Random(); // randomize speed
    mv3Speed.X = 1.0f + randomNumber.Next(3);
    mv3Speed.Z = 1.0f + randomNumber.Next(3);
}
```

The speed can be randomized at the beginning of the game by calling init_speed() from the Initialize() method:

```
init_speed();
```

If updates to the airplane's position are not monitored and adjusted, the airplane is going to fly off into outer space. A check is needed to determine if the X and Z world boundaries are exceeded—in which case the corresponding speed on X or Z is reversed. To allow the airplane to travel, the update_position() method is added to the game class. This method updates the airplane's position for every frame. A time scale is obtained by dividing the total milliseconds between frames by 1000. Multiplying this scaled time value by the speed ensures that the animation will run at the same rate regardless of the system. For this example, the outcome ensures that the airplane will take the same time to travel from point A to point B regardless of the computer's processing power, the varying demands of your game each frame, and the background processing on your system outside your game.

```
void update_position(){
    // change corresponding speed if beyond world's X and Z boundaries
    if (mv3AirplanePos.X > BOUNDARY || mv3AirplanePos.X < -BOUNDARY)
        mv3Speed.X *= -1.0f;
    if (mv3AirplanePos.Z > BOUNDARY || mv3AirplanePos.Z < -BOUNDARY)
        mv3Speed.Z *= -1.0f;

    // increment position by speed * time scale between frames
    float fTimeScale = (float)TargetElapsedTime.Milliseconds / 1000.0f;
    mv3AirplanePos.X += mv3Speed.X * fTimeScale;
    mv3AirplanePos.Z += mv3Speed.Z * fTimeScale;
}
```

The update_position() method is called from the Update() method to ensure the airplane's position variable is adjusted for each frame:

```
update_position();
```

When this updated vector variable is applied—in a translation matrix against the airplane's body—it moves the airplane to the current position. Replacing the existing CreateTranslation() instruction inside draw_airplane_body() will include the updated translation in the transformation:

```
matTransl = Matrix.CreateTranslation(mv3AirplanePos);
```

This same translation needs to be implemented inside draw_propeller() to move the propeller with the airplane:

```
matTransl = Matrix.CreateTranslation(mv3AirplanePos);
```

When you run this program, the airplane will fly around the world and remain within the boundaries. However, there is still one problem with this version of the example. The airplane has no sense of direction and therefore appears to fly sideways.

Setting the Angle of Direction with Math.Atan()

This portion of the example adds in the ability to point the airplane in the direction it is traveling. The rotation implemented in this get_rotation_angle() method uses quadrants to calculate the angle of rotation about the Y axis:

```
float get_rotation_angle(){
    float fPI = (float)Math.PI;
    float fRotY;
    // 1st quadrant
    if (mv3Speed.X <= 0.0f && mv3Speed.Z >= 0.0f)
        fRotY = (float)Math.Atan(mv3Speed.Z /-mv3Speed.X);
    // 2nd quadrant
    else if (mv3Speed.X >= 0.0f && mv3Speed.Z >= 0.0f)
        fRotY =  fPI / 2.0f + (float)Math.Atan(mv3Speed.X / mv3Speed.Z);
    // 3rd quadrant
    else if (mv3Speed.X >= 0.0f && mv3Speed.Z <= 0.0f)
        fRotY = fPI + (float)Math.Atan(-mv3Speed.Z / mv3Speed.X);
    // 4th quadrant
    else
        fRotY = 3.0f*fPI/2.0f + (float)Math.Atan(-mv3Speed.X /-mv3Speed.Z);
    return fRotY - fPI / 2.0f;
}
```

Replacing the instruction for the creation of the Y rotation matrix—inside draw_airplane_body()—creates a rotation about Y that matches the direction of the aircraft:

```
matRotY = Matrix.CreateRotationY(get_rotation_angle());
```

This same replacement must be applied in the draw_propeller() method to rotate the propeller properly about the Y axis:

```
matRotY = Matrix.CreateRotationY(get_rotation_angle());
```

When you compile and run this code, the airplane will fly through the world and will point in the direction it is traveling.

Setting the Angle of Direction with Math.Atan2()

You could actually replace the existing get_rotation_angle() method with this simpler version to get the same result. The longer version was shown first to demonstrate how this simpler version actually works:

```
float get_rotation_angle(){
    float fAngle =(float)Math.Atan2((double)mv3Speed.X,(double)mv3Speed.Z);
    return fAngle;
}
```

This finished example shows an airplane that flies within the boundaries of the 3D world and points in the direction it is traveling. The only difference with this last change is the simplified instruction.

Setting the Angle of Direction Using Vectors

As explained earlier, the direction vectors can be used to generate a rotation matrix. To use the Look (speed), Up, and Right vectors to calculate the angle of direction, add this method to your game class:

```
Matrix get_rotation_Matrix(){
    Vector3 v3L = mv3Speed;
    v3L.Normalize();

    // Default Up in this case is (0, 1, 0)
    Vector3 v3U = new Vector3(0.0f, 1.0f, 0.0f);
    v3U.Normalize();

    // Right = Up x Look
    Vector3 v3R = Vector3.Cross(v3U, v3L ); // right = up x look
    v3R.Normalize();

    Matrix mat = new Matrix(); // compute direction rotation matrix
    mat.M11= v3R.X; mat.M12= v3R.Y; mat.M13= v3R.Z; mat.M14=0.0f;//Right
    mat.M21= v3U.X; mat.M22= v3U.Y; mat.M23= v3U.Z; mat.M24=0.0f;//Up
    mat.M31= v3L.X; mat.M32= v3L.Y; mat.M33= v3L.Z; mat.M34=0.0f;//Look
    mat.M41= 0.0f;  mat.M42= 0.0f;  mat.M43= 0.0f;  mat.M44=1.0f;

    return mat;
}
```

Then, to replace the trigonometry reference in calculating the Y rotation angle, in both draw_propeller() and draw_airplane_body(), replace the instruction that creates the Y rotation matrix with the following instruction:

```
matRotY = get_rotation_Matrix();
```

When you run your code now, the airplane exhibits the same behavior flying through the world pointing in the direction it is traveling.

Once you become comfortable with the code in this chapter and the previous one for animation, you will have more control over the look and feel of your game. Being able to control the movement of your vehicles, objects, and other beings will lead to many interesting avenues for creating great graphics effects and game play.

CHAPTER 6 REVIEW EXERCISES

1. Implement the step-by-step exercises presented in this chapter.

2. Create a helicopter with a spinning top and side rotor, like the one shown in the following illustration. Make the helicopter fly continuously within the boundaries of your world and ensure that it points in the direction it is traveling. Use the Look, Up, and Right vectors to calculate the helicopter's angle of direction.

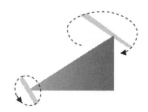

CHAPTER 7

Texturing Your Game World

ANYTHING

that appears in a video game should be textured; this includes everything from plants to people. If things aren't textured well, your game just won't look right. But don't worry because we've got you covered. After completing this chapter, you will be able to cover your virtual surfaces with images, create tiling patterns, shade images with color, add transparency to images, and make 2D images appear as 3D objects.

TEXTURE INTRODUCTION

Textures are images applied to the surfaces of primitive objects. The wide variety of texture attributes within the XNA platform gives developers the power to blend and manipulate textures to create an infinite number of exciting visual effects. For example, textures can be colored, filtered, blended, and transformed at run time. Considering the importance of quality texturing, it's no surprise that XNA offers impressive support for presenting and manipulating texture data. XNA supports .bmp, .dds, .dib, .hdr, .jpg, .pfm, .png, .ppm, and .tga image formats for textures.

UV Coordinates

UV coordinates specify a point in the texture; they are commonly referred to as texture coordinates. Texture coordinates are different from X, Y, and Z position coordinates because a texture is a two-dimensional object that is mapped onto a three-dimensional polygon. The texture's two-dimensional coordinate data is stored inside the vertex along with each X, Y, and Z position coordinate. When a texture is mapped on a one-to-one basis to a rectangular object, both U and V coordinates take a minimum value of 0 and a maximum value of 1. Figure 7-1 shows the UV coordinate settings of textures that are mapped on a one-to-one basis in three different planes.

Texture C# Syntax

Textures are loaded and manipulated in C# using a Texture2D object. The object is declared with the following syntax:

```
private Texture2D TextureObject;
```

Using the ContentManager Class to Load Textures

The ContentManager class is an XNA component used for loading binary content such as images. The ContentManager's Load() method can load image files into Texture2D objects once the images have been added to your project. The Load() method only requires the directory path and image name. The image file extension (*.bmp for example) is not required. In this example, the image folder is located in

FIGURE 7-1

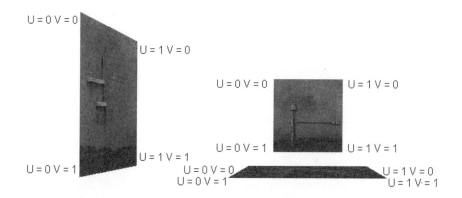

UV coordinates when mapping textures on the X, Y, and Z axes

the same directory as the C# source files. The syntax shown here is used to load an image from the game project's Images folder:

```
Texture2D texture = content.Load<Texture2D>(".\\Images\\imageName");
```

VertexPositionColorTexture, VertexPositionNormalTexture, and VertexPositionTexture

Previous examples used a VertexPositionColor variable for storing vertex data. This variable type lacked the ability to store image information, so the graphics until now have been limited to basic shapes and colors. Three vertex formats allow for storage of image coordinates; they will literally add another dimension to your graphics:

> **)** VertexPositionColorTexture
>
> This format allows you to apply image textures to your primitive shapes, and you can even shade your images with color. For example, with this vertex type you could draw a rectangle with an image texture and then you could show it again with a different shade of color. The vertex variable declaration syntax is:
>
> ```
> VertexPositionColorTexture  vertex = new
> VertexPositionColorTexture(Vector3 pos, Color Color.color, Vector2 uv);
> ```

> **)** VertexPositionNormalTexture
>
> This format allows you to add textures to your primitive objects. The normal data enables lighting for this textured format. The vertex variable declaration syntax is:
>
> ```
> VertexPositionNormalTexture  vertex = new
> VertexPositionNormalTexture(Vector3 pos, Vector3 normal, Vector2 uv);
> ```

> ❱ VertexPositionTexture
> This format only permits storage of position and texture data. It may be useful if you didn't need lighting and were concerned about saving space or performance for large amounts of vertices. The vertex variable declaration syntax is:

```
VertexPositionTexture  vertex = new
VertexPositionTexture(Vector3 pos, Vector2 uv);
```

Shader Implementation for Textures

Texturing is applied in the shader. The shader code needed to texture objects is similar to the shader explained in Chapter 4, "Shaders." However, some changes to the code are required to enable textures. The additions required are:

> ❱ A global Texture variable

> ❱ A Sampler object for filtering the texture

> ❱ Vertex shader input and output data types that include UV coordinates

> ❱ Pixel shader code that applies the texture data to the pixels that are output

High Level Shader Language Texture Variable

The Texture data type is used to store and apply the image within the shader. The declaration for a texture is usually made in the global section of the shader:

```
uniform    extern    Texture    ShaderVariableName;
```

High Level Shader Language Sampler Object

A Sampler object defines properties or filters in the shader for drawing. The Sampler is like a brush type that can be used to apply the texture to the primitive surface. Here is the Sampler used in the texture shaders throughout this book:

```
Sampler TextureSampler = sampler_state{
    Texture   = < ShaderVariableName >;
    magfilter = LINEAR;
    minfilter = LINEAR;
    mipfilter = LINEAR;
};
```

In this code, you can see that the filter properties are declared. A minfilter tells the shader how to draw the texture on the object if the object is smaller than the actual texture. A magfilter tells the program how to draw the texture if the object is larger than the texture. A mipfilter assists in resizing the image up close and far away so your surfaces will not be as jagged around the edges. This method of sampling is actually very common and applies the image clearly against a primitive surface, as you would expect to see in a standard photo that can be printed in both small and large sizes. In this case, the filter properties for the shader are LINEAR. A linear Sampler state tells the shader to take the portion of the texture defined by the UV coordinates and spread it evenly over the area defined by the corresponding X, Y, and Z values for each vertex. This process of projecting image data between vertices is known as *linear interpolation*.

UV Coordinates Within the Shader   Until now, the input and output data declarations in the vertex shader only enabled vertices for color and position. For textures, the vertex shader input and output must be declared to handle not only position and color but also UV coordinate data. The following struct defines the structure of each vertex that is passed to the vertex shader:

```
struct VS_INPUT{
    float4 f4Position        : POSITION0; // position semantic x,y,z,w
    float2 textureCoordinate : TEXCOORD0; // texture semantic u,v
    float4 f4Color           : COLOR0;    // color semantic r,g,b,a
};
```

The following struct defines the output from the vertex shader. The output data type will also serve as the pixel shader's input data type.

```
struct VS_OUTPUT{
    float4 f4Position        : POSITION0;
    float4 f4Color           : COLOR;
    float2 textureCoordinate : TEXCOORD0;
};
```

The texture output for the vertex shader is defined in the vertex shader with the instruction:

```
OUT.textureCoordinate = IN.textureCoordinate;
```

tex2D   If a pixel shader is used when texturing is applied, the tex2D() function is often used to return output that combines the texture information with the filter. The syntax for the conversion would appear as:

```
OUT.f4Color = tex2D(TextureSampler, IN.textureCoordinate);
```

Shader Code for Applying Textures

This complete listing of shader code applies textures to vertices and renders objects built from vertices that store X, Y, and Z positions, as well as UV texture coordinates and color. This shader is very similar to the initial shader used in the preceding examples. However, the shader used previously could only render objects constructed from position and color data. The new shader also applies image textures to your objects, making them more visually appealing. You can find this shader code in the TextureShader.fx file in the Shaders folder in the download from this book's website.

```
float4x4 fx_WVP : WORLDVIEWPROJ;              // world view projection matrix
uniform extern texture fx_Texture;           // stores texture for shader

// filter texture
sampler textureSampler = sampler_state{
    Texture = <fx_Texture>;
    magfilter = LINEAR; // magfilter when image bigger than actual size
    minfilter = LINEAR; // minfilter when image smaller than actual size
};

struct VS_INPUT{                             // input to vertex shader
    float4 f4Position          : POSITION0; // position semantic x,y,z,w
    float4 f4Color             : COLOR0;    // color semantic   r,g,b,a
    float2 textureCoordinate   : TEXCOORD0; // texture semantic  u,v
};

struct VS_OUTPUT{                           // vertex shader output
    float4 f4Position          : POSITION0; // position semantic x,y,z,w
    float4 f4Color             : COLOR;     // color semantic   r,g,b,a
    float2 textureCoordinate   : TEXCOORD0; // texture semantic  u,v
};

struct PS_OUTPUT{                           // pixel shader output
    float4 f4Color             : COLOR0;    // colored pixel is output
};

void vertex_shader(in VS_INPUT IN, out VS_OUTPUT OUT){
    OUT.f4Position = mul(IN.f4Position, fx_WVP);// transform object
    OUT.f4Color = IN.f4Color;                   // send color as is to p.s.
    OUT.textureCoordinate= IN.textureCoordinate;// send uv coords to p.s.
}

// alter vs output and send to hardware one pixel at a time
void pixel_shader(in VS_OUTPUT IN, out PS_OUTPUT OUT){
    // use texture for coloring object
    OUT.f4Color = tex2D(textureSampler, IN.textureCoordinate);
```

```
        // this next line is optional - you can shade the texturized pixel
        // with color to give your textures a tint. Do this by multiplying
        // output by the input color vector.
        OUT.f4Color *= IN.f4Color;
}


// the shader starts here
technique mytechnique{
    pass p0{
        // texture sampler initialized
        sampler[0] = (textureSampler);

        // declare and initialize vs and ps
        vertexshader = compile vs_1_1 vertex_shader();
        pixelshader = compile ps_1_1 pixel_shader();
    }
}
```

That's all of the shader code needed to receive vertices with position, color, and texture coordinates to transform this data into textured objects.

C# EffectParameter for Setting the Shader's Texture Value

An EffectParameter object for the texture is required in the C# code to tell the shader what image to use when rendering a textured polygon. As discussed in Chapter 4, "Shaders," the EffectParameter object is declared in the C# application with the following syntax:

```
private     Effect              effect;
private     EffectParameter     texture;
```

When the program begins, the EffectParameter object is assigned the name of the Texture variable in the shader:

```
texture = effect.Parameters["ShaderVariableName"];
```

Later, when an image needs to be selected for rendering, the EffectParameter object is assigned a texture using the SetValue() method. Immediately after the assignment takes place, the Texture value is set in the shader with the CommitChanges() method. Remember to always use CommitChanges() immediately after assigning a shader variable, or it will not be set in the shader.

```
texture.SetValue(Texture2D    texture2D);
effect.CommitChanges();
```

An image texture is not applied to an object until the object is drawn from the shader. You might consider keeping your texture objects organized by assigning and committing them from the same methods where their corresponding primitive objects are rendered.

TRANSPARENT TEXTURES

You may at some point want to create a transparency effect. For example, to make the background pixels of an image invisible while all other pixels in the texture are rendered in their original color. You likely have seen this transparency effect applied with tree images, a heads-up display, or a stylish custom dashboard that always faces the viewer. It is possible to create this effect when using a mask that is stored in the *.dds format. It is also possible to create *.png or *.tga images with transparent pixels in your favorite photo editor, such as Adobe Photoshop, and then draw them using XNA code so that the transparent pixels do not appear.

Alpha Channel

An alpha channel can be used to "mask" all pixels of a specific color in an image. Alpha data is stored in the last color byte of a pixel—after the red, green, and blue bytes. When alpha blending is enabled in your XNA code and the alpha channel is active, transparency is achieved for the pixels where the alpha setting is set to 0.

Texture Example

This example begins with either the WinMGHBookBaseCode project or the Xbox360MGHBookBaseCode project, which can be found in the BaseCode folder of the book's download from the website. This project already has textured ground and uses the TextureShader.fx file described earlier in this chapter. Aside from the shader already being present, this demonstration adds in new textured objects from scratch to show the texturing process from start to finish. Each surface will be transformed into place, and the accompanying textures will be applied to each. By the time Part A of this example is complete, a textured side wall, a textured back wall, and matching ground will be visible.

In Part B of this example, a tree texture with transparency will be added. This tree will use a "billboarding" technique so that it always faces the viewer regardless of the camera's angle. Figure 7-2 shows the billboard tree from different camera angles.

Texture Example, Part A: Opaque Textures

When you are applying textures, a shader that can handle the texture data is required. The TextureShader.fx code presented earlier in this chapter can do the job. This shader has already been added to the base code project. In addition, an Effect

FIGURE 7-2

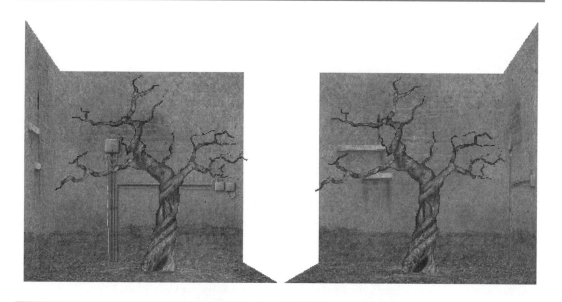

Texturing, transparency, and billboarding

object and Effect parameters are included in the base code to reference the shader from your XNA code.

When drawing objects that have textures, the GraphicsDevice needs to retrieve data from the vertex variable in the proper format. A new VertexDeclaration object is declared in the module declarations section so that the graphics device can later retrieve the correct position, color, and UV data.

```
private      VertexDeclaration      mVertPosTexColor1;
```

Later, in the Initialize() method, add code to set the VertexDeclaration object to a VertexPositionColorTexture format:

```
mVertPosTexColor1 = new VertexDeclaration(gfx.GraphicsDevice,
VertexPositionColorTexture.VertexElements);
```

Identifiers are used to identify the Texture2D objects and the set of transformations required when drawing the textured surface. Add these identifiers to the top of the game class:

```
const int BACKWALL = 0; const int GROUND = 1;
const int SIDEWALL = 2;
```

To store each image, Texture2D objects are required. To do this, add declarations for the texture objects in the module declarations area:

```
private Texture2D mTexGround;
private Texture2D mTexBackwall;
private Texture2D mTexSidewall;
```

The ground.tga, backwall.tga, and sidewall.tga images will be used to texture the ground and two walls. They can be found in the Images folder in the download from the website. They are loaded in your project using the Load() method when the program begins. The code here works under the assumption that the three image files have been copied to the Images folder of your project and have been added to your project from the *Solution Explorer*. To reference the image files from your project, right-click the Images folder, select Add, and then navigate and select each of the image files. Add these instructions to load each texture inside the LoadGraphicsContent() method:

```
mTexGround      = content.Load<Texture2D>(".\\Images\\ground");
mTexBackwall    = content.Load<Texture2D>(".\\Images\\backwall");
mTexSidewall    = content.Load<Texture2D>(".\\Images\\sidewall");
```

The vertex data is stored in the vertex variable mVert. The type declaration of mVert needs to be set to store image data with each vertex. In the module declarations section, add the declaration for mVert to make the vertex variable available throughout the game class:

```
private VertexPositionColorTexture[] mVert = new
VertexPositionColorTexture[4];
```

The method init_surface() initializes the vertices with the position, color, and UV coordinates that will be used to create a rectangular surface for each wall. The UV coordinates will be mapped with U along the X axis and with V along the Z axis.

Add init_surface() to the game class to create these vertices with position, color, and UV coordinates:

```
private void init_surface(){
    Vector2 uv  = new Vector2(0.0f, 0.0f);
    Vector3 pos = new Vector3(0.0f, 0.0f, 0.0f);
    Color color = Color.White;

    // set for vertices of surface with uv, pos, and color data
    uv.X=1.0f; uv.Y=1.0f; pos.X =-BOUNDARY; pos.Y = 0.0f; pos.Z =-BOUNDARY;
    mVert[0] = new VertexPositionColorTexture(pos, color, uv);//front right
```

```
    uv.X=1.0f; uv.Y=0.0f; pos.X =-BOUNDARY; pos.Y = 0.0f; pos.Z = BOUNDARY;
    mVert[1] = new VertexPositionColorTexture(pos, color, uv);//back right
    uv.X=0.0f; uv.Y=1.0f; pos.X = BOUNDARY; pos.Y = 0.0f; pos.Z =-BOUNDARY;
    mVert[2] = new VertexPositionColorTexture(pos, color, uv);//front left
    uv.X=0.0f; uv.Y=0.0f; pos.X = BOUNDARY; pos.Y = 0.0f; pos.Z = BOUNDARY;
    mVert[3] = new VertexPositionColorTexture(pos, color, uv);//back left
}
```

The data for the surface should be assigned at the beginning of the program. To do this, call init_surface() from the Initialize() method:

```
init_surface();
```

You will need to add draw_surface() to the game class to transform each surface into position, to apply a texture, and to render each textured surface using the same set of vertices. Each time the method is called, an identifier parameter is passed to this method to indicate which surface is being rendered. The draw_surface() method uses a switch to select the specific transformations and texture for each surface based on the identifier that it receives. When the texture is selected, it is set in the shader using the EffectParameter object's SetData() method. Then, after the cumulative transformation has been set, the WorldViewProjection matrix is set in the TextureShader using another EffectParameter object, mfxTex_WVP. The WorldViewProjection matrix is used in the shader to position each surface so that it can be seen properly by the camera. Once the shader variables have been set, the CommitChanges() method must be called to finalize the state change in the shader. Before the surface is rendered, an assignment of the VertexDeclaration format to the GraphicsDevice allows for retrieval of X, Y, and Z positions, as well as UV texture data and color information. When the primitive is drawn, a <VertexPositionColorTexture> reference in the DrawUserPrimitives() method ensures that a texture is applied to the primitive object.

```
private void draw_surface(int iSurface){
    // 1: declare matrices
    Matrix matIdentity, matScale, matTransl, matYrot, matXrot;

    // 2: initialize matrices
    matIdentity = Matrix.Identity; // always start with identity matrix
    matTransl   = Matrix.CreateTranslation(0.0f, -0.9f, 10.0f);
    matScale    = Matrix.CreateScale(0.1f, 0.1f, 0.1f);
    matXrot     = Matrix.CreateRotationX(-(float)Math.PI / 2.0f);

    matYrot     = Matrix.CreateRotationY(0.0f);

    // create transformations and set texture for each object
```

```
switch (iSurface){
    case GROUND:      // ground centered at origin
        matXrot = Matrix.CreateRotationX(0.0f);
        mfxTexture.SetValue(mTexGround);    // set texture
        break;
    case BACKWALL:  // rotate -90 Deg on X and move back & up.
        matTransl    = Matrix.CreateTranslation(0.0f, 0.70f , 11.6f);
        mfxTexture.SetValue(mTexBackwall); // set texture
        break;
    case SIDEWALL:   // rotate -90 Deg on X and +90 on Y.move left & up.
        matYrot      = Matrix.CreateRotationY((float)Math.PI / 2.0f);
        matTransl    = Matrix.CreateTranslation(1.6f, 0.70f, 10.0f);
        mfxTexture.SetValue(mTexSidewall); // set texture
        break;
}

// 3: build cumulative world matrix using I.S.R.O.T. sequence
// identity, scale, rotate, orbit(translate & rotate), translate
mMatWorld = matIdentity * matScale * matXrot * matYrot * matTransl;

// 4: pass wvp matrix to shader
mfxTex_WVP.SetValue(mMatWorld * mMatView * mMatProj);
mfxTex.CommitChanges(); // commit changes to set wvp and texture vars

// 5: draw object - select vertex type, primitive type, # of primitives
gfx.GraphicsDevice.VertexDeclaration = mVertPosTexColor1;
gfx.GraphicsDevice.DrawUserPrimitives<VertexPositionColorTexture>
    (PrimitiveType.TriangleStrip, mVert, 0, 2);      // use texture type
}
```

Inside the Draw() method, delete the call to draw_ground() to remove the existing surface. If you do not remove this line, the old ground will cover the new ground surface.

When rendering the new textured surfaces, you need to select the correct shader, but it is possible to use more than one shader for drawing. Just be certain of two things:

> When an effect is selected, all code for rendering is triggered between the shader effect's Begin() and End() methods.

> The shader effect's End() method must be executed before another shader effect begins.

This new code belongs in the Draw() method to select and apply the new effect object when calling draw_surface() to render each new textured surface. draw_surface() is called each time with the identifier of the textured surface to be rendered. A new textured ground surface will be drawn along with the two textured walls, so replace the existing draw_ground() instruction with these instructions:

```
// draw objects
draw_surface(GROUND);
draw_surface(BACKWALL);
draw_surface(SIDEWALL);
```

When you compile and run the program, the output will show the two walls and ground texture.

Texture Example, Part B: Transparent Textures

This example shows how to draw a tree without the background pixels. This example continues with the code created for Part A. Some extra setup is required to load the tree texture. A Texture2D object declaration at the top of the game class is required to store the tree texture so that it can be referenced throughout the class:

```
private Texture2D mTexTree;
```

An identifier definition at the module level is used to allow the draw_surface() method to select the tree texture and to apply the appropriate transformations:

```
const int TREE = 3;
```

The tree.png file used to create the tree texture must be loaded when the program begins. Once your tree.png file has been added to the Images folder of your project and is referenced in the *Solution Explorer*, this file can be loaded in your XNA code using the LoadGraphicsContent() method:

```
mTexTree = content.Load<Texture2D>(".\\Images\\tree");
```

The draw_surface() method can be used to draw the tree using the same vertices that were used to create the wall and ground textures. An additional case is required inside the switch to handle the texture selection and transformations that move the tree into place:

```
case TREE:
    matTransl  = Matrix.CreateTranslation(0.0f, 0.5f, 10.0f);
    matScale   = Matrix.CreateScale(0.09f, 0.09f, 0.09f);
    mfxTexture.SetValue(mTexTree); // set texture
    break;
```

To draw the tree, alpha blending is applied so that the transparent pixels will not be rendered. The SourceBlend property selects the image pixel and masks it with the DestinationBlend layer. Pixels with an active alpha channel will be made transparent after the masking operation. Once the tree is drawn, the alpha blending property, AlphaBlendEnable, is turned off. You must add this code inside the Begin() and End() methods for the mfxTex effect since draw_surface() references this effect. Also, you must add the code to draw the tree after the code that draws the opaque surfaces; this allows the transparent object to overlay the opaque objects.

```
gfx.GraphicsDevice.RenderState.AlphaBlendEnable = true;
gfx.GraphicsDevice.RenderState.SourceBlend      = Blend.SourceAlpha;
gfx.GraphicsDevice.RenderState.DestinationBlend = Blend.InverseSourceAlpha;
draw_surface(TREE);
gfx.GraphicsDevice.RenderState.AlphaBlendEnable = false;
```

With the right adjustments to your game application, you will now be able to look through the branches of the tree and see what's on the other side. However, if you ran the code now, you would notice that while the tree appears with a transparent background, it only looks real when the camera is facing the texture directly. When the camera faces another direction, the illusion is spoiled because the viewer can easily see that a two-dimensional image is being used. At some angles, the surface will appear to be paper thin to the viewer. In *Halo 2*, you can see an example of how this can happen. On the Delta Halo level, it is possible to climb onto a cliff that overlooks the level; the cliff was not intended to be accessible, but once you climb up, you can clearly see that the bushes on the cliff are 2D. In fact, you can walk right through them to see that they are 2D.

Billboarding can help solve the two-dimensional problem. Billboarding is a common technique that makes two-dimensional images appear as though they are three-dimensional objects; this works regardless of the camera position or angle. The algorithm for billboarding involves rotating the texture about the Y axis by the angle of the camera's look direction. (Refer to Chapter 15, "Building a Graphics Engine Camera," for an explanation on how the look vector is obtained.) For the billboarding effect to work, the vertices that create the textured face must be centered at the origin. Also, the tree must be centered in the image (see Figure 7-3).

Billboarding Example

This example begins with the solution from the transparency code example. Chapter 6, "Character Movement," explained the logic used to animate a game object about the Y axis so it points in the direction it travels. This same logic can be used to rotate the tree about the Y axis so it always faces the viewer and will consequently always looks like a robust bushy tree at any camera angle. As in Chapter 6, "Character Movement," the Atan2() function uses the changes in direction on X and Z as parameters to calculate the angle of direction about the Y axis. However, for this case, the camera's Look vector is used to obtain the direction parameters. The Look direction equals the View position minus the camera position. (Refer to Chapter 15, "Building a Graphics Engine Camera," for more detail on the Look vector that stores the direction of the camera.)

Adding get_billboard_angle() to the game class provides a method that returns the rotation angle about the Y axis. This angle matches the camera's angle about the Y axis. When the tree is rotated about the Y axis, by the amount returned by this function, the tree will always face the viewer.

FIGURE 7-3

Objects within billboarded images must be centered on the X axis.

```
float get_billboard_angle(){
    // make third person so it always faces user
    float f_rads;
    float f_change_x = cam.m_vView.X - cam.m_vPos.X;
    float f_change_z = cam.m_vView.Z - cam.m_vPos.Z;

    f_rads = -(float)Math.Atan2(f_change_z , f_change_x)
            + (float)Math.PI / 2.0f;
    return f_rads;
}
```

Inside draw_surface(), in the case that handles the TREE identifier, you need to add code to reset the Y rotation matrix based on the camera's rotation about the Y axis. This creates the billboard effect that makes the tree look real from a distance.

```
matYrot = Matrix.CreateRotationY(get_billboard_angle());
```

After you have made these changes, try running the program. The tree will appear like a nice, full bushy tree, regardless of the angle of the camera.

TEXTURE COLORING

It is possible to color your image textures at run time. This technique might be handy for a number of instances—maybe you need your texture to be darker and you can't wait for the artist to fix it, so you shade it yourself in code. Maybe you want to create a stone pattern; you could use the same image to draw all stones but alternate the shade of the stones to create more contrast on your surface.

The TextureShader.fx shader is already able to apply colors that are stored in the vertices to any textured item. If a non-white color is stored in the vertices, the image in the texture will be shaded by this color.

To see how this works, it helps to examine the vertex shader and pixel shader. The vertex shader input receives the color stored in the vertices. The user-defined struct that stores the vertex shader output stores this color information. The vertex shader output, by design, serves as the input for the pixel shader. This vertex shader code receives the color from the vertices that are set in your C# code and passes it to the pixel shader:

```
void vertex_shader(in VS_INPUT IN, out VS_OUTPUT OUT){
    OUT.f4Position          = mul(IN.f4Position, fx_WVP);
    OUT.f4Color             = IN.f4Color; // send color from vertex to p.s.
    OUT.textureCoordinate   = IN.textureCoordinate;
}
```

The pixel shader can only return colored pixels as output. On the first line within the shader, the texture is applied to each vertex using the tex2D() function, which uses the textureSampler filter and UV coordinates as input parameters. The pixel shader uses linear interpolation to shade and texture the area between the vertices. On the second line, this optional instruction is added, which multiplies the colored pixel by the color that is stored in the vertices. This modification, in effect, applies a color to the image texture:

```
void pixel_shader(in VS_OUTPUT IN, out PS_OUTPUT OUT){
    // apply texture to vertices using textureSampler filter
    OUT.f4Color             = tex2D(textureSampler, IN.textureCoordinate);

    // apply color from v.s. to output - p.s. interpolates between verts
    OUT.f4Color             *= IN.f4Color;
}
```

This example shows how to colorize your image textures. It begins with the solution from the previous example. You can also find this solution in the Solutions folder in the download from the website. The discussion in this section shows how to change the color of the texture for the back wall.

In the init_surface() method, replace the line that sets the color for the vertices from white to red:

```
Color color = Color.Red;
```

When you run the program, the surfaces will be shaded red.

TEXTURE TILING

Tiling is a very simple effect that creates a repeating pattern of an image on the primitive object surface. Tiling is a performance-friendly effect that looks great on brick or stone surfaces, such as walls and streets. However, tiling can even be implemented for grass and soil as long as the image is created so that the edges of the image match the neighboring edges of the same image. In fact, the grass texture in the WinMGHBookBaseCode and Xbox360MGHBookBaseCode projects is tiled ten times horizontally and vertically to make the grass look more dense and lush. If you look at the UV coordinates inside draw_ground(), you will notice they range between 0 and 10 instead of between 0 and 1:

```
// set for vertices of surface with uv, pos, and color data
uv.X=10.0f; uv.Y=10.0f; pos.X = -BOUNDARY; pos.Y = 0.0f; pos.Z = -BOUNDARY;
mVertGround[0] = new VertexPositionColorTexture(pos, color, uv);//front R
uv.X=10.0f; uv.Y= 0.0f; pos.X = -BOUNDARY; pos.Y = 0.0f; pos.Z = BOUNDARY;
mVertGround[1] = new VertexPositionColorTexture(pos, color, uv);//back R
uv.X= 0.0f; uv.Y=10.0f; pos.X = BOUNDARY; pos.Y = 0.0f; pos.Z = -BOUNDARY;
mVertGround[2] = new VertexPositionColorTexture(pos, color, uv);//front L
uv.X= 0.0f; uv.Y= 0.0f; pos.X = BOUNDARY; pos.Y = 0.0f; pos.Z = BOUNDARY;
mVertGround[3] = new VertexPositionColorTexture(pos, color, uv);//back L
```

Figure 7-4 shows an example of tiling where the image is repeated ten times along both the rows and columns. The original texture is on the left, and the tiled surface is on the right. Using a small image to cover a large surface makes tiling a useful way to increase the performance of your textures and decrease the size of your image files.

By now, you should see that applying images makes the 3D world a lot more interesting. Simple effects such as tiling, color, transparency, and billboarding can be applied with little effort.

FIGURE 7-4

Tiling effect

CHAPTER 7 REVIEW EXERCISES

Try these exercises to focus on some of the key points for applying texture effects:

1. Try the step-by-step examples presented in this chapter.

2. State four differences between a shader that enables texturing and a shader that only handles position and color.

3. List the objects that need to be added to the C# code to add in a second shader that allows textures.

4. List the states that must be set to enable transparency.

5. Create a building and apply textures to the sides. Add a billboarded tree, cactus, or flower that you create with transparency.

THIS

chapter explains how to create a realistic sky effect with an infinite horizon. By the time you finish working through this chapter, the sunny blue atmosphere you create will look so tranquil and inviting, you may want to crawl inside your 3D world and never leave.

THE SKYBOX

The structure that houses the images that create the sky and horizon is often referred to as a *skybox*. When the skybox is built properly, it is seamless—you can't tell where it begins or ends. Figure 8-1 shows three different camera views of a 3D world from within a skybox.

A skybox is built using six images to create the sides, sky, and ground for the horizon. Each individual image is shown in Figure 8-2.

To create the effect of an infinite horizon, each of the four wall images and the sky image translate with the camera, but the ground image remains stationary. The result allows you to see the ground move underneath you as you travel, but you will never reach the horizon.

The walls of your virtual world are draped so that they fall slightly below the ground, so the bottom edges of the walls are hidden. Figure 8-3 illustrates the stationary ground and its position relative to the moving ceiling and draped walls.

FIGURE 8-1

Viewing a skybox from different camera angles

FIGURE 8-2

Six images used to make the skybox

TERRAGEN PHOTOREALISTIC SCENERY-RENDERING SOFTWARE

Excellent tools are available to create your skybox. Terragen (http://www.planetside.co.uk/) from Planetside is a popular utility for generating photorealistic scenery for creating spectacular landscapes, seascapes, and skyscapes. The beauty of Terragen is also evident in its ease of use.

Thanks to Planetside, a link to the download for the noncommercial edition of Terragen is included at the website for this book. The noncommercial version is free for personal use. However, the registered commercial version offers access to support, the ability to render larger and higher quality images, enhanced anti-aliasing modes, and, of course, permission to deploy works created using Terragen for commercial purposes. Refer to the Planetside website for licensing details.

FIGURE 8-3

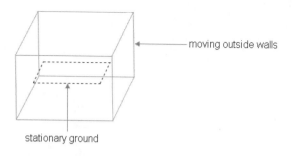

moving outside walls

stationary ground

Moving ceiling and draped walls with a stationary ground of skybox

USING TERRAGEN TO CREATE A SKYBOX

This demonstration explains the steps needed to create the six images used to make a skybox.

When you open Terragen, the application launches the main window, presented in Figure 8-4.

Setting Up the Terragen Project

When you are setting up a Terragen project, you should assign several properties before you create your images. This ensures consistency among the images you generate. The properties you need to set govern image size, magnification, quality, camera position, and target position for generating land and sky scenery.

Sizing the Image

To ensure consistent sizing for all images, you should give each image in the skybox the same pixel width and height dimensions. To set the dimensions, click the *Image Size* button to open the *Render Settings* dialog. On the *Image* tab of the *Render Settings* dialog, you can enter numeric values for *Width* and *Height* (both values are in pixels). For this demonstration, a size of 512 pixels by 512 pixels is recommended.

FIGURE 8-4

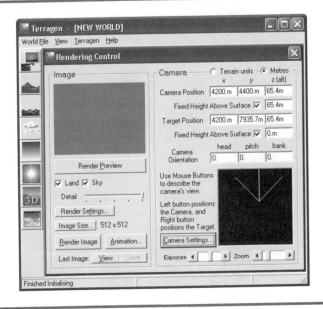

Terragen main window

A higher pixel count enables better quality images, but higher pixel counts also reduce the memory available for processing. This may lower the frame rate in your game because it takes more processing power for the game engine to render the sky.

Setting the Zoom Magnification

The camera's zoom magnification must be set to 1 to ensure the images are scaled properly when you create each snapshot for the sides of the skybox. This setting can be adjusted using the *Zoom Magnification* slider in the *Camera Settings* dialog, which is launched by clicking the *Camera Settings* button on Terragen's main window.

Setting the Image Quality

You can specify additional filter settings to improve image quality. For example, you can adjust values for atmosphere and cloud effects. To do this from Terragen's main window, click the *Render Settings* button. This opens the *Render Settings* dialog. In this dialog, you can increase the *Accuracy* settings for *Atmosphere* and *Cloud Shading* from the *Quality* tab. If you want to avoid pixilation, it is strongly recommended that you select high levels of accuracy for *Atmosphere* and *Cloud Shading*.

Setting the Detail Level

If you want to ensure that your images are rendered with minimal pixilation, you must set the *Detail* slider on Terragen's main window to full strength. Leaving the slider at a lower setting reduces the image-generation time, but the pixilation is noticeably worse; this problem will be magnified when used for the skybox. Figure 8-4 shows Terragen's main window with the Detail setting at full strength.

Setting the Camera and Target Positions

While working in the main window of your Terragen project, it is possible to specify the position of the camera and target position viewed by the camera. You can experiment with these settings if you choose. The settings used while creating the skybox images for this chapter are summarized in Table 8-1. If you are new to Terragen, we recommend that you try these settings; they will allow you to create a skybox similar to the one shown in Figure 8-1. These settings are also visible in Terragen's main window (see Figure 8-4).

Checking the Land and Sky Options

Select the *Land* and *Sky* options in Terragen's main window to generate ground and cloudscapes for your scenery.

TABLE 8-1

	X	Y	Z
Camera Position	4200.m	4400.m	65.4m
Fixed Height Above Surface		Yes	65.4m
Target Position	4200.m	7935.7m	65.4m
Fixed Height Above Surface		Yes	0.0m

Camera Position and Target Position Settings

Creating Each Image: Assigning Head, Pitch, and Bank Properties

If you followed the instructions in the previous section, your global settings for the Terragen project will be set. Each individual image, in the skybox, will have specific settings that generate a unique picture that fits with the other images that make the skybox.

Setting Up Each Snapshot

When all of your images are assembled together in the box, the edges of each picture must match up with the edges of the neighboring picture. To achieve a perfect set of matching images, you must give the camera a carefully planned and unique angle for each snapshot. Terragen refers to these camera direction settings as *Head*, *Pitch*, and *Bank* attributes. These attributes set direction on the X, Y, and Z planes. Later in this chapter, a code example shows you how to load and display Terragen images in your game project. For the code example to work properly, you must generate the named image files and their corresponding *Head*, *Pitch*, and *Bank* properties with the settings summarized in Table 8-2.

TABLE 8-2

Image Name	Camera Orientation		
	Head	**Pitch**	**Bank**
front.bmp	0	0	0
left.bmp	90	0	0
back.bmp	180	0	0
right.bmp	−90	0	0
sky.bmp	−90	90	0
ground2.bmp	−90	−90	0

Camera Direction Settings for Each Image of the Skybox

Rendering and Saving Each Image

To create each image from Terragen's main window, enter the *Head*, *Pitch*, and *Bank* settings and then click *Render Image*. A bitmap appears in the resulting *Image* dialog. You can then save the image by clicking the *Save* button in the top-left corner of the *Image* dialog.

After completing the steps for creating each image, you should have a directory that contains your brand-new front.bmp, back.bmp, left.bmp, right.bmp, sky.bmp, and ground2.bmp images. You can now load these into your game project and create the skybox.

Skybox Code Example

This example takes your new images and renders them to create a seamless sky with an endless horizon. For this example, you can use either the WinMGHBook project or the Xbox360MGHBook project at the BaseCode link.

Once the base project is ready, you will need to load the images you created with Terragen. To add the images to your project, copy them into the Images directory that already exists in your project. Next, click the *Show All Files* button in the *Solution Explorer*, select the new images that appear under the Images folder, and then right-click and choose *Include in Project*. When you are done, you will see all of your skybox images referenced under the Images folder in the *Solution Explorer*.

Now that your images are referenced in your game project; the next step is to declare variables for storing them. These must be declared at the top of your game class.

```
Texture2D mTexFront, mTexBack, mTexGround, mTexLeft, mTexRight, mTexSky;
```

To assign these images at startup, place the image-loading code inside the LoadGraphicsContent() method:

```
mTexFront   = content.Load<Texture2D>(".\\Images\\front");
mTexBack    = content.Load<Texture2D>(".\\Images\\back");
mTexLeft    = content.Load<Texture2D>(".\\Images\\left");
mTexRight   = content.Load<Texture2D>(".\\Images\\right");
mTexGround  = content.Load<Texture2D>(".\\Images\\ground2");
mTexSky     = content.Load<Texture2D>(".\\Images\\sky");
```

Textured ground already exists in the base project. It is currently tiled ten times, but the skybox ground texture is not designed for tiling. Inside init_ground(), all uv.X or uv.Y values set to 10.0f must be replaced with code that sets them to 1.0f to ensure the texture is mapped to the ground surface on a one-to-one basis. Also, to replace the existing image with the ground2.bmp image from Terragen, in step 4 of draw_ground(), marked by the comments in the code, replace the instruction that sets the texture using *mTexGrass* with an instruction to use the *mTexGround* texture:

```
mfxTexture.SetValue(mTexGround);
```

If you try the program now, you will see the same 3D world, but this time the ground will be covered with the texture you created in Terragen.

Once the ground is properly rendered with the texture, the surrounding walls and ceiling of the skybox can be added. By design, the edges of the skybox surround the outer perimeter of the world, so the skybox walls must be bigger than the world walls. A class-level definition for the skybox panel size must be proportionately larger than the world boundary size:

```
private const float          EDGE = BOUNDARY * 2.0f;
```

A set of vertices is required to store the vertex position, texture, and color information for a rectangle that can be used to make each surface of the skybox. This same surface can be redrawn using a different set of rotations and translations to create each panel of the skybox as long as the appropriate texture is used each time it is drawn. Because only one rectangular surface is required to draw all sides of the skybox, the vertex array only needs to be declared with room for four sets of coordinates:

```
private VertexPositionColorTexture[] mVertSkybox = new
VertexPositionColorTexture[4];
```

The init_skybox() method contains the necessary code to set up the vertices that can be used to render a skybox panel. As mentioned earlier, the same four vertices are used to draw each panel. Remember that the length of the panels must be greater than the length of the world size. The module-level definition, EDGE, is used to set the X and Z values of each vertex to ensure that the panels are large enough to surround the perimeter of the 3D world.

Each time these coordinates are used to draw a panel, they must be rotated and translated into position. Notice how the rectangle's X, Y, and Z coordinates are centered about the origin where X=0, Y=0, and Z=0. This enables easier rendering.

Note that the UV coordinates that enable texture mapping are between 0.003f and 0.997f. This shortened range from the usual 0.0f to 1.0f setting removes the white seam that outlines each bitmap. The UV offset of 0.003f preserves the illusion of the skybox.

```
private void init_skybox()
{
    Vector3 pos = new Vector3(0.0f, 0.0f, 0.0f);
    Vector2 uv  = new Vector2(0.0f, 0.0f);
    const float max = 0.997f; // offset to remove white seam at top edge
```

```
const float min = 0.003f; // offset to remove white seam at bottom edge

// set position, image, and color data for each vertex in rectangle
pos.X = +EDGE; pos.Y = -EDGE; uv.X = min; uv.Y = max; //Bottom L
mVertSkybox[0] = new VertexPositionColorTexture(pos, Color.White, uv);
pos.X = +EDGE; pos.Y = +EDGE; uv.X = min; uv.Y = min; //Top L
mVertSkybox[1] = new VertexPositionColorTexture(pos, Color.White, uv);
pos.X = -EDGE; pos.Y = -EDGE; uv.X = max; uv.Y = max; //Bottom R
mVertSkybox[2] = new VertexPositionColorTexture(pos, Color.White, uv);
pos.X = -EDGE; pos.Y = +EDGE; uv.X = max; uv.Y = min; //Top R
mVertSkybox[3] = new VertexPositionColorTexture(pos, Color.White, uv);
}
```

To be sure the skybox is initialized only once, add the call statement to the Initialize() method:

```
init_skybox();
```

To draw each panel of the skybox, you must add the draw_skybox() method to the game class. This method is designed to iterate through all five moving panels of the skybox, transform each panel into place, and render it with the correct texture. Step 1 declares a set of matrices and initializes each matrix with a default value. In step 2, the transformations are assigned so that the sides and the ceiling of the skybox are drawn where they belong. Also in step 2, the corresponding texture for each panel is set. In step 3, the I.S.R.O.T. sequence is used to calculate the cumulative transformation. Of course, this order of transformations is crucial and cannot change. The last extra translation, *matCam*, translates the skybox panels so that they move with the camera and give the illusion of an unreachable horizon.

```
private void draw_skybox()
{
    const float kfDrop = -1.2f;

    // 1: declare matrices and set defaults
    Matrix matIdentity  = Matrix.Identity;
    Matrix matRotY      = Matrix.CreateRotationY(0.0f);
    Matrix matRotX      = Matrix.CreateRotationX(0.0f);
    Matrix matTransl    = Matrix.CreateTranslation(0.0f, 0.0f, 0.0f);
    Matrix matScale     = Matrix.CreateScale(1.0f, 1.0f, 1.0f);
    Matrix matCam       //move box with camera to make horizon unreachable.
        = Matrix.CreateTranslation(cam.m_vPos.X,0.0f, cam.m_vPos.Z);

    // 2: set transformations and also texture for each wall
```

```
for (int i = 0; i < 5; i++){ // front, right, left, right, & sky
    switch (i){
        case 0: // back wall
            matTransl = Matrix.CreateTranslation( 0.0f, kfDrop, EDGE);
            mfxTexture.SetValue(mTexBack);    break;
        case 1: // right wall
            matTransl = Matrix.CreateTranslation(-EDGE, kfDrop, 0.0f);
            matRotY   = Matrix.CreateRotationY(-(float)Math.PI / 2.0f);
            mfxTexture.SetValue(mTexRight);    break;
        case 2: // front wall
            matTransl = Matrix.CreateTranslation(0.0f, kfDrop, -EDGE);
            matRotY   = Matrix.CreateRotationY((float)Math.PI);
            mfxTexture.SetValue(mTexFront);    break;
        case 3: // left wall
            matTransl = Matrix.CreateTranslation( EDGE, kfDrop, 0.0f);
            matRotY   = Matrix.CreateRotationY((float)Math.PI / 2.0f);
            mfxTexture.SetValue(mTexLeft);     break;
        case 4: // sky
            matTransl = Matrix.CreateTranslation(0.0f,EDGE+kfDrop,0.0f);
            matRotX   = Matrix.CreateRotationX(-(float)Math.PI / 2.0f);
            matRotY   =
            Matrix.CreateRotationY( 3.0f*(float)Math.PI / 2.0f);
            matScale  = Matrix.CreateScale(1.0f, 1.0f, 1.0f);
            mfxTexture.SetValue(mTexSky);      break;
    }

    // 3: build cumulative world matrix using I.S.R.O.T. sequence

    mMatWorld = matIdentity*matScale*matRotX*matRotY*matTransl*matCam;

    // 4: pass wvp matrix to shader
    mfxTex_WVP.SetValue(mMatWorld * mMatView * mMatProj);
    mfxTex.CommitChanges();

    // 5: draw object - select vert type, primitive type, # primitives
    gfx.GraphicsDevice.VertexDeclaration = mVertPosColorTex;
    gfx.GraphicsDevice.DrawUserPrimitives<VertexPositionColorTexture>(
    PrimitiveType.TriangleStrip, mVertSkybox, 0, 2);
}
}
```

To trigger the code to draw the skybox from the Draw() method, you must place the call statement between the Begin() and End() statements for the *mfxTex* object, which references the TextureShader.fx file:

```
draw_skybox();
```

When you run this project, your majestic skybox will surround your world. As you move, you discover that you can never reach the horizon.

This example is not yet complete, however. You may have discovered that you can travel over the edge of the ground and see the bottom of the skybox—this spoils the illusion. To fix this problem, Chapter 16, "Collision Detection," shows how to add collision detection just inside the outer edges of your world to prevent players from reaching the world's edge where they can see the bottom of your skybox.

There is another common method for building a skybox, which involves creating a model of the top half of a sphere and mapping a sky texture to it. However, there are some advantages to using Terragen. Terragen generates the images for you and also has the ability to create terrain to match your sky and horizon. The creation of terrain with height detection will be explained in Chapter 25.

Whether you use Terragen or a 3D model, coding a skybox is easy, and the skybox will make your world look much more real.

CHAPTER 8 REVIEW EXERCISES

1. Create your own skybox by following the steps outlined in this chapter.

2. In your code solution from Exercise 1, change the min and max declarations so that the range falls between 0.0f and 1.0f. Then run the project and look at the seams around the bitmaps. Notice how the original offset prevents the white seam from appearing.

CHAPTER 9

Index Buffers

ON the surface, a chapter dedicated to building an indexed grid of vertices might not seem very exciting, but once you see what's underneath, you'll change your mind. The index buffer is a powerful and efficient structure for referencing large amounts of vertex data. The index buffers in conjunction with vertex buffers also enable dynamic updates to position, texture, color, and surface normal data. Together, these two functions enable great effects such as water and hilly terrain. Remember what water looked like in *Frogger?* Now, think of what water looks like in *Halo 2*. Which do you prefer? If water ripples do not interest you, how about terrain that isn't flat or beautifully lit surfaces that use per-vertex lighting? These are the sort of effects you can create with index buffers.

INDEX BUFFERS

If you rendered a surface or polygon with a large set of data to construct a series of line or triangle strips, you would run into a problem. Using the methods you have applied until now, you would find that much of the vertex data needs to be stored twice. The diagram on the left in Figure 9-1 shows how non-indexed vertices are duplicated when drawing a line strip where multiple rows of data are used to create a rectangular surface. The diagram on the right in Figure 9-1 shows how indexing reduces storage requirements because each vertex used only needs to be stored once.

All indexed vertices in the vertex buffer must be stored in a sequence that enables proper rendering of the 3D object being drawn. The sequence must be arranged so

FIGURE 9-1

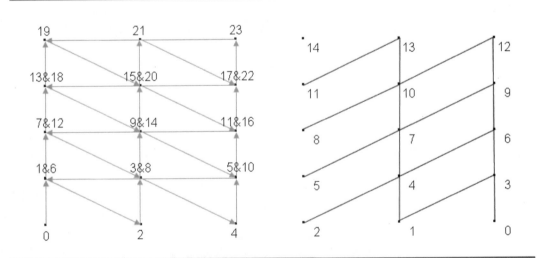

Total vertices stored for non-indexed data (left) versus indexed data (right)

several subsets of vertices can be used for drawing in succession to render the complete surface. When the index buffer is declared, it is sized to store one subset of vertices. The vertices are referenced using a short array:

```
short[] indexArray = new short[int subsetVertexCount];
```

In Figure 9-2, indices for a subset of six vertices are stored in a short array. Later, while the surface is being rendered, the index reference will be applied four times to reference four subsets of six vertices to build the rectangle.

The index buffer is declared using the IndexBuffer class. Here is the syntax:

```
IndexBuffer indexBuffer = new IndexBuffer
(    GraphicsDevice            graphicsDevice,
     Type                      indexType,
     int                       subsetLength,
     ResourceUsage             resourceUsage,
     ResourceManagementMode    resourceManagementMode );
```

The first three parameters of the index buffer are self-explanatory. The last two parameters allow you to customize how the index buffer is stored in memory to optimize efficiency. For the material in this book, WriteOnly usage is required and a ResourceManagementMode setting of Automatic is applied to allow the index buffer to be copied to memory as needed.

FIGURE 9-2

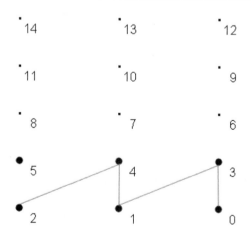

The index buffer references two rows of data in the grid at a time.

Once the indices have been defined, the SetData() method stores the index references in the index buffer:

```
IndexBuffer indexBuffer.SetData< VertexType >
(    short             indexArray,
     int               startElement,
     int               elementCount,
     SetDataOptions    options);
```

The SetDataOptions parameter allows you to specify whether existing buffer data may be overwritten during the SetData() operation. For the demonstrations in this book, a setting of None is suitable, which allows portions of the buffer to be overwritten.

DYNAMICALLY UPDATING DATA WITH INDEX BUFFERS AND VERTEX BUFFERS

By themselves, the VertexPositionColor, VertexPositionColorTexture, VertexPositionTexture, and VertexPositionNormalTexture objects that you have used until now will not permit live updates to the position, color, texture, and normal data after they are initially set. Dynamic vertex buffers in combination with index buffers, on the other hand, will permit updates to large amounts of vertex data. You are going to want a structure like this when creating an effect such as water.

When initialized, the constructor for the vertex buffer takes parameters for the current graphics device, vertex type, element count, resource properties, and resource management:

```
VertexBuffer vb = new VertexBuffer(
     GraphicsDevice            graphicsDevice,
     Type                      vertexType,
     int                       elementCount,
     ResourceUsage             usage,
     ResourceManagementMode    resourceManagementMode
);
```

The ResourceUsage parameter provides the option ResourceUsage.Dynamic | ResourceUsage.WriteOnly to create a vertex buffer that can be written to and updated at run time. Dynamic vertex buffers require a ResourceManagementMode setting of Manual so they can be updated after they are initialized.

After the vertex data is loaded into an array, the vertex data is moved into the vertex buffer with the SetData() method. Here is the syntax:

```
VertexBufferObject.SetData<VertexType>(
     VertexType[]              vertexArray,
     int                       startIndex,
```

```
int                     elementCount,
SetDataOptions          options);
```

Rendering Vertex Buffers with an Index Buffer Reference

The draw method you use for dynamic vertex buffers—using index buffers—differs in three ways from the draw methods you have used until now:

▶ The SetSource() method is used to set the vertex buffer that stores the grid, the starting element, and the size of the vertex type in bytes:

```
gfx.GraphicsDevice.Vertices[0].SetSource
(       VertexBuffer vb,
        int             startingElement,
        int             sizeOfVertex (in bytes));
```

▶ The GraphicsDevice's Indices object is set with the corresponding IndexBuffer object you defined during the program setup:

```
gfx.GraphicsDevice.Indices = indexBuffer;
```

▶ The DrawIndexedPrimitives() method is used to reference a series of vertex subsets that are rendered in succession to draw the entire polygon or surface. DrawIndexedPrimitives() is called for each vertex subset.

```
gfx.GraphicsDevice.DrawIndexedPrimitives(
        PrimitiveType   primitiveType,
        int     startingPointInVertexBuffer,
        int     minimumVerticesInBuffer,
        int     totalVerticesInBuffer,
        int     indexBufferStartingPoint,
        int     indexBufferEndPoint  );
```

Grid Using Index Buffer Example

This code will implement an index buffer and dynamic vertex buffer to draw a rectangle from a set of vertices that is three vertices wide and five vertices long (see Figure 9-3). Drawing a rectangle with a set of vertices that uses index buffers might seem like a lackluster chore, but don't be fooled. Index buffers have grit. This little example serves as the foundation for creating water waves in Chapter 10, "Combining Images for Better Visual Effects"; creating terrain with height detection in Chapter 25, "Terrain with Height Detection"; and enabling better lighting across primitive surfaces in Chapter 20, "Lighting."

This example begins with either the WinMGHBook or Xbox360MGHBook project in the BaseCode directory in the download from this book's website.

To make this vertex reference system work, an index buffer to reference a grid of vertices is required. Also, a vertex buffer object is needed to store the vertices. A vertex declaration type is used to set up the buffer when it is being initialized. Add these object declarations to the module area of your game class:

FIGURE 9-3

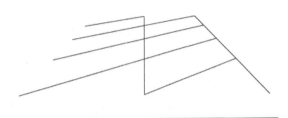

Grid rendered from an index buffer

```
private IndexBuffer      mIB;                    // reference vertices
private VertexBuffer     mVB;                    // dynamic vertex storage
private VertexPositionColorTexture[] mVertGrid;  // store vertices
```

The rows and columns used to draw the rectangle will be referenced with identifiers to help explain how the vertices are arranged. Add these identifiers to the module level of the game class.

```
const    int     NUM_COLS = 3;
const    int     NUM_ROWS = 5;
```

Indices for referencing the vertex buffer are initialized when the program begins. The index buffer array is sized to store the total number of vertices contained in one subset of the vertex buffer. The code that you need to set up the index reference is contained in the init_indices() method. Add this method to set up your index reference:

```
private void init_indices(){
    short[] shrtIndexArray;                      // stores indices for 1 subset

    shrtIndexArray = new short[2*NUM_COLS]; // sized to store 1 subset
    mIB = new IndexBuffer(gfx.GraphicsDevice,    // our gfx device
            typeof(short),                       // set type to short
            shrtIndexArray.Length,               // int size in bytes
            ResourceUsage.WriteOnly,             // memory use options
            ResourceManagementMode.Automatic);

    int i = 0;
```

```
    // store indices for one subset of vertices
    // see Figure 9-2 for the first subset of indices
    for (int col = 0; col < NUM_COLS; col++){
        shrtIndexArray[i++] = (short)col;
        shrtIndexArray[i++] = (short)(col + NUM_COLS);
    }
    mIB.SetData<short>(shrtIndexArray,
                       0,                          // element start
                       shrtIndexArray.Length,      // element count
                       SetDataOptions.None);       // options
}
```

To initialize the short array and index buffer when the program begins, add the call statement to the Initialize() method:

```
init_indices();
```

A dynamic VertexBuffer object is declared to store the vertices used to build the rectangle. The properties ResourceUsage.Dynamic | ResourceUsage.WriteOnly, in the buffer's declaration, allow the buffer's data to be changed for each frame. This dynamic property won't actually be used for this demonstration, but it is being set here for use later. A vertex type array, mVertGrid, assists with the setup of the vertex data, which is then transferred into the vertex buffer. mVertGrid stores all position, texture, and color data for the grid. When the vertex buffer is initialized or updated, the mVertGrid array is referenced to obtain the data for each vertex in the grid. To set up your vertices in this efficient and dynamic buffer, add init_dynamic_vb() to your game class:

```
private void init_dynamic_vb(){
    // initialize dynamic vertex buffer that can be updated at run time
    mVB     = new VertexBuffer(
        gfx.GraphicsDevice,                     // gfx device
        typeof(VertexPositionColorTexture),     // vertex type
        NUM_COLS * NUM_ROWS,                    // element count
        ResourceUsage.Dynamic | ResourceUsage.WriteOnly,
        ResourceManagementMode.Manual);         // memory use

    // size to store all verts in rectangle
    mVertGrid = new VertexPositionColorTexture[NUM_ROWS * NUM_COLS];

    float f_x = (float)2 * BOUNDARY / (NUM_COLS - 1); // column width
    float f_z = (float)2 * BOUNDARY / (NUM_ROWS - 1); // row height
```

```
    // store x, y, and z for each point in rectangle
    for (int iRow = 0; iRow < NUM_ROWS; iRow++){
        for (int iCol = 0; iCol < NUM_COLS; iCol++){
            // generate x, y, z in rectangle
            float fx, fy, fz;
            fx = -BOUNDARY + iCol * (f_x);
            fy = 0.0f;
            fz = -BOUNDARY + iRow * (f_z);

            // set X, Y, Z
            mVertGrid[iCol + iRow*NUM_COLS].Position =new Vector3(fx,fy,fz);

            // set color
            mVertGrid[iCol + iRow * NUM_COLS].Color = Color.White;

            // set uv coordinates to map texture 1:1
            float u, v;
            u = 1.0f - ((float)iCol / ((float)NUM_COLS - 1));
            v = 1.0f - ((float)iRow / ((float)NUM_ROWS - 1));
            mVertGrid[iCol+iRow*NUM_COLS].TextureCoordinate
                = new Vector2(u,v);
        }
    }
    // commit data to vertex buffer
    mVB.SetData<VertexPositionColorTexture>
        (mVertGrid, 0, mVertGrid.Length, SetDataOptions.None);
}
```

The vertices must be set when the program begins, so add a call to initialize the grid vertices in the Initialize() method:

```
init_dynamic_vb();
```

When a dynamic vertex buffer is being rendered, the SetSource() method reads data from the vertex buffer mVB, which was initialized earlier. The vertex format is passed into the SetSource() method, so the GraphicsDevice knows how to extract the data, and the GraphicsDevice's Indices property is assigned the index buffer mIB. Finally, DrawIndexedPrimtives() is executed once for each subset of strips in the grid. Add draw_grid() to the games class:

```
private void draw_grid(){
    // 1: declare matrices
    Matrix matIdentity, matTransl;
```

```
matTransl = Matrix.CreateTranslation(0.0f, -0.5f, 0.0f);

// 2: initialize matrices
matIdentity = Matrix.Identity;

// 3: build cumulative world matrix using I.S.R.O.T. sequence

mMatWorld = matIdentity * matTransl;

// 4: pass wvp matrix to shader
mfxTex_WVP.SetValue(mMatWorld * mMatView * mMatProj);
mfxTex.CommitChanges();

// 5: draw object - select vertex type, primitive type, index, and draw
gfx.GraphicsDevice.VertexDeclaration = mVertPosColorTex;
gfx.GraphicsDevice.Vertices[0].SetSource(mVB, 0,
    VertexPositionColorTexture.SizeInBytes);
gfx.GraphicsDevice.Indices = mIB;

// draw grid one row at a time
for (int z = 0; z < NUM_ROWS - 1; z++){
    gfx.GraphicsDevice.DrawIndexedPrimitives(
    PrimitiveType.LineStrip,// primitive
    z * NUM_COLS,                    // start point in buffer for drawing
    0,                               // minimum vertices in vertex buffer
    NUM_COLS * NUM_ROWS,             // total vertices in buffer
    0,                               // start point in index buffer
    2 * (NUM_COLS - 1));             // end point in index buffer
    }
}
```

To draw the grid using the texture shader, call draw_grid() from between the Begin() and End() statements for the TextureShader.fx object inside the Draw() method:

```
draw_grid();
```

Also, you will need to comment out the instruction to draw the ground, draw_ground(), to see the grid when it renders.

When you run the program, the grid appears as shown back in Figure 9-3. However, if the grid is drawn with triangle strips, by changing LineStrip to TriangleStrip in draw_grid(), the output will fill in the area between the vertices and display a rectangle.

Bystanders might not be impressed that you just created a rectangular surface, but don't be bothered. Let's put this demo on the backburner for now. We'll return to it in later chapters to let it rip.

CHAPTER 9 REVIEW EXERCISES

1. Try the step-by-step example in this chapter. Change the number of rows to 125 and the number of columns to 55. View the project using line strips and triangle strips.

2. How many vertices can be stored in a vertex buffer that houses a grid 60 rows high and 35 rows wide?

3. Name the property that is set in the vertex buffer to allow its data to be updated at run time.

4. List three ways that the DrawIndexedPrimitives() method is different from the DrawUserPrimitives() method.

FIGURE 10-1

An animated sprite in the game window

animation on the left at each interval. To the gamer, the image of the light appears to blink on and off every 0.5 seconds.

This example begins with either the WinMGHBook project or the Xbox360MGHBook project found in the BaseCode download from this book's website. This example uses a SpriteBatch object to access methods for drawing a 2D sprite on the 2D game window. The Texture2D object is used to load and reference the image. To try this example, first add these two declarations to the modules level of the game class:

```
private SpriteBatch mSpriteBatch;   // SpriteBatch object
private Texture2D   mTex2DSprite;   // load and set image that is rendered
```

A timer is used to trigger the frame change for the sprite which creates the blinking light animation. To implement the timer, module-level declarations are required to store the frame number (mIFrameNum), the time spent in the current timer interval (mDblCurrentFrame), and the time lapse since the last interval (mDblPreviousFrame):

```
int            mIFrameNum      = 1;
private double mDblCurrentFrame  = 0; // time in current interval
private double mDblPreviousFrame = 0; // interval saved as of last frame
```

Next, the Timer() method is added to the methods section to check for the completion of each 0.5 second interval. The Timer() method calculates the remainder of the amount of time since the interval started, divided by 500 milliseconds. When the remainder has increased compared to the remainder calculated for the previous frame, the interval is incomplete. When the remainder has decreased since the previous frame, a new interval has been entered, and the Timer() method returns a positive result. The positive result triggers a frame swap for the sprite. Checking the remainders in this manner prevents the variable from growing beyond the variable's storage capacity because it is reset every interval. Even though the remainder is usually positive when a new interval is detected, the overshot from the interval start is miniscule, and tracking the remainder makes this algorithm self-correcting. In this manner, the Timer() implements animations that appear to be synchronized with real time:

```
bool Timer(GameTime gameTime){
    bool bNewInterval;
    double dblMS = (double)gameTime.ElapsedRealTime.Milliseconds;

    // increment by time lapse between frames and stop var overflow
    mDblCurrentFrame += dblMS;
    mDblCurrentFrame  = mDblCurrentFrame % 500;

    // used up time increasing so interval is incomplete
    if (mDblCurrentFrame >= mDblPreviousFrame)
        bNewInterval = false;
    // current time was reset to zero so interval complete
    else
        bNewInterval = true;
    mDblPreviousFrame = mDblCurrentFrame;
    return bNewInterval;
}
```

The SpriteBatch object is initialized when the program begins in Initialize():

```
mSpriteBatch = new SpriteBatch(this.gfx.GraphicsDevice);
```

The warninglight.png file is also loaded by code into the Texture2D object in the LoadGraphicsContent() method. The warninglight.png file can be downloaded from this book's website. The image needs to be added to your project so it can be loaded by the content pipeline. To reference this in your project, right-click the Images folder in the Solution Explorer, choose Add, and then select Existing Item. A dialog will appear that allows you to navigate to the image and select it. Once the warninglight.png file is selected, it will appear in your project within the Solution Explorer, and you can then load it with the following instruction:

```
mTex2DSprite = content.Load<Texture2D>(".\\Images\\warninglight");
```

To ensure the sprite is positioned properly in the game window, add the routine that was discussed earlier to retrieve the starting pixel for drawing in the window:

```
Vector2 get_titleSafe_bottomLeft_pixel(){
    const int MARGIN = 20;    // bottom and left margin for PC
    const int IMAGEFRAME_H = 61;
    int ipcYpx = gfx.GraphicsDevice.Viewport.Height
                        - MARGIN - (IMAGEFRAME_H);
    Vector2 v2px = new Vector2(MARGIN, ipcYpx);

    #if XBOX                      // adjust - tv may only show 80% of window
        const float kPercent = 0.2f;
        v2px.X = gfx.GraphicsDevice.Viewport.Width * kPercent/2.0f;
        v2px.Y = gfx.GraphicsDevice.Viewport.Height*(1 - kPercent/2.0f);
        v2px.Y -= IMAGEFRAME_H;
    #endif
    return v2px;
}
```

The next method to add is draw_2D_sprite(). This method is simple to implement, as is explained in the code comments. This current example shows a sprite
with only two frames, but this can easily be changed if needed. Also, the three constant values—kTotalFrames, kFrameW, and kFrameH—can be modified to handle
a new image with a different frame count and pixel dimension size.

draw_2D_sprite() checks the timer to see if the set interval has completed. If the
timer returns a true value, indicating that it just ticked into a new interval, the frame
in the image is incremented or reset. The SpriteBatch() calls the Begin() method to start
the drawing. Begin() allows the developer to set the SpriteBlendMode option to specify the type of blending. This could include:

> **AlphaBlend**   For removing masked pixels

> **Additive**   For summing source and destination colors

> **None**   For standard rendering

If you want to remove the transparent pixels, you will use
SpriteBlendMode.AlphaBlend as a parameter in the SpriteBatch's Begin() method.
The picture in the warninglight.png file was created with a transparent background
so the pixels will not appear when the image is drawn with alpha blending.

The SpriteBatch's Draw() method applies four parameters. The first parameter is
the Texture2D object. In this case, the mTex2DSprite object is used to store the
warninglight.png file. The drawing position and pixel area covered in the window
are set in the second parameter. Then, the starting pixel and corresponding height
and width for the image frame are set in the third parameter. Finally, you could set a
color in the fourth parameter to shade the sprite, but in this case white is used to draw

the sprite with the original image color. To make all of this happen, add draw_2D_sprite() to your project:

```
void draw_2D_sprite(GameTime gameTime, Vector2 v2pixel){
    // change pixel h&w and frame count if different sprite used
    const int kFrameW      = 61;             const int kFrameH = 61;
    const int kTotalFrames = 2;

    if (Timer(gameTime)){                    // adjust frame every 500ms
        mIFrameNum += 1;
        if (mIFrameNum >= kTotalFrames)
            mIFrameNum = 0;                  // restart if last frame
    }

    int iWinX = (int)v2pixel.X; int iWinY = (int)v2pixel.Y;
    mSpriteBatch.Begin(SpriteBlendMode.AlphaBlend);
    mSpriteBatch.Draw(
        mTex2DSprite,                        // sprite image
        new Rectangle(iWinX,    iWinY,       // X, Y window position
                    kFrameW,  kFrameH),      // pixel W&H area used on window
        new Rectangle(0,mIFrameNum*kFrameH,  // starting X&Y pixels in image
                    kFrameW,  kFrameH),      // pixel W&H used in image
                    Color.White);            // color
    mSpriteBatch.End();
}
```

draw_2D_sprite() needs to be called in the Draw() method after methods for drawing the 3D objects are called so that the 2D sprite can overlay the 3D graphics:

```
draw_2D_sprite(gameTime, get_titleSafe_bottomLeft_pixel());
```

As mentioned earlier, the SpriteBatch object automatically adjusts the render state of the GraphicsDevice object to draw in 2D but does not change it back. To draw in 3D, the original settings must be reset in the Draw() method after the SpriteBatch object is drawn:

```
gfx.GraphicsDevice.RenderState.CullMode= CullMode.None;//see both sides
gfx.GraphicsDevice.RenderState.DepthBufferEnable= true;//re-enable 3D on Z
gfx.GraphicsDevice.RenderState.AlphaBlendEnable=false;//disable transparent
gfx.GraphicsDevice.RenderState.AlphaTestEnable =false;//per pixel testing
// re-enable tiling
gfx.GraphicsDevice.SamplerStates[0].AddressU    =TextureAddressMode.Wrap;
gfx.GraphicsDevice.SamplerStates[0].AddressV    =TextureAddressMode.Wrap;
```

When you run the program, the light will appear as shown back in Figure 10-1.

Sprite Texture Example

The previous example is useful for implementing 2D sprites in the game window. This example shows how to create a sprite inside your 3D world. When the example is complete, a flashing "danger" sign will appear in your game. Maybe you don't need a flashing danger sign, but you need a flashing billboard on your speedway, or maybe you want to display scrolling text on one of the objects in your 3D world. A sprite texture can do this. You could even use a similar effect to create a cartoon in your game.

To get these effects off the window and inside your game world, you will need to use textured primitive objects. The frames in the sprite are swapped by modifying the UV coordinates at the start of each interval. The fraction of the image displayed in each frame is based on the total frames stored in the image. The sprite used for this example has just two frames. Figure 10-2 shows the two frames of the image on the left and the animation on the right at different intervals.

FIGURE 10-2

Two frames of an image (left) and animation (right)

This example begins with either the WinMGHBook project or the Xbox360MGHBook project in the BaseCode folder of this book's download. Also, the dangersign.png must be downloaded from this book's website and referenced in your project from the Solution Explorer.

An array of four vertices, mVertSprite, will be used to render a triangle strip with a danger sign sprite texture. This vertex object declaration is needed at the module level of the game class so the vertices can be stored, updated, and used for drawing while the game runs:

```
private VertexPositionColorTexture[] mVertSprite = new
VertexPositionColorTexture[4];
```

The position, texture, and color data are set when the program begins. Add init_3DSprite_surface() to the game class to set up these vertices for the rectangle used to display the danger sign:

```
private void init_3DSprite_surface(){
    // initialize when program starts
    mVertSprite = new VertexPositionColorTexture[4];

    // bottom right
    Vector2 uv  = new Vector2(1.0f, 1.0f);
    Vector3 pos = new Vector3(-0.5f, 0.0f, 0.0f);
    mVertSprite[0] = new VertexPositionColorTexture(pos, Color.White, uv);
    // bottom left
    pos.X = 0.5f; pos.Y = 0.0f; pos.Z = 0.0f; uv.X = 0.0f; uv.Y = 1.0f;
    mVertSprite[1] = new VertexPositionColorTexture(pos, Color.White, uv);
    // top right
    pos.X = -0.5f; pos.Y = 1.0f; pos.Z = 0.0f; uv.X = 1.0f; uv.Y = 0.0f;
    mVertSprite[2] = new VertexPositionColorTexture(pos, Color.White, uv);
    // top left
    pos.X = 0.5f; pos.Y = 1.0f; pos.Z = 0.0f; uv.X = 0.0f; uv.Y = 0.0f;
    mVertSprite[3] = new VertexPositionColorTexture(pos, Color.White, uv);
}
```

The four vertices that are used to draw the rectangle with the danger sign texture must be initialized when the program launches. To do this, inside Initialize(), add the following call to init_3DSprite_surface():

```
init_3DSprite_surface();
```

Also, a Texture2D object is required to store the texture, so a declaration for mTexDanger needs to be in the module declarations area of the game class:

```
private Texture2D mTexDanger;
```

The sprite contained in the dangersign.png file (shown in Figure 10-2) must be read into memory when the program begins. To do this, add a statement to load the image in the LoadGraphicsContent() method:

```
mTexDanger = content.Load<Texture2D>(".\\Images\\dangersign");
```

The texture's frame must alternate every 500 milliseconds, so a timer is used to track when these intervals are completed. To assist with setting up the timer and swapping texture frames, module-level declarations are used to store the current frame number as well as times of the current and previous frame:

```
private int mICurrentFrame      = 0;
private double mDblPreviousFrame = 0; // interval saved as of last frame
private double mDblCurrentFrame  = 0;
```

The timer code used for this example follows the same algorithm used in the previous example. This time, it will set the interval for the textured sprite. Add Timer() to enable frame swapping every 500 milliseconds:

```
bool Timer(GameTime gameTime) {
    bool bNewInterval;
    double dblMS = (double)gameTime.ElapsedRealTime.Milliseconds;

    // increment by time lapse between frames and stop var overflow
    mDblCurrentFrame += dblMS;
    mDblCurrentFrame = mDblCurrentFrame % 500;

    // used up time increasing so interval is incomplete
    if (mDblCurrentFrame >= mDblPreviousFrame)
        bNewInterval = false;
    // current time was reset to zero so interval complete
    else
        bNewInterval = true;
    mDblPreviousFrame = mDblCurrentFrame;
    return bNewInterval;
}
```

When animating sprites, you must update the UV coordinates to switch frames. Since the texture frames are arranged vertically in this example, when the timer signals the completion of an interval, the V coordinate for each vertex is adjusted to switch frames. If you need to use a different sprite, with a different number of frames or dimensions, this method could easily be employed by adjusting the constants kIFrameHeight and kITotalFrames. Add update_sprite_uv() to your game class:

```
void update_sprite_uv(GameTime gameTime){
    const int kIFrameHeight = 512;   // image frame height
    const int kITotalFrames = 2;     // total frames in image

    if (Timer(gameTime)){
        mICurrentFrame += 1;

        if (mICurrentFrame >= kITotalFrames)
            mICurrentFrame = 0;
    }
```

```
    float u, v;
    // bottom right
    u = mVertSprite[0].TextureCoordinate.X;
    v = ((mICurrentFrame + 1.0f) * kIFrameHeight) / (2.0f * kIFrameHeight);
    mVertSprite[0].TextureCoordinate = new Vector2(u, v);

    // bottom left
    u = mVertSprite[1].TextureCoordinate.X;
    v = ((mICurrentFrame + 1.0f) * kIFrameHeight) / (2.0f * kIFrameHeight);
    mVertSprite[1].TextureCoordinate = new Vector2(u, v);

    // top right
    u = mVertSprite[2].TextureCoordinate.X;
    v = (kIFrameHeight * mICurrentFrame * 0.5f) / kIFrameHeight;
    mVertSprite[2].TextureCoordinate = new Vector2(u, v);

    // top left
    u = mVertSprite[3].TextureCoordinate.X;
    v = (kIFrameHeight * mICurrentFrame * 0.5f) / kIFrameHeight;
    mVertSprite[3].TextureCoordinate = new Vector2(u, v);
}
```

update_sprite_uv() is called from Update() to ensure the texture frames are swapped at the completion of each interval:

```
update_sprite_uv(gameTime);
```

The draw_3D_sprite() routine is identical to the routines used for drawing any textured object that you have used until now. Check the comments in this code for details:

```
private void draw_3D_sprite(){
    // 1: declare matrices
    Matrix matIdentity, matTransl;
    matTransl = Matrix.CreateTranslation(0.0f, -0.9f, 2.0f);

    // 2: initialize matrices
    matIdentity = Matrix.Identity;

    // 3: build cumulative world matrix using I.S.R.O.T. sequence
    mMatWorld = matIdentity *  matTransl;

    // 4: pass wvp matrix to shader
```

```
mfxTex_WVP.SetValue(mMatWorld * mMatView * mMatProj);
mfxTex.CommitChanges();

// 5: draw object - select vertex type, primitive type, index, and draw
gfx.GraphicsDevice.VertexDeclaration = mVertPosColorTex;
mfxTexture.SetValue(mTexDanger);            // set texture
mfxTex.CommitChanges();                     // commit texture

gfx.GraphicsDevice.DrawUserPrimitives<VertexPositionColorTexture>
(PrimitiveType.TriangleStrip,               // triangle strips
mVertSprite,                                // use sprite vertex
0,                                          // vertex offset
2);                                         // two primitive objects
}
```

Inside the Draw() method, just before the EndScene() method for the texture shader, the texture sprite needs to be drawn. When transparency is involved, these transparent objects must be rendered last after the opaque 3D objects have been drawn. To enable transparency, several RenderStates for the GraphicsDevice must be adjusted. Alpha blending must be enabled by setting AlphaBlendEnable = true. The opaque pixels are drawn by setting SourceBlend = Blend.SourceAlpha, and the masked portion of the image is filtered out by setting DestinationBlend = Blend.InverseSourceAlpha. Alpha blending is disabled when the drawing is complete.

Add this code to set up transparency for your textured sprite and to render it as the last item in your list of 3D objects that are drawn:

```
gfx.GraphicsDevice.RenderState.AlphaBlendEnable  = true;
gfx.GraphicsDevice.RenderState.SourceBlend       = Blend.SourceAlpha;
gfx.GraphicsDevice.RenderState.DestinationBlend  = Blend.InverseSourceAlpha;
draw_3D_sprite();
gfx.GraphicsDevice.RenderState.AlphaBlendEnable  = false;
```

When you run the program, it will show a flashing danger sign in the 3D world, as shown earlier in Figure 10-2. Unlike the sprite example, this sign can be viewed from different angles as a player travels through the world.

MULTITEXTURING

Multitexturing is a technique that blends two or more images into one texture. Multitexturing offers interesting possibilities for creating graphics effects, such as adding detail texturing to terrain, simulating moving currents of water, and changing the appearance of existing textures at run time.

Multitexturing uses multipass rendering to draw the same object more than once for each frame. Each render of the object is triggered during one *pass* in the shader. (There are several references to shaders in this example, so you may find a review of Chapter 4, "Shaders," to be helpful.) The developer can set each pass to specify how the object is filtered, textured, and drawn.

Multipass Rendering from the Shader's Technique

A shader that implements multitexturing is almost identical to the shader used for applying textures in Chapter 7, "Texturing Your Game World." The only difference with a multipass shader is that the technique implements more than one pass. In each pass, different blending and filtering can be triggered and different functions within the shader can be executed. This technique demonstrates typical syntax for a multitexturing shader:

```
technique MultiTexture
{
    pass p0 // first routine
    {
        // filtering
        vertexshader = compile vs_1_1 vs();
        pixelshader = compile ps_1_1 ps();
    }

    pass p1 // second routine
     {
        // filtering
        // call same or different vs
        vertexshader = compile vs_1_1 vs2();
        // call same or different ps
        pixelshader = compile ps_1_1 ps2();
    }
}
```

Calling the Pass from the Draw() Method

Each pass is called from the XNA application's Draw() method between the BeginScene() and EndScene() methods for the shader.

You must select the shader's passes between the effect's Begin() and End() methods. The code syntax presented here is similar to code that would be used to select and execute two passes within the shader. Note that the same draw_object() method is called, but a different texture is assigned and is committed to the shader in each pass.

```
mfxTex.Techniques[0].Passes[1].Begin();  // *START 2ND PASS
    mfxTexture.SetValue(mTexWater1);      // set 2nd texture
    mfxTex.CommitChanges();               // set change in shader
    draw_grid();
mfxTex.Techniques[0].Passes[1].End();    // *END 2ND PASS


    // disable image blending
    gfx.GraphicsDevice.RenderState.AlphaBlendEnable = false;
mfxTex.End();
```

Finally, in draw_grid(), replace the primitive type in the DrawIndexedPrimitives() method with TriangleStrip. Compile and run the program. The output will show a clear, bright moving surface that appears to be water (see Figure 10-4).

Water Using Multitexturing Example, Continued:
Adding Waves

This next portion of the example adds waves to the water. The algorithm uses a sine function, shown here, to update the Y value of each vertex in the grid at every frame.

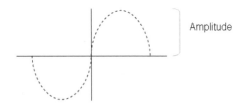

The sine wave equation offers properties to control the wave frequency, number of waves, and height (amplitude).

Start with the code from the last solution, "Water Using Multitexturing Example."

FIGURE 10-4

Clear water, no waves

To generate the effect of more naturally rounded waves, more vertices are required. At the top of the game class, replace the existing definitions for the total number of columns and rows, in the vertex grid, with these revised declarations:

```
private const int NUM_COLS = 30;
private const int NUM_ROWS = 30;
```

Also, add a float to store the sine wave cycle increment:

```
private float            mfCycleIncrement;
```

get_point_in_cycle() traces a floating-point value through a sine wave's cycle over time. The function is only executed once per frame but is used to update each Y value for all vertices in the grid. Add this function to your game class:

```
float get_point_in_cycle(GameTime gameTime) {
    // retrieves between 0 and 1. Full cycle for sine wave is 2*PI
    double dblMS = gameTime.ElapsedGameTime.Milliseconds;

    // less than full cycle of sine wave
    if (mfCycleIncrement < 1)
        mfCycleIncrement += 0.0000005f * (float)dblMS;
    // adjust when sine wave cycle complete
    else
        mfCycleIncrement = mfCycleIncrement - 1;
    return mfCycleIncrement;
}
```

As discussed, get_point_in_cycle() is called only once per frame to trace a value on the sine wave over time. The point on the sine wave that is returned is added to the V coordinate for each point in the grid. This sum is used for setting the Y value of each point in the grid. The result is a set of oscillating Y values that follow the sine wave as it rises and falls over time.

set_water_height() receives the sum of the texture's V coordinate plus the point in the sine wave over time. This sine wave equation returns a Y value for the coordinate that corresponds with the V coordinate:

$$\text{Height} = \text{Amplitude} = \sin(\text{WaveCountPerCycle} * \text{PointInCycle} * 2\pi)$$

Add the set_water_height() method to the game class:

```
float set_water_height(float fCycleTime){
    const float kFrequency    = 6.0f;                // wave count per cycle
```

Combining Images for Better Visual Effects

```
const float kAmplitude    = 1.0f / 15.0f;    // wave height

// by definition each cycle is 2PI
const float k2PI          = (float)2.0f * (float)Math.PI ;

// generates height based on V coord and sine equation
return (kAmplitude*(float)Math.Sin(kFrequency*fCycleTime*k2PI)-0.4f);

}
```

The X, Y, Z, information is the same for both the stationary image layer and the moving image layer. Since the stationary layer is drawn first, the Y value that changes with the sine wave over time can be set for this layer and the changes will apply to both image layers. Adding this code to reset the X, Y, and Z coordinates inside a nested for-loop for update_stationary_layer() will create a dynamically changing Y value that simulates the wave for both layers over time:

```
float X, Y, Z;
Y = set_water_height(v + get_point_in_cycle(gameTime));
X = mVertGrid[iCol + iRow * NUM_COLS].Position.X;
Z = mVertGrid[iCol + iRow * NUM_COLS].Position.Z;

mVertGrid[iCol + iRow * NUM_COLS].Position =
    new Vector3(X, Y, Z);
```

When you run this program, it shows the moving dynamic texture and the waves rippling through the object. The effect is actually quite beautiful (see Figure 10-5). You can try building this example, or you can download the completed example from the Solutions folder in the download from this book's website.

FIGURE 1 0 - 5

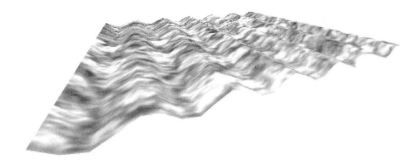

Surf's up!

There are various ways to combine images for creating exciting graphics effects. Sprites are used to animate a series of image frames that are stored in an image file. Multitexturing can be used to blend two images together and provide more detail or dynamic movement for the texture.

CHAPTER 10 REVIEW EXERCISES

1. Try the step-by-step examples presented in this chapter.

2. For your solution to the SpriteBatch example, remove the code that manually resets the RenderState properties for the GraphicsDevice in the Draw() method. Then add code to automatically restore the render states after the SpriteBatch object is drawn. Automatically restoring the render states can be done in draw_2D_sprite() by replacing the SpriteBatch object's Begin() instruction with code similar to this:

```
spriteBatch.Begin(SpriteBlendMode.AlphaBlend,
                SpriteSortMode.Immediate,SaveStateMode.SaveState);
```

Try running your code and notice that the output appears to be the same as before.

3. Replace your Begin() statement in Exercise 2 with an instruction similar to the following statement and then run your project:

```
spriteBatch.Begin();
```

Notice how the ground and all other 3D objects disappear when the render states are not restored.

4. With the solution for the 2D sprite and the original 2D sprite settings, call draw_2D_sprite() before draw_ground(). Notice you cannot see the sprite unless the view is changed so the ground is not covering it.

5. Create your own sprite with three or more frames. In the same project, show the sprite as a 2D SpriteBatch object. Display your sprite in the 3D world using a textured sprite.

6. Use multitexturing to make it appear as if moving shadows cast from the clouds are traveling across the ground.

Score Tracking and Game Statistics

BEING able to display status information about players and their scores is fundamental to any game dashboard. For example, you might need to show statistics such as health, fuel level, the current map name, or maybe even the opponents' names. In the end, your ability to present this information boils down to having access to a font library that can overlay 2D text on your game's 3D environment.

When this book was written (just after the first full release of Microsoft's Game Studio Express), fonts were not included in the XNA library. Understandably, the Microsoft XNA team was focused on getting XNA to market for their promised release date of December 11, 2006. Microsoft delivered on their promise, and the product release was excellent. However, to get GSE to market on time, fonts were dropped from the features list. By the time you read this book, the XNA team will have already added a font library in their latest build of GSE.

If Microsoft's library is anything like XNA's predecessor, Managed DirectX, you can expect that the XNA font class will be easy to use and require the addition of only a few lines of code to your game class. However, even if you have a GSE version that implements fonts, you still may want to build a custom font to match the theme of your game. For example, if your game has a haunted house theme, you may want to construct a set of alphanumeric characters using images of human bones. Or maybe your game has a jungle theme and you want to create a character set made from images of bamboo. This chapter shows you how to create a custom font class that enables 2D text on your game dashboard.

CREATING A CUSTOM IMAGE FONT

A custom image font is a set of characters stored in an image file. The custom image font presented in this chapter is based on the image shown in Figure 11-1.

This image was actually converted to a mask so each character in the font set is opaque and the background is transparent. The opaque characters must be colored white if you want the ability to assign different text foreground colors at run time.

To create your own font with a transparent background, you could use a photo editor such as Adobe Photoshop to create a character set using the *.png or *.tga format. You could also achieve the same result by creating a mask with a *.dds format.

FIGURE 11-1

```
abcdefghijklmnopqrstuvwxyz0123456789  .:
ABCDEFGHIJKLMNOPQRSTUVWXYZ+-*/|,=^
```

Custom character set stored in the fonts.dds image file

The fonts.dds image was created with the Courier New font. This is an even-spaced font, which means each character in the font set is designed to take up the same column width. Unlike a Times New Roman font or an Arial font, an even-spaced character set such as Courier New makes it easy to right-align words and numbers. The process of storing and retrieving an even-spaced character set is simplified since every character in the font set has the same height and width. For the font class presented in this chapter, an area of 10 pixels wide by 13 pixels high is used for all characters in the set.

CUSTOM FONT CLASS

The font class contains a fair amount of code, but it is easy to understand. The constructor receives the total pixel height and width for each character. Then, all of the work is handled by two methods: getStartingXPixel() and getStartingYPixel(). Both of these methods are called once for each character in the display string. Each time a character is passed in, these methods work together to return the top-left pixel for the corresponding character in the font image.

```
using System;
using System.Collections.Generic;
using System.Text;

namespace NS_Font
{
    class Font
    {
        private int miWidth, miHeight;

        // constructor (receives width and height of each character)
        public Font(int w, int h)
        {
            miWidth = w; miHeight = h;
        }
        // return starting X pixel in font.dds
        public int get_pixel_startingX(char ch)
        {
            switch (ch)
            {
                case 'a': case 'A': return 0;
                case 'b': case 'B': return 1 * miWidth;
                case 'c': case 'C': return 2 * miWidth;
                case 'd': case 'D': return 3 * miWidth;
```

```
                case 'e': case 'E': return 4 * miWidth;
                case 'f': case 'F': return 5 * miWidth;
                case 'g': case 'G': return 6 * miWidth;
                case 'h': case 'H': return 7 * miWidth;
                case 'i': case 'I': return 8 * miWidth;
                case 'j': case 'J': return 9 * miWidth;
                case 'k': case 'K': return 10 * miWidth;
                case 'l': case 'L': return 11 * miWidth;
                case 'm': case 'M': return 12 * miWidth;
                case 'n': case 'N': return 13 * miWidth;
                case 'o': case 'O': return 14 * miWidth;
                case 'p': case 'P': return 15 * miWidth;
                case 'q': case 'Q': return 16 * miWidth;
                case 'r': case 'R': return 17 * miWidth;
                case 's': case 'S': return 18 * miWidth;
                case 't': case 'T': return 19 * miWidth;
                case 'u': case 'U': return 20 * miWidth;
                case 'v': case 'V': return 21 * miWidth;
                case 'w': case 'W': return 22 * miWidth;
                case 'x': case 'X': return 23 * miWidth;
                case 'y': case 'Y': return 24 * miWidth;
                case 'z': case 'Z': return 25 * miWidth;
                case '0': case '+': return 26 * miWidth;
                case '1': case '-': return 27 * miWidth;
                case '2': case '*': return 28 * miWidth;
                case '3': case '/': return 29 * miWidth;
                case '4': case '|': return 30 * miWidth;
                case '5': case ',': return 31 * miWidth;
                case '6': case '=': return 32 * miWidth;
                case '7': case '^': return 33 * miWidth;
                case '8': return 34 * miWidth;
                case '9': return 35 * miWidth;
                case ' ': return 36 * miWidth;
                case '.': return 37 * miWidth;
                case ':': return 38 * miWidth;
            }
        return 0;
    }


    // return starting Y pixel in font.dds
    public int get_pixel_startingY(char ch)
    {
```

```
        switch (ch)
        {
            case 'A': case 'B': case 'C': case 'D': case 'E': case 'F':
            case 'G': case 'H': case 'I': case 'J': case 'K': case 'L':
            case 'M': case 'N': case 'O': case 'P': case 'Q': case 'R':
            case 'S': case 'T': case 'U': case 'V': case 'W': case 'X':
            case 'Y': case 'Z': case '+': case '-': case '*': case '/':
            case '|': case ',': case '=': case '^':
                return miHeight;
            default:
                return 0;
        }
    }
  }
}
```

Notice how simple the code is—most of it is repetitious. Of course, this routine can be streamlined, and it could easily be tailored to fit your needs if you chose to create a different font. All of this font class code can be found in the Fonts.cs file in the BaseCode folder in the download from the book's website.

Font Example: Displaying Text in the Game Window

Implementing the font class to draw text in your game window is also easy. This example explains the steps to display the string "Score Tracking and Game Stats" in the game window.

This example begins by using either the WinMGHBook or Xbox360MGHBook project in the BaseCode folder in the download from the book's website. You will use the font class that has just been described, so the Font.cs source file must be referenced in your project. You can find it in the BaseCode folder in the download.

The code inside Font.cs is designed to work with the fonts.dds image, so the fonts.dds image must also be copied to the Images folder for your project. The fonts.dds file can be found in the Images folder in the download.

Now that the Font.cs and fonts.dds files are referenced from the project, you can make modifications inside Game1.cs to draw some text. You will need a reference to access the font class, so the namespace must be included at the top of the file:

```
using NS_Font;
```

To declare an object that can use the font class methods, a module-level declaration for the font class object is required in the game class. As explained, the font created for this chapter is 10 pixels wide by 13 pixels high. When creating an instance of the font class, you pass in the width and height of each character area in the font mask to ensure that the font class returns the correct pixel values for each character. The font size of 10 by 13 is quite small, so you will magnify it by 1.3 to make it a bit more prominent:

```
const int    FONT_W  = 10;      // character pixel width
const int    FONT_H  = 13;      // character pixel height
const float  MAGNIFY = 1.3f;    // increase the font size
private Font mFont    = new Font(FONT_W, FONT_H);
```

Class-level declarations are needed to store the font mask as a texture to load and display it as a SpriteBatch object:

```
private Texture2D mtexFont;
private SpriteBatch mspriteFont;
```

The instruction to load the mask either from a Windows or Xbox 360 Games project with all of the other graphics files is made from the LoadGraphicsContent() method:

```
mtexFont = content.Load<Texture2D>(".\\Images\\fonts");
```

The sprite object must be set up at the beginning of the program, so you will need to add the following code to the Initialize() method:

```
mspriteFont = new SpriteBatch(this.gfx.GraphicsDevice);
```

Next, you will add the draw_string() method to the game class. This method receives a string and draws each character as text in the window. Inside the method, a for-loop iterates through each character in the string and draws it. The upper bound of the loop is obtained using the String.Length attribute. For each character that is rendered in the window, the SpriteBatch's Draw() method selects the font object, assigns the area of the window where the drawing takes place, selects the area of the font mask to be rendered, and assigns a color to the character that is output. When the loop is finished, the entire string is displayed as a perfect 2D text overlay on top of the game window.

```
void draw_string(string str, int iStartingX, int iStartingY, Color color)
{
    mspriteFont.Begin(SpriteBlendMode.AlphaBlend); // enable transparency

    for (int i = 0; i < str.Length; i++)
    {
        mspriteFont.Draw(
            mtexFont,
            // x window pos, y window pos, window w in px, window h in px
             new Rectangle(iStartingX + i * (int)(MAGNIFY * FONT_W),
              iStartingY, (int)(MAGNIFY * FONT_W), (int)(MAGNIFY * FONT_H)),

            // start x image px, start y image px, image w, image h
            new Rectangle(mFont.get_pixel_startingX(str[i]),
                mFont.get_pixel_startingY(str[i]), FONT_W,FONT_H),
```

```
            color);
    }
    mspriteFont.End();
}
```

As explained in Chapter 10, "Combining Images for Better Visual Effects," when rendering SpriteBatch objects to the window, you position these items using pixel references. Since most CRT televisions only show 80% to 90% of the game window, an additional adjustment is needed to ensure the text appears in the visible region of the window. To be sure the text displays on all televisions, this algorithm assumes that only 80% of the CRT screen is visible. Adding the get_titleSafe_topLeft_pixel() method to your game class provides a routine to return the top-left X, Y pixel coordinate that falls within the title safe region. This X, Y coordinate is obtained by multiplying the GraphicsDevice.Viewport's Height and Width attributes by 20%, which is the total portion of the game window that could potentially be truncated by the television screen. The resulting product is then divided by 2 to create equal spacing for each margin. This adjustment is not required for PCs since the PC window will display all the pixels. An #ifdef structure selects the appropriate routine depending on whether the code implementation is for the PC or the Xbox 360.

```
Vector2 get_titleSafe_topLeft_pixel()
{
    const float kPercent   = 0.2f;              // non visible 20%
    Vector2     v2px        = new Vector2(20, 20); // PC shows all pixels

    #if XBOX  // automatically predefined by 360 project
        float fMargin = kPercent / 2;            // adjust 360 visibility
        v2px.X = (float)(fMargin * gfx.GraphicsDevice.Viewport.Width);
        v2px.Y = (float)(fMargin * gfx.GraphicsDevice.Viewport.Height);
    #endif
    return v2px;
}
```

Before the text is drawn, the get_titleSafe_topLeft_pixel() method is called to obtain the starting X and Y pixel for the text in the game window. The instruction to trigger the rendering of the 2D sprite must be placed at the end of the Draw() method, but before the base.Draw() instruction. This rendering order ensures the 2D text will not be covered by any 3D objects that are drawn.

```
Vector2 v2px0 = get_titleSafe_topLeft_pixel();
draw_string("Score Tracking and Game Stats", (int)v2px0.X, (int)v2px0.Y,
            Color.Red);
```

When the font is drawn, the 2D SpriteBatch automatically resets the GraphicsDevice's render states to draw 2D graphics in the window (see Chapter 10,

"Combining Images for Better Visual Effects"). If these settings are not restored, your 3D graphics may not display properly. After the font is drawn, the following states need to be reset to enable 3D graphics after drawing the SpriteBatch:

```
gfx.GraphicsDevice.RenderState.CullMode= CullMode.None;//see both sides
gfx.GraphicsDevice.RenderState.DepthBufferEnable= true;//re-enable 3D on Z
gfx.GraphicsDevice.RenderState.AlphaBlendEnable= false;//stop transparency
gfx.GraphicsDevice.RenderState.AlphaTestEnable = false;//per pixel testing
// re-enable tiling
gfx.GraphicsDevice.SamplerStates[0].AddressU    = TextureAddressMode.Wrap;
gfx.GraphicsDevice.SamplerStates[0].AddressV    = TextureAddressMode.Wrap;
```

When you compile and run this code, the words "Score Tracking and Game Stats" appear in the window.

Font Example: Displaying a Frames-per-Second Count

This next example takes fonts a little further by demonstrating how to display numeric data in the window. For this case, a frame count per second will be shown at the bottom of the window.

To create the frames-per-second count, you will use a timer like the one presented in Chapter 10, "Combining Images for Better Visual Effects." The total frames rendered during one-second intervals are counted. When each one-second interval is complete, the total frame count generated is displayed on the screen for the second that follows—until a new count is tallied and displayed.

Some setup is required to store the count and interval times, so you will need to add the following module-level variable declarations (for storing the counter and time values) to the game class:

```
private int miFPS, miFPScounter;
private double mdblTimeLapsed, mdblTimeLapsedPreviousFrame;
```

The timer method discussed in Chapter 10, "Combining Images for Better Visual Effects," must also be added to measure the frame count in one-second intervals. A value of 1000 milliseconds is assigned for the interval to ensure the timer returns a true value for every one second.

```
bool Timer(GameTime gameTime)
{
    bool bIntervalIsFinished;

    // get total milliseconds since the last frame
    double dblMS = gameTime.ElapsedGameTime.Milliseconds;
```

```
    // increment time within interval
    mdblTimeLapsed += dblMS;
    // take remainder of the time lapse divided by the fixed interval to
    // prevent variable overflow
    mdblTimeLapsed = mdblTimeLapsed % 1000; // fixed interval =1000 ms =1s

    // if time in the interval is increasing the interval is incomplete
    if (mdblTimeLapsed >= mdblTimeLapsedPreviousFrame)
        bIntervalIsFinished = false;
    // current time was reset to zero so the interval was completed
    else
        bIntervalIsFinished = true;

    // store the time lapse for comparison with the next frame
    mdblTimeLapsedPreviousFrame = mdblTimeLapsed;
    return bIntervalIsFinished;
}
```

The Update() method is not necessarily called the same number of times as the Draw() method. As a result, when displaying the frame count, you must add code within the Draw() method to check the timer and increment the frame count:

```
if (Timer(gameTime))         // check if 1 second is up
{
    miFPS = miFPScounter; // 1 second complete so assign new FPS to display
    miFPScounter = 0;     // reset counter to 0 to start new interval
}
else
    miFPScounter += 1;    // increment counter when interval incomplete
```

Since the frame count string is displayed at the bottom of the window, a get_titleSafe_bottomLeft_pixel() method is needed in the game class to ensure the text appears in an area that is visible to the user. This method returns a Vector2 object that stores an X and Y value for the lower-left starting pixel coordinate of the text string. If you run this code on the PC, the left margin is set to be 20 pixels wide and the bottom margin is set to be 20 pixels high. If you run the code on the Xbox 360, the Viewport's Height and Width attributes are used to ensure the text is positioned 10% from the left of the window and 10% above the bottom of the window.

```
Vector2 get_titleSafe_bottomLeft_pixel()
{
    const float kPercent = 0.2f;                    // non visible area
    int ipcYpx = gfx.GraphicsDevice.Viewport.Height
                - 20 - (int)(FONT_H * MAGNIFY); // 20 px & font height
```

```
    Vector2 v2px = new Vector2(20, ipcYpx);         // bottom left px on PC

#if XBOX                                            // adjust if on Xbox 360
        v2px.X = gfx.GraphicsDevice.Viewport.Width  * kPercent / 2.0f;
        v2px.Y = gfx.GraphicsDevice.Viewport.Height
            * (1 - kPercent / 2.0f);
        v2px.Y -= (int)(FONT_H * MAGNIFY);
#endif
    return v2px;
}
```

Before the text is drawn, the pixel coordinate at the bottom-left margin is obtained. Then, the frame count total is converted to a String object using the ToString() method. Next, the frame count string is appended to the "FPS: " label. This combined string is rendered using the draw_string() method—which implements the font class to output the string as 2D text.

The frames-per-second string is rendered at the end of the Draw() method but before the RenderStates and SamplerStates are restored for 3D graphics. This logic in effect sets an appropriate rendering order that allows the 2D layer to appear on top after the 3D layer is drawn.

```
Vector2 v2px1 = get_titleSafe_bottomLeft_pixel();
draw_string("FPS: " + miFPS.ToString(), (int)v2px1.X, (int)v2px1.Y,
Color.Yellow);
```

When you run this example, the frame count appears at the bottom of the window.

Building a custom font is an easy way to customize the look and feel of your game. You will definitely want a dynamic method like this to display game scores and other game data. You may find the frames-per-second routine useful when testing your code's performance.

CHAPTER 11 REVIEW EXERCISES

1. Try the step-by-step examples presented in this chapter.

2. Try creating your own custom font using different graphic resources.

3. Create a custom score board. Increment the score every time the space bar is pressed.

4. Replace the code that restores the GraphicsDevice's RenderState properties with code that resets the RenderState properties after the SpriteBatch object is drawn. This restore can be automated by replacing the Begin() statement inside draw_string() with the following code:

```
mspriteFont.Begin(SpriteBlendMode.AlphaBlend,
            SpriteSortMode.Immediate,SaveStateMode.SaveState);
```

CHAPTER 12

3D Models

BY now, you may be thinking that you'd like to add some more realistic models to your game world—maybe an airplane, a rocket, or a castle. You could add them by hand-coding a bunch of textured primitive objects, but that would be way too much work. The obvious way to efficiently develop a complex 3D object is with a 3D modeling application. Learning to work with 3D models is a giant step in understanding game development. It allows you to add realistic and exciting-looking objects to your game world. By the end of this chapter—after you have created your own models and animated them in code—you will certainly choose the use of 3D models over hand-coded primitive objects when possible.

Once you have developed a 3D model, you can import it into your game and control it with your code. The two supported model formats currently for XNA are .x and .fbx. Microsoft has provided a library of code to load these models into XNA for you. If you really wanted, you could use other model file formats in your game, but you'd have to write a model loader.

3D MODELING TOOLS

Autodesk's Maya, Autodesk's 3D Studio Max, and Softimage's XSI are three of the most popular modeling tools for professional game artists, but these packages are expensive. That's not to say they aren't worth their cost; these packages are definitely worth it if you can afford them. If you are a student, you may be able to purchase an educational license for a fraction of the cost of a commercial license.

Most high-end modeling tools, such as Maya or 3ds Max, have the ability to export to Microsoft's .x format or Alias's .fbx format if you install the right combination of plug-ins. However, converting other model formats to .x or .fbx can be a finicky process. If you plan to use a modeling tool, then experiment with it first so that you are sure about the tool's requirements for successful conversions.

An inexpensive, but popular, lightweight 3D modeling program is MilkShape, by chUmbaLum sOft. MilkShape is used for the examples in this book because it is one of the easiest modeling tools to learn. In addition, MilkShape's support for the .fbx format is excellent. MilkShape also imports from and exports to over 70 relevant model file types for games. Even if you decide later that you prefer a different modeling tool, MilkShape is a great application to use when you are learning how to create 3D models. chUmbaLum sOft offers a free 30-day trial version. The purchase price is surprisingly inexpensive—$25 (U.S.) at the time this book was written. A link to their 30-day trial version is available in the download from this book's website.

MILKSHAPE 3D INTRO EXAMPLE: CREATING A WINDMILL

This first example shows you how to create a windmill using MilkShape. Later, a code demo will show you how to load and animate the windmill in your game application.

When you finish creating the model and program the animation in code, it will look similar to the one in Figure 12-1.

The process of creating a 3D model helps to demonstrate how models can be loaded and manipulated in your code. But, if you decide that you are not interested in 3D modeling, or if you use other modeling tools, you can skip this section. All of the models presented in this chapter can be found in the Models folder in the download from this book's website. On the other hand, you might find you actually enjoy the break from programming. MilkShape is such a great utility, even if you use other modeling tools, you might discover a feature that can assist you in your model creation, such as converting one model format to another or performing quick edits to your model.

FIGURE 12-1

A windmill model animated in code

Creating a New Project

Starting MilkShape automatically opens the designer studio environment. Most of the controls can be found in the gray panel on the right. Four different viewports are located on the left, as shown in Figure 12-2.

Each viewport offers a view of the model from a different angle. As with similar applications, the viewport serves to guide you when you're working with your model. Different views can also offer easier access to specific sets of vertices when you're adding, modifying, or deleting parts of the model. You can change the view in each of the four ports by right-clicking the port and choosing between Front, Back, Left, Right, Top, Bottom, and 3D (from the Projection drop-down menu). The first six views are self-explanatory. The 3D view offers you the ability to see a solid model as it would appear in a game. When in 3D view, right-clicking the viewport and choosing Textured will show the model with the texture applied.

In the *Window* menu is the *Show Viewport Caption* option, which is useful because it labels each view as Front, Left, Right, and so on. You can easily lose your bearings after switching between views, so this option can help you keep track of your model from different angles.

FIGURE 12-2

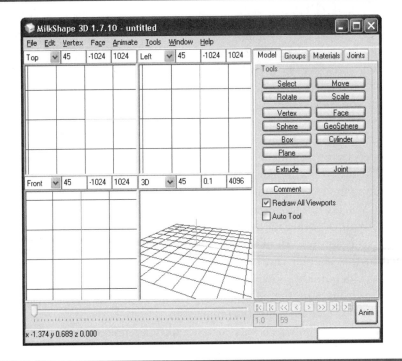

MilkShape 3D designer studio

Adding a Box

Now it's time to start designing. First, you need to create a base for the windmill. To do this, find the *Model* tab, click the *Box* button, and click and drag in one of the viewports. A box will emerge as you drag your mouse with the left mouse button pressed down. After you have added the box and resized it, the box shape will resemble the one in Figure 12-3.

If the box is incorrectly sized, you can always scale it into shape. In order to scale it, the box must be selected. To select the box, on the *Model* tab, click the *Select* button and choose *Group* under the *Select Options* area. Then click inside one of the viewports and drag the mouse over the box. When the box is selected, it will be highlighted in red.

You can scale the box using either the *Scale* button or the mouse. The *Scale* button is used for intricate scaling and it is located on the right gray panel of the *Model* tab. When the *Scale* button under the *Tools* group is clicked, a *Scale Options* group will appear further down on the right panel. You can enter scale amounts here for the X, Y, and Z planes. Repeatedly clicking the *Scale* button under the *Scale Options* group will resize the selected group(s) according to the values that are set for the X, Y, and Z planes. You may find it easier to manually scale the box using the mouse. To use the mouse for scaling, choose *Scale* on the *Model* tab and then resize the object by dragging the cursor in the viewport to compress or stretch the box as needed.

FIGURE 12-3

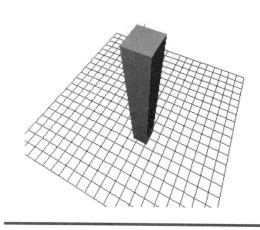

Scaled box positioned at origin

Adding a Sphere

The next step is to add a pin to your windmill. The windmill needs a pin to fasten the windmill fan to the base. Once the pin has been added, scaled, and moved into place, it will appear similar to the one in Figure 12-4.

Your pin will be a sphere added to the top face of the windmill base. To add your pin, select the *Model* tab and click the *Sphere* button—it's under the *Tools* group in the right panel. Then, click into one of the viewports and drag with your left mouse button down. The sphere will grow as the cursor is dragged outward from the center. You may need to resize the sphere. If you do, when you finish scaling, the pin size should be proportionate to the windmill base. The next step is to move the sphere into the correct position. On the *Groups* tab in the right panel, select the sphere group. Click the *Move* button. Then, click in a viewport and use the mouse to drag the sphere to the place where it belongs.

FIGURE 12-4

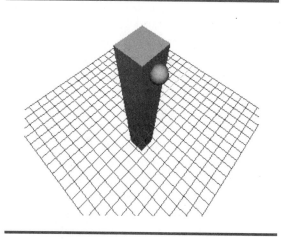

Sphere sized and positioned relative to the box

Adding a Cylinder

Next, you will add a cylinder to serve as one of the blades for the windmill's fan. You will use scaling to flatten and shape the blade in a proportion similar to what is shown in Figure 12-5.

On the *Models* tab in the right panel, click the *Cylinder* button. Then click in one of the viewports and drag the mouse. In one continuous movement, with the left mouse button pressed, size the cylinder so it is proportionate to the windmill base created by the box and pin.

You'll notice that the cylinder looks too round to be a windmill blade. You definitely need to flatten it. It is also possible that your cylinder is too short or too long, so you may need to scale it up or down accordingly. You could scale it using *Scale Options* or manually adjust it by dragging your mouse in the viewport. You may scale the entire cylinder or only a select group of vertices. On the *Model* tab, after clicking *Select,* you may choose *Vertex, Face, Group,* or *Joint* to isolate your vertices for scaling or transforming your cylinder in a manner that is most efficient. When the scaling is done, you should have a relatively flat blade with a point at the end.

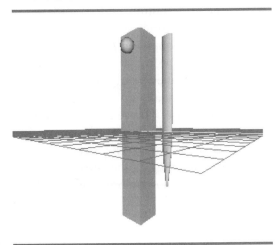

FIGURE 12-5

Modified cylinder to create a fan blade

Applying a Texture

Now that the pieces of the windmill appear to be in good form, you may be tempted to duplicate the blades and finish creating the fan. However, first you should apply a texture to your windmill. It is easier to texture your model at this point because the pieces of the model are separate. Applying the texture piece by piece is easier than trying to get the texture right with one large piece. After one blade is textured the way you want, it can be duplicated two more times and rotated into place to complete the windmill fan. Having a windmill with three identical well-textured fans will look very impressive. To texture the fan, you will apply a windmill.bmp file. A copy can be found in the Images folder in the download from the book's website.

It is common for one image to contain the textures for an entire 3D model. Having all of the textures in one file greatly simplifies the code required to load and apply the textures to a model. With this in mind, 3D modelers often combine a cross-section of different textures in one image file. The windmill.bmp contains a cross-section of images to map the texture on different parts of the model.

In MilkShape, textures can be set up on the *Materials* tab in the right panel. On the *Materials* tab, click *New*. A gray ball will appear when the material has been generated.

Two-thirds of the way down the right panel on the *Materials* tab, you will find two buttons labeled *<none>*. Click on the top one to launch the *Open* dialog, which will prompt you to select an image. In this case, a bitmap (.bmp file) is being used, but any image format that is supported by XNA will work. These image formats include .bmp, .dds, .dib, .jpg, .png, and .tga. Navigate to the windmill.bmp file. Select the image and click *Open* in the *Open* dialog. The name of the loaded image will appear on the *Materials* tab.

To reduce any difficulties during model format conversions and exporting to *.fbx, it is recommended that you use only one texture for your model. After you export to .fbx from MilkShape, XNA will demand that you use images that have height and width pixel dimensions that are a power of 2. Before creating the model, it is further recommended that you first test your texture by exporting a simple model that uses this image to *.fbx and then load and display it from your XNA code. When the program loads your model and tries to draw it, GSE will inform you if there are any issues with the image. Test your model by loading it in your game on a regular basis to ensure it continues to load and display properly from your code. You may experience issues with compressed image formats such as .jpg, so consider sticking with the .bmp, .tga, or .png format where possible.

Assigning the Material to the Blade

Now that an image has been loaded, you can start texturing your model with it. You could start by giving the cylinder a texture to make it appear as if it has been painted with a decal. To do this, on the *Groups* tab, click on the cylinder group in the group listing and then click *Select*. The cylinder should be the only object that is selected; this is indicated by a red highlight in the viewports.

Now that the cylinder is the only object selected, return to the *Materials* tab and click *Assign*. Then, from the *Window* menu select *Texture Coordinate Editor*. The *Texture Coordinate Editor* dialog will open.

Choose *Front* in the lower drop-down menu. Make sure that the cylinder is selected in the top drop-down menu. If the model and image do not appear, select the cylinder from the drop-down and click *Remap*. After you select the cylinder group and do the remapping, if the image and cylinder group do not appear in the Texture Coordinate Editor, the group wasn't assigned properly. To correct this, exit from the Texture Coordinate Editor and reselect the cylinder group only. Then on the *Materials* tab, click *Assign* and return to the Texture Coordinate Editor.

Once the cylinder appears in the Texture Coordinate Editor, the cylinder wireframe can be moved, scaled, and rotated into place over the section of the image that contains the decal for the windmill blade. (This section of the image is the rectangular strip that runs along the left side of the image.) The section of image underneath the cylinder's vertex group automatically wraps around the entire group of vertices. Figuring out how to wrap textures around your models may require some trial and error. But with a little practice, you will be able to plan your model components so that they're easier to texture. You may find that your model groups need to be split apart or revised so that you can map textures on them as you had originally intended. The buttons in the right panel of the Texture Coordinate Editor allow you to select your group or individual vertices to move, rotate, and scale them to find the best possible fit over the image section that is needed for the texture. In this case, the windmill fan blade fits nicely on top of the image section. Figure 12-6 shows the windmill blade before and after it is positioned over the corresponding section of image used to texture it.

Once the best fit has been achieved for the selected group, close the Texture Coordinate Editor. When you close the Texture Coordinate Editor, texture coordinates are assigned to the model where the model was last placed. The 3D viewport on the bottom right will show how the texture wrapped on the model component. Right-click the 3D viewport and choose *Textured*. The windmill fan blade will appear with the texture on it as in Figure 12-7.

Assigning the Material to the Box and Sphere

Repeat the process described previously to map the box and sphere groups individually to other sections in the texture.

Duplicating the Blade

Now that everything has been textured properly, you can complete the fan. The first blade is already textured. When this blade is duplicated, the copy will also be textured in an identical manner. Because of this, the matching blades will look sharp in the final product. To do this, on the *Model* tab, click the *Select* button. Then, under *Select Op-*

FIGURE 12-6

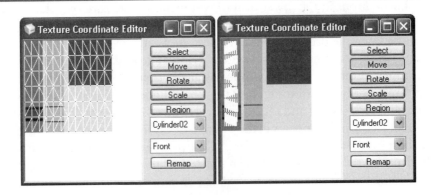

Texture Coordinate Editor while texturing the fan blade

FIGURE 12-7

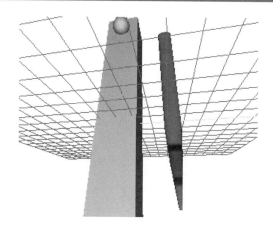

Properly textured windmill fan blade viewed in 3D viewport

tions choose *Group*. Once there, click into the viewport and drag over the group of vertices in the blade. The entire blade is now highlighted. Finally, under the *Edit* menu choose *Duplicate Selection*. A new blade will appear on top of the original one.

Rotating the Duplicate Blade about the Z Axis

At this point, the duplicate blade is selected. Before doing anything else, choose the *Rotate* button on the *Model* tab. In the *Rotate Options* area that appears midway down the right panel, enter **120** in the Z plane, set X and Y to 0, and then click the *Rotate* button. This will rotate the new blade by 120 degrees on the Z axis. The result will be two duplicate blades that appear at different angles around the Z axis.

Next, you will create the third blade. While the new blade is still selected, under the *Edit* menu choose *Duplicate Selection* again. A new blade will appear on top of the original one. Next, choose the *Rotate* button on the right panel. In the *Rotate Options* area enter **120** in the Z plane and then click *Rotate*. This will rotate the new blade.

The three blades have now been forged. It is time to move them into position. Select one of the blades, and choose the *Move* button on the *Model* tab. Click into the top-right viewport. Make sure you have a front view by right-clicking the viewport and selecting *Front*. While holding down the left mouse button, drag the selected blade so the base matches up with the base of one of the other blades. Repeat these steps to join the remaining blade with the other two. The three blades should now be positioned together as shown in Figure 12-8.

FIGURE 12-8

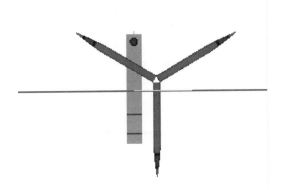

Original blade with two duplicate blades

Merging the Groups

Now that the blades are all textured with identical markings and are placed together, you should merge them into one group. Having the blades in one group will help later when you write code to animate the fan. It will be a lot easier to transform one fan rather than three separate blades. On the *Groups* tab, select each of the cylinders in the groups list. Click the *Regroup* button on the *Groups* tab. When you do this, the three blades will be merged into one. Select the new merged group and enter the name, *fan*, beside the *Rename* button and then click *Rename*.

FIGURE 12-9

Deselect the fan and select the box and sphere. Repeat the regroup process for the box and sphere to weld them together. When the merged box and sphere are selected on the *Groups* tab, enter the name, *base*, beside the *Rename* button. Click the *Rename* button to assign the name to the newly merged group, as shown in Figure 12-9.

Group listing after merging and renaming

Positioning the Model at the Point of Origin

Before exporting your model pieces, make sure they are centered at the origin (X = 0, Y = 0, Z = 0). If you do not center your models at the origin, complex animations will be very difficult to implement. Any extra distance away from the origin will create a translation that may cause trouble if you rotate the object in code. As explained in Chapter 6, "Character Movement," a translation followed by a rotation creates an orbit. When you create objects that are animated programmatically, the unwanted orbit will be very hard to fix in code. If you don't move the model to the origin in the designer, you might waste a lot of time trying to debug this issue when the problem isn't actually in your code. To avoid these pitfalls, professional game developers will usually ask the modeler to position the model so it rests at the point of origin. Both the fan and windmill base should be moved to the origin, as shown in Figure 12-10.

FIGURE 12-10

Windmill fan and base positioned so their connection point meets at the origin

Adding a Joint

A *joint* is the root of the model hierarchy. It is used to identify the center of the mesh.

The XNA model loader currently does not require that a joint exist when exporting to *.fbx. However, adding a joint to your MilkShape model in your project is still strongly recommended in case it is required for a future export or by a different format. When MilkShape was used for creating models for XNA's predecessor, DirectX, most DirectX Software Developers Kit releases required a joint for the .x format, but a few releases did not. This made it confusing for MilkShape designers who discovered their models would not load in certain releases of DirectX. To ensure your model exports can load in your XNA code for future releases, take the extra 30 seconds to add the joint.

The joint can be added from the *Model* tab. To do this, click on the *Joint* button and then left-click once over the origin in one of the viewports. If you don't quite get your joint in the exact center of origin, click the *Select* button. In the *Select Options* area that appears, choose *Joint*. Left-click into a viewport and drag around the joint to select it so the joint is highlighted in red. Next, click the *Move* button on the *Model* tab. Once in *Move* mode, you can left-click on the selected joint with your mouse and drag it into place. The joint should appear where the two model pieces are centered at the point of origin, as shown in Figure 12-11.

FIGURE 12-11

Joint placed at origin where windmill fan and base connect

Saving the Project

Your MilkShape project is now complete. You should save the project and keep it archived in case you decide that you want to modify it. MilkShape projects save as *.ms3d files. Using the ms3d project file type is strongly recommended in case you want to reopen your project later for editing. It is possible to import other file formats into MilkShape, but you may discover unwanted alterations, such as lost group information. Save the project with the name Windmill.ms3d to the same directory where the windmill.bmp file is located. Make sure you store the Windmill.ms3d and windmill.bmp files in a safe place.

Exporting the Model from the Project to the .fbx Format

Next, you are going to export your model to the .fbx format. To keep things simple, you are going to export the fan and windmill base separately. Exporting each piece separately to its own .fbx file allows you to load the pieces separately and animate them individually in your code. After you export the model, you will be able to load and display the windmill base as a stationary object. To create a rotation animation, you will load the fan separately and give it a constant rotation around the Z axis. When the windmill base and the rotating fan are positioned properly, the model will look like an animating windmill in your 3D game.

Exporting the Windmill Base

To prevent the loss of any valuable models, create a copy of your archived project. Open the copy and delete the fan. Next, click on *File* then *Export*. Choose *Alias FBX File format* in the lengthy list of available model formats that appears. Enter **base.fbx** in the *Filename* text area of the *Export* dialog. Export the base.fbx file to the same directory where the windmill.bmp file is located using the default options. Close the project and do not save it. You have now exported the base of the windmill. The next step is to export the fan.

Exporting the Fan

Reopen your copy of the MilkShape project. This time, delete the windmill base from your project. Next, click on *File* then *Export*. Choose the Alias FBX format from the export list that appears. Enter **fan.fbx** in the *Filename* area of the *Export* dialog. Export the fan.fbx file to the same directory where the windmill.bmp file is located. Close the project, but do not save it.

Concluding the MilkShape Demonstration

After working through this chapter, you will have created four files: fan.fbx, base.fbx, windmill.bmp, and windmill.ms3d. The *.fbx and *.bmp files will be loaded in the game project in the next example.

Naturally, you encounter a learning curve when you first create models with MilkShape, but at this point, you probably agree that the job of creating a simple model was not too challenging. If your first few models turn out lousy, do not be alarmed. Most model design newbies do not produce stellar models on their first few tries. But with a little bit of practice, it will not take long for you to ramp up on MilkShape. You can create incredible models in MilkShape once you experiment, learn its limitations, and then learn to push its limits. The simplicity of MilkShape, and its flexibility, makes this a product well worth the low price requested after the free 30-day trial ends.

The windmill you created using the modeling tool is certainly more interesting and easier to build than coding it with a series of textures and primitive objects. With only a little bit of practice, you could probably build the same windmill presented in this demo in 5 minutes or less.

LOADING THE MODEL IN XNA

Now that your windmill is built and exported, you can load and animate your masterpiece in code.

The Model class was introduced in version 1.0 of GSE. It provides a simple and effective way to quickly load models, transform them, and of course draw them. Currently the .x and .fbx formats are supported.

The Model class uses a skeletal hierarchy to store and draw the vertices of a model. The skeleton is made of bones, and each bone has a transformation associated with it. Mesh data containing vertices with position, normals, and texturing information are attached to each bone in the model and move with the bone when it is transformed.

Loading the Models

Models are loaded through the content pipeline with the Load() method:

```
Model model = content.Load<Model>(".\\model directory\\modelName");
```

To successfully load each model, you must reference each one in the Solution Explorer in your project.

Skeletal Hierarchy

A matrix array stores the transformation matrices for positioning each bone in the model skeleton. For nonanimated models, usually the bone count is 1, so only one transformation is applied to the entire model.

```
Matrix   BoneTransformations = new Matrix[int   model.Bones.Count];
```

The skeletal hierarchy is designed for bone animation. But, as mentioned, currently there is no official animated model loader code for the XNA release. Even so, when drawing static models, it is possible to have more than one bone in your model that has a separate mesh attached to each bone. Each bone has a transformation, and the transformations are cumulative as you travel down the hierarchy from the skeleton's root. As an example, you could think of the spine as the root. The upper leg takes on the transformation of the spine and adds a transformation of its own. The lower leg takes on the cumulative transformation of the spine and upper leg in addition to adding its own transformation. The foot takes on the cumulative transformations of all these bones, plus it adds its own transformation to the series. The foot is a child of the lower leg, and the lower leg is a child of the upper leg, and so on. Conversely, the spine is the parent of the upper leg, which in turn is the parent of the lower leg. This hierarchy of bones is ideal for transforming and animating multiple meshes.

When the model is created, the bone transformation matrices associated with the model are stored in the Model class using the CopyAbsoluteBoneTransformsTo() method exposed by the Model object:

```
Model   model.CopyAbsoluteBoneTransformsTo(Matrix   boneTransformations);
```

DRAWING THE MODEL IN XNA

It is possible to have more than one mesh in a model where each mesh is considered a separate unit of vertex position, texture, and normal data. While rendering the model, the routine searches the Model object for each ModelMesh object, transforms it according to the World matrix, sets lighting (if desired), and draws it. To iterate through each mesh of the Model object, a foreach loop searches through each ModelMesh object:

```
foreach (ModelMesh mesh in model.Meshes);
```

Another loop nested inside the ModelMesh loop is required to properly show your model in the game world and to add lighting (if desired):

```
foreach (BasicEffect effect in mesh.Effects);
```

Before drawing the model, you can apply lighting to the model using XNA's BasicEffect class, which was introduced in Chapter 4, "Shaders." Once inside the effect loop, to show all objects in your game properly relative to the camera, you must store the game class's View and Projection matrices in the BasicEffect shader through the effect parameters:

```
BasicEffect   effect.View       = Matrix world;
BasicEffect   effect.Projection = Matrix world;
```

To apply transformations to all meshes within the model, you must multiply each mesh's bone transformation matrix by the cumulative transformation matrix, or *World matrix*. The product is stored in the BasicEffect shader, which applies the final transformation to the mesh drawn.

```
effect.World = mMatCarTransforms[mesh.ParentBone.Index] * WorldMatrix;
```

You can use XNA's BasicEffect class to also add lighting to the model. More information will be provided in Chapter 20, "Lighting," to explain how to customize your lighting. For this chapter, the default lighting is applied to the model:

```
effect.EnableDefaultLighting();
```

When you are ready to draw the model, call the ModelMesh's Draw() method to render it:

```
ModelMesh   mesh.Draw();
```

Loading and Animating the Windmill in Code

This example takes the windmill you made in MilkShape and animates it in code. When you are finished working through this example, your windmill will look like the one presented earlier in Figure 12-1.

This code example begins with either the WinMGHBook or Xbox360MGHBook project found in the BaseCode folder in the download from this book's website. Also, your fan.fbx and base.fbx files, along with the windmill texture (windmill.bmp) models, must be added to your project so they can be loaded in the content pipeline. Or, if you don't want to build these models, you can find the fan.fbx, base.fbx, and windmill.bmp files in the Models folder. These three files need to be placed in a Models folder in your project so they can be loaded properly.

To store the fan and base models separately, two separate Model objects are declared at the module level of the game class. Matrices for transforming the meshes in each model are also included with this declaration so they can be set later when the models are loaded.

```
Model    mModBase;    Model    mModFan;
Matrix[] matFan;      Matrix[] matBase;
```

The same code will be reused to draw each model, so identifiers are needed to distinguish between the windmill base and fan model. These definitions are used throughout the game class, so they need to be added at the top of the game class.

```
const int WINDMILL_BASE = 0; const int WINDMILL_FAN = 1;
```

The two models are loaded separately with the ContentManager's Load() method using a <model> identifier. When each model is loaded, the bone matrices are stored in a Matrix object for that model. These examples have only one bone, so any transformations applied to them will apply to the entire model. The CopyAbsoluteBoneTransformsTo() method copies the transformations for all bones in the model into an array that the model object can use.

```
void initialize_windmill_model(){
    mModBase = content.Load<Model>(".\\Models\\base");
    matBase = new Matrix[mModBase.Bones.Count];
    mModBase.CopyAbsoluteBoneTransformsTo(matBase);

    mModFan = content.Load<Model>(".\\Models\\fan");
    matFan = new Matrix[mModFan.Bones.Count];
    mModFan.CopyAbsoluteBoneTransformsTo(matFan);
}
```

To set the model up when the program begins, call initialize_windmill_model() from the Initialize() method:

```
initialize_windmill_model();
```

To create a continuous rotation for the windmill fan, a module-level variable, *mfFanRotation*, is used. The module-level variable stores the total rotation in radians and is incremented each frame. Adding it at the module level allows you to store the variable and read its updated value each frame:

```
private float mfFanRotation = 0.0f; // stores rotation of windmill fan
```

Drawing the windmill base is actually very simple. The first three steps for rendering a model are identical to the steps used to draw a primitive object using vertex types. The transformation matrices are declared and initialized just as you have done before when you rendered primitive objects from vertex types. As described in Chapter 5, "Animation Introduction," the same I.S.R.O.T. sequence of transformations applies here to transform each Model object. In this case, scaling and a translation will be performed for both models. Every time you load a model, you have to resize it so it is proportionate to your game world. The fan is rotated about the Z axis too, so an additional transformation on the Z axis is required. A time-scaled value is used to perform the rotation to keep the rotation speed constant regardless of the system used. The scaled time lapse is added to *mfFanRotation,* which stores total radians for the rotation. *mfFanRotation* is reset to equal the remainder of *mfFanRotation* divided by 2π. This extra step to store the remainder rather than the true value maintains the same rotation about the Z axis while preventing variable overflow.

In step 4 of draw_windmill(), once the cumulative transformation matrix has been built, it is multiplied against the transformation matrix for each mesh in the model. If you are working with a model that is centered at the origin and only has one mesh, the mesh's matrix would be equivalent to the identity matrix. If your model is not centered at the origin, your transformations are going to take on an additional translation, so you may need to check this if your models are not animating properly. The product of the bone matrix and the World matrix is passed to the World matrix variable in XNA's BasicEffect shader. At the same time, you also need to store the View and Projection matrices from your game class in the BasicEffect's variables. The shader needs this information to position your models so they can be seen properly by the camera.

Lighting is also enabled in step 4 using the EnableDefaultLighting() method. Refer to Chapter 20, "Lighting," for more information on how to use the different lighting options that come with the BasicEffect class.

Finally, the model can be drawn using the ModelMesh object's Draw() method. Add draw_windmill() to your game class to transform and render your fan and windmill:

```
void draw_windmill(Model model, int iModel, GameTime gameTime){
    foreach (ModelMesh mesh in model.Meshes){
            // 1: declare matrices
            Matrix matWorld,matIdent,matScale,matRotY,matRotZ,matTransl;

            // 2: initialize matrices
            matIdent = Matrix.Identity;
            matScale    = Matrix.CreateScale(0.1f, 0.1f, 0.1f);
            matTransl   = Matrix.CreateTranslation(0.0f, 0.0f, 1.5f);
            matRotY     = Matrix.CreateRotationY((float)Math.PI);
            matRotZ     = Matrix.CreateRotationZ(0.0f);

            if (iModel == WINDMILL_FAN){
                // calculate t between frames for system independent speed
                mfFanRotation += gameTime.ElapsedRealTime.Ticks/6000000.0f;
                // prevent var overflow - store remainder
                mfFanRotation=mfFanRotation%(2.0f*(float)Math.PI);
                matRotZ = Matrix.CreateRotationZ(mfFanRotation);
            }

            // 3: build cumulative world matrix using I.S.R.O.T. sequence
            // identity, scale, rotate, orbit(translate&rotate), translate
            matWorld = matIdent*matScale*matRotZ*matRotY * matTransl;

            foreach (BasicEffect effect in mesh.Effects){
            // 4: pass wvp to shader
            if(iModel == WINDMILL_BASE)
                effect.World = matBase[mesh.ParentBone.Index] * matWorld;
            if(iModel == WINDMILL_FAN)
                effect.World = matFan[mesh.ParentBone.Index] * matWorld;
            effect.View       = mMatView;
            effect.Projection = mMatProj;

            // 4b. set lighting
            effect.EnableDefaultLighting();
            effect.CommitChanges();
        }
        // 5: draw object
```

```
      mesh.Draw();
   }
}
```

To draw both models, call them from the Draw() method:

```
draw_windmill(mModBase, WINDMILL_BASE, gameTime);
draw_windmill(mModFan, WINDMILL_FAN, gameTime);
```

When you run this program, you will see how great the windmill looks in your game. The output shows your windmill with the fan rotating about the Z axis (refer to Figure 12-1). You may find that additional scaling, rotations, or translations are needed to move your own models into place depending on how your windmill was built. In the end, you will find you can create, load, and render 3D models with very little effort.

Adding a Car as a Third-person Object

This example shows how to draw a model car as a third-person object. When you use the third-person view, your camera is behind the object wherever you travel in the 3D world. When this example is complete, not only will the car drive in front of you as you move the camera through the 3D world, but the wheels of the car will spin when you move and the front wheels will pivot about the Y axis as you turn.

One car model and one tire model will be used for this example. They can be found in the Models folder in the download from this book's website. Note that these models are intentionally positioned at the origin with the joint, as shown in Figure 12-12. Having everything centered at the origin ensures that the transformations done in code generate the expected behavior.

Figure 12-13 shows the car after the wheel has been transformed and drawn once in each wheel well.

When this demonstration is complete, the model car and wheel will be drawn as the third person, so your camera will always be positioned behind it.

The code example begins with the WinMGHBook project or the Xbox360MGHBook project found in the BaseCode folder.

You can find the hotrod.fbx, wheel.fbx, and car.tga files in the Models folder in the download from this book's website. To reference them in your project, add a Models folder and place these files there. You will need to add a reference to the two *.fbx files from the Models folder inside the Solution Explorer. To do this, right-click the project name in the Solution Explorer. Then choose *Add* and then *New Folder*. This will create a Models folder. Next, right-click the Models folder and choose *Add an Existing Item*. Finally, navigate to the hotrod.fbx and wheel.fbx files and select them. When you do this, they will be added to the Models folder. You will also need to add the car.tga file to this Models directory in your project.

FIGURE 12-12

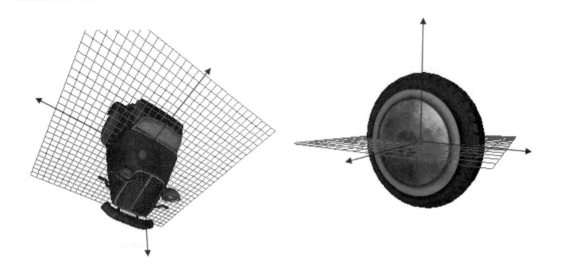

Models centered at the origin with a joint in the middle

In code, two separate model objects are used to draw the model car. One object stores the car, and the other stores a wheel. Also, a matrix array for each model is needed to store the bone transformations for their meshes when the two models are loaded. These bone transformations will be implemented later when the models are

FIGURE 12-13

One model car and one model wheel redrawn four times

drawn to position them so they can be seen properly by the camera. Add these declarations for the model objects and their matrix arrays at the top of the game class so the two models can later be loaded, transformed, and drawn:

```
Model       mModCar;              Model       mModWheel;
Matrix[]    mMatCarTransforms;    Matrix[]    mMatWheelTransforms;
```

Adding the initializeModels() method to your game class will load the models using the ContentManager object. The transformation matrices for each mesh in both models will be stored in a mesh array with the CopyAbsoluteBoneTransformsTo() method. The code loads your models from the Models folder referenced from your project. The wheel.fbx, hotrod.fbx, and car.tga files need to be there for a successful load.

```
void initializeModels(){
    mModCar = content.Load<Model>(".\\Models\\hotrod");
    mMatCarTransforms = new Matrix[mModCar.Bones.Count];
    mModCar.CopyAbsoluteBoneTransformsTo(mMatCarTransforms);

    mModWheel = content.Load<Model>(".\\Models\\wheel");
    mMatWheelTransforms = new Matrix[mModWheel.Bones.Count];
    mModWheel.CopyAbsoluteBoneTransformsTo(mMatWheelTransforms);
}
```

The two models must be loaded when the program begins, so this method is called from Initialize():

```
initializeModels();
```

To obtain a better look at the car from behind so you can see the front wheels pivot, an adjustment to the camera is made so it looks slightly downward toward the ground. In the constructor for the camera class, replace the view direction on the Y plane with this instruction to angle the camera downward:

```
m_vView.Y = -0.07f;
```

To further enable a better view of the car from behind, the ground is lowered slightly on the Y axis. Replacing the translation in draw_ground() with this revision will lower the ground by 0.099f units:

```
matTransl = Matrix.CreateTranslation(0.0f, -0.99f, 0.0f);
```

The look and feel of the camera needs to change when a car is used as a third person so that the movement through the world feels more like you are driving rather than just panning the view. To prevent the view from shifting up and down when the user shifts the right thumbstick or moves the mouse, change the call to modify the view in set_view_matrix() with this instruction (the 0.0f parameter prevents any changes to the camera's view on Y):

```
cam.changeView(v2View.X, 0.0f);
```

Still on the topic of adapting the camera's look and feel for a car, obviously you cannot strafe with a car, so in the Update() method comment out the instruction that triggers strafing:

```
// cam.strafe(strafe());.
```

To position the car and wheels ahead of the camera, a translation on the Z axis is needed. A variable declared at the class level to store this translation is required so that the methods that draw the tires and wheels can use the same variable. Using the same translation amount variable in both methods makes it easy to adjust the car's distance from the camera.

```
private float mfTransl     =  2.10f;
```

To understand the logic behind turning the wheels and the response of the controls, consider the process behind parallel parking a car. You have to consider the car's direction when turning the steering wheel while moving backward and forward as you position the car beside the roadside curb. You have to look where you're going too, so you don't hit the cars around you. The logic is similar when programming a third-person car.

For this routine, if the game pad is in use, the left thumbstick's Y property is obtained to determine if the car is moving forward or backward. The left thumbstick's Y value ranges from –1 for reverse to +1 for forwards. If the left thumbstick is resting at the center, where Y = 0.0f, the car is not moving so the view is not changed. If the game pad is not connected, the up and down arrow keys are used to move the car and the right and left arrow keys are used to turn it. If the up or down arrow key is pressed, the view will not change because the car is not moving. To coordinate the changes in view with the game controls, the following code is added to the end of the changeView() method immediately before the return statement:

```
// use game pad
if (mGamePadState[0].IsConnected == true){
    // no forwards or backwards so don't change view
    if (mGamePadState[0].ThumbSticks.Left.Y == 0.0f)
        v2Change.X = 0.0f;
    // driving in reverse - the view must match the wheel pivot
```

```
        else if (mGamePadState[0].ThumbSticks.Left.Y < 0.0f)
            v2Change.X *= -1.0f;
}
// no game pad so using keyboard
else{
    // RIGHT
    if (kbState.IsKeyDown(Keys.Right)){
        v2Change.Y = 0.0f; v2Change.X = SENSITIVITY; // camera change
    }
    // LEFT
    else if (kbState.IsKeyDown(Keys.Left)){
        v2Change.Y = 0.0f; v2Change.X = -SENSITIVITY;
    }
    // no forwards or backwards
    if (!kbState.IsKeyDown(Keys.Down) && !kbState.IsKeyDown(Keys.Up))
        v2Change.X = 0.0f;
    // driving in reverse - the view must match the wheel pivot
    else if (kbState.IsKeyDown(Keys.Down))
        v2Change.X *= -1.0f;
}
```

When you turn your car, you are changing the view with a rotation on the Y axis. The rotation for the default camera is a little too fast for turning a car, so an adjustment is required to slow down the change in view. To slow the change in view, a replacement of the SENSITIVITY definition is made inside changeView():

```
const float SENSITIVITY = 200.0f;
```

The code used to draw the car is similar to the code used to draw the windmill base and fan. The transformations are a little more complex, but they still follow the I.S.R.O.T. sequence. The references used to create the car in the modeling tool were different from the XNA environment. The car needs to be scale down to 0.2% of its original size so it is proportionate to the 3D world generated in the base code. Also, to make the car bottom horizontal with the ground, it must be rotated on the X axis. Once these initial transformations have been performed, some additional translations and a rotation are needed to move the car out ahead of the camera so you can see it at all times as a third person wherever you go. Figure 12-14 explains the transformations to make viewing the car as a third person possible.

As explained in the windmill model example, when the model is drawn, the BasicEffect shader is used, so the World, View, and Projection matrices must be set to transform it. Also, when the car is drawn, default lighting is enabled since the

FIGURE 12-14

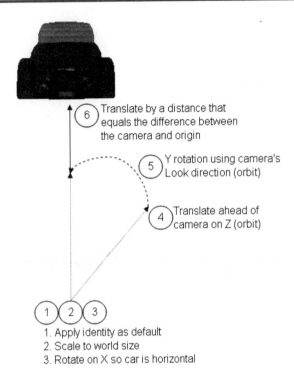

6 Translate by a distance that equals the difference between the camera and origin

5 Y rotation using camera's Look direction (orbit)

4 Translate ahead of camera on Z (orbit)

1 2 3
1. Apply identity as default
2. Scale to world size
3. Rotate on X so car is horizontal

Transformations for positioning the car in front of the camera

BasicEffect shader makes this easy to do. Add drawCar() to transform, light, and draw your car so it appears as a third person you can always see in front of your camera:

```
void drawCar(Model model){
    foreach (ModelMesh mesh in model.Meshes){
        // 1: declare matrices
        Matrix matWorld, matIdent, matScale, matRotX, matTransl;
        Matrix matTransOrb, matRotYorb;

        // 2: initialize matrices
        matIdent = Matrix.Identity;
        matScale = Matrix.CreateScale(0.002f, 0.002f, 0.002f);
        matRotX  = Matrix.CreateRotationX(-(float)Math.PI / 2.0f);
        float fYrot = (float)Math.Atan2(cam.m_vView.X - cam.m_vPos.X,
                                        cam.m_vView.Z - cam.m_vPos.Z);
```

```
matRotYorb = Matrix.CreateRotationY(fYrot);
matTransl  = Matrix.CreateTranslation(cam.m_vPos.X, -0.81f,
                                      cam.m_vPos.Z);
matTransOrb = Matrix.CreateTranslation(0.0f, 0.0f, mfTransl);

// 3: build cumulative world matrix using I.S.R.O.T. sequence
// identity, scale, rotate, orbit(translate & rotate), translate
matWorld = matIdent * matScale * matRotX
            * matTransOrb * matRotYorb * matTransl;

foreach (BasicEffect effect in mesh.Effects){
    // 4: pass wvp to shader
    effect.World=mMatCarTransforms[mesh.ParentBone.Index]*matWorld;
    effect.View =mMatView;
    effect.Projection = mMatProj;

    // set lighting
    effect.EnableDefaultLighting();
    effect.CommitChanges();
}
// 5: draw object
mesh.Draw();
    }
}
```

The car is ready for rendering. To draw it, add the call statement to the end of Draw():

```
drawCar(mModCar);
```

When you run the program now, you will see the car but without the wheels. The code for adding the wheels is not much different from the code used to load and draw the car model. However, the wheels must also spin when the car moves and they must pivot when the car turns.

A variable *mfTireRotation* is declared at the top of the game class to store and update the current spin value in radians:

```
private float mfTireRotation;
```

The wheels are spun forward as long as you shift the left thumbstick up or press the up arrow key. The wheels spin backward if you shift the left thumbstick down or press the down arrow key. Add spinWheel() to spin your wheels as your car moves forward or backward:

```
private float spinWheel(GameTime t){
    KeyboardState kbState = Keyboard.GetState();
    GamePadState gpState = getNewState(mGamePadState[0]);

    // generate time scaled increment for tire rotation
    float fTimeScale = t.ElapsedGameTime.Milliseconds / 170.0f;

    // game pad connected - car not moving forward or reverse
    if (mGamePadState[0].ThumbSticks.Left.Y == 0.0f
        && mGamePadState[0].IsConnected)
        return 0.0f; // don't spin wheels

    // game pad not connected - car not moving forward or reverse
    else if (!mGamePadState[0].IsConnected && !kbState.IsKeyDown(Keys.Up)
            && !kbState.IsKeyDown(Keys.Down))
        return 0.0f; // don't spin wheels

    // down key or left stick down so reverse tires
    if (kbState.IsKeyDown(Keys.Down)
        || mGamePadState[0].ThumbSticks.Left.Y < 0.0f)
        fTimeScale *= -1.0f;

    // increment tire and prevent variable overflow with modulus
    mfTireRotation += fTimeScale;
    mfTireRotation = mfTireRotation % (2.0f * (float)Math.PI);

    // return increment to X rotation for tire
    return mfTireRotation;
}
```

Next, some extra code is needed to pivot the front wheels when you turn the car. While the car is moving forward or backward, an adjustment to the view either from shifting the right thumbstick left or right or from pressing the left or right arrow key will cause the wheels to pivot. You can also pivot the wheels when the car is stationary and there is no change to the view.

If the game pad is in use, the right thumbstick's X property is obtained to adjust the rotation angle about the Y axis for both wheels. The right thumbstick's X property ranges from –1 to 1. This X value is scaled to provide a suitable pivot angle in radians for the front wheels.

If you are using the keyboard only, the change in view from pressing the right or left arrow key is used to set the rotation angle. When you're using the keyboard, the change in view is used to obtain the rotation angle. Since the change in view is determined before the pivot angle is calculated, matching the wheel pivot to the change in view avoids conflicts in direction if you are pressing the up and down arrow keys at the same time. The pivot angle in radians is negated if the car is driving in reverse, so the front wheels pivot properly while you back up.

Add pivotWheel() to the game class to rotate your front tires about the Y axis when you want to turn your wheels:

```
private float pivotWheel(GameTime t){
    float fYRotation = 0.0f;

    KeyboardState kbState = Keyboard.GetState();
    GamePadState gpState = getNewState(mGamePadState[0]);

    // turn wheel about Y axis if right stick shifted on X
    if (mGamePadState[0].IsConnected == true)
        fYRotation = mGamePadState[0].ThumbSticks.Right.X / 2.7f;
    // turn wheel about Y axis if LEFT or RIGHT keys pressed
    else{
        Vector2 v2 = changeView(t);
        fYRotation = v2.X / 470.0f;

        if (move() < 0.0f)              // driving in reverse
            fYRotation *= -1.0f;
        else if (move() == 0.0f){   // car stopped but pivot tires
            if (kbState.IsKeyDown(Keys.Right))
                fYRotation = 0.41f;
            else if (kbState.IsKeyDown(Keys.Left))
                fYRotation = -0.41f;
        }
    }
    return fYRotation;
}
```

The code for drawing the wheel is structurally identical to all other draw routines presented in this chapter. Only one wheel model is actually being used, but it is being drawn four times. The transformations to rotate, spin, and position each wheel into place may look hefty, but they are actually simple when you realize they, too, follow the I.S.R.O.T. sequence. Figure 12-15 summarizes the transformations applied to each wheel.

FIGURE 12-15

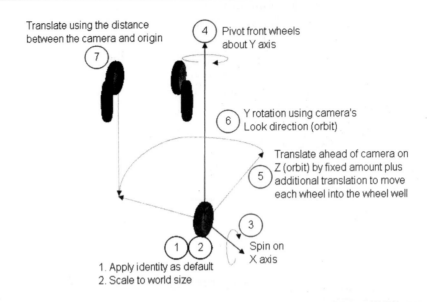

Translate using the distance between the camera and origin (7)

4 Pivot front wheels about Y axis

6 Y rotation using camera's Look direction (orbit)

5 Translate ahead of camera on Z (orbit) by fixed amount plus additional translation to move each wheel into the wheel well

3 Spin on X axis

1 2

1. Apply identity as default
2. Scale to world size

Transformations for each wheel

Add drawWheels() to transform, light, and draw the wheel model four times so that each wheel is positioned properly around the car:

```
void drawWheels(Model model, GameTime t){
const int FRONTL = 0;   const int FRONTR = 1;
const int BACKL  = 2;   const int BACKR  = 3;

for (int i = 0; i < 4; i++) // draw each tire
{
foreach (ModelMesh mesh in model.Meshes){
    // 1: declare matrices
    Matrix matWorld, matIdent, matScale, matRotX, matRotY,
            matTransOrb, matRotYOrb, matTransl;

    // 2: initialize matrices
    matIdent = Matrix.Identity;

    // model is huge when loaded - scale it down
    matScale = Matrix.CreateScale(0.002f, 0.002f, 0.002f);
```

```
// look direction of camera about the Y axis
// so car always faces in direction it moves
float fYrot = (float)Math.Atan2(cam.m_vView.X - cam.m_vPos.X,
                                cam.m_vView.Z - cam.m_vPos.Z);

// move wheels with camera
matTransl = Matrix.CreateTranslation(cam.m_vPos.X,-0.8f, cam.m_vPos.Z);

// defaults
matRotY = Matrix.CreateRotationY(0.0f);
matRotX = Matrix.CreateRotationX(0.0f);

// same wheel is drawn four times
// translate and rotate wheels into position from car center
// spin wheels on X axis
// pivot front tires on Y when user selects left and right
matTransOrb = Matrix.CreateTranslation(0.0f, 0.0f, 0.3f);
matRotYOrb  = Matrix.CreateRotationY(fYrot);
switch (i)
{
case FRONTL:
matTransOrb = Matrix.CreateTranslation(0.23f,-0.08f, mfTransl+0.26f);
matRotY     = Matrix.CreateRotationY(+(float)Math.PI-pivotWheel(t));
matRotX     = Matrix.CreateRotationX(-spinWheel(t));
    break;
case FRONTR:
matTransOrb = Matrix.CreateTranslation(-0.23f,-0.08f, mfTransl+ 0.26f);
matRotY     = Matrix.CreateRotationY(-pivotWheel(t));
matRotX     = Matrix.CreateRotationX(spinWheel(t));
    break;
case BACKL:
matTransOrb = Matrix.CreateTranslation(0.24f,-0.08f, mfTransl-0.29f);
matRotY     = Matrix.CreateRotationY(+(float)Math.PI);
matRotX     = Matrix.CreateRotationX(-spinWheel(t));
    break;
case BACKR:
matTransOrb = Matrix.CreateTranslation(-0.24f,-0.08f,mfTransl-0.29f);
matRotX     = Matrix.CreateRotationX(spinWheel(t));
    break;
}
```

```
// 3: build cumulative world matrix using I.S.R.O.T. sequence
// identity, scale, rotate, orbit(translate & rotate), translate
matWorld = matIdent * matScale * matRotX * matRotY
         * matTransOrb * matRotYOrb * matTransl;

foreach (BasicEffect effect in mesh.Effects){
    // 4: pass world view and projection to default model shader
    effect.World = mMatWheelTransforms[mesh.ParentBone.Index]*matWorld;
    effect.View        = mMatView;
    effect.Projection = mMatProj;
    effect.EnableDefaultLighting();

    effect.CommitChanges();
}
// 5: draw object
mesh.Draw();
}
}
}
```

Now the wheels are ready to be drawn. Inside Draw(), add the call statement to draw the wheels to view them with your car:

```
drawWheels(mModWheel, gameTime);
```

After compiling and running your project, you will be able to drive through the 3D world in comfort. Driving around in this model hot rod is definitely a lot more interesting than driving around in a hand-coded primitive object. Point your wheels and go.

CHAPTER 12 REVIEW EXERCISES

1. Follow the step-by-step examples presented in this chapter.

2. Explain how models that are not saved at the origin cause unbalanced transformations.

3. Replace the primitive objects in the airplane example shown in Chapter 6, "Character Movement," with an airplane model and propeller model that you create in MilkShape. When you create the airplane model, be sure to use only one image for the texture as explained in the guidelines in this chapter.

CHAPTER **13**

Vectors

A *vector* is a multidimensional object that stores data such as position, distance, and speed. Vectors are a key pillar in the structure of any 3D graphics engine because they are used to create animations, implement collision detection, set lighting, launch ballistics, and more. Understanding vector math is essential if you want to invent impressive special effects for your games. The good news is that vector math is simple.

VECTOR CLASS

A three-dimensional vector stores X, Y, and Z coordinates, which are often used for describing position and direction. However, a vector could be two dimensional, in which case it would only store X and Y coordinates. A two-dimensional vector is often used for setting position coordinates for 2D sprites or UV coordinates for textures. A vector could even have four dimensions (that is, it would store X, Y, Z, and W coordinates). The W coordinate might be used to specify the alpha color for setting transparency along with red, green, and blue parameters in the X, Y, and Z values of the same vector. Alternatively, the W coordinate might be added on to the end of a three-dimensional vector to ensure the total vector columns match the total rows of a 4×4 matrix so the objects are compatible for multiplication.

The Microsoft.Xna.Framework library provides three vector class types: Vector2, Vector3, Vector4. Each vector class contains a similar set of methods to perform mathematical operations on the vectors, but each set of operators is tailored for total dimensions in the class. You will see these vector operations in various graphics and game algorithms, so it is worth understanding them—and it's even better when you can use them to customize your own graphics algorithms. The logic behind vector math operations is the same for each of the three vector classes, and each vector class makes it easy to perform addition, subtraction, and scaling. The vector classes also provide methods for performing more complex operations. This includes calculating a vector's length, calculating a perpendicular vector from a surface, and finding the angle between two vectors.

VECTOR ADDITION

Vector addition is essential for many game algorithms. You have already been using vector addition to move an object by updating its coordinates. This technique was first covered in Chapter 6, "Character Movement." Here is the formula for summing two 3D vectors (A and B):

A + B = {Ax + Bx, Ay + By, Az + Bz}

Here's an example of vector addition. If vector A stores a direction of X=5, Y=3, Z=0, and vector B stores a direction of X=4, Y=−2, Z=0, then the sum equals X=9, Y=1, Z=0. This is the manual calculation:

$$
\begin{vmatrix} 5 \\ 3 \\ 0 \end{vmatrix} + \begin{vmatrix} 4 \\ -2 \\ 0 \end{vmatrix} = \begin{vmatrix} 9 \\ 1 \\ 0 \end{vmatrix}
$$

To perform this calculation in code, start with the "Font Example: Displaying Text in the Game Window" solution in Chapter 11, "Score Tracking and Game Statistics," and add the calculate_to_string() method to the game class. This new method adds vectors A and B and then displays their sum as text in the game window:

```
String calculate_to_string()
{
    Vector3 vA = new Vector3(5.0f, 3.0f, 0.0f);                    // A
    Vector3 vB = new Vector3(4.0f,-2.0f, 0.0f);                    // B
    Vector3 vC;

    vC.X = vA.X + vB.X;    vC.Y = vA.Y + vB.Y;    vC.Z = vA.Z + vB.Z;



    return          "X = "   + vC.X.ToString()
             +   "   Y = "   + vC.Y.ToString()
             +   "   Z = "   + vC.Z.ToString();
}
```

To trigger the calculation and show the result in the top of the game window, inside the Draw() method, replace the line

```
draw_string("Score Tracking and Game Stats", (int)v2px0.X, (int)v2px0.Y,
            Color.Red);
```

with this revised version that calls the calculate_to_string() method:

```
draw_string(calculate_to_string(), (int)v2px0.X, (int)v2px0.Y, Color.Red);
```

When you run this code, the output will show the same sum for X, Y, and Z that was demonstrated earlier in the manual addition.

You could actually replace the three lines that separately assign values to vC.X, vC.Y, and vC.Z to perform the sum in calculate_to_string() with this revision:

```
vC = vA + vB;
```

When you run this program, you will see the same output as before, but there is considerably less code behind the addition.

VECTOR SUBTRACTION

Vector subtraction is essential any time you wish to calculate the distance between two vectors. If vector A (5, 3, 0) is decremented by B (4, –2, 0), the resulting vector would be defined by X=1, Y=5, Z=0:

```
|5| - | 4| = |1|
|3|   |-2|   |5|
|0|   | 0|   |0|
```

To implement vector subtraction in your code, start with the solution from the previous example and make the following changes. To calculate the difference between vector A and vector B, replace the instruction that performs the addition for vC inside calculate_to_string() with the following:

```
vC = vA - vB;
```

When you run this code, the vector that results from the subtraction is displayed in the game window as X = 1, Y=5, Z = 0. Notice that these totals for X, Y, and Z match the difference you calculated manually.

VECTOR SCALING

Scaling a vector's magnitude up or down involves multiplying a vector by a scalar value. When you're working with the Vector2, Vector3, and Vector4 objects, the scalar must be a floating-point number. Of course, there are endless possibilities for using vector scaling in your game and graphics routines. In Chapter 5, "Animation Introduction," vector scaling was used to maintain an animation at a constant rate. To regulate the animation speed so that it runs at the same rate on both fast and slow machines, the direction vector is multiplied by the time lapse between frames.

Vector Scaling, Example 1

To demonstrate vector scaling, consider a vector where X=9, Y=1, and Z=0. Then multiply the vector by 2. The product equals

$$X = 9*2 \ Y = 1*2 \ Z = 0*2$$

The new vector is X = 18, Y = 2, Z = 0.

To perform this scaling in code, replace the calculate_to_string() method from the previous example with this new version:

```
String calculate_to_string()
{
```

```
Vector3 v        = new Vector3(9.0f, 1.0f, 0.0f);
float    fScale = 2.0f;

v *= fScale;  // multiply float and vector

return        "X = " + v.X.ToString()
        + "   Y = " + v.Y.ToString()
        + "   Z = " + v.Z.ToString();
}
```

When you compile and run this code, the text output will show the same product that you calculated manually: X = 18 Y = 2 Z = 0.

You may also use a divisor to scale a vector by a fraction. One common example of this operation is in the creation of unit vectors to scale the range so each vector component is between −1 and 1. Unit vectors are essential for ensuring consistency when working with direction vectors and even when using vectors for graphics effects such as lighting.

Vector Scaling, Example 2

To demonstrate vector scaling with a divisor, consider vector A (9, 1, 0) divided by 2; you would end up with the following calculation:

X = 9/2 Y = 1/2 Z = 0/2

The new vector is defined with the coordinates X = 4.500, Y = 0.500, and Z = 0.000. The direction information is the same, but the magnitude is reduced to half the original amount.

To implement this vector operation in code, begin with the solution for the preceding scaling example. Then, replace the instruction to multiply the vector with a float to apply the divisor:

```
v /= fScale;  // multiply float and vector
```

The output of this code reads "X=4.5 Y = 0.5 Z = 0," which is equivalent to the quotient from your manual calculation.

NORMALS

A *normal* is a special type of vector that is perpendicular to a flat surface. In other words, a normal is a vector that points outward from a face at an angle of 90 degrees. The normal represents direction, so the position is irrelevant. Figure 13-1 shows a normal vector pointing outward from a face. In game programming, normal vectors have uses that range from implementing lighting to building a camera.

FIGURE 13-1

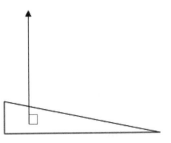

Normal vector

When you're computing normal vectors from a flat surface, the simplest flat surface possible is built by two vectors joined at the tail end.

Cross Product

The cross product formula is used to calculate a normal vector for a surface that is created by two vectors. It uses the two surface vectors as inputs. The cross product between vectors A and B equals the following:

$$A \times B = (A_y{}^*B_z - A_z{}^*B_y, A_z{}^*B_x - A_x{}^*B_z, A_x{}^*B_y - A_y{}^*B_x)$$

The set of coordinates generated from the cross product represents the normal direction vector. The order of the surface vectors used in the cross product will affect the direction of the normal vector. When applying the cross product using the Right Hand Rule, you can use a mnemonic device to determine the direction of the normal vector. You can determine the direction of the normal by positioning your right thumb so it runs in the direction of vector A. Then position your hand so your right index finger points in the direction of vector B. The palm of your right hand will point in the direction of the normal vector that results from the cross product between vector A and vector B.

XNA's Cross() method automates the process of calculating the cross product to generate the normal. The syntax is

```
Vector3 crossproduct = Vector3.Cross(Vector3 vectorA, Vector3 vectorB);
```

Cross Product Example

This example shows you how to calculate a normal in both directions. The surface is defined by vector A (9, 1, 0) and vector B (9, 0, 0). Here is the manual cross product calculation to generate the normal direction vector:

$$A \times B$$
$$= (A_y{}^*B_z - A_z{}^*B_y, A_z{}^*B_x - A_x{}^*B_z, A_x{}^*B_y - A_y{}^*B_x)$$
$$= (1{}^*0 - 0{}^*0, 0{}^*9 - 9{}^*0, 9{}^*0 - 1{}^*9)$$
$$= (0, 0, -9)$$

The manual calculation verifies the prediction that X and Y equal 0. Also, the normal vector is traveling in a negative direction (on the Z axis) from the surface created by vectors A and B. The image on the left in Figure 13-2 shows the two surface vectors together with the negative normal vector that was just calculated.

To show this cross product calculation in code, use the solution from the previous code example and replace the calculate_to_string() method with this version:

```
String calculate_to_string()
{
    Vector3 vA = new Vector3(9.0f, 1.0f, 0.0f);          // A
    Vector3 vB = new Vector3(9.0f, 0.0f, 0.0f);          // B

    Vector3 vC = new Vector3(vA.Y * vB.Z - vA.Z * vB.Y, // compute normal
                            vA.Z * vB.X - vA.X * vB.Z,
                            vA.X * vB.Y - vA.Y * vB.X);

    return          "X = "  + vC.X.ToString()            // string output
            +    "   Y = "  + vC.Y.ToString()
            +    "   Z = "  + vC.Z.ToString();
}
```

FIGURE 13-2

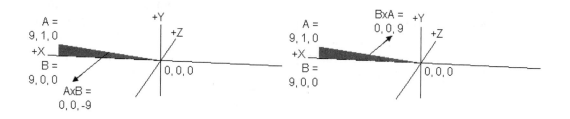

Cross product A × B (left) and cross product B × A (right)

The output of this code will show the values "X = 0 Y = 0 Z = –9."

This cross product calculation code can be simplified further. The definition for vector C, *vC*, can be replaced with a definition that uses the Cross() method:

```
Vector3 vC = Vector3.Cross(vA, vB);
```

Once again, after you insert and run this code, the resulting vector is computed as X = 0 Y = 0 Z = – 9.

So far, in this example, you have generated a normal vector with a negative direction. You can reverse the normal vector's direction by swapping the vector parameters in the Cross() method. Swapping vector A and vector B parameters in the Cross() method reverses the order in which the surface vectors are used in the cross product. To try this, replace the existing definition for vector C, *vC*, with this revision in the calculate_to_string() method:

```
Vector3 vC = Vector3.Cross(vB, vA);
```

The result of swapping vector parameters in the Cross() method will output a normal vector that points in a positive direction on Z with the coordinates X = 0 Y = 0 Z = 9. The image on the right in Figure 13-2 shows how the normal vector points outwards from the face in a positive direction.

NORMALIZATION

The process of scaling vectors to unit vectors is known as *normalization*. A *unit vector* is a set of numbers that have been expressed in the same ratio as the original vector, but the vector components are scaled to a fraction that ranges between –1 and +1. The vector length is scaled to 1. Often, when you're comparing properties such as direction or speed, magnitude is not important, but relative change on the X, Y, and Z planes is important. A normalized vector allows such comparisons on a uniform scale while the individual vector components (X, Y, Z) retain the same relative size to each other as the original vector.

The normal vector is calculated by dividing the X, Y, and Z coordinates of a vector by the total vector length:

UnitVector.X = Vector.X / VectorLength
UnitVector.Y = Vector.Y / VectorLength
UnitVector.Z = Vector.Z / VectorLength

The vector length is calculated using the Pythagorean Theorem.

Pythagorean Theorem

As you'll remember from math class, the Pythagorean Theorem states that for a right-angle triangle, $A^2 + B^2 = C^2$ (where C is the length of the hypotenuse, and A and B represent the lengths of the other two sides). In the context of three-dimensional vectors, the vector length can be calculated with the equation

$$\text{Vector length} = \sqrt{X^2 + Y^2 + Z^2}$$

To apply the Pythagorean Theorem for vectors, you create a right-angle triangle by dropping a line from the head of the vector so that it intersects the nearest axis at 90 degrees. Together, the original vector, the right-angle line, and the axis create a right-angle triangle.

Using the Pythagorean Theorem to Calculate the Vector Length

This example shows how you can use the Pythagorean Theorem to calculate the vector length. It starts with a vector having values of X = 9, Y=1, and Z=0. Calculating the length of the hypotenuse, in effect, returns the vector length.

Implementing the Pythagorean Theorem gives you the following:

$$\text{VectorLength} = \sqrt{9^2 + 1^2 + 0^2} = 9.055$$

To compute and display vector length in code, replace the existing calculate_to_string() method (in the code solution from the last example) with this new version:

```
String calculate_to_string()
{
    Vector3 v         = new Vector3(9.0f, 1.0f, 0.0f);
    float fLength     = (float)Math.Sqrt(v.X * v.X + v.Y * v.Y + v.Z * v.Z);
    return "Vector length   = " + fLength.ToString("N3"); // 3 decimals
}
```

When you run this code, the vector length 9.055 is generated and displayed in the game window.

XNA provides the Length() method to automate the vector's length calculation. If you replace the declaration for fLength in calculate_to_string() with this instruction, the same result will be generated:

```
float fLength      = (float)v.Length();
```

When you run the code now, the vector length that appears in the game window will remain the same. The length of 9.055 is still computed and shown in the window.

Using Normalization to Compute the Unit Vector

After the length has been calculated, you can scale the original vector to a unit vector by dividing the X, Y, and Z values in the original vector by the vector length. Here is the manual calculation:

```
UnitVector.X = Vector.X / VectorLength = 9 / 9.055  = 0.99
UnitVector.Y = Vector.Y / VectorLength = 1 / 9.055  = 0.11
UnitVector.Z = Vector.Z / VectorLength = 0 / 9.055  = 0.00
```

In this case, the calculated unit vector is much smaller than the original vector, but the unit vector contains the same proportion of direction or speed information. The angle of the vector remains the same as the original vector (9, 1, 0), but the vector is shorter.

To calculate the unit vector in code, and show it in the window, replace the current calculate_to_string() method from the previous example's solution with this version:

```
String calculate_to_string()
{
    Vector3 v      = new Vector3(9.0f, 1.0f, 0.0f);
    float fLength = (float)v.Length();
    Vector3 vUnit = v / fLength;

    return       "X = " + vUnit.X.ToString("N3")
         + "     Y = " + vUnit.Y.ToString("N3")
         + "     Z = " + vUnit.Z.ToString("N3");    // 3 decimals
}
```

When you run this version of the code, the text in the window reads "X = 0.994 Y= 0.110 Z = 0.000."

Using the Normalize() Method to Compute the Unit Vector

XNA provides the Normalize() method to automate the generation of the unit vector so that you no longer need to divide the original vector by the length. The syntax for the Normalize() method is

```
Vector3 unitVector = Vector3.Normalize(Vector3 vector);
```

A Normalize() method also exists for objects derived from the Vector2 and Vector4 classes. The syntax is identical to that for the Vector3 class:

```
Vector2 unitVector = Vector2.Normalize(Vector2 vector);
Vector4 unitVector = Vector4.Normalize(Vector4 vector);
```

Vectors

The solution from the previous example can be reimplemented using the Normalize() method. To use this method, replace the declaration for vUnit in calculate_to_string() with this version:

```
Vector3 vUnit = Vector3.Normalize(v);
```

Also, in calculate_to_string(), delete the vector-length calculation because it is no longer required. The output from this revised method generates the same unit vector as before, but with less code.

DOT PRODUCT

The dot product is used to find the angle between vectors and is essential for many 3D graphics routines. The dot product can be used for calculating trajectory angles, angles of reflection, or even light intensity. If you have two vectors, as in Figure 13-3, the dot product can be computed with the following equation:

$\cos \theta$
$= \text{UnitVectorA} . \text{UnitVectorB}$
$= \text{UnitVectorA.x} * \text{UnitVectorB.x} + \text{UnitVectorA.y} * \text{UnitVectorB.y}$
$\quad + \text{UnitVectorA.z} * \text{UnitVectorB.z}$

The dot product formula can be rearranged to give the angle:

$\theta = \cos^{-1}(\text{UnitVectorA} . \text{UnitVectorB})$

For the material in this book, the dot product is used in Chapter 16, "Collision Detection," and in Chapter 20, "Lighting."

FIGURE 13-3

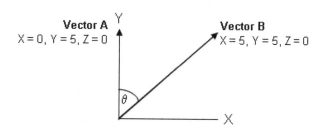

Calculating the angle between vectors using the dot product

Dot Product Method

XNA provides the Dot() method to help automate the calculation of the dot product:

```
float dotproduct = Vector3.Dot(Vector3 unitVectorA, Vector3 unitVectorB);
```

Dot Product Example

This example shows how to use the dot product to calculate the angle between vector A where X = 0, Y = 5, Z = 0 and vector B where X = 5, Y = 5, and Z = 0, as shown back in Figure 13-3.

To perform this calculation manually, first calculate the unit vector for A:

$$\text{UnitVectorA} = \text{A} / \text{LengthA}$$
$$\text{LengthA} = \sqrt{0^2 + 5^2 + 0^2} = 5$$
$$\text{Ax} / \text{LengthA} = 0.000, \text{Ay} / \text{LengthA} = 1.000, \text{Az} / \text{LengthA} = 0.000$$

Then, calculate the unit vector for B:

$$\text{UnitVectorB} = \text{B} / \text{LengthB}$$
$$\text{LengthB} = \sqrt{5^2 + 5^2 + 0^2} = 7.072$$
$$\text{Bx} / \text{LengthB} = 0.707, \text{By} / \text{LengthB} = 0.707, \text{Bz} / \text{LengthB} = 0.000$$

Next, using the dot product definition, you can calculate the value for $\cos \theta$:

$$\cos \theta.$$
$$= \text{UnitVectorA} . \text{UnitVectorB}$$
$$= \text{UnitVectorA.x} * \text{UnitVectorB.x} + \text{UnitVectorA.y} * \text{UnitVectorB.y}$$
$$+ \text{UnitVectorA.z} * \text{UnitVectorB.z}$$
$$= 0.000 * 0.707 + 1.000 * 0.707 + 0.0000 * 0.000$$
$$= 0.707$$

The result can be rearranged to isolate the value for θ, which is the angle being sought:

$$\theta. = \cos^{-1}(0.707) = 0.785 \text{ radians}$$
$$2\pi \text{ radians} = 360 \text{ degrees}$$
$$\theta. = 0.785 \text{ radians} * (360 \text{ degrees} / 2\pi \text{ radians}) = 45 \text{ degrees}$$

To perform this calculation for the angle between the two vectors in code, replace the old calculate_to_string() method with this revision:

```
String calculate_to_string(){
    Vector3 vA      = new Vector3(0.0f, 5.0f, 0.0f);
    Vector3 vB      = new Vector3(5.0f, 5.0f, 0.0f);
    Vector3 vUnitA  = Vector3.Normalize(vA);
    Vector3 vUnitB  = Vector3.Normalize(vB);
    float   vDot    = Vector3.Dot(vUnitA, vUnitB);

    float fRadians  = (float)Math.Acos((double)vDot);
    float fDegrees  = fRadians * 360.0f / (float)(Math.PI * 2.0);
    return "Angle in Degrees = " + fDegrees.ToString("N3");
}
```

When you run the code, the text in the window will read "Angle in Degrees = 45.000."

Vector lingo is daunting if you haven't used it before or studied it for many years. If you studied vectors in high school, chances are you never associated them with cool graphics and game code, so they may not have stuck with you. As far as game code goes, you can get a lot of mileage from the formulas presented in this chapter. The formulas covered here appear in all types of game algorithms and effects in the wide world of games programming.

CHAPTER 13 REVIEW EXERCISES

1. Implement the step-by-step examples shown in this chapter.

2. Create a pyramid, composed of line lists, that is centered at the origin. Generate normals for each of the five faces and render them as line lists. Draw each of the five normal vectors as line lists as well.

3. Normalize the normal vectors in Exercise 2. Run and view your project after the normals have been converted to unit vectors.

Matrices

MATRIX

math is a branch of linear algebra, and all 3D graphics programmers can benefit from understanding it. In video game development, matrices are used to store data, vertices, and information about how to transform an object. Matrices are simply grids of rows and columns, but they are essential for scaling, rotating, and translating objects in 3D space. You will have noticed by now that matrix calculations are used throughout your XNA and shader code for performing transformations, controlling your camera, and even for drawing 3D models. Understanding how these matrix methods work will provide you with better comprehension of how 3D game engines work. Most of the time, you can get away with just using XNA matrix methods to automatically create matrices and to implement your transformations. However, for complex vector transformations, you will sometimes need to be able to build your own matrices to implement the calculations.

In Chapter 6, "Character Movement," a matrix is manually created to compute an airplane's angle of direction. In Chapter 17, "Ballistics," a matrix is manually built to implement a vector transformation to determine the starting position and direction of a rocket. In cases like these, understanding the matrix math can definitely help to simplify your transformations.

MATRIX MULTIPLICATION

This section introduces matrix multiplication and prepares you for performing manual transformations later in the chapter. The product of two matrices is obtained by multiplying the rows of matrix A against the columns of matrix B, where matrix A is located on the left side of the operator. For the multiplication to be possible, the total number of columns in matrix A must equal the total number of rows in matrix B.

Matrix Class

XNA's Matrix class enables storage of a 4x4 matrix (4 rows by 4 columns). Each cell in the matrix grid can be accessed by referencing the matrix and suffixing it with the cell's row and column, where the top-left cell begins at row 1, column 1. Each cell stores a float:

```
float cellvalue = Matrix matrix.MRC
```

For example, matrix.M11 represents the value in row 1, column 1. Matrix.M13 represents the value in row 1, column 3.

Matrix Multiplication Example: 1×4 Matrix * 4×4 Matrix

This example shows how to multiply a 1×4 matrix by a 4×4 matrix. We'll first show the multiplication done by hand so that you can see each step of the calculation. Later, the same operation will be shown in code. For this example, a vector with X=2, Y=1, Z=0, and W=0 will be multiplied by a 4×4 matrix.

Manual Calculation

To set up the equation, the vector is placed on the left side of the multiplication operator, and the 4×4 matrix is placed on the right, as shown here:

```
| 2   1   0   0 |  X  |  2   1   3   1  |
                     |  1   2   4   1  |
                     |  0   3   5   1  |
                     |  2   1   2   1  |
```

The row on the left is multiplied by each column on the right. The following formula is used for each of the four columns of vector C, where A represents the matrix on the left and B represents the matrix on the right:

```
for(int c=1; c<=4; c++)
    C1c =A11*B1c + A12*B2c + A13*B3c + A14*B4c
```

Implementing the formula gives you the following:

```
|( 2*2 + 1*1   ( 2*1 + 1*2   ( 2*3 + 1*4   ( 2*1 + 1*1
|+ 0*0 + 0*2)  + 0*3 + 0*1)  + 0*5 + 0*2)  + 0*1 + 0*1)
=
| 5   4   10   3  |
```

The product of $A*B$, therefore, is a new vector with X=5, Y=4, Z=10, and W=3.

Calculation in Code

The previous computation will now be performed in code. To be able to print the calculation results in the game window, use the solution from the "Font Example: Displaying Text in the Game Window" section of Chapter 11, "Score Tracking and Game Statistics." This solution can be found in the Solutions folder in the download available from this book's website.

When you open the solution, you must add the multiply_matrix() method to the game class so it can initialize two matrices and calculate their product. For this example, the code declares matrix A and initializes it to store the vector in the first row. Initially, when the constructor for the Matrix class is referenced, all cells in matrix A are initialized to 0. The vector's X, Y, Z, and W components are assigned to the four cells of the first row of matrix A. The cell data for the matrix on the right side of the operator is assigned to matrix B; then A and B are multiplied together to generate the product matrix.

```
public void multiply_matrix(){
    Matrix A = new Matrix();
    Matrix B = new Matrix();
```

```
    Matrix C = new Matrix();

    // store vector in first row - all other cells equal 0
    A.M11 = 2.0f; A.M12 = 1.0f; A.M13 = 0.0f; A.M14 = 0.0f;

    // init matrix B
    B.M11 = 2.0f; B.M12 = 1.0f; B.M13 = 3.0f; B.M14 = 1.0f;
    B.M21 = 1.0f; B.M22 = 2.0f; B.M23 = 4.0f; B.M24 = 1.0f;
    B.M31 = 0.0f; B.M32 = 3.0f; B.M33 = 5.0f; B.M34 = 1.0f;
    B.M41 = 2.0f; B.M42 = 1.0f; B.M43 = 2.0f; B.M44 = 1.0f;

    C = A * B;
    draw_matrix(C);
}
```

To display the cell data (for the product matrix) as text in the game window, you require the draw_matrix() method. Add it to your game class so that you can convert each cell of the product matrix to a string, combine cells to form each row of the matrix, and then draw each row of the matrix in the window.

```
public void draw_matrix(Matrix C){
    String[] sOut = new String[4];

    sOut[0] = sCell(C.M11)+sCell(C.M12)+sCell(C.M13)+sCell(C.M14); // row 1
    sOut[1] = sCell(C.M21)+sCell(C.M22)+sCell(C.M23)+sCell(C.M24); // row 2
    sOut[2] = sCell(C.M31)+sCell(C.M32)+sCell(C.M33)+sCell(C.M34); // row 3
    sOut[3] = sCell(C.M41)+sCell(C.M42)+sCell(C.M43)+sCell(C.M44); // row 4

    Vector2 v2px0 = get_titleSafe_topLeft_pixel();  // starting left pixel

    for (int i = 0; i < 4; i++)                      // draw 4 matrix rows
        draw_string(sOut[i], (int)v2px0.X,
                    (int)v2px0.Y + i * (FONT_H + 2), Color.Black);
}
```

To improve readability, add sCell() so that you can create a string for each cell. This will right-align the columns when they are displayed in a matrix grid. sCell() first formats the data in each cell so it appears as a floating-point number with two decimal places, then sCell() compares the length of the data string with the amount allotted for each cell. sCell() does this by adding extra spaces until the total character count for the string matches the amount allotted for each cell. When the string has been created, it is returned to the calling function.

```
public string sCell(float fCell){
    string      strCell = fCell.ToString("N2"); // 2 decimal places
    const int   CELL_W  = 8;                     // each cell takes 8 chars
    int         iLen    = strCell.Length;        // original cell length

    // right align text based on string length. Add padding on left
    for (int i = 0; i < CELL_W - iLen; i++)
        strCell = " " + strCell;

    return strCell;
}
```

To trigger the methods that calculate the matrix product and display the output, replace the line

```
draw_string("Score Tracking and Game Stats",
            (int)v2px0.X, (int)v2px0.Y, Color.Red);
```

inside Draw() with the following:

```
multiply_matrix();
```

When you run this code, the product matrix will appear in the window:

```
5.00    4.00    10.00    3.00
0.00    0.00     0.00    0.00
0.00    0.00     0.00    0.00
0.00    0.00     0.00    0.00
```

This result verifies that the code, C = A * B (where A, B, and C are Matrix objects), generates the same product as shown in the lengthy manual calculation.

Matrix Multiplication Example: 4×4 Matrix * 4×4 Matrix

This next example shows how to multiply a 4×4 matrix by a 4×4 matrix. Knowing how to do this by hand is very useful because all of the transformations you have been implementing in your XNA code involve multiplying 4×4 matrices by 4×4 matrices. You will first see how the multiplication can be performed manually, and then how you can do it in code.

Manual Calculation

For this case, the following two matrices, A and B, are to be multiplied:

```
A   X   B   =
| 2   1   0   0  | X |  2   1   3   1  |
```

```
| -1   -2    0    0  |        |  1    2    4    1  |
|  3    1    0    0  |        |  0    3    5    1  |
| -3    2    2    0  |        |  2    1    2    1  |
```

When you're calculating the product of a 4x4 matrix by a 4x4 matrix, the formula to multiply the rows of matrix A by the columns of matrix B is

```
for(r=1; r<=4; r++)
    for(c=1; c<=4;c++)
        Crc =A1*B1c + A2*B2c + A3*B3c + A4*B4c
```

When the formula is implemented by hand, the calculation looks like this:

```
|( 2*2 + 1*1      ( 2*1 + 1*2      ( 2*3 + 1*4      ( 2*1 + 1*1
|+ 0*0 + 0*2)     + 0*3 + 0*1)     + 0*5 + 0*2)     + 0*1 + 0*1)
|(-1*2 - 2*1      (-1*1 - 2*2      (-1*3 - 2*4      (-1*1 - 2*1
|+ 0*0 + 0*2)     + 0*3 + 0*1)     + 0*5 + 0*2)     + 0*1 + 0*1)
|( 3*2 + 1*1      ( 3*1 + 1*2      ( 3*3 + 1*4      ( 3*1 + 1*1
|+ 0*0 + 0*2)     + 0*3 + 0*1)     + 0*5 + 0*2)     + 0*1 + 0*1)
|(-3*2 + 2*1      (-3*1 + 2*2      (-3*3 + 2*4      (-3*1 + 2*1
|+ 2*0 + 0*2)     + 2*3 + 0*1)     + 2*5 + 0*2)     + 2*1 + 0*1)
=
|  5    4    10    3  |
| -4   -5   -11   -3  |
|  7    5    13    4  |
| -4    7     9    1  |
```

Calculation in Code

After performing the long-winded manual calculation, you can appreciate the simplicity of being able to compute the same result with the instruction C = A * B.

Using the code solution from the previous example, in multiply_matrix() replace the instructions that initialize matrix A with the following version (matrix B remains the same as the previous example, so no changes are required to it):

```
A.M11 = 2.0f;    A.M12 = 1.0f;    A.M13 = 0.0f;    A.M14 = 0.0f;
A.M21 =-1.0f;    A.M22 =-2.0f;    A.M23 = 0.0f;    A.M24 = 0.0f;
A.M31 = 3.0f;    A.M32 = 1.0f;    A.M33 = 0.0f;    A.M34 = 0.0f;
A.M41 =-3.0f;    A.M42 = 2.0f;    A.M43 = 2.0f;    A.M44 = 0.0f;
```

When you run the code, you will see the result does indeed match the manual calculation:

```
|  5.00    4.00    10.00    3.00  |
| -4.00   -5.00   -11.00   -3.00  |
|  7.00    5.00    13.00    4.00  |
| -4.00    7.00     9.00    1.00  |
```

At this point, we can say when multiplying a 4×4 matrix by a 4×4 matrix that the manual calculation can be executed in one line with the following instruction:

Matrix C = A * B

TRANSFORMATION MATRICES

When drawing primitive shapes and 3D models, you use matrices to transform sets of vertices. Through the study of linear algebra, specific matrices have been defined to scale, rotate, and translate sets of vertices. In Chapter 5, "Animation Introduction," the I.S.R.O.T. (Identity, Scale, Revolve, Orbit [translation and rotation], Translate) sequence of matrices was introduced as the way to ensure balanced transformations. The same logic applies when you are using transformation matrices that have been created manually. If the matrices are multiplied in an incorrect order, the transformations will also be incorrect.

When matrix calculations are performed in XNA, they are applied using the Right Hand Rule perspective, which was explained in Chapter 5, "Animation Introduction." This chapter applies the transformation matrices from a Right Hand Rule perspective to suit the XNA framework.

When you perform transformations on an object, the data matrix containing the X, Y, Z, and W coordinates is located on the left of the multiplication operator. The transformation matrix is located on the right.

Translation Matrix

Translation matrices store lateral transformations along the X, Y, and Z planes. Here is the format for the translation matrix:

```
|  1    0    0    0  |
|  0    1    0    0  |
|  0    0    1    0  |
|  X    Y    Z    1  |
```

Without even performing any calculations, when you are presented with a 4×4 matrix with 1s along the diagonal, values for X, Y, Z at the bottom, and 0s elsewhere, you can conclude the matrix will perform a translation of X units along the X plane, Y units along the Y plane, and Z units along the Z plane.

Handling the W Component

When a vector representing the X, Y, and Z coordinates of an object is transformed using a translation matrix, the W component in the fourth column of the data matrix must be set to 1.

 Failing to set all values in the fourth column of the data matrix to 1 will lead to inaccurate translations.

Translation Matrix Example

Imagine the vertex (X=2, Y=1, Z=0) is transformed by the matrix on the right. The vector data matrix is located on the left. Note that the fourth column representing the W component is set to 1. The translation matrix for the format described here must be located on the right side of the operator for the calculation to work properly.

$$
\begin{vmatrix} 2 & 1 & 0 & 1 \end{vmatrix} \times \begin{vmatrix} 1 & 0 & 0 & 0 \\ 0 & 1 & 0 & 0 \\ 0 & 0 & 1 & 0 \\ 3 & 5 & 0 & 1 \end{vmatrix}
$$

Viewing this vertex and translation matrix gives you enough information to determine that the vertex with the coordinates X=2, Y=1, and Z=0 will be transformed three units in the positive X direction and five units in the positive Y direction. If this is correct, the product of the vertex and translation matrix should move the vertex to X=5, Y=6, and Z=0. Figure 14-1 shows the coordinate in its original position before the predicted translation (on the left) and after the predicted translation (on the right).

To verify the prediction, this calculation will be performed in code. To set up the data matrix, replace the code that initializes matrix A with this revision to initialize the vector data. The remaining rows will take on the default of 0 in each cell.

```
// store vector in first row - all other cells equal 0 by default
A.M11 = 2.0f; A.M12 = 1.0f; A.M13 = 0.0f; A.M14 = 1.0f;
```

Next, to set up the translation matrix, replace the code that assigns matrix B with this revision:

```
B.M11 = 1.0f;    B.M12 = 0.0f;    B.M13 = 0.0f;    B.M14 = 0.0f;
B.M21 = 0.0f;    B.M22 = 1.0f;    B.M23 = 0.0f;    B.M24 = 0.0f;
B.M31 = 0.0f;    B.M32 = 0.0f;    B.M33 = 1.0f;    B.M34 = 0.0f;
B.M41 = 3.0f;    B.M42 = 5.0f;    B.M43 = 0.0f;    B.M44 = 1.0f;
```

FIGURE 14-1

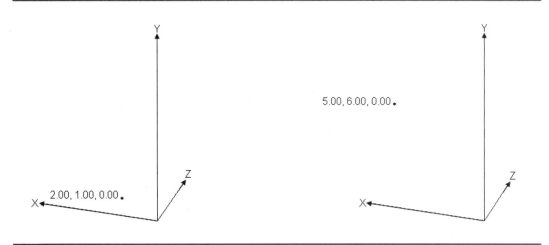

Translating an object with the translation matrix

If you run this code, the output that appears in the window matches the prediction that the new coordinates are X=5, Y=6, and Z=0:

```
5.00    6.00    0.00    1.00
0.00    0.00    0.00    0.00
0.00    0.00    0.00    0.00
0.00    0.00    0.00    0.00
```

The translation moved the original vertex three units in the positive X direction and five units in the positive Y direction.

Translation Matrix Example Using the CreateTranslation() Method

Since Chapter 5, "Animation Introduction," we have used the method CreateTranslation(float x, float y, float z) to automatically generate the translation matrix. This method actually generates a translation matrix that is identical to the translation matrix we just created manually. If you replace the code inside multiply_matrix() that assigns cell values to matrix B with the following instruction, you will generate an identical matrix:

```
B = Matrix.CreateTranslation(3.0f, 5.0f, 0.0f);
```

Therefore, when you compile and run the code, the product matrix will also be identical.

Scaling Matrix

Scaling matrices are used any time an object needs to be resized. You will almost always need to scale your 3D models because modeling tools usually generate them in a size that is different from the size needed for your game project. The following matrix represents a standard matrix for performing scaling operations. At a glance, this scaling matrix contains information to expand or shrink an object in the X plane by a factor of A units, in the Y plane by a factor of B units, and in the Z plane by a factor of C units. The A, B, and C scaling factors on the diagonal down to the right, a 1 in the bottom-right corner, and 0s elsewhere mark this matrix as a scaling matrix.

A	0	0	0
0	B	0	0
0	0	C	0
0	0	0	1

Scaling Matrix Example

In this example, you will use a scaling matrix to double the size of a triangle. A triangle is represented with the matrix containing the triangle vertices on the left. The vertex coordinates used to build the triangle are ((0, 0, 0), (1, 4, 0), (4, 2, 0)). The scaling matrix that doubles the size of the triangle is on the right. In the first three rows of the data matrix on the left, the X, Y, and Z coordinates for the three triangle vertices are stored. One triangle vertex is stored in each of the first three rows. When multiplying the triangle vertices by the scaling matrix (to double the size), you can use the following matrix equation:

$$
\begin{vmatrix} 0 & 0 & 0 & 0 \\ 1 & 4 & 0 & 0 \\ 4 & 2 & 0 & 0 \\ 0 & 0 & 0 & 0 \end{vmatrix} \times \begin{vmatrix} 2 & 0 & 0 & 0 \\ 0 & 2 & 0 & 0 \\ 0 & 0 & 2 & 0 \\ 0 & 0 & 0 & 1 \end{vmatrix}
$$

By looking at the scaling matrix—and without performing any calculations—it is apparent that the size of the existing triangle is going to be doubled. In Figure 14-2, you can see the size of the triangle has doubled when a vector set was transformed with the scaling matrix.

FIGURE 14-2

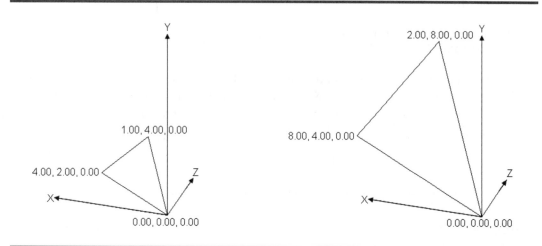

Before scaling and after scaling

Inside matrix_multiply(), replace the code that assigns values to the cells of matrix A with the following revision to initialize the data matrix for the triangle:

```
A.M11 = 0.0f;   A.M12 = 0.0f;   A.M13 = 0.0f;   A.M14 = 0.0f;
A.M21 = 1.0f;   A.M22 = 4.0f;   A.M23 = 0.0f;   A.M24 = 0.0f;
A.M31 = 4.0f;   A.M32 = 2.0f;   A.M33 = 0.0f;   A.M34 = 0.0f;
A.M41 = 0.0f;   A.M42 = 0.0f;   A.M43 = 0.0f;   A.M44 = 0.0f;
```

Next, replace the code that initializes matrix B with this version to initialize a scaling matrix:

```
B.M11 = 2.0f;   B.M12 = 0.0f;   B.M13 = 0.0f;   B.M14 = 0.0f;
B.M21 = 0.0f;   B.M22 = 2.0f;   B.M23 = 0.0f;   B.M24 = 0.0f;
B.M31 = 0.0f;   B.M32 = 0.0f;   B.M33 = 2.0f;   B.M34 = 0.0f;
B.M41 = 0.0f;   B.M42 = 0.0f;   B.M43 = 0.0f;   B.M44 = 1.0f;
```

When the program is run, the output displays coordinates for the triangle that has been doubled:

```
0.00    0.00    0.00    0.00
2.00    8.00    0.00    0.00
8.00    4.00    0.00    0.00
0.00    0.00    0.00    0.00
```

The triangle coordinates in the output matrix are graphed on the right side of Figure 14-2.

Translation Matrix Example Using the CreateScale() Method

In Chapter 5, "Animation Introduction," the CreateScale(float x, float y, float z) method was introduced as a way to automatically generate the scaling matrix. Replace the instructions that manually assign the scaling matrix with this simpler revision to generate an identical matrix:

```
B = Matrix.CreateScale(2.0f, 2.0f, 2.0f);
```

When you run the code, the output will be the same as before.

Rotation Matrix X Axis

The X rotation matrix is used to transform sets of vertices by an angle of θ radians about the X axis:

$$
\begin{vmatrix}
1 & 0 & 0 & 0 \\
0 & \cos\theta & \sin\theta & 0 \\
0 & -\sin\theta & \cos\theta & 0 \\
0 & 0 & 0 & 1
\end{vmatrix}
$$

Rotation Matrix X Axis Example

This example applies the X rotation matrix to rotate a triangle by 45 degrees ($\pi/4$). The original set of coordinates (before the rotation) is in the left matrix, and the X rotation matrix is located on the right:

$$
\begin{vmatrix}
0 & 0 & 0 & 0 \\
1 & 4 & 0 & 0 \\
4 & 2 & 0 & 0 \\
0 & 0 & 0 & 0
\end{vmatrix}
\;\text{X}\;
\begin{vmatrix}
1 & 0 & 0 & 0 \\
0 & \cos(\pi/4) & \sin(\pi/4) & 0 \\
0 & -\sin(\pi/4) & \cos(\pi/4) & 0 \\
0 & 0 & 0 & 1
\end{vmatrix}
$$

If you were to multiply this out by hand, the result would be

```
0.00   0.00   0.00   0.00
1.00   2.83   2.83   0.00
4.00   1.41   1.41   0.00
0.00   0.00   0.00   0.00
```

Figure 14-3 shows how the triangle would be positioned before and after the rotation.

FIGURE 14-3

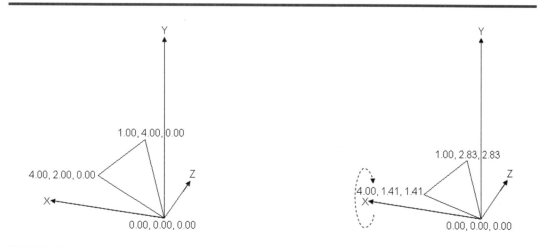

Rotation of a triangle using the X rotation matrix

Now we will show this implementation of the rotation matrix in code by using the solution from the previous example. To create a rotation matrix of π/4 radians about the X axis, replace the instructions that initialize matrix B with the following version inside matrix_multiply():

```
float sin = (float)Math.Sin(Math.PI / 4.0);
float cos = (float)Math.Cos(Math.PI / 4.0);
B.M11 = 1.0f;    B.M12 = 0.0f;    B.M13 = 0.0f;    B.M14 = 0.0f;
B.M21 = 0.0f;    B.M22 =  cos;    B.M23 = sin;    B.M24 = 0.0f;
B.M31 = 0.0f;    B.M32 = -sin;    B.M33 = cos;    B.M34 = 0.0f;
B.M41 = 0.0f;    B.M42 = 0.0f;    B.M43 = 0.0f;    B.M44 = 1.0f;
```

When you compile and run this code, the product matrix equals the result that is computed by hand:

```
0.00   0.00   0.00   0.00
1.00   2.83   2.83   0.00
4.00   1.41   1.41   0.00
0.00   0.00   0.00   0.00
```

This matrix stores the coordinates of the triangle after it has been rotated about the X axis, as shown in Figure 14-3.

X Axis Rotation Example Using the CreateRotationX() Method

Prior to this chapter, the CreateRotationX(float radians) method has been used to generate the same X rotation matrix as the manually created matrix. To calculate the same transformation for the triangle, replace the initial declaration for the X rotation matrix with a matrix that is generated using the CreateRotationX() method:

```
B = Matrix.CreateRotationX((float)(Math.PI / 4.0));
```

The resulting product is obviously the same, but the calculation requires less code.

Rotation Matrix Y Axis

The matrix shown here is a predefined matrix that rotates a set of vertices around the Y axis by θ radians:

```
| cosθ    0   -sinθ    0 |
| 0       1   0        0 |
| sinθ    0   cosθ     0 |
| 0       0   0        1 |
```

Rotation Matrix Y Axis Example

This example demonstrates the use of the Y rotation matrix to rotate a set of triangle coordinates by π/4 radians about the Y axis. The data matrix is on the left, and the Y rotation matrix is on the right:

```
| 0   0   0   0 |   X   | cos(π/4)   0   -sin(π/4)   0 |
| 1   4   0   0 |       | 0          1   0           0 |
| 4   2   0   0 |       | sin(π/4)   0   cos(π/4)    0 |
| 0   0   0   0 |       | 0          0   0           1 |
```

If you multiplied this out by hand, the result would be

```
| 0       0   0       0 |
| 0.71    4   -0.71   0 |
| 2.83    2   -2.83   0 |
| 0       0   0       0 |
```

Figure 14-4 shows the triangle coordinates before and after the multiplication that performs the rotation.

FIGURE 14-4

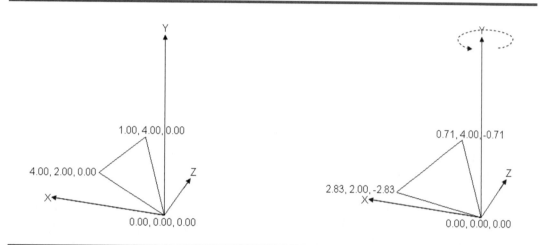

Y axis rotation before and after the transformation matrix is applied

To implement the Y rotation in code, replace the code that initializes matrix B with a rotation matrix to rotate the vertices by π/4 radians:

```
float sin = (float)Math.Sin(Math.PI / 4.0);
float cos = (float)Math.Cos(Math.PI / 4.0);
B.M11 =  cos;   B.M12 = 0.0f;   B.M13 = -sin;   B.M14 = 0.0f;
B.M21 = 0.0f;   B.M22 = 1.0f;   B.M23 = 0.0f;   B.M24 = 0.0f;
B.M31 =  sin;   B.M32 = 0.0f;   B.M33 =  cos;   B.M34 = 0.0f;
B.M41 = 0.0f;   B.M42 = 0.0f;   B.M43 = 0.0f;   B.M44 = 0.0f;
```

When you run this program, the product matrix stores the triangle's new coordinates after they are rotated by π/4 units around the Y axis (see Figure 14-4).

Y Axis Rotation Example Using the CreateRotationY() Method

Before this chapter, the CreateRotationY(float radians) method has been used to generate an identical Y rotation matrix as the one presented in this chapter. You can replace the code that initializes matrix B with the following instruction and it will produce the same result:

```
B = Matrix.CreateRotationY((float)(Math.PI / 4.0));
```

When you run this code, the product matrix will be the same as before, but this version requires less code.

Rotation Matrix Z Axis

The following matrix is the classic matrix for rotations of θ radians on the Z axis:

$$
\begin{vmatrix}
\cos\theta & \sin\theta & 0 & 0 \\
-\sin\theta & \cos\theta & 0 & 0 \\
0 & 0 & 1 & 0 \\
0 & 0 & 0 & 1
\end{vmatrix}
$$

Rotation Matrix Z Axis Example

In this example, the triangle coordinates on the left are transformed with the Z rotation matrix by π/4 radians (45 degrees) about the Z axis:

$$
\begin{vmatrix}
0 & 0 & 0 & 0 \\
1 & 4 & 0 & 0 \\
4 & 2 & 0 & 0 \\
0 & 0 & 0 & 0
\end{vmatrix}
\; X \;
\begin{vmatrix}
\cos(\pi/4) & \sin(\pi/4) & 0 & 0 \\
-\sin(\pi/4) & \cos(\pi/4) & 0 & 0 \\
0 & 0 & 1 & 0 \\
0 & 0 & 0 & 1
\end{vmatrix}
$$

When you calculate the multiplication by hand, the new triangle coordinates—after the rotation—will appear in the product matrix:

```
 0.00    0.00    0.00    0.00
-2.12    3.54    0.00    0.00
 1.41    4.24    0.00    0.00
 0.00    0.00    0.00    0.00
```

Figure 14-5 shows the triangle before and after the rotation.

To try this in code, replace the assignment of matrix B with the following code to create a rotation about the Z axis of π/4 radians:

```
float sin = (float)Math.Sin(Math.PI / 4.0);
float cos = (float)Math.Cos(Math.PI / 4.0);
B.M11 =  cos;    B.M12 =  sin;    B.M13 = 0.0f;    B.M14 = 0.0f;
B.M21 = -sin;    B.M22 =  cos;    B.M23 = 0.0f;    B.M24 = 0.0f;
B.M31 = 0.0f;    B.M32 = 0.0f;    B.M33 = 1.0f;    B.M34 = 0.0f;
B.M41 = 0.0f;    B.M42 = 0.0f;    B.M43 = 0.0f;    B.M44 = 1.0f;
```

Z Axis Rotation Example Using the CreateRotationZ() Method

The CreateRotationZ(float radians) matrix will generate a matrix identical to the one just declared for matrix B. Replacing the existing matrix assignment with this instruction will generate the same result:

```
B = Matrix.CreateRotationZ((float)(Math.PI / 4.0));
```

Matrices

FIGURE 14-5

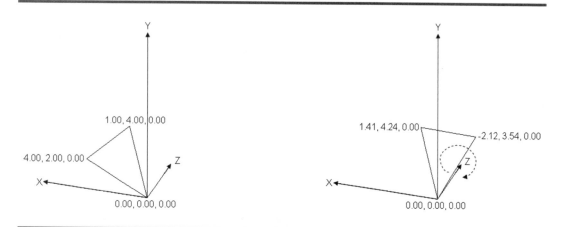

Z axis rotation before and after the transformation matrix is applied

IDENTITY MATRIX

When a set of vertices is multiplied by the identity matrix, the product equals the original vertex matrix. In other words, nothing changes in the original data matrix. It may seem pointless to use the identity matrix since it does not actually perform a transformation. However, the identity matrix is included in the recommended I.S.R.O.T. sequence of transformations to ensure that the World matrix is initialized properly when no other transformation matrix is applied. By default, an identity matrix is used in the World matrix to initialize it. The World matrix is explained in more detail in Chapter 15, "Building a Graphics Engine Camera."

The identity matrix is defined for a matrix that has 1s on the diagonal from the top left to the bottom right, and 0s elsewhere, as shown here:

```
|  1   0   0   0  |
|  0   1   0   0  |
|  0   0   1   0  |
|  0   0   0   1  |
```

Identity Matrix Example

This example shows that when a data matrix is multiplied by an identity matrix, the result equals the data matrix. In other words, A * B = A, where B is an identity matrix. In this case, the vertices for a triangle are multiplied by the identity matrix. The product equals the original set of vertices for the triangle:

```
|  0   0   0   0  |   X   |  1   0   0   0  |   =   |  0   0   0   0  |
|  1   4   0   0  |       |  0   1   0   0  |   =   |  1   4   0   0  |
```

$$\begin{vmatrix} 4 & 2 & 0 & 0 \\ 0 & 0 & 0 & 0 \end{vmatrix} \quad \begin{vmatrix} 0 & 0 & 1 & 0 \\ 0 & 0 & 0 & 1 \end{vmatrix} = \begin{vmatrix} 4 & 2 & 0 & 0 \\ 0 & 0 & 0 & 0 \end{vmatrix}$$

To perform this calculation in code, replace the assignment for matrix B with this revision:

```
B.M11 = 1.0f;   B.M12 = 0.0f;   B.M13 = 0.0f;   B.M14 = 0.0f;
B.M21 = 0.0f;   B.M22 = 1.0f;   B.M23 = 0.0f;   B.M24 = 0.0f;
B.M31 = 0.0f;   B.M32 = 0.0f;   B.M33 = 1.0f;   B.M34 = 0.0f;
B.M41 = 0.0f;   B.M42 = 0.0f;   B.M43 = 0.0f;   B.M44 = 1.0f;
```

When you run this code, the product matrix displayed in the game window equals matrix A, which defines the triangle.

Identity Matrix Example Using Matrix.Identity

Until now, the predefined matrix, Matrix.Identity, has been used for the identity matrix. This matrix is equivalent to the one you just created manually. If you replace the assignment for matrix B with

```
B = Matrix.Identity;
```

the outcome will be the same.

Matrices enable transformations in 3D space. Understanding linear algebra and the defined transformation matrices will allow you to develop better graphics algorithms and have deeper control of your graphics engine. This will be especially helpful when you need to build your own matrices to perform transformations for vectors. See Chapter 6, "Character Movement," and Chapter 17, "Ballistics," for examples of when this technique is necessary.

CHAPTER 14 REVIEW EXERCISES

1. Try the step-by-step examples discussed in this chapter.

2. Starting with a triangle with the coordinates

```
A{-0.23f,  -0.2f,  -0.1f)
B{ 0.23f,  -0.2f,  -0.1f)
C{ 0.0f,    0.2ff, 0.1f)
```

manually compute the unit normal. Then manually translate the triangle, together with its unit normal, 2 units on Z and –0.35 units on X. Scale the triangle and normal by 3.5 on X, Y, and Z. Rotate the triangle and normal by π/3 radians on X and π/4 radians on Z. When performing this transformation, do not use any variations of the following methods:

```
CreateScale(float X, float Y, float Z);
CreateRotationX(float radians);
CreateRotationY(float radians);
CreateRotationZ(float radians);
CreateTranslation(float X, float Y, float Z);
Cross();
Normalize();
```

When the program is run, the final result shows both the triangle and the triangle's unit normal pointing out from it. Both the triangle and normal vector are

> Translated 2 units on Z and –0.35 units on X.

> Scaled by 3.5 on X, Y, and Z.

> Rotated π/3 radians on X.

> Rotated π/4 radians on Z.

Building a Graphics Engine Camera

A great number of elements contribute to the "feel" of a video game. The physics, sounds, music, graphics, 3D models, and many other factors influence the gamer's experience. All of these things are important, but possibly none is as important as the camera you create for your game. The camera is the heart of the graphics engine. This book shows how to add and customize all the components you need for decent graphics, but it's the camera that allows your players to see your world.

A camera lets your viewer travel through a virtual world; it can be thought of as the player's lens. The camera includes logic for responding to the game's controls so the user can adjust their view and position within the 3D world. How you code your camera will determine much of how the controls "feel" to the player.

The 3D camera code is so fundamental that it is included in the base code for all of this book's examples. This chapter explains how the base code camera was created. You can use this step-by-step explanation to add this camera to any of your own game projects.

CAMERA VECTORS

Most cameras are constructed with logic that applies a common set of camera vectors and camera matrices. The camera structure is often described and manipulated with a set of five vectors:

```
View     -- Stores the target position focused on by the camera.
Position -- Stores the camera's position.
Up       -- Stores the camera's upright direction.
Look     -- Stores the direction of the camera lens (View - Position).
Right    -- Stores the normal vector from the Look and Up vectors.
```

Figure 15-1 shows the position and directional vectors that describe a camera's position and orientation.

FIGURE 15-1

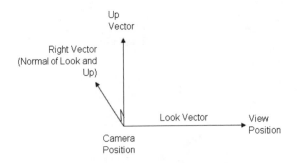

Position and directional vectors that make a camera

CAMERA MATRICES

For a camera to function properly (so all objects in the world are seen correctly), three matrices are used. Together, they transform the objects seen by the camera, the angle at which these objects appear, and the range of visibility, respectively. These three matrices are known as the World matrix, the View matrix, and the Perspective matrix. The WVP matrix you have been sending to your shader in this book's examples thus far is a product of these three matrices.

World Matrix

You have already been working with the World matrix to transform vertices and 3D models. The World matrix converts model and vertex coordinates to world coordinates, so they properly map to the 3D world space. You have used both XNA transformation functions for creating the rotations, translations, and scaling, and you have also seen how to perform these calculations manually.

View Matrix

The View matrix defines what the camera sees by setting the camera's direction.

Perspective Matrix

The Perspective matrix sets the visibility for the camera. A large perspective creates a wide-angle lens. Another way to say this is that the Perspective matrix describes the *frustum*, which is the cone-shaped view seen by the camera. The frustum has front and back boundaries on the Z axis known as the *near clip plane* and the *far clip plane*, respectively.

The Perspective matrix builds the frustum using the function Matrix .CreatePerspectiveFieldOfView(), which takes five parameters:

```
mMatProj  = Matrix.CreatePerspectiveFieldOfView(
float     fieldOfView,// angle of visibility
float     aspectRatio,// width / height
float     nearClip,   // first visible point from camera on Z
float     farClip)    // last visible point from camera on Z
```

Figure 15-2 shows a diagram of the frustum created with the Perspective matrix.

FIGURE 15-2

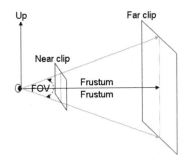

Perspective described by field of view, aspect ratio, and clip space

CAMERA EXAMPLE

The camera code presented in this example shows everything you need to implement a camera that can be used for a first-person shooter game, a racing game, and more. In fact, the code explained here is the same code used in the WinMGHBook and Xbox360MGHBook base code projects. You can begin with either the Windows Game project or Xbox 360 Game project template to generate your game application shell. The camera you add will move and strafe with arrow keypress events or left stick shift events. The camera's view will change with either mouse movements or right thumbstick shift events.

Creating the Camera Class Shell

You will first need to add an empty CCamera.cs file to your project. It needs the following class structure:

```
using System;
using System.Collections.Generic;
using Microsoft.Xna.Framework;

namespace NS_Camera{
    public class CCamera{}
}
```

When you have created your bare CCamera class, it will need some module-level variables for storing the camera vectors and a time variable for moving the camera at a regulated speed:

```
public  Vector3 m_vPos, m_vUp, m_vView;
private float    mfTimeLapse;
```

Obviously, the CCamera() constructor initializes the class. It starts by creating a camera that uses the vectors m_vView, m_vPos, and m_vUp; these vectors store the direction, position, and orientation of the camera, respectively:

```
public CCamera(){
    m_vPos.X   = 0.0f; m_vPos.Y   = 0.0f; m_vPos.Z   = 0.0f;
    m_vView.X  = 0.0f; m_vView.Y  = 0.0f; m_vView.Z  = 0.5f;
    m_vUp.X    = 0.0f; m_vUp.Y    = 1.0f; m_vUp.Z    = 0.0f;
}
```

In the camera class, set_frame_interval() provides an interface for setting a scaled measure based on the time difference between the current frame and the previous frame. This scaled time measure is then used to increment or decrement the position of the camera when it is moved. The time scale enables smooth lateral and diagonal camera translations along the X axis and the Z axis. Because you're measuring the time between frames, the translations are performed at the same speed regardless of the system running the application.

```
public void set_frame_interval(GameTime gameTime){
    mfTimeLapse = (float)gameTime.ElapsedGameTime.Milliseconds;
}
```

Referencing the Camera from Your Game Class

To reference the camera in your game class, include the camera's namespace in your Game1.cs file:

```
using   NS_Camera;
```

The camera is instantiated from the game class with the following line:

```
private CCamera      cam = new CCamera();
```

Every frame, a call to set_frame_interval() from the Update() method sets the time lapse between frames so the camera will move at uniform speed on any system:

```
cam.set_frame_interval(gameTime);
```

Matrices used for storing the camera's World, View, and Projection matrices are declared at the class level so they can be referenced throughout the class:

```
private Matrix       mMatWorld, mMatView, mMatProj;
```

After initializing your camera class, you must create a Perspective matrix to define what the camera lens sees. This method sets the frustum:

```
void set_proj_matrix(){
    // parameters are field of view, aspect ratio, near clip, far clip
    mMatProj = Matrix.CreatePerspectiveFieldOfView((float)Math.PI / 4.0f,
    (float)Window.ClientBounds.Width/(float)Window.ClientBounds.Height,
    0.005f, 1000.0f);
}
```

set_proj_matrix () is called from Initialize(). This is necessary because the frustum for most single-player games normally only needs to be defined once:

```
set_proj_matrix(); // only need to set at beginning of program
```

set_view_matrix() is added to define what the camera sees according to the camera's direction or orientation:

```
void set_view_matrix(GameTime gameTime){
    mMatView = Matrix.CreateLookAt(cam.m_vPos, cam.m_vView, cam.m_vUp);
}
```

set_view_matrix() is called from the Update() method in the game class to account for any changes to the camera's Look direction at each frame:

```
set_view_matrix(gameTime);
```

Moving and Strafing

Once you have defined the basic camera structure, you can add methods to enable the viewer to move forward, backward, or sideways (strafing) in the 3D world. Updating the camera's position while moving also requires an update to change the scenery that is visible.

Enabling Forward, Backward, and Sideways Movement in CCamera.cs

update_cam_pos_and_view() is added to the camera class to increment the camera position along X and Z. This increment is taken from the direction vector, which is scaled by the time between frames. The camera's view is also incremented by the same amount to ensure updates to the scenery match the changes to the camera's position:

```
public void update_cam_pos_and_view(Vector3 vCam, float f_speed){
    f_speed    *= (float)mfTimeLapse;
    vCam       *= f_speed;
```

```
    m_vPos.X  += vCam.X;     m_vPos.Z  += vCam.Z;
    m_vView.X += vCam.X;     m_vView.Z += vCam.Z;
}
```

The camera's move() method allows the viewer to move forward and backward whenever the user presses the up or down arrow key or when shifting the left thumbstick on the game controller. The actual "move" is implemented by incrementing the camera's View and Position vectors by the camera's Look direction. The Look direction is normalized to ensure a uniform comparison of elements in the direction vector:

```
public void move(float fCamSpeed){
    Vector3 v3Look       = Vector3.Zero;
    Vector3 v3UnitLook   = Vector3.Zero;

    const float SPEEDSCALE = 0.005f;
    fCamSpeed *= SPEEDSCALE;

    v3Look.Y = m_vView.Y;
    v3Look.X = m_vView.X - m_vPos.X;
    v3Look.Z = m_vView.Z - m_vPos.Z;

    v3UnitLook = Vector3.Normalize(v3Look);
    update_cam_pos_and_view(v3UnitLook, fCamSpeed);
}
```

A similar feature to add to your camera is the ability to strafe. A *strafe* is a side-to-side camera movement. If you're a fan of first-person shooter games, you know how fundamental strafing can be to a game. Whether you're playing *Quake*, *Doom*, *Halo*, or *Call of Duty*, moving side to side is often your only defense against taking enemy fire.

The code needed to perform this action is almost identical to the code used for creating forward and backward movement. Only one extra instruction is needed to convert the forward direction vector into a strafe direction vector:

```
Vector3 v3Strafe = Vector3.Cross(v3UnitLook, m_vUp);
```

The strafe vector is perpendicular to the surface created by the Look and Up vectors. This new vector is referred to as the Right vector. A time-scaled increment based on the Right vector is then used to update the camera's position and view from the strafe() method. Adding the strafe() method to the camera class provides the code needed to generate sideways camera movement:

```
public void strafe(float fCamSpeed){
    Vector3 v3Look           = new Vector3(0.0f, 0.0f, 0.0f);
```

```
Vector3 v3UnitLook;

const float SPEEDSCALE = 0.005f;    // time scale
fCamSpeed *= SPEEDSCALE;

v3Look.Y = m_vView.Y;                        // camera direction
v3Look.X = m_vView.X - m_vPos.X;
v3Look.Z = m_vView.Z - m_vPos.Z;

// update cam and view with time-scaled Right vector
v3UnitLook       = Vector3.Normalize(v3Look);        // unit Look
Vector3 v3Strafe = Vector3.Cross(v3UnitLook, m_vUp); // unit Right
update_cam_pos_and_view(v3Strafe, fCamSpeed);        // update
}
```

Triggering Forward, Backward, and Sideways Movement from the Game Class

Before you add code to trigger changes to the view and position, some references are needed to enable the keyboard, mouse, and game pad. A class-level declaration is required to store the states for each game pad:

```
private GamePadState[]  mGamePadState = new GamePadState[4];
```

The code that retrieves the states is also added to this game class:

```
GamePadState getNewState(GamePadState state){
    return state;
}
```

With the getNewState() method in place, the UpdateGamePad() method can be added to retrieve the states of each of the controls on the game pad:

```
private void UpdateGamePad(){
    mGamePadState[0] = GamePad.GetState(PlayerIndex.One);
    mGamePadState[1] = GamePad.GetState(PlayerIndex.Two);
    mGamePadState[2] = GamePad.GetState(PlayerIndex.Three);
    mGamePadState[3] = GamePad.GetState(PlayerIndex.Four);
}
```

By placing the following code at the top of the Update() method, you can now retrieve both the keyboard and the game pad events:

```
KeyboardState kbState = Keyboard.GetState(); // update controls
UpdateGamePad();
```

With the code for handling the keyboard and game pad in place, you should add some code to the Update() method to allow the game player to exit the game gracefully when pressing the X button on the controller or the ESC key on the keyboard:

```
if (GamePad.GetState(PlayerIndex.One).Buttons.X == ButtonState.Pressed
   || kbState.IsKeyDown(Keys.Escape))
   this.Exit();
```

Forward and backward movement is triggered by shifting the game pad's left thumbstick up and down, or by pressing the up and down arrow keys on the keyboard. This move() method handles user input from the game class:

```
float move(){
    KeyboardState kbState = Keyboard.GetState();
    GamePadState gpState    = getNewState(mGamePadState[0]);
    float fMove            = 0.0f;
    const float kScale     = 1.50f;

    if (mGamePadState[0].IsConnected){  // left stick shifted left / right
        if (gpState.ThumbSticks.Left.Y != 0.0f)
            fMove = (kScale * gpState.ThumbSticks.Left.Y);
    }
    else                                        // no gamepad
        if (kbState.IsKeyDown(Keys.Up))         // UP   - move ahead
            fMove = (1.0f);
        else if (kbState.IsKeyDown(Keys.Down))  // DOWN - move back
            fMove = (-1.0f);
    return fMove;
}
```

The code that gets the strafe amount in the game class is executed when the user shifts the left thumbstick on the controller from side to side, or when the user presses the left or right arrow key. This code returns an amount between –1.0f and +1.0f when the user shifts the left thumbstick. If the game controller is not connected, either –1 is returned when the left arrow key is pressed or +1 is returned when the right arrow key is pressed:

```
float strafe(){
    KeyboardState kbState = Keyboard.GetState();
    GamePadState  gpState = getNewState(mGamePadState[0]);

    // using gamepad. left stick shifted left / right for strafe
    if (mGamePadState[0].IsConnected){
```

```
        if(gpState.ThumbSticks.Left.X != 0.0f)
            return gpState.ThumbSticks.Left.X;
    }
    // using keyboard - strafe with X and Z keys
    else if (kbState.IsKeyDown(Keys.Left))   // strafe left
        return -1.0f;
    else if (kbState.IsKeyDown(Keys.Right)) // strafe right
        return 1.0f;
    return 0.0f;
}
```

The camera's move() and strafe() methods are triggered from Update() to enable continuous checks for these events:

```
cam.move(move());
cam.strafe(strafe());
```

If you have implemented all of the code shown so far in your project, you have a camera that moves forward, backward, and sideways.

Rotating the View

This next portion of the example explains how to rotate the camera's View vector about the X and Y axes—based on the position of the mouse or right thumbstick. Be aware that the camera Position vector and camera Up vector are not changed by the mouse movements or shifts of the right thumbstick; only the View vector is modified by this section of code. This enables the ability to rotate the view around the camera without actually moving the camera.

But before you dive into the code, here's a description of quaternion theory that enables changes to the view.

Quaternion Theory

The section of code, which updates the camera view for the mouse movement, is based on quaternion theory. By definition, a *quaternion* is a special type of vector that stores a rotation around an axis. Quaternion math is used to calculate an increment to update the camera's Look vector.

Because

Look   = View - Position.

we can say the following:

View   = Look + Position.

If the quaternion represents the updated Look vector, then

```
Updated View = Updated Look Vector + Position
```

Updated Look Vector

The formula for calculating the updated Look vector is:

```
qRotation * qLook * qRotation' (qRotation' is the conjugate of qRotation)
```

Each of the three operands will be discussed next.

Local Rotation Quaternion

The first quaternion that is used to calculate the updated Look vector, qRotation, is a local rotation. Quaternion theory provides a formula for computing the local rotation. In this case, the local rotation is generated using a direction vector for X, Y, and Z. Rotations about the X axis are applied using the Look vector. Rotations about the Y axis are applied using the Right direction vector. The rotation angle stored in the W component is obtained from the deviation of the mouse (or thumbstick) from the center of the window. With this information, we can generate the local rotation by saying the following:

```
qRotation.W = cos(MouseDeviationFromCenter/2)
qRotation.X = UnitDirection.X * sin(MouseDeviationFromCenter/2)
qRotation.Y = UnitDirection.Y * sin(MouseDeviationFromCenter/2)
qRotation.Z = UnitDirection.Z * sin(MouseDeviationFromCenter/2)
```

Using the Look Vector as a Quaternion

The next quaternion used in the formula for the updated Look vector is based on the Look direction:

```
qLook.X = Look.X    qLook.Y = Look.Y    qLook.Z = Look.Z    qLook.W = 0
```

Conjugate Quaternion

A conjugate quaternion is used to calculate the updated Look vector. The conjugate is created by negating a quaternion vector's X, Y, and Z components:

```
Quaternion conjugate
= (-Quaternion.X, -Quaternion.Y, -Quaternion.Z, Quaternion.W)
```

Quaternion Product

The equation for multiplying two quaternion is as follows:

```
(Quaternion₁*Quaternion₂).W = W₁W₂ - X₁X₂ - Y₁Y₂ - Z₁Z₂
(Quaternion₁*Quaternion₂).X = W₁X₂ + X₁W₂ + Y₁Z₂ - Z₁Y₂
(Quaternion₁*Quaternion₂).Y = W₁Y₂ - X₁Z₂ + Y₁W₂ + Z₁X₂
(Quaternion₁*Quaternion₂).Z = W₁Z₂ + X₁Y₂ - Y₁X₂ + Z₁W₂
```

Updating the View

The updated Look vector is obtained using the product of local rotation, look, and conjugate quaternions.

```
Updated Look Vector = qRotation * qLook * qRotation'
```

With the result from this product, the View can be updated:

```
Updated View        = Updated Look Vector + Position
```

Now you will apply this logic to the graphics engine to update your view.

Updating the View in the Camera Class

get_rotation_quaternion() can be added to the camera class to generate the local rotation quaternion based on the direction vector. The first parameter of this method represents the shift of the mouse or thumbstick from the resting position. The second parameter is a direction vector that can be either the Look or Right vector:

```
private Vector4 get_rotation_quaternion(float f_deg, Vector3 vAxisA){
    Vector4 vAxisUnit;
    Vector4 vAxis = new Vector4(vAxisA.X, vAxisA.Y, vAxisA.Z, 0.0f);

    // only normalize if necessary
    if ((vAxis.X != 0 && vAxis.X != 1) ||
        (vAxis.Y != 0 && vAxis.Y != 1) || (vAxis.Z != 0 && vAxis.Z != 1))
        vAxisUnit = Vector4.Normalize(vAxis);

    float f_angle = f_deg * (float)Math.PI/180.0f;
    float f_sin   = (float)Math.Sin(f_angle/2.0f);

    // create the quaternion
    Vector4 vQT = new Vector4(0.0f, 0.0f, 0.0f, 0.0f);
    vQT.X = vAxis.X * f_sin;
```

```
    vQT.Y = vAxis.Y * f_sin;
    vQT.Z = vAxis.Z * f_sin;
    vQT.W = (float)Math.Cos(f_angle/2.0f);

    Vector4 vQTUnit = Vector4.Normalize(vQT);
    return vQTUnit;
}
```

Next, you'll add the update_camera_view() method. update_camera_view() computes the product of these three quaternions and uses it to update the player's view:

```
private void update_camera_view(float f_angle, Vector3 vDirection){
    Vector4 vLookQT;
    Vector4 vQT;

    // create rotation quaternion for axis being rotated
    vQT = get_rotation_quaternion(f_angle, vDirection);

    // the look quaternion
    vLookQT.X = m_vView.X - m_vPos.X;
    vLookQT.Y = m_vView.Y - m_vPos.Y;
    vLookQT.Z = m_vView.Z - m_vPos.Z;
    vLookQT.W = 0;

    // conjugate is made by negating quaternion x, y, and z
    Vector4 vConj = new Vector4(-vQT.X, -vQT.Y, -vQT.Z, vQT.W);

    // quaternion product
    Vector4 vQuat;
    vQuat.X = vQT.W * vLookQT.X + vQT.X * vLookQT.W + vQT.Y * vLookQT.Z -
            vQT.Z * vLookQT.Y;
    vQuat.Y = vQT.W * vLookQT.Y - vQT.X * vLookQT.Z + vQT.Y * vLookQT.W +
            vQT.Z * vLookQT.X;
    vQuat.Z = vQT.W * vLookQT.Z + vQT.X * vLookQT.Y - vQT.Y * vLookQT.X +
            vQT.Z * vLookQT.W;
    vQuat.W = vQT.W * vLookQT.W - vQT.X * vLookQT.X - vQT.Y * vLookQT.Y -
            vQT.Z * vLookQT.Z;

    // complete the quaternion
    Vector4 qNewView;
    qNewView.X = vQuat.W * vConj.X + vQuat.X * vConj.W + vQuat.Y * vConj.Z
            - vQuat.Z * vConj.Y;
```

```
qNewView.Y = vQuat.W * vConj.Y - vQuat.X * vConj.Z + vQuat.Y * vConj.W
             + vQuat.Z * vConj.X;
qNewView.Z = vQuat.W * vConj.Z + vQuat.X * vConj.Y - vQuat.Y * vConj.X
             + vQuat.Z * vConj.W;
qNewView.W = vQuat.W * vConj.W - vQuat.X * vConj.X - vQuat.Y * vConj.Y
             - vQuat.Z * vConj.Z;

// cap view at ground and sky
if (qNewView.Y > -0.49f && qNewView.Y < 0.49f){
    // update the view. add position to the quaternion
    m_vView.X = m_vPos.X + qNewView.X;
    m_vView.Y = m_vPos.Y + qNewView.Y;
    m_vView.Z = m_vPos.Z + qNewView.Z;
}
}
```

The camera class uses the changeView() method to receive changes in View direction from the game class and apply them to the camera orientation. changeView() checks if the mouse or right stick has been shifted. If no movement is detected, the method exits and no changes to the view are performed. Otherwise, a relative measure for the X and Y rotations are generated based on the deviation of the mouse from the center of the window. Rotations about the X axis are applied using the Right vector. Rotations about the Y axis are applied using the Up vector:

```
public void changeView(float fXcontrol, float fYControl){
    float fYRotation = 0.0f;
    float fXRotation = 0.0f;

    Vector3 vLook, vRight, vRightUnit;
    vLook = m_vView - m_vPos;

    // don't rotate view if no change in thumbstick or mouse
    if ((fXcontrol == 0) && (fYControl == 0))
        return;

    // rotate around Y axis using a time scale for smooth rotation
    fYRotation = (float)(fXcontrol) * (mfTimeLapse/2000.0f);

    // response is immediate for tilting camera up and down
    fXRotation = (float)(fYControl)/50.0f;
```

```
    // view about X calculated with Right vector
    vRight      = Vector3.Cross(vLook, m_vUp);
    vRightUnit = Vector3.Normalize(vRight);
    update_camera_view(fXRotation, vRightUnit);

    // view about the Y axis calculated with Up vector
    Vector3 vYrotation = new Vector3(0.0f, 1.0f, 0.0f);
    update_camera_view(-fYRotation, vYrotation);
}
```

Triggering Changes to the View from the Game Class

Back inside the game class, the camera needs to be enabled for manipulation from the game controller, keyboard, and mouse. The camera will function on the PC like a first-person shooter, where a typical configuration uses the mouse to change the view. XNA does not include code to handle the mouse, so to enable it in C#, you need to import some Windows DLLs, but obviously only if the game is running on a PC.

The mouse has to be enabled in the game class when run on the PC. The mouse will adjust the view by checking the distance from the center of the window to the mouse. At the top of the game class, GetCursorPos() retrieves the X and Y coordinates of the mouse position over the window:

```
#if !XBOX
    MouseState mMouse;         // store Mouse X and Y

    // dll ref to use API for setting and getting cursor pos
    [DllImport("user32.dll")]
    static extern bool SetCursorPos(int X, int Y);
    [DllImport("user32.dll")]
    static extern int GetCursorPos(ref tPoint lpPoint);

    // stores cursor X and Y as integer
    struct tPoint { public int X, Y; }

    // converts cursor coordinates to integers
    // this is used to adjust the view with the mouse on the PC
    public static Point GetCursorPoint(){
    tPoint point;
    point.X = 0; point.Y = 0;
    GetCursorPos(ref point);
```

```
        return new Point(point.X, point.Y);
    }
#endif
```

To enable the DLL import on the PC, the following reference to the system InteropServices is required:

```
using System.Runtime.InteropServices;
```

The game class's changeView() method receives changes in view on X and Y that are triggered from the game class by mouse movements, or by shifts to the right thumbstick. After the relative changes in view have been captured and processed on the PC, SetCursorPos() moves the cursor back to the center of the window so the mouse's relative change from the center of the window can be calculated in the next frame. Otherwise, the camera will use the right stick's deviation from the center to calculate the change in view:

```
Vector2 changeView(GameTime gameTime){
    const float SENSITIVITY = 250.0f;

    // handle change in view using right and left keys
    KeyboardState kbState = Keyboard.GetState();

    int iWidthMiddle  = Window.ClientBounds.Width / 2;
    int iHeightMiddle = Window.ClientBounds.Height / 2;

    Vector2 v2Change = new Vector2(0.0f, 0.0f);

    if (mGamePadState[0].IsConnected == true){ // gamepad on PC / Xbox
        float kScaleY = (float)gameTime.ElapsedGameTime.Milliseconds/50.0f;
        v2Change.Y     = kScaleY*mGamePadState[0].ThumbSticks.Right.Y
                         * SENSITIVITY;
        v2Change.X     = mGamePadState[0].ThumbSticks.Right.X * SENSITIVITY;
    }
    else{          // mouse only (on PC)
#if !XBOX        // PC has mouse which isn't recognized on Xbox
        float kScaleY =(float)gameTime.ElapsedGameTime.Milliseconds/100.0f;
        float kScaleX =(float)gameTime.ElapsedGameTime.Milliseconds/400.0f;

        // get cursor position
```

```
        Point point = GetCursorPoint();
        int iY = point.Y;
        int iX = point.X;

        // change X is cursor not at center of X
        if (iX != iWidthMiddle){
            v2Change.X = iX - iWidthMiddle;
            v2Change.X /= kScaleX;
        }
        // change Y is cursor not at center of Y
        if (iY != iHeightMiddle){
            v2Change.Y = iY - iHeightMiddle;
            v2Change.Y /= kScaleY;
        }
        // reset cursor back to center
        SetCursorPos(iWidthMiddle, iHeightMiddle);
#endif
    }
    return v2Change;
}
```

The mouse coordinates are maintained in the game class each frame from Update:

```
#if !XBOX
            mMouse = Mouse.GetState();
#endif
```

To update your camera's view from the game class each frame, add this code to the start of set_view_matrix():

```
// define how objects are placed in our world relative to camera
Vector2 v2View = changeView(gameTime);
cam.changeView(v2View.X, v2View.Y);
```

If you run your code now, your project will have a fully functional camera enabled. To actually see it moving, you need to add some kind of reference, such as ground, a triangle, or a 3D model. Of course, you will also need to reference a shader in your project to render this object. The camera moves and strafes with the left thumbstick or arrow keys. It changes view with the right thumbstick or the mouse.

With this camera, your game players now have full access to journey into the world hosted by your graphics engine.

CHAPTER 15 REVIEW EXERCISES

1. Follow the step-by-step example presented in this chapter.

2. Add an option to "invert" the camera. This is a common first-person shooter game feature that allows players to reverse the direction of the Up and Down view control.

CHAPTER 1

Collision Detection

COLLISION

detection determines whether two objects overlap and therefore are colliding in your virtual world. Having accurate collision detection is fundamental to a solid game engine. Without collision detection, your cars would drive off the road, your people would walk through buildings, and your camera would travel through cement walls. Collision detection is also fundamental when dealing with any sort of missiles. For example, if you had faulty detection in a first-person shooter (FPS), you might successfully hit your target and not receive credit—or possibly even worse, your enemies might miss a shot at you and still be credited with a hit. These sorts of problems are still evident in commercial games, but to avoid player frustration, you should strive to have excellent collision detection. This chapter shows you how to use collision detection to add boundaries around your game objects.

BOUNDING SPHERES

The use of bounding spheres is one of the most common methods for collision detection. It isn't a perfect solution, but it is suitable for many cases and doesn't require as much processing power as more advanced solutions.

The bounding sphere method involves creating an invisible sphere around each object that requires collision detection. If the distance between the centers of the two spheres is less than the sum of their radii, a collision is detected (see Figure 16-1).

This example implements collision detection for two flying birds and a stationary gray wall. Each of these items will be assigned a radius that is large enough so the sphere around it surrounds the object. The actual collision code for this example is very compact, and most of it is spent setting up and implementing the animations.

FIGURE 16-1

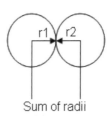

Collision detected when the distance between sphere centers is less than the sum of their radii

This example can start with either the base code for the WinMGHBook example or the Xbox360MGHBook example.

To store vertex data for the birds and wall, these module-level vertex declarations are required at the top of the game class:

```
private VertexPositionColor[]    mVertBird0  = new VertexPositionColor[3];
private VertexPositionColor[]    mVertBird1  = new VertexPositionColor[3];
private VertexPositionColor[]    mVertWall   = new VertexPositionColor[4];
```

These next three methods initialize the vertices for the two birds and the wall. Each method initializes the X, Y, and Z coordinates and the color. To set up each vertex set, you will need to add init_bird0(), init_bird1(), and init_wall() to your game class:

```
private void init_bird0(){
    mVertBird0[0] = new VertexPositionColor(
                    new Vector3(0.0f, 0.0f, -0.02f), Color.Red);
    mVertBird0[1] = new VertexPositionColor(
                    new Vector3(0.1f, 0.0f,  0.00f), Color.Red);
    mVertBird0[2] = new VertexPositionColor(
                    new Vector3(0.0f, 0.0f,  0.02f), Color.Red);
}
private void init_bird1(){
    mVertBird1[0] = new VertexPositionColor(
                    new Vector3(0.0f, 0.0f, -0.02f), Color.Blue);
    mVertBird1[1] = new VertexPositionColor(
                    new Vector3(0.1f, 0.0f,  0.00f), Color.Blue);
    mVertBird1[2] = new VertexPositionColor(
                    new Vector3(0.0f, 0.0f,  0.02f), Color.Blue);
}
private void init_wall(){
    mVertWall[0] = new VertexPositionColor(                     // bottom R
    new Vector3(-BOUNDARY / 2.0f, 0.0f, 0.0f), Color.LightGray);
    mVertWall[1] = new VertexPositionColor(                     // top R
    new Vector3(-BOUNDARY / 2.0f, 2.0f, 0.0f), Color.LightGray);
    mVertWall[2] = new VertexPositionColor(                     // bottom L
    new Vector3(BOUNDARY / 2.0f, 0.0f, 0.0f), Color.LightGray);
    mVertWall[3] = new VertexPositionColor(                     // top L
    new Vector3(BOUNDARY / 2.0f, 2.0f, 0.0f), Color.LightGray);
}
```

To load the vertex data for each bird and the wall when the program begins, call init_bird0(), init_bird1(), and init_wall() from the Initialize() method.

```
init_bird0();
init_bird1();
init_wall();
```

A collision class will be used to track the position, speed, radius, and angle about the Y axis for each bird and the wall. You can add the class by right-clicking the project name in the Solution Explorer and choosing *Add,* then *New Item.* Next, select the *Class* icon and type **Collision.cs** in the *Name* textbox. When you click the *Add* button, GSE will generate the Collision class file with a class shell.

In this example, you will use vectors for storage in the Collision class, so the Microsoft.Xna.Framework code namespace must be included at the top of Collision.cs:

```
using Microsoft.Xna.Framework;
```

To ensure that your collision detection is realistic, it is necessary for you to track the radius and position of all collision objects in every frame. This allows you to determine whether any two radii make contact with each other. You will also add speed and rotation properties so that you can translate the objects, reverse their direction when a collision is detected, and make them point in that direction when they move. Adding this code inside the new Collision class enables storage of the position, speed, sphere radius, and the rotation angle for each collision object:

```
public Vector3   pos;
public Vector3   speed;
public float     radius;
public float     yrotation;


// constructor
public Collision(){
    // defaults - set the speed to 0 for stationary objects
    speed       = new Vector3(0.0f, 0.0f, 0.0f);
    yrotation   = 0.0f;
}
```

Creating collision-tracking objects, in the game class, requires a reference to the Collision class, so the namespace must be added at the top of the game class with the other namespace references:

```
using MGHBook;
```

In this example, an array is used to track all of the collision-tracking objects—a collision object will be created for each bird and the wall. Definitions are also required to identify each individual collision object in the array, and to track the total number of objects. Adding these declarations to the module level of the game class will make the collision objects and identifiers available to the entire class.

```
const int BIRD0 = 0; const int BIRD1 = 1; const int WALL = 2;
const int NUMCOLLIDER              = 3;
const int NUMBIRDS                 = 2;
private Collision[] collider       = new Collision[NUMCOLLIDER];
```

Each object is given a position, speed, and radius when they are created. A default speed of X=0, Y=0, and Z=0 is assigned in the constructor. Stationary objects, such as the wall, have zero speed, so they are assigned the 0 default. Add the init_collision_objects() method to your game class to set up collision-tracking objects for the two birds and the wall:

```
public void init_collision_objects(){
    collider[BIRD0]         = new Collision();
    collider[BIRD0].radius = 0.1f;
    collider[BIRD0].speed  = new Vector3(0.7f, 0.0f, -0.9f);
    collider[BIRD0].pos    = new Vector3(-2.0f, 0.2f, 3.0f);

    collider[BIRD1]         = new Collision();
    collider[BIRD1].radius = 0.1f;
    collider[BIRD1].speed  = new Vector3(-0.8f, 0.0f, -0.8f);
    collider[BIRD1].pos    = new Vector3( 0.0f, 0.2f, 3.0f);

    collider[WALL]          = new Collision();
    collider[WALL].radius  = BOUNDARY / 2.0f;
    collider[WALL].pos     = new Vector3(BOUNDARY/2.0f,0.0f,BOUNDARY/3.0f);
}
```

Ensure the collision objects are initialized when the program begins by calling init_collision_objects() from the Initialize() method:

```
init_collision_objects();
```

Next, the draw_wall() method is required in the game class to render the wall from the vertices that were created earlier:

```
private void draw_wall(int i){
    // 1: declare matrices
    Matrix matIdentity, matTransl;

    // 2: initialize matrices
    matIdentity = Matrix.Identity; // always start with identity matrix
    matTransl   = Matrix.CreateTranslation(
                collider[i].pos.X, -0.9f, collider[i].pos.Z);

    // 3: build cumulative world matrix using I.S.R.O.T. sequence
    // identity, scale, rotate, orbit(translate & rotate), translate
    mMatWorld = matIdentity * matTransl;
```

```
    // 4: pass wvp matrix to shader
    worldViewProjParam.SetValue(mMatWorld * mMatView * mMatProj);
    mfx.CommitChanges();

    // 5: draw object - select vertex type, primitive type, # of primitives
    gfx.GraphicsDevice.VertexDeclaration = mVertPosColor;
    gfx.GraphicsDevice.DrawUserPrimitives<VertexPositionColor>(
                    PrimitiveType.TriangleStrip, mVertWall, 0, 2);
}
```

When drawing the birds, you use the same triangle to draw both wings. To make the wings flap, variables that track the wing tip's rotation angle on the Z axis and the wing's up or down direction are required in the module area of the game class:

```
private float mfWingTip = 0.0f; // flap angle about Z axis
private bool  mbWingUp  = true; // up or down direction
```

The routine loops twice to draw both wings. A rotation of π radians about the Y axis is applied during the second loop to draw the second wing on the side that is opposite to the first. Add the draw_bird() method to render both wings and to create their flying and flapping animation:

```
private void draw_bird(VertexPositionColor[] vertBird, int j){
    // 1: declare matrices
    Matrix matIdentity, matTransl, matRotZ, matRotY, matYDir;

    // 2: initialize matrices
    matIdentity = Matrix.Identity;  // initialize with identity matrix
    matTransl   = Matrix.CreateTranslation(
                  collider[j].pos.X, collider[j].pos.Y, collider[j].pos.Z);
    matYDir     = Matrix.CreateRotationY(collider[j].yrotation);
    matRotZ     = Matrix.CreateRotationZ(mfWingTip);

    for (int i = 0; i < 2; i++){     // draw both wings
        if(i==0) // draw first wing
                matRotY = Matrix.CreateRotationY(0.0f);
        else     // draw second wing (rotated 180 Degrees about Y)
                matRotY = Matrix.CreateRotationY((float)Math.PI);

        // 3: build cumulative world matrix using I.S.R.O.T. sequence
        // identity, scale, rotate, orbit(translate & rotate), translate
            mMatWorld = matIdentity*matRotZ*matRotY*matYDir*matTransl;
```

```
        // 4: pass wvp matrix to shader
        worldViewProjParam.SetValue(mMatWorld * mMatView * mMatProj);
        mfx.CommitChanges();

        // 5: draw object-select vertex type, primitive type, # primitives
        gfx.GraphicsDevice.VertexDeclaration = mVertPosColor;
        gfx.GraphicsDevice.DrawUserPrimitives<VertexPositionColor>(
                        PrimitiveType.TriangleStrip, vertBird, 0, 1);
    }
}
```

The code to draw the wall and birds is triggered from Draw() between the Begin()
and End() methods for the BasicShader.fx file. Add these call statements to render
each object:

```
draw_wall(WALL);
draw_bird(mVertBird0, BIRD0);
draw_bird(mVertBird1, BIRD1);
```

If you run this code, the birds and wall will appear, but nothing will move. Some
extra code is required to animate the birds and to implement the collision detection.

To animate the birds, you need code to translate them, keep them within the
boundaries of the world, flap their wings, and ensure they point in the right direction.
Add the animate_birds() method to your game class to perform these tasks:

```
void animate_birds(GameTime gameTime){
    float fTimeLapse= (float)gameTime.ElapsedGameTime.Milliseconds/1000.0f;

    // increment position to create animation
    for (int i = 0; i < NUMBIRDS; i++){
        // scale increment by time between frames to keep speed constant
        // and system independent
        collider[i].pos += collider[i].speed * fTimeLapse;

        // if boundaries of world exceeded reverse the direction
        if (collider[i].pos.Z > BOUNDARY || collider[i].pos.Z < -BOUNDARY)
            collider[i].speed.Z = -collider[i].speed.Z;
        if (collider[i].pos.X > BOUNDARY || collider[i].pos.X < -BOUNDARY)
            collider[i].speed.X = -collider[i].speed.X;

        // point bird in direction that it moves
        // use change in X and Z to get rotation about the Y axis
```

```
        if(collider[i].speed.Z != 0) // prevent divide by zero
            collider[i].yrotation = (float)Math.Atan(collider[i].speed.X
                                          / collider[i].speed.Z);
        update_wingtip(gameTime);
    }
}
```

Remember that when you are checking for collisions between two bounding spheres, a collision is detected when the distance between the two collision objects is less than the sum of their radii. The collision checking is performed in a nested loop that checks each collision-tracking object with all other collision-tracking objects. Add check_collisions() to implement this routine:

```
void check_collisions(){
    // compare object with all others and reverse direction if collision
    for (int i = 0; i < NUMCOLLIDER - 1; i++)
        for (int j = i + 1; j < NUMCOLLIDER; j++){
            Vector3 v3Distance = collider[i].pos - collider[j].pos;
            if ( v3Distance.Length()
                 < collider[i].radius + collider[j].radius )
                reverse_direction(i, j);
        }
}
```

When collisions are detected for the birds, their directions will be reversed. Of course, reversing the wall's speed has no effect because the speed of a stationary object is zero anyway. Add the reverse_direction() method to your game class to provide code that negates the speed of the collision objects when collisions are detected:

```
void reverse_direction(int i, int j){
    collider[i].speed.X *= -1.0f; collider[i].speed.Z *= -1.0f;
    collider[j].speed.X *= -1.0f; collider[j].speed.Z *= -1.0f;
}
```

To create a wing-flapping animation, add the update_wingtip() method to your game class to increment or decrement the rotation angle of each wing about the Z axis. A time-scaled increment or decrement is applied based on whether the wing is moving upward or downward. When the upper maximum or lower minimum rotation angle about Z is reached, the direction is reversed.

```
void update_wingtip(GameTime gameTime){
    const float WINGSPEED = 2.5f;
    const float WINGLIMIT = 0.5f;
```

```
float fTimeLapse= (float)gameTime.ElapsedGameTime.Milliseconds/1000.0f;

if (mbWingUp && mfWingTip > WINGLIMIT)
    mbWingUp = false;                // reverse if upper max
else if (mbWingUp == false && mfWingTip < -WINGLIMIT)
    mbWingUp = true;                 // reverse if lower min

// position wing tip by incrementing it each frame
// scale the increment by a time lapse between frames to keep
// speed constant regardless of system running this program
if (mbWingUp)
    mfWingTip += WINGSPEED * fTimeLapse;
else
    mfWingTip -= WINGSPEED * fTimeLapse;
}
```

To animate the collision objects and to check for their collisions each frame, call animate_birds() and check_collisions() from the Update() method:

```
animate_birds(gameTime);
check_collisions();
```

When you run this version of the example, you will see two birds flying. When the birds are close to each other, they reverse their directions to avoid a collision. When the birds are near the gray wall, they also reverse their direction to avoid flying into the wall.

As you can see, with a small amount of code, implementing collision detection using bounding spheres is simple.

COLLISION DETECTION BETWEEN A SPHERE AND A PLANE

A bounding sphere algorithm may provide accurate enough collision detection for round objects, or for small, fast-moving objects—such as a bullet—but it is not effective for larger rectangular objects. Maybe you have an 18-wheeler truck driving through your world; this truck is not going to fit nicely inside a sphere. Or maybe you have buildings with large stone walls. You want to stop your camera from traveling through these walls, and you don't want your birds to fly through them either. A bounding sphere around your brick walls leaves too much wasted space. From a gamer's perspective, a poorly applied bounding sphere will result in false collisions. It could mean that a missed shot counts as a hit, or an object might seem to be surrounded by an invisible force field.

To remedy this problem, you can implement collision detection between a sphere and a plane. For large rectangular objects, and even more complex shapes that do not fit nicely in a sphere, this next type of collision detection is more suitable—a series of lines to establish the bounding planes can be set around the object to enable collision detection. This algorithm calculates the point on the collision plane that is closest to the sphere center. The distance between the sphere and the closest point on the line is then compared to the sphere radius to determine whether a collision has occurred.

Implementing the Sphere and Plane Collision-Detection Routine

When implementing the bounding sphere and plane algorithm, you first need to set up planes by defining collision lines around the objects that need detection. Then you add bounding spheres around the objects that you don't want to cross these lines—such as the camera. Each frame, every line is checked to determine whether a sphere overlaps it.

The point of intersection, *t*, on the collision vector, *Vcl1*, represents the closest point between the sphere and the collision line. A line drawn from the closest point on the collision line to the sphere by definition is a normal. Two instances when this definition is not true are when the sphere is closest to the starting point of the collision line or when the sphere is closest to the ending point of the collision line. Figure 16-2 shows the location of the intersect, t, between the perpendicular from the collision line to the sphere.

To obtain this value for t, the sphere vector, *Vsp1*, is scaled by the length of the line vector. The result from this scaling calculation expresses the sphere vector, also known as a *ray*, as a fraction of the line vector length. When the X and Z components of the scaled sphere vector are multiplied by the unit direction of the line vector, you end up with the point of intersection on the line vector. To simplify these calcula-

FIGURE 16-2

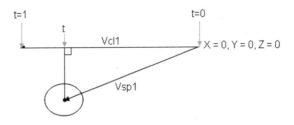

Intersect t of perpendicular from collision line to sphere

tions, the sphere vector and the line vector have been expressed as rays that start at the origin:

```
Vsp_Scaled      = Vsp1 / Vcl_Length
V_CollisionUnit = Normalize(Vcl)
t               = Vsp_Scaled.X * V_CollisionUnit.X + Vsp_Scaled.Z * V_CollisionUnit.Z
```

The intersection, t, indicates the percentage of the collision line where the intersection is made.

Checking for Collisions When 0 < t < 1

When $0 < t < 1$, the distance between the collision line and the sphere center is at a minimum. In this case, this distance is compared with the sphere radius to check for collisions. Figure 16-3 demonstrates collision detection when the intersection falls between the beginning and ending of the collision line vector.

Checking for Collisions When t < 0

When the sphere's center precedes the start of the line vector, the intersect, t, is less than zero. When $t < 0$, the distance between the sphere center and the origin is compared with the sphere radius. If the distance is less than the radius, a collision is detected. Figure 16-4 shows this case where the sphere's relative position is before the origin.

FIGURE 16-3

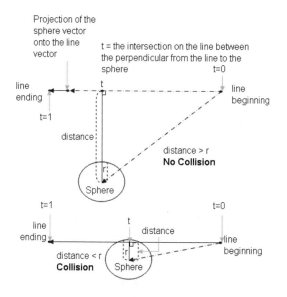

Collision detection when 0 < t < 1

FIGURE 16-4

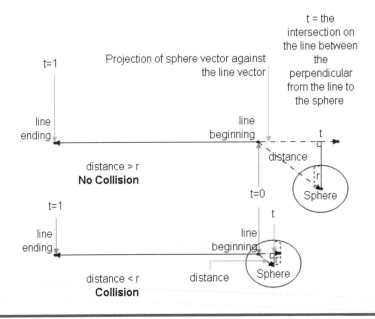

Collision detection when t < 0

Checking for Collisions When t > 1

When the sphere is positioned after the line, the closest point of intersection is calculated by taking the difference between the sphere center and the end of the collision line vector. In this case, t will be greater than 1 because the vector to the sphere is projected to a point that falls after the line vector. Figure 16-5 shows how collisions are detected when t > 1.

Collision Detection Using Lines and Spheres

This example modifies the solution from the previous example to implement a sphere and plane collision-detection algorithm. This sphere and plane routine will implement better collision detection to check if the bird, or camera, collides with the four outer world boundaries or the left middle wall. The bounding spheres algorithm already effectively handles collision detection when the two birds collide with each other, so you can leave that code untouched.

A line array is needed to store the starting and ending points for each of the four world boundaries and for the middle left wall. Then, at each frame, the bounding spheres around the camera and around each bird are checked to ensure there is no

FIGURE 16-5

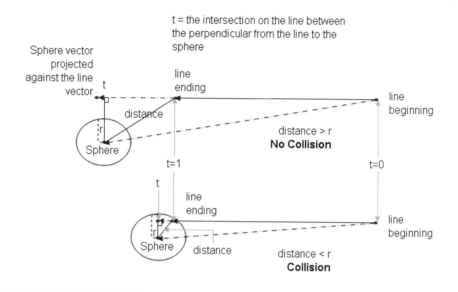

t = the intersection on the line between the perpendicular from the line to the sphere

Collision detection when t > 1

overlap with any collision lines in the array. If the sphere around the camera touches one of the five lines, it will be pushed back to prevent it from going through the object. Also, if one of the birds hits one of these five lines, the bird's direction will be reversed.

Identifiers are needed at the top of the game class to reference the arrays storing the collision line coordinates:

```
const int NUMLINES = 5;
private Vector3[] mv3LineBeg = new Vector3[NUMLINES];
private Vector3[] mv3LineEnd = new Vector3[NUMLINES];
```

The arrays that store the collision line coordinates are initialized in the init_collision_lines() method. Note that the starting and ending points for each line must be arranged so that the difference between the ending coordinate and the starting coordinate yields a positive result.

Add init_collision_lines() to store the end points for each of the five lines:

```
public void init_collision_lines(){
    // keep user from going over edge of world
    const float kfLine = 1.0f * BOUNDARY;

    mv3LineBeg[0].X = -kfLine; mv3LineBeg[0].Z = -kfLine;  //R front
```

```
mv3LineEnd[0].X = -kfLine; mv3LineEnd[0].Z =  kfLine;   //R back
mv3LineBeg[1].X =  kfLine; mv3LineBeg[1].Z = -kfLine;   //L front
mv3LineEnd[1].X =  kfLine; mv3LineEnd[1].Z =  kfLine;   //L back
mv3LineBeg[2].X = -kfLine; mv3LineBeg[2].Z = -kfLine;   //F right
mv3LineEnd[2].X =  kfLine; mv3LineEnd[2].Z = -kfLine;   //F left
mv3LineBeg[3].X = -kfLine; mv3LineBeg[3].Z =  kfLine;   //B right
mv3LineEnd[3].X =  kfLine; mv3LineEnd[3].Z =  kfLine;   //B left

// set up line where gray wall is located
mv3LineBeg[4].X = 0.0f;        mv3LineBeg[4].Z = BOUNDARY / 3.0f;
mv3LineEnd[4].X = BOUNDARY;    mv3LineEnd[4].Z = BOUNDARY / 3.0f;
}
```

To ensure the line arrays are loaded when the program begins, call init_collision_lines() from the Initialize() method:

```
init_collision_lines();
```

This next block of code implements the algorithm explained earlier in the "Implementing the Sphere and Plane Collision-Detection Routine" section of this chapter. The code scales the vector to the sphere by the length of the collision line. Then, the X and Z components of the scaled vector are each multiplied by the unit X and Z directions stored in the normalized line collision vector. The X and Z products are summed to give the point of intersection of the perpendicular on the collision line that runs to the sphere center. Three cases are considered. If $t < 0$, a collision is detected when the sphere radius is greater than the distance between the sphere and the origin. If $0 < t < 1$, a collision is detected if the sphere radius is greater than the distance between the sphere center and t. If $t > 1$, a collision is detected if the radius is greater than the distance between the sphere center and the end of the collision line. Add the is_line_collision() method to check if any bounding spheres collide with any of the collision lines:

```
bool is_line_collision(int i, float x, float z, float radius){
    float t;                            // line intersect (%)
    Vector3 v3Line, v3UnitLine;         // line vector from origin
    v3Line = v3UnitLine = mv3LineEnd[i] - mv3LineBeg[i];

    Vector3 v3SphereAbs = new Vector3(x, 0, z);       //original position
    Vector3 v3SphereRel = v3SphereAbs - mv3LineBeg[i]; //rel to line at 000

    // vector to sphere / line len ( remember len = sqrt(x^2 + y^2 + z^2) )
    Vector3 v3SphereScaled = v3SphereRel / v3Line.Length();

    v3UnitLine.Normalize();                            // line unit vector
```

```
    // intersect on line (in %) between line perpendicular and sphere ctr
    t = v3SphereScaled.X * v3UnitLine.X + v3SphereScaled.Z * v3UnitLine.Z;

    Vector3 v3Distance;                                 // distance to line

    if (t < 0)        // sphere precedes line vector
        v3Distance = v3SphereAbs - mv3LineBeg[i];
    else if (t > 1) // sphere follows line vector
        v3Distance = v3SphereAbs - mv3LineEnd[i];
    else{           // intersect falls somewhere on the line vector
        Vector3 v3intersect = mv3LineBeg[i] + t * v3Line;// abs intersect
        v3Distance = v3SphereAbs - v3intersect;         // distance
    }

    if (v3Distance.Length() < radius)                   // if distance < r
        return true;                                    // collision
    return false;                                       // no collision
}
```

To add code that checks whether the birds collide with the collision lines, replace the check_collisions() method with this new version. The bounding spheres algorithm is left to check whether the birds collide because the algorithm is efficient for that case.

```
void check_collisions(){
    // compare birds and reverse direction if collision
    for (int i = 0; i < NUMBIRDS; i++)
        for (int j = i + 1; j < NUMBIRDS; j++){
            Vector3 v3Distance = collider[i].pos - collider[j].pos;
            if (v3Distance.Length()
                < collider[i].radius + collider[j].radius)
                reverse_direction(i, j);
        }
    // compare birds with lines at wall and outer boundaries
    for (int i = 0; i < NUMBIRDS; i++)
        for (int j = 0; j < NUMLINES; j++){
            if (is_line_collision(j, collider[i].pos.X, collider[i].pos.Z,
                collider[i].radius))
                reverse_direction(i); // reverse direction if hit
        }
}
```

Because the birds are being checked individually for collisions between each of the outer boundaries and the left wall, an overloaded reverse_direction() method is required in the game class to prevent them from flying through the line:

```
void reverse_direction(int i){
    collider[i].speed.X *= -1.0f; collider[i].speed.Z *= -1.0f;
}
```

The code that checks for collisions between the camera and each of the lines is triggered whenever the game player moves forward, backward, or strafes to the side. If a collision is detected, the user is forced to move back by the same amount in the opposite direction. Adding the handle_camera_collision() method to the game class allows you to prevent the camera from moving through a line:

```
void handle_camera_collision(float fMoveAmount, bool bStrafe){
    for (int i = 0; i < NUMLINES; i++){
        // if border hit move the user back
        if (is_line_collision(i, cam.m_vPos.X, cam.m_vPos.Z, 0.2f)){
            if(!bStrafe)
                cam.move(-fMoveAmount);
            else
                cam.strafe(-fMoveAmount);
            break;
        }
    }
}
```

Collisions are triggered when the player moves forward or backward using the up or down arrow key on the keyboard, or when strafing sideways with the right or left arrow key. When the game pad is used, shifting the left thumbstick up and down will trigger forward and backward movement. Shifting the thumbstick to the side will trigger a strafe sideways. The code to detect a collision between the camera and the line must be called from the Update () method. If a collision is detected, the camera will be forced back in the opposite direction. Replace the existing instructions to move the camera and strafe the camera in Update() with this revision to force the user back if the camera collides with the wall or boundary of the world:

```
float    fMove;            // store amount of movement back & forth or side
bool     bStrafe = false;  // indicate if strafe is being checked

// handle forwards and backwards movement
fMove = move();
```

```
cam.move(fMove);
handle_camera_collision(fMove, bStrafe);

// handle sideways movement
bStrafe = true;
fMove = strafe();
cam.strafe(fMove);
handle_camera_collision(fMove, bStrafe);
```

When you run this version of the code, your camera will no longer travel past the wall or the boundaries of the world. Also, the birds will not fly into each other and they will not fly into the wall or past the outer boundaries of the world. Using lines to detect collisions with spheres offers a better fit for rectangular and irregular shapes.

As discussed in this chapter, collision detection can be implemented in many different ways. Algorithms for implementing collision detection can range from simple to complex. For advanced collision detection, the algorithm may start with a simple check to see whether two objects are close to each other. Advanced algorithms can be called once a close proximity between objects has been established. If the objects are not in close proximity, the advanced algorithms can be skipped to save on processing time. The algorithms presented in this chapter are simple, but they offer a solid first line of collision checking and in most cases will provide all you need for detection.

CHAPTER 16 REVIEW EXERCISES

1. Try the step-by-step examples discussed in this chapter.

2. After completing the example of collision detection using lines and a sphere, add a black bird that is larger than the first two. Be sure to adjust the size of the radius about the bird and ensure collision detection is implemented so that it does not fly through the other birds. Also, be sure to adjust the code so the bird does not fly though the wall or the outer boundaries of the world.

3. Add a diagonal wall across one of the corners of the world and create a collision line to prevent the birds and camera from traveling past this wall.

CHAPTER 17

Ballistics

BALLISTICS

describes the flight of projectiles. When considering ballistics in the context of a game, you might think of obvious choices such as grenades, bullets, cannon balls, or rockets. Ballistics could even include throwing bananas, shooting squirt guns, or throwing baseballs. Regardless of the implementation, ballistics certainly will liven up your game.

This chapter explains two common ballistics algorithms. The first algorithm, referred to as the *Linear Projectile algorithm,* provides a routine for launching a fast-moving projectile where its speed on the X, Y, and Z planes remains constant. This first algorithm is suitable for projecting a laser beam, a bullet, or an extremely fast-moving missile that only needs to be shown over a short range. The second algorithm, referred to in this book as the *Arcing Projectile algorithm,* builds on the first algorithm. The difference is that the second algorithm considers the gravitational pull that acts on the projectile until it hits the ground.

LINEAR PROJECTILES

The Linear Projectile algorithm works under the assumption that the projectile will maintain a constant speed on the X, Y, and Z planes until the object is out of sight. For example, Figure 17-1 shows rockets flying in a linear path from the camera.

FIGURE 17-1

When the projectile is launched, the linear projectile travels in a path that follows the camera's Look direction. The Look vector gives us constant speeds for X, Y, and Z. Remember from Chapter 15, "Building a Graphics Engine Camera," the Look direction vector equals the difference between the View position vector and the camera position vector.

The initial rate of change (in distance over time on the X, Y, and Z planes) when a projectile takes flight is known as the launch speed. Launch speed is based on the Look direction to ensure the object projects outward from the camera toward the target. The total launch speed is scaled by each Look vector component in each of the corresponding X, Y, and Z planes. Figure 17-2 illustrates how the individual velocity components are derived.

Rockets following a linear path with a constant speed and direction

FIGURE 17-2

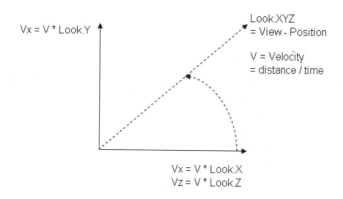

$$Vx = V * Look.Y$$

Look.XYZ
= View - Position

V = Velocity
= distance / time

$$Vx = V * Look.X$$
$$Vz = V * Look.Z$$

Deriving X, Y, and Z velocities using the Look direction

At every frame during the projectile's flight, the position of the projectile is updated by summing the projectile's current position with the projectile velocity multiplied by time, as shown here:

$$\text{Projectile Position}_{xyz} = \text{Launch Position}_{xyz} + \text{Velocity}_{xyz} * \text{Time}$$

ARCING PROJECTILE

The Linear Projectile routine only works for bullets or other objects that appear to fly in a straight line. For events where the effects of gravity are apparent—such as a catapult launch or a grenade toss—the Arcing Projectile algorithm is needed to make the ballistic look real and to give the player control over the trajectory, height, and distance traveled. Higher launch speeds and trajectories help to overcome gravity, and ensure that the ballistic has a longer flight before hitting the ground.

Figure 17-3 shows several rockets at various elevations (on the Y axis) and at different stages of flight. Over time, the projectiles lose momentum and gravity pulls them to the ground. The overall effect creates a nice arcing projectile path.

FIGURE 17-3

Considering the effect of gravity over time

Game developers will often use real-world physics to create more realistic graphics effects. The physical properties that they consider may include gravity, friction, force, velocity, acceleration, viscosity, and much more. In case you're wondering, game development companies will often implement pseudo-physics in their algorithms. As long as the effect looks correct and is efficient, an approximation of the laws of physics is usually the faster and more effective alternative. After all, as a simulation approaches reality, it can become so complex that it loses its value. However, even when the code deviates from the laws of physics, realistic algorithms usually consider some portion of the real physical model.

Once the launch velocity and direction have been obtained, the effect of gravity can be computed and the X, Y, and Z positions of the projectile can be calculated over time. The X and Z positions are calculated using the same equations as the Linear Projectile algorithm to obtain the projectile's position over time:

$$X_t = X_{start} + V_x * t$$
$$Z_t = Z_{start} + V_z * t$$

The Arcing Projectile algorithm treats the calculation of the Y position over time as a special case that also considers gravity. Initially, the projectile's velocity is powerful enough to defy gravity—otherwise, there would insufficient energy to launch the projectile into the air. However, over time, the projectile loses its momentum and gravity becomes the strongest force on the object. This gravitational pull is defined by a constant value of acceleration, g, which represents the Earth's gravity. The accepted value for g equals 9.8 meters / second ^{2} (32 ft/s^2). After the Earth's gravity is factored in, the equation used for calculating the Y position over time becomes:

$$Y_t = Y_{start} + V_y * t - 0.5 * g * t^2$$

Implementing these projectile algorithms in code is simple. The first example in this chapter implements the Linear Projectile algorithm. Then, in the example that follows, the Linear Projectile algorithm is converted into an Arcing Projectile algorithm.

LINEAR PROJECTILES EXAMPLE

This example demonstrates how to add in projectiles that can be launched on a linear path from a rocket launcher, as shown back in Figure 17-1.

In this example, you will shoot ten rockets into the air at a time. When a trigger or spacebar event occurs, the first available rocket (that is not already in flight) is launched. At the time of launch, the rocket is given a position, speed, and direction to start it on an outward journey from the tip of the rocket launcher. The rocket launcher's position and direction are based on the camera's current position and Look direction. Also, during the launch, the activation state for the projectile is set to true, and remains set to true until the projectile reaches the end of the path. The activation state prevents the projectile from being reused while it is in flight. The projectile properties are reset every time the projectile is launched.

This example begins with either the WinMGHBook or Xbox360MGHBook project located in the BaseCode folder of the book's download available from the website.

You will create a Projectile class to assist with the implementation of your projectiles. You will use Projectile to keep track of each rocket and to update its position. The Projectile class can be created from scratch in the Solution Explorer. To generate it, right-click the project and choose *Add New Item*. Then, choose the Class icon and enter **Projectile.cs** as the Name in the *Add New Item* dialog. When you click *Add*, GSE will generate a shell for your Projectile class.

The Projectile class needs to perform vector calculations that determine direction and speed, so a reference to Microsoft.Xna.Framework is required at the top of the Projectile.cs file:

```
using Microsoft.Xna.Framework;
```

Module-level declarations are also required for storing the position, direction, angle, and activation state of each projectile. An additional variable, for storing the size of the world, enables a check to determine whether the projectile has flown out of sight. This tells you when to deactivate the projectile. To allow access to these variables throughout the class, we place their declarations at the top of the Projectile class:

```
public   Vector3 mv3Pos, mv3PosPrev;// position of projectile
public   Vector3 mv3Dir;            // direction of projectile on x,y,z
public   bool    mbActive;          // active or inactive state
public   float   mfRotation;        // rotation about X axis
private  float   mfBoundary;        // + & - edge of world on x and z
public   Matrix  mmatDir;           // direction matrix
```

When the program begins, each projectile needs to be created only once. After they are created, the projectiles remain inactive until the user launches them. Later, you will add a method to deactivate a projectile when it flies past the boundaries of the world. To set the projectile flight range and activation state when the projectile is initialized, add this constructor to the Projectile class:

```
public Projectile(float fBoundary){
    mfBoundary  = fBoundary;
    mbActive    = false;
}
```

The projectile's position, direction, and activation state are set according to the camera's position and Look direction at the time of the launch. The rocket is angled about the X axis according to the angle used by the rocket launcher. Including the stage_projectile() method in the Projectile class will enable proper initialization of these attributes during the launch.

```
public void stage_projectile(Vector3 v3Look,Vector3 v3Start,float fRotX){
    mv3Pos       = v3Start;                    // starting xyz = camera xyz
    mv3Dir       = Vector3.Normalize(v3Look);// unitize it
    mfRotation   = fRotX;
    mbActive     = true;
}
```

As discussed in Chapter 6, "Character Movement," an object's direction can be calculated from the object's speed vector. Adding setDirectionMatrix() to your Projectile class will provide the method you need to make your rocket point in the direction it is traveling. This routine applies to both the Linear Projectile algorithm and the Arcing Projectile algorithm. For the Linear Projectile algorithm, the rocket direction remains constant as the rocket travels outwards. For the Arcing Projectile algorithm, setDirectionMatrix() will launch the rocket with the original launcher direction and then it will gradually drop the rocket, nose downwards, as the gravitational pull takes over:

```
public void setDirectionMatrix(){
    // speed = difference between current and past position
    Vector3 v3Speed = mv3Pos - mv3PosPrev;

    Vector3 v3L = v3Speed;                     // look vector
    v3L.Normalize();

    Vector3 v3U = new Vector3(0.0f, 1.0f, 0.0f);// up vector
    v3U.Normalize();

    Vector3 v3R = Vector3.Cross(v3U, v3L);     // right vector
    v3R.Normalize();

    Matrix mat = new Matrix(); // compute direction matrix
    mat.M11=v3R.X; mat.M12=v3R.Y; mat.M13=v3R.Z; mat.M14=0.0f; //Right
    mat.M21=v3U.X; mat.M22=v3U.Y; mat.M23=v3U.Z; mat.M24=0.0f; //Up
    mat.M31=v3L.X; mat.M32=v3L.Y; mat.M33=v3L.Z; mat.M34=0.0f; //Look
    mat.M41=0.0f;  mat.M42=0.0f;  mat.M43=0.0f;  mat.M44=1.0f;
    mmatDir = mat;
}
```

The projectile's position is updated before being drawn each frame. Also, in every frame, the projectile's position is incremented by a time-scaled direction vector,

FIGURE 17-4

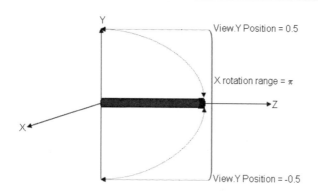

Rocket launcher rotation range around the X axis

The launcher must also be rotated about the Y axis to match the camera's Look direction about the Y axis. And finally, to finish the transformation using the I.S.R.O.T. sequence, the launcher must be translated by an amount that is equivalent to the distance from the origin to the camera. An extra shift downward on the Y axis is added to this translation to move the launcher downward slightly so it does not block your view.

Add draw_launcher() to your game class to move and rotate the rocket launcher with your camera:

```
private void draw_launcher(Model model){
    // 1: declare matrices
    Matrix matIdent, matTransl, matScale, matRotX, matRotY;

    // 2: initialize matrices
    matIdent  = Matrix.Identity; // always start with identity matrix
    matScale  = Matrix.CreateScale(0.20f, 0.20f, 0.20f);
    matTransl = Matrix.CreateTranslation(cam.m_vPos.X, -0.3f,cam.m_vPos.Z);
    matRotX   = Matrix.CreateRotationX(-(float)Math.PI * cam.m_vView.Y);
    Vector3 v3Look = cam.m_vView - cam.m_vPos;
    matRotY = Matrix.CreateRotationY((float)Math.Atan2(v3Look.X,v3Look.Z));

    foreach (ModelMesh mesh in model.Meshes){
        // 3: build cumulative matrix using I.S.R.O.T. sequence
        // identity,scale,rotate,orbit(translate & rotate),translate
        mMatWorld = matIdent * matScale * matRotX * matRotY * matTransl;
```

```
foreach (BasicEffect effect in mesh.Effects){
    effect.World      =matLauncher[mesh.ParentBone.Index]*mMatWorld;
    effect.View       =mMatView;
    effect.Projection=mMatProj;

    // 4b. set lighting
    effect.EnableDefaultLighting();
    effect.SpecularPower    = 0.01f;
    effect.CommitChanges();
}
// 5: draw object
mesh.Draw();
    }
}
```

To actually see the rocket launcher, you obviously need to call the method to draw it. Adding draw_launcher() to the end of the Draw() method will draw the rocket when other objects are rendered:

```
draw_launcher(mModLauncher);
```

Because the rocket launcher's rotation angle about the X axis changes with the view position on Y, if the right thumbstick or mouse shifts the view all the way up or all the way down, you can actually see the base of the launcher, which spoils the effect. Inside the camera class in the update_camera_view() method, you'll replace the code that caps the Y view position so it can no longer exceed 0.20 or fall below –0.10, which prevents you from pointing the launcher into the ground. The end result is whatever angle you point, it looks as though you are always holding the rocket launcher:

```
if (qNewView.Y > -0.10f && qNewView.Y < 0.20f)
```

At this point, the projectile objects are initialized and your launcher is in place. Your rockets are ready, but a mechanism is required to trigger their launch. In this case, you will add code to initiate their launch when the left mouse button is pressed, or when the right trigger on the controller is pressed. To ensure that all ten rockets are not launched during this press event—which lasts over several frames—a time delay between launches is added. The time delay allows the user enough time to press and release the trigger so that only one projectile is launched at a time. To enable the time delay, you must add a declaration for a *GameTime* variable and a *double* variable at the top of the game class to store the time of the last press event:

```
private GameTime        mgameTime;
private double          mdblLastPress;
```

The projectile trigger events can now be handled at the end of the Update() method. In this block of code, you will add a delay of 250 milliseconds to the user's input. This delay allows the user time to press and release the trigger or left-click the mouse to launch one projectile during this period.

```
if ((GamePad.GetState(PlayerIndex.One).Triggers.Right > 0
#if !XBOX
 || // check left-click mouse event only on PC - won't work on xbox
    mMouse.LeftButton == ButtonState.Pressed
#endif // provide 250 ms delay before next launch
 ) && mgameTime.TotalGameTime.TotalMilliseconds - mdblLastPress > 250){
    mdblLastPress = mgameTime.TotalGameTime.TotalMilliseconds;
    launch_rocket();
}
```

The code that you use to launch the rocket (from the game class) is contained in the launch_rocket() method. This routine searches through the array of projectiles and finds the first inactive projectile available. When an inactive projectile is found, launch_rocket() sets the starting position and direction to equal the camera position and Look direction.

The transformations use the I.S.R.O.T. sequence. Their implementation to angle and position the rocket at the tip of the launcher is summarized in Figure 17-5.

The starting position is needed to help track the location of each rocket. To create the required transformation, and record the initial starting position of the rocket, we can use the Matrix math discussed in Chapter 14, "Matrices." Once the starting position is computed using matrices, the first row of the matrix that contains the position information is stored in a vector. This position vector can be used later to update

FIGURE 17-5

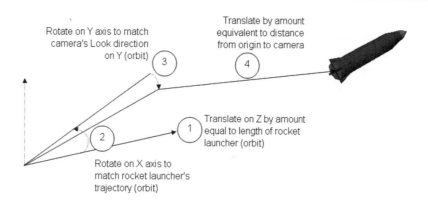

Calculating the launch direction and angle of the rocket

the position of the rocket by incrementing the position by a time-scaled direction vector. As you can see, it really does pay to understand how to employ linear algebra beyond just using the Matrix objects and methods that are shipped with XNA.

Add launch_rocket() to your game class to find the first available rocket when a launch is triggered and to calculate and store the starting position and direction of the rocket:

```
private void launch_rocket(){
for (int i = 0; i < NUM_ROCKETS; i++){
    if (mProj[i].mbActive == false){
        Matrix matTransOrb, matTransl, matRotX, matRotY, matPos;

        matPos = new Matrix(); // must be initialized for Xbox

        Vector3 v3Look = cam.m_vView - cam.m_vPos;       // look direction
                    // translate on Z by length of rocket
        matTransOrb = Matrix.CreateTranslation(0.0f, 0.0f, 1.25f);
        matTransl   = Matrix.CreateTranslation(cam.m_vPos.X, -0.34f,
                      cam.m_vPos.Z); // translate rocket to cam position
        matRotX     = Matrix.CreateRotationX(-(float)Math.PI *
                      cam.m_vView.Y);// match rotation of launcher about X
        matRotY     = Matrix.CreateRotationY((float)Math.Atan2(v3Look.X,
                      v3Look.Z));    // rotate about Y to match direction

        // rocket's starting position must be at the tip of the launcher
        // first use matrix to store origin vector in first row
        matPos.M11=0.0f; matPos.M12=0.0f; matPos.M13=0.0f; matPos.M14=1.0f;
            matPos.M21 = matPos.M22 = matPos.M23 = matPos.M24
        =   matPos.M31 = matPos.M32 = matPos.M33 = matPos.M34
        =   matPos.M41 = matPos.M42 = matPos.M43 = matPos.M44 = 0.0f;
        // this uses the I.S.R.O.T. sequence to get rocket start position
        matPos = matPos * matTransOrb * matRotX * matRotY * matTransl ;
        // convert from matrix back to vector so it can be used for updates
        Vector3 v3start = new Vector3(matPos.M11, matPos.M12, matPos.M13);

        float fRotX = -(float)Math.PI * cam.m_vView.Y +(float)Math.PI/2.0f;
        mProj[i].stage_projectile(v3Look, v3start , fRotX);

        break;
    }
}
}
```

Ballistics

In each frame, the locations of all projectiles must be updated so each can be animated properly along its trajectory path. The code used to trigger the update for each projectile position belongs at the end of the Update() method in the game class:

```
mgameTime = gameTime;


for(int i=0; i<NUM_ROCKETS; i++){
    if (mProj[i].mbActive)
        mProj[i].update_projectile(gameTime);
}
```

Only one method is used to draw each projectile. draw_rockets() loops through all projectile objects and translates the active ones to their current position. The details are explained in the comments:

```
private void draw_rockets(Model model){
    // 1: declare matrices
    Matrix matIdent, matScale, matRotX, matTransl;

    // 2: initialize matrices
    matIdent = Matrix.Identity;                        // default matrix
    matScale = Matrix.CreateScale(0.33f, 0.33f, 0.33f); // reduce size
    matRotX  = Matrix.CreateRotationX((float)Math.PI / 2.0f);// rotate on X

    for (int i = 0; i < NUM_ROCKETS; i++){
        if (mProj[i].mbActive){
        foreach (ModelMesh mesh in model.Meshes){
            matTransl    = Matrix.CreateTranslation(mProj[i].mv3Pos);

            // 3: build cumulative matrix using I.S.R.O.T. sequence
            // identity,scale,rotate,orbit(translate & rotate),translate

            mMatWorld = matScale * matRotX * mProj[i].mmatDir * matTransl;
            foreach (BasicEffect effect in mesh.Effects){
                // store matrices for transformation in BasicEffect shader
                effect.World  = matRocket[mesh.ParentBone.Index]*mMatWorld;
                effect.View      = mMatView;
                effect.Projection= mMatProj;

                // apply lighting using XNA's BasicEffect shader
                effect.EnableDefaultLighting();
                effect.SpecularPower = 16.5f;    // add highlights
```

```
                    effect.CommitChanges();
                }
                // 5: draw object
                mesh.Draw();
            }
        }
    }
}
```

To ensure projectiles are actually drawn, draw_rockets() needs to be called from the Draw() method:

```
draw_rockets(mModRocket);
```

When you compile and run this program, it shows the Linear Projectile algorithm in action. Whenever the left mouse button is pressed, or a game controller trigger is pulled, a rocket is launched. Each projectile shoots outward until it reaches an arbitrary boundary located at the outer limits of the world.

ARCING PROJECTILES EXAMPLE

This Arcing Projectiles example picks up where the Linear Projectile algorithm ends. When this example is complete, and the effect of gravity is factored in, the flight of each projectile will rise to a peak and then follow a descending path to the ground. Most of the code in this revised routine remains the same. However, the method that updates the rocket position will be replaced so that the gravitational pull over time is taken into consideration. To enable this revised method, we need an additional variable declaration for tracking time at the module level for the projectile class:

```
private    float    mfTime;          // time since launch
```

One extra line of code is needed in stage_projectile() to reset the time to *zero* when each projectile is launched.

```
mfTime = 0.0f;
```

Another significant change to the update_projectile() method involves placing code to factor in gravitational pull on the Y position over time. The equations used to change the X and Z positions remain the same as in the Linear Projectile algorithm:

$$mv3Pos.X \mathrel{+}= v3LookVel.X * mfTime;$$
$$mv3Pos.Z \mathrel{+}= v3LookVel.Z * mfTime;$$
$$mv3Pos.Y \mathrel{+}= v3LookVel.Y * mfTime$$
$$- 0.5f * kfGravity * mfTime * mfTime;$$

The setDirectionMatrix() adjusts the rocket's direction on the X and Y axes. The transformation matrix returned when calling this method from update_projectile() enables the rocket to shoot outward from the launcher at a suitable angle on the Y axis. In addition, the rocket is tilted on the X axis, so it points upward as it climbs and then lowers as the rocket descends to the ground.

Replace the existing update_projectile() method with this one to implement the change:

```
public void update_projectile(GameTime gameTime){
    const float kfGravity = 9.8f;    // 9.8 m/s^2
    float fvel            = 7.0f;    // 7.0 m/s

    // cumulative seconds - scaled to slow projectile down
    const float kfTimeScale = 4.0f;
    mfTime = mfTime + (float)(gameTime.ElapsedGameTime.Milliseconds)
            / (kfTimeScale * 1000);

    // velocity on x, y, and z
    Vector3 v3LookVel = mv3Dir * fvel;

    mv3PosPrev= mv3Pos; // store position at last frame

    // current position updated over time
    mv3Pos.X += v3LookVel.X * mfTime;
    mv3Pos.Z += v3LookVel.Z * mfTime;

    // increment on Y also affected by gravity
    float fY = v3LookVel.Y * mfTime
            - 0.5f * kfGravity * mfTime * mfTime;
    mv3Pos.Y += fY;
    setDirectionMatrix(); // generate matrix for direction angle

    // de-activate if projectile falls below ground level
    if (mv3Pos.Y < -1.0f)
        mbActive = false;
}
```

Running the program now shows the projectiles rising in an arc. When the peak is reached, they rotate gradually so they point downward and fall back to the ground. On reaching the ground, they are deactivated and made ready for the next launch.

Whether you are allowing your players to throw a ball or deploy weaponry, your ballistics are ready for launch.

CHAPTER 17 REVIEW EXERCISES

1. Follow the step-by-step examples shown in this chapter to implement the Linear Projectile algorithm and Arcing Projectile algorithm.

2. State how the projectile update routine for linear projectiles differs from that for arcing projectiles.

3. Replace the model rocket with your own 3D object and make it point in the direction that it travels. Add bounding sphere collision detection to an object in your world so something happens when you hit it.

CHAPTER 18

Particle Effects

PARTICLE algorithms enable effects such as rain, explosions, fire, smoke, sparkles, and much more. The effects created by the particle algorithm are only limited by your imagination. Compare the non-particle-based explosions in *Space Invaders* with an explosion that uses a particle algorithm—like a rocket explosion in id Software's *Quake*. *Quake*'s rocket effect is substantially more interesting.

A *particle* is a user-defined object that sets, stores, and updates properties for a group of related items. Each group or class of particles shares a similar but slightly randomized set of properties (for example, a group of rain particles, snow particles, fire particles, or smoke particles). Particles are usually assigned properties for life, size, color, position, and speed. As an example, a snowflake would have a starting position somewhere up in the sky, so the X and Z positions would be random but the starting position for Y would definitely be positive. The snow particle's life starts at the beginning of the particle's descent and ends when the snowflake reaches the ground. The snowflakes are small, but each one varies slightly in size. The snowflake's color property would be set to a shade of white. The snowflake's speed would definitely be negative on the Y axis, but the X and Z speeds are random. The Y speed of the snowflake particle is varied and slow enough to allow for the snow to drift to the ground.

There is no set syntax or rule for defining particles—they have different properties based on their implementation. Particles are usually regenerated on a continuous basis, but some randomization is normally present for creating a dynamic and ever-changing special effect.

When drawing particles, you often need transparency to remove background pixels. This generates the image you need for your effect—such as rain, fire, or an explosion. You could use billboarded triangle strips for this task, or you might consider using point sprites.

Because particle algorithms can be expensive in terms of system bandwidth, you should be careful not to create too many particles. Game developers use particle algorithms when they want to show off brilliant special effects, but when performance is an issue, they may choose a textured sprite instead of a particle algorithm.

POINT SPRITES

To improve performance, point sprites are often used for particle algorithms. A *point sprite* is a resizable textured vertex that always faces the camera. There are three good reasons for choosing a point sprite surface to render your particles:

- A point sprite only uses one vertex, so it saves space and boosts performance.
- When point sprites are enabled, textures are automatically mapped to them, so there is no need to store or set UV coordinates in your XNA code. Once again, this saves memory and boosts performance.
- Point sprites always face the camera, so there is no need to implement code to adjust their angle to view them from various directions.

The behavior of point sprites is slightly different from other textured primitive objects. Up close, point sprites appear to be more sparse and scattered. Also, scaling point sprites to a size that is proportionate to your other primitive objects and 3D models can be tricky. Even so, with careful planning around these differences, point sprites can be very effective. When they are set up properly, point sprites work like magic.

Point sprites can only be enabled through a shader. Much of the shader code is similar to code you have used before in this book to draw a textured primitive surface. As discussed in Chapter 4, "Shaders," the shader begins with global variables that can be set from your XNA application:

```
float4x4    fx_WVP : WORLDVIEWPROJ; // world view projection matrix
texture     fx_Texture;             // stores texture
float       fx_DistanceScale;       // scale by distance from camera
float       fx_Fade;                // fade as particle nears end of life
```

The same texture sampler used throughout this book, and explained in Chapter 7, "Texturing Your Game World," will also work for this point sprite shader:

```
// filter (like a brush) for showing texture
sampler textureSampler = sampler_state{
    Texture = <fx_Texture>;
    magfilter = LINEAR; // magfilter when bigger than actual size
    minfilter = LINEAR; // minfilter when smaller than actual size
    mipfilter = LINEAR; // to resize images close and far away
};
```

Until now, your XNA code has been using XNA's preset VertexDeclarations to define the type of vertex data for drawing primitive-based surfaces using data such as texture coordinates, position, color, or normal information. These preset definitions are convenient, but sometimes you will want to customize your vertex definitions. To be able to access features such as setting the point sprite size, you need to create your own custom vertex definition in your XNA code. This ensures the data sent from your XNA project is compatible with your vertex shader inputs. This will allow you to size your point sprite from your XNA code.

The vertex shader input for a point sprite still receives color and position information from your XNA application—as has been done in previous shader examples. However, the texture coordinate mapping is automatic, so you don't need to set UV coordinates in your XNA code or send them to the vertex shader. For you to pass the point sprite size to your vertex shader from your XNA code, the size variable defined for your vertex shader input must be tagged with the PSIZE semantic:

```
struct VS_INPUT{
    float4 f4Position   : POSITION0;
    float4 f4Color      : COLOR0;
```

```
    float1 Size          : PSIZE0;
};
```

The output from the vertex shader is also different from the shader code that is used for texturing objects. When texturing primitive surfaces, the output from our vertex shader includes elements for color, position, and texture data. When implementing point sprites, the vertex shader also outputs the size element, and this must be denoted by the PSIZE semantic. You actually have to invent some data for the texture coordinate, which might seem weird, but some graphics cards require UV coordinates to exist when they leave the vertex shader.

```
// vertex shader output
struct VS_OUTPUT{
    float4 f4Position    : POSITION0;
    float1 Size          : PSIZE;
    float4 f4Color       : COLOR0;
    float4 UV            : TEXCOORD0;
};
```

Because of differences in point sprite handling on the Xbox 360 and on the PC, we need to create a separate set of output specifically for the pixel shader. This allows you to use your shader on either platform. The Xbox 360 requires that UV coordinates be handled with a four-float vector denoted by a SPRITETEXCOORD semantic, and Windows requires the UV coordinates to be handled with a two-float vector denoted by a TEXCOORD0 semantic. You may think having the extra output from the vertex shader is odd—and it is odd. However, being able to channel the VS_OUTPUT data to the graphics pipeline and the PS_INPUT data to the pixel shader is necessary to run the same shader code on both your PC and Xbox 360.

```
struct PS_INPUT{
    #ifdef XBOX
        float4 UV    : SPRITETEXCOORD;
    #else
        float2 UV    : TEXCOORD0;
    #endif
        float4 Color : COLOR0;
};
```

The vertex shader is similar to ones you've used before. Some extra values are added in here to set up the point sprite for creating 3D fire in the next demonstration. The extras in this case include two coefficients used to scale the point sprite. The first scale value, *fx_DistanceScale,* sizes the point sprite by the relative distance from the camera. The second scale value, *fx_Fade,* reduces the size of each fire particle as it rises in the air and diminishes before being regenerated. *fx_Fade* is also used to darken the color of the particle as it rises away from the core of the fire.

Handling the texture data output for a point sprite from the vertex shader is notably different from a shader that just applies the usual texturing. The point sprite texture is automatically applied to the point sprite when it is sent to the pixel shader, so it doesn't matter what UV coordinates you set in the vertex shader. The data structure for the texture coordinate output from the vertex shader just needs to be in place. A vector with four floats is assigned to the texture output variable. This works both on the PC and on the Xbox. In the case of the PC, the vector will be truncated to a two-float vector.

The pixel shader actually performs the final processing on the color and texture data. However, to appease graphics card differences, and to allow this code to run on the PC and Xbox, two separate output streams have been created. Depending on your graphics card, if you leave this code out, your point sprites may not appear on your PC. The VS_OUTPUT data is sent into the graphics pipeline, and the PS_INPUT data is sent to the pixel shader for further processing of color and UV data:

```
void vertex_shader(in VS_INPUT IN, out VS_OUTPUT OUT){
    OUT.f4Position      = mul(IN.f4Position, fx_WVP);
    OUT.Size            = IN.Size*fx_DistanceScale*fx_Fade;
    OUT.f4Color         = (1.0f, 1.0f, 1.0f, 1.0f);
    OUT.UV              = (1.0f, 1.0f);

    // pass these values to the pixel shader
    PS_INPUT ps;
    ps.Color            = IN.f4Color * fx_Fade;
    ps.UV               = (1.0f, 1.0f, 0.0f, 0.0f);
}
```

In the pixel shader, the texture coordinate values are extracted from the XY coordinates of the texture input. On the Xbox 360, these values are extracted from the ZW coordinates, and they may be negative. This tip is attributed to Shawn Hargreaves, an XNA project developer at Microsoft and very knowledgeable blogger on XNA. (Awesome work, Shawn.) Shawn sums up this strangeness with a simple "Crazy, huh?" We agree it is crazy, but it works. Microsoft is working on documentation to provide more detail on the HLSL extensions on the Xbox 360, but for now have confidence that if you try this on your Xbox 360, it will function properly:

```
float4 pixel_shader(PS_INPUT IN) : COLOR0{
    float2 f2UV;

#ifdef XBOX
    f2UV = abs(IN.UV.zw);
#else
    f2UV = IN.UV.xy;
```

```
    #endif
    return tex2D(textureSampler, f2UV) * IN.Color;
}
```

Finally, in the technique, some rendering states need to be set to create a shiny particle with a transparent background. Point sprites can be enabled in the shader by setting the PointSpriteEnable state to true. AlphaBlendEnable must be set to true to enable transparency. An SrcBlend setting of SrcAlpha and a DestBlend property of 1 will make the point sprite very shiny. If you just need a transparent point sprite texture but without the shiny filter, you could set the destination blend to InvSrcAlpha. When the DestBlend state is 1, the shiny particle will only appear against dark backgrounds because the brightness does not offer enough contrast to make it visible against lighter backgrounds. An additional PointSize_Min render state property has been added to enable scaling the point sprite to 0. You may not need this on your PC, but you will need it on the Xbox 360. Add this technique to set up your shader to run on both platforms:

```
technique mytechnique{
    pass p0{
        // texture sampler initialized
        sampler[0]  = (textureSampler);
        PointSpriteEnable    = true;       // needed for point sprite
        PointSize_Min        = 0;          // enable scaling to 0 on xbox

        AlphaBlendEnable     = true;       // enable transparency
        SrcBlend             = SrcAlpha;   // turn off transparent pixels
        DestBlend            = One;        // shiny blending
        ZWriteEnable         = false;      // disable 3D rendering

        // declare and initialize vs
        vertexshader = compile vs_1_1 vertex_shader();

        // declare and initialize ps
        pixelshader = compile ps_1_1 pixel_shader();
    }
}
```

For this case, the default state of ZWriteEnable is set to false; this disables the Z plane for 2D rendering and blends the sprites together. Without blending, the transparency effect for the point sprites may be spoiled for larger particles because the transparent edges will appear layered on top of each other when rendered with other sprites. Figure 18-1 shows how this layering appearance can backfire. Note how the top of the flame is distorted by poor layering.

If you set ZWriteEnable to false (to blend the point sprites), you will also need to ensure that you draw your point sprites after your other models and primitive surfaces are rendered. Otherwise, any 3D objects that you draw later will appear to be on top of the point sprites. This drawing order issue is demonstrated later in the chapter.

This shader can now be used to create great flashy effects.

FIGURE 18-1

Unwanted layering of point sprites when ZWriteEnable is true

CUSTOM VERTEX DECLARATIONS

As mentioned earlier, XNA's preset VertexDeclarations are convenient but limited. For example, these preset vertex formats do not include an element for storing point sprite size. To set the point size from your XNA code, you will need to create a custom vertex to include this element. You may actually want to customize your vertex format to include other information—such as additional texture data, blend weights, fog, and much more. In other words, you create a vertex format to store the elements you need. Each data field in your vertex declaration is referred to as a *VertexElement*. An example of how to add VertexElement objects to your custom vertex definition appears later in this chapter. To set this up, you need to create a struct that stores data for each VertexElement. When declaring each VertexElement in your custom format definition, you use the following parameters:

```
VertexElement(
short stream,                       // stream read from - 0 if only 1 stream
short offset,                       // offset in bytes for current element
VertexElementFormat elementFormat,  // data type
VertexElementMethod elementMethod,  // which data to calculate during render
VertexElementUsage elementUsage,    // Color, PointSize, TextureCoordinate,
                                    // Normal, Depth, Fog, BlendWeight, etc
byte usageIndex);                   // semantic instance of elementUsage
```

To initialize your data, you use your struct type to declare a vertex variable. Data is then stored in the fields of this vertex variable. Once your data is set, a VertexBuffer object is then initialized to store your custom vertex format. The contents of your vertex variable array are then assigned to this vertex buffer for use when rendering.

A VertexDeclaration object is also declared to store your custom definition:

```
VertexDeclaration vertexDeclaration = new VertexDeclaration(
GraphicsDevice device, VertexElement[] customVertex.VertexElements);
```

This VertexDeclaration object is used later to set this property for the GraphicsDevice object, so it can read the data and render graphics using the newly defined vertex format. When you are drawing with the new vertex format, the vertex data is read from the VertexBuffer object and is rendered using the DrawPrimitives() method. The point sprite uses the PointList primitive type because only one vertex is needed for each point sprite.

```
gfx.GraphicsDevice.DrawPrimitives
(PrimitiveType.PointList, int startVertex, int primitiveCount);
```

FIRE EXAMPLE USING POINT SPRITES

This example takes the PointSprite.fx shader described earlier, creates a compatible custom vertex format in your XNA code, and shows you how to create a fire effect. It begins with either the WinMGHBook or Xbox360MGHBook base code project. This example is kept simple for easy learning, but the intent is to also inspire you with new ideas about how to create great effects. This example takes one image of a fire particle with a transparent background and turns it into fire. Figure 18-2 shows the fire from a torch at different frames.

In the Solution Explorer, reference the PointSprite.fx shader just described in this chapter. You can find this shader file in the Shaders folder in the download from this book's website.

In your XNA code, this shader is referenced with the Effect object, *mfxPtSpt*. This Effect object needs to be declared at the class level of your game class so it can be used throughout the class. Along with this declaration, some EffectParameters are also

FIGURE 18-2

Fire from a torch during different frames

needed so you can set the WVP matrix, texture value, point sprite size, and scaling values in this shader from your XNA code:

```
private Effect mfxPtSpt;                  // shader object
private EffectParameter mfxPtSptWVP;  // cumulative matrix w*v*p
private EffectParameter mfxPtSptTex;  // texture param
private EffectParameter mfxPtSptSize; // ptsprite size relative to cam
private EffectParameter mfxPtSptFade; // fade size & color as fire rises
```

With these objects in place, your shader can be loaded and compiled, and your XNA code can be given access to its global variables. This setup needs to be done when the program begins. Therefore, in Initialize(), add the instructions to load your shader and to reference the shader's global variables:

```
mfxPtSpt = content.Load<Effect>(@"shaders\PointSprite");
mfxPtSptWVP  = mfxPtSpt.Parameters["fx_WVP"];
mfxPtSptTex  = mfxPtSpt.Parameters["fx_Texture"];
mfxPtSptSize = mfxPtSpt.Parameters["fx_DistanceScale"];
mfxPtSptFade = mfxPtSpt.Parameters["fx_Fade"];
```

The shader is now in place and ready for use, but a custom vertex format that is compatible with the shader inputs is required. Here is the class-level struct that stores the VertexElements (color, position, and point sprite size, as described earlier):

```
private struct tCustomVertex{
    // struct fields
    private Vector3    pos;
    private Vector4    color;
    private float      size;

    // create a new format with pos, color, and size elements
    public static readonly VertexElement[] VertexElements
    = new VertexElement[]{
    new VertexElement(0,0,VertexElementFormat.Vector3,          // pos
        VertexElementMethod.Default,VertexElementUsage.Position,0),
    new VertexElement(0,sizeof(float)*3,VertexElementFormat.Vector4,// col
        VertexElementMethod.Default,VertexElementUsage.Color,0),
    new VertexElement(0,sizeof(float)*7,VertexElementFormat.Single ,// size
        VertexElementMethod.Default,VertexElementUsage.PointSize,0),
    };
```

```
    // constructor for custom vertex element
    public tCustomVertex(Vector3 v3pos,  Vector4 v4color, float fSize){
        this.pos    = v3pos;
        this.color  = v4color;
        this.size   = fSize;
    }
}
```

With the new vertex type in place, we can create an array that stores vertices using this new format. We'll also need to create a VertexBuffer object to serve as a data source while rendering our vertices. A VertexDeclaration object is also required to set the GraphicsDevice object, so it can read and draw using your new vertex format. Adding their declaration to the game class will make them available later:

```
tCustomVertex[]     mvtPtSprite = new tCustomVertex[1]; // store data
VertexBuffer        mVB;                                // data stream
VertexDeclaration   mCustomVtDeclaration;               // format description
```

Now you can initialize the particle vertex. You actually only need one vertex to do this. Once the data is set, it is then stored in a vertex buffer that serves as the data source during rendering. The vertex declaration is also initialized here, so the custom definition can be referenced by the GraphicsDevice when reading and drawing primitive surfaces with this new vertex format:

```
void initParticleVertex(){
    Vector3 pos= new Vector3(0.0f, 0.0f, 0.0f);          // origin
    Vector4 col= new Vector4(0.7f, 0.8f, 0.0f, 1.0f);    // yellow color
    float fSize= 10.0f;                                  // point sprite size
    mvtPtSprite[0]= new tCustomVertex(pos, col, fSize);// set the data

    // initialize and set the vertex buffer with data
    mVB = new VertexBuffer(gfx.GraphicsDevice, mvtPtSprite.Length * 32,
           ResourceUsage.WriteOnly, ResourceManagementMode.Automatic);
    mVB.SetData(mvtPtSprite);

    // define format for data retrieval & drawing
    mCustomVtDeclaration = new VertexDeclaration(gfx.GraphicsDevice,
                                        tCustomVertex.VertexElements);
}
```

To initialize your custom vertex data, vertex buffer stream, and VertexDeclaration object when the program begins, call initParticleVertex() from Initialize():

```
initParticleVertex();
```

Next, the texture used for the point sprite needs to be loaded. Only one image is needed to create a flashy fire effect, but you could add more to make the effect even flashier and varied. The image shown here is the one used for the particle texture.

To load your image using the ContentManager, you must reference the image file, particle.png, in your project's Images folder as well as in the Solution Explorer. The particle.png file can be obtained from the Images folder in the download from this book's website. The image is stored in a Texture2D object called *mTexParticle*. Add this declaration to the modules area of your game class:

```
private Texture2D mTexParticle;
```

To load your texture with other textures when the program starts, add the load statement to the LoadGraphicsContent() method:

```
mTexParticle = content.Load<Texture2D>(".\\Images\\particle");
```

To store and update the fire particles, you use a particle class. To store this class, add a Particle.cs source file to your project. Here is the class shell:

```
using System;
using System.Collections.Generic;
using System.Text;

namespace MGHBook{
    class Particle
    {    }
}
```

To access vital XNA functions from your new class, you need to include the XNA graphics framework declarations at the top of the Particle.cs file:

```
using Microsoft.Xna.Framework;
```

Declarations for the classic particle properties described at the beginning of the chapter belong in the module level of your particle class. Position, speed, life, and a fade rate in your particles are essential to build a fire.

```
public  Vector3  position;    // X, Y, Z
public  Vector3  speed;       // rate of movement on X, Y, Z plane
```

```
public  float     fLife;      // die when life=0.0f. reborn with life = 1.0f
private float     fadeRate;   // every particle dies at a different rate
```

You are also going to need to add a constructor; otherwise, your class will not compile when you reference it from another class:

```
// constructor
public Particle(){}
```

It would not make sense to continuously create a new particle each time an old particle has run its course. Instead, processing time is saved by forcing the particles to be effectively "reborn" after they die. In the case of a fire algorithm, the fire particles start at the base and rise upward. As each particle leaves the furnace core, it cools down and grows faint until it finally burns out and dies. The function reset_particle() then rejuvenates the particle and it begins a new life. Every time the particle is regenerated, it is given a randomized position, fade rate, and speed. This randomization makes the fire more interesting.

Also note that these particle properties will often need a minimum or a maximum value to ensure they fall within an acceptable range. For example, if the fade rate is not set to a minimum of 60, you discover very quickly that the longer-living particles will take over. These longer-living particles are like mutants that won't die off as nature intended. If your fire is overtaken by longer-living particles, eventually the core of your fire will become so dispersed, the flames will burn out and you will be left with a scattering of particles floating off into the atmosphere.

When you're customizing your own particle algorithms, these properties won't just jump into your head. Give yourself time for trial and error when setting up your particle properties and then see what looks best during your test phase. For this example, the properties have been provided for you. Here is the reset_particle() procedure to add to your particle class:

```
public void reset_particle(Random rand){
    // set life to 1 for new full life
    fLife = 1;

    // set positions back to x=0, y=0, z=0
    position.X = 0; position.Y = 0; position.Z = 0;

    // set fade rate
    int iFadeFactor = 60 + rand.Next(0, 70); // between 60 and 129
    fadeRate = (1 + (float)iFadeFactor) / 50.0f;

    // calculate X speed
    int iXspeedRand = rand.Next(-40, 40); // min -40 and max 39
```

```
speed.X = (float)(iXspeedRand + 1) / 300.0f;

// calculate Y speed
int iYspeedRand = rand.Next(0, 15); // min 0 and max 14
speed.Y = (float)(iYspeedRand + 1) / 23.0f;

// set Z speed
speed.Z = 0.0f;
}
```

A method is required to update the particles. The particle position property is incremented by the speed scaled by the time between frames. The scale regulates the speed so that the animation appears at the same rate regardless of the processing power of the machine that runs the algorithm.

Particle life is reduced by the fade rate at each frame. If the life value falls below zero, then the particle is reincarnated. In this case, the fire particle is born at the bottom by the fire source, and it then rises upward on a randomized path. Eventually, the particle gets too far away from the fire, grows smaller, and dims until it is invisible. At this point, the particle is regenerated again. To achieve this effect, add the update() procedure to your particle class. This code ensures that the particles live according to their destiny.

```
public void update(int iTimeBetweenFrames, Random rand){
    float fTimeBetweenFrames = (float)iTimeBetweenFrames/1000.0f;
    position   += speed    * fTimeBetweenFrames; // update position
    fLife      -= fadeRate * fTimeBetweenFrames; // update speed

    // regenerate particle if life falls below zero
    if (fLife < 0)
        reset_particle(rand);
}
```

Back in Game1.cs, a reference to this new particle class is required. The particle class's namespace must be added at the top of Game1.cs so the game class can find it:

```
using MGHBook;
```

Several particles are needed to collectively build the fire. Through trial and error while experimenting with different numbers of particles when writing this algorithm, we found that 100 particles appeared to simulate a decent fire, both up close and from a distance. You may find as you customize your own particle algorithms that you don't need as many particles, especially if the effect is only viewed from a distance. Sometimes you may need more to create a fuller bodied particle effect. For this routine, 100 particles look good from different distances. Declaring 100 particle objects in your game class will allow you to track and update each particle's size, location, and color while drawing one point sprite in each particle's place.

```
private const int NUM_PARTICLES = 100;
private Particle[] cParticle;
```

A Random object is declared and initialized at the class level to seed the random generation of properties for each particle:

```
Random mRand = new Random();
```

All particles are born when the game application begins. An array of particle objects makes it easy to generate fire particles when your program kicks into gear. By the time your window opens, you will likely catch the tail end of the particles springing to life in a full-fledged fire. The fire is started from the game application's Initialize() method:

```
// initialize particles
cParticle = new Particle[NUM_PARTICLES];

for (int i = 0; i < NUM_PARTICLES; i++){
    cParticle[i] = new Particle();
    cParticle[i].reset_particle(mRand);
}
```

For every frame, the position for each fire particle must be adjusted so that the particle rises at the object's own random rate. Of course, after each frame, the particle is one step closer to its own death as its life is gradually reduced by its fade rate. The particle object's update method will check whether the life is reduced to zero—in which case a new life and entirely different set of properties will be generated to start the particle on a new path from the core of the fire. This ensures that your particles don't stand still. Add this routine to update your particle objects inside the Update() method of your game class:

```
// update particles
int iTimeLapseBetweenFrames = this.TargetElapsedTime.Milliseconds;
for(int i=0; i<NUM_PARTICLES; i++)
    // pass in time between frames to regulate speed & random seed
    cParticle[i].update(iTimeLapseBetweenFrames, mRand);
```

Scaling point sprites is different from scaling other primitive surfaces. In this setup, with a custom vertex format, you cannot use the usual matrix methods to scale them as part of the cumulative World transformation. Here is one alternative for scaling the point sprite size that considers the length between the camera and the point sprite:

```
private void scale_particles(Vector3 v3TranslateGroup){
    Vector3     v3Len = cam.m_vPos - v3TranslateGroup;
    float       fLen = (float)v3Len.Length();
    float       fSize;
    const float MAX_DISTANCE = 40.0f;

    if (fLen >= MAX_DISTANCE)   // don't show it after max distance
        fSize = 0.0f;
    else                        // shrink sprite as camera moves away
        fSize = (MAX_DISTANCE - fLen) /MAX_DISTANCE;
    mfxPtSptSize.SetValue(fSize);
}
```

The code required to draw the particle using point sprites is very similar to code that draws any textured primitive surface. Scaling for the entire group of particles is triggered once—based on the distance between the camera and the group of particles. Each fire particle is rendered individually. The group of particles is moved into position and then each individual particle is translated from the fire base to its own position in the roaring fire. The particle's life level, which ranges between 0 for dead and 1 for full life, is passed to the shader so it can be used to fade the color of the flame and shrink the size as each particle rises away from the core of the fire.

Before the fire is drawn, the GraphicsDevice object is set to retrieve vertex buffer data from and render data using the new vertex format. The data is then read from the vertex buffer, and the vertex is drawn using a point list. These steps are repeated for each fire particle:

```
private void draw_particles(){
    // 1: declare matrices
    Matrix matIdentity, matTranslParticle, matTranslateGroup;

    // scale the point sprite by cam distance to the group of particles
    Vector3 v3TranslateGroup = new Vector3(0.0f, -0.53f, 5.0f);
    scale_particles(v3TranslateGroup);

    // 2: initialize matrices
    matIdentity        = Matrix.Identity; // always start with identity
    matTranslateGroup  = Matrix.CreateTranslation(v3TranslateGroup);

    for (int i = 0; i < NUM_PARTICLES; i++){
```

```
        // translate each individual particle
        matTranslParticle =
        Matrix.CreateTranslation(cParticle[i].position);

        // 3: build cumulative world matrix using I.S.R.O.T. sequence
        // identity, scale, rotate, orbit(translate & rotate), translate
        mMatWorld = matIdentity * matTranslateGroup * matTranslParticle;

        // 4: pass wvp matrix and texture to shader
        mfxPtSptWVP.SetValue(mMatWorld * mMatView * mMatProj);
        mfxPtSptTex.SetValue(mTexParticle);
        mfxPtSptFade.SetValue(cParticle[i].fLife);
        mfxPtSpt.CommitChanges();

        // 5: draw object-select vertex type, primitive type, # primitives
        gfx.GraphicsDevice.VertexDeclaration = mCustomVtDeclaration;
        gfx.GraphicsDevice.Vertices[0].SetSource(mVB, 0, 32);
        gfx.GraphicsDevice.DrawPrimitives(PrimitiveType.PointList, 0, 1);
    }
}
```

Inside the Draw() method, a call can be made to draw the fire. A SaveStateMode.SaveState parameter is needed in the Begin() method to restore the GraphicsDevice settings after the point sprites have been rendered. Performing this restore is necessary; otherwise, the GraphicsDevice object's depth setting is disabled. Your other non–point sprite objects will look strange if the original GraphicsDevice states are not restored. Try running the code with SaveStateMode enabled to see the code work correctly. Then run your code without including this parameter to see how the background is off color and 3D models have no depth when the GraphicsDevice settings have been thrown out after the point sprite is drawn:

```
// SaveState needed to restore GraphicsDevice properties
// so other non-point sprite objects can be rendered properly
mfxPtSpt.Begin( SaveStateMode.SaveState);
mfxPtSpt.Techniques[0].Passes[0].Begin();
    draw_particles();
// end shader - PointSprite.fx
mfxPtSpt.Techniques[0].Passes[0].End();
mfxPtSpt.End();
```

Finally, as one last touch to make the example a little more interesting, we'll add a model torch. For this to work, the torch.fbx file must be referenced from the Models folder in the Solution Explorer. The torch.bmp texture will also need to be placed in the Models folder in your project but not referenced. If the torch.bmp texture is referenced from the Solution Explorer, it will be confused with the torch.fbx model because they both use the same name. The torch.fbx and torch.bmp files can be found in the Models folder in the download from the website.

The logic and methods used to load and draw the models are the same as explained in Chapter 12, "3D Models," so the details behind these next steps will be minimal. First, declarations in the game class are required to store the torch model object and the array for the torch's bone transformations:

```
Model        mModTorch;
Matrix[]     matTorch;
```

This init_torch() method includes the code to load the torch and set the transformation matrix for the meshes in it. Placing this in the game class allows you to load the model:

```
void init_torch(){
    mModTorch = content.Load<Model>(".\\Models\\torch");
    matTorch = new Matrix[mModTorch.Bones.Count];
    mModTorch.CopyAbsoluteBoneTransformsTo(matTorch);
}
```

init_torch() can be called from the Initialize() method to read in the torch.fbx file when the program begins:

```
init_torch();
```

You can add this next method to your game class to draw the torch:

```
private void draw_torch(Model model){
    // 1: declare matrices
    Matrix matIdent, matTransl, matScale;

    // 2: initialize matrices
    matIdent    = Matrix.Identity; // always start with identity matrix
    matScale    = Matrix.CreateScale(0.50f, 0.50f, 0.50f);
    matTransl   = Matrix.CreateTranslation(0.0f, -0.60f, 5.0f);

    foreach (ModelMesh mesh in model.Meshes){
        // 3: build cumulative matrix using I.S.R.O.T. sequence
        // identity,scale,rotate,orbit(translate & rotate),translate
        mMatWorld = matIdent * matScale * matTransl;
```

```
        foreach (BasicEffect effect in mesh.Effects){
            effect.World        = matTorch[mesh.ParentBone.Index]*mMatWorld;
            effect.View         = mMatView;
            effect.Projection   = mMatProj;

            // 4b. set lighting
            effect.EnableDefaultLighting();
            effect.SpecularPower= 0.01f;
            effect.CommitChanges();
        }
        // 5: draw object
        mesh.Draw();
    }
}
```

The method to draw the torch model is triggered from Draw() along with the other draw routines that are called. draw_torch() must be called before the point sprites are rendered to ensure that the point sprites are layered properly over the 3D model:

```
draw_torch(mModTorch);
```

FIGURE 18-3

To observe deviant layering when ZWriteEnable is false, try calling draw_torch() after drawing the point sprites. You will notice the flame no longer appears to come from the torch, as shown in Figure 18-3.

Setting ZWriteEnable in the shader to false ensures the point sprites will be blended together. However, sometimes setting ZWriteEnable to true looks good when the background is colored the same as the pixels that are supposed to be transparent, or when the particles are small or disperse. You can always experiment to see what looks good, but remember that a PC game may be played in several different environments—on different-sized windows.

Draw order issues for point sprites when ZWriteEnable is false

You should consider this in your decision as to whether or not to use ZWriteEnable.

With the DestBlend state set to 1 in the shader, shiny blending is applied. As a result, the point sprite can only be seen against darker backgrounds. To ensure you can see the fire against the background, replace the instruction that clears the background and resets the color inside the Draw() method with this new instruction:

```
gfx.GraphicsDevice.Clear(Color.CornflowerBlue);
```

When you run your program, it will show a steady, ever-changing body of fire. As you back away from the fire, the size of the particles will scale properly to match the size of the primitive ground surface and model torch. At any angle the fire particles will face the camera, so you don't need to have any billboarding code.

Up close, the particles will appear to be scattered and disperse. This is normal behavior for a particle algorithm based on point sprites. To work around this limitation, you may consider limiting access to areas around the particles or only showing them from a distance, or you might increase the number of particles drawn when the viewer is nearby.

This is a cool effect, but it's really only the beginning of what you can do with point sprites and particle effects. This particle effect would be ideal for creating explosions, exhaust trails from missiles, star dust, and more. You could even increase the number of textures used or the particle types to make the fire more interesting.

CHAPTER 18 REVIEW EXERCISES

1. Try the step-by-step examples provided in this chapter.

2. Starting with the existing algorithm, create an additional particle stream to simulate smoke from your fire.

3. Modify your fire algorithm to create an explosion.

19

Keyframe
Animations

KEYFRAME

animations combine a timer and interpolation to project the location of game objects. The term *keyframe* comes from the world of hand-drawn animation. The senior artists would draw the "key frames" and then other artists would create the "in-betweens." In computer games, the keyframes still define the most important stages of the animation, but interpolation is used to fill in the frames in between. This can mean interpolating the position or orientation of an object. For example, in a racing game, you might want to include a pace car when the cars are under a caution flag. Using keyframes, you can control the course that the pace car follows as it leads the pack and then eventually drives off into the pit. By the end of this chapter, you will be able to use keyframes to map out a route and regulate the speed of this sort of animation.

The proper technique is to use a timeline to control the speed of animations; this allows the animation to be rendered at the same speed regardless of the system that runs it. Until now, the examples in this book have generated translational animations by incrementing X, Y, and Z coordinates by a product of the increment unit and the difference in time between the current and previous frame. Interpolation is a similar process, but it offers other possibilities for moving objects on linear and curved paths. For translations or rotations, a path may be defined for the object and a specific duration of time may be assigned for completing the path.

INTERPOLATION

Interpolation can be used to project the location of a game object based on the expected time of arrival at the destination. For example, if the time between the starting frame and ending frame of an object is 10 seconds, and the object is expected to travel 5 units on the X plane and 10 units on the Z plane, then interpolation can be used to estimate the object's location at any time between 0 and 10 seconds. At 4 seconds, interpolation would project the object to be at X = 2 and Z = 4.

CURVES

When mapping out keyframes on your timeline, you probably won't always want your vehicles traveling in a straight line. You might want to use a curve to map out a path for a keyframe animation. This chapter uses Bézier curves to fulfill this role, but you could use other types of curves for the same task. Most splines are calculated by similar methods as the Bézier curve, so the Bézier curve provides a good example of how this family of curves can be implemented in your game algorithms.

The Bézier curves in this chapter use four points: a start point, an end point, and two control points (see Figure 19-1). The control points provide the user with a way to stretch or compress the curve. Stretching the control points will "push" or "pull" the curve into different shapes.

FIGURE 19-1

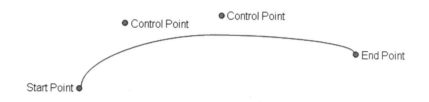

A Bézier curve

The formula for finding a point on a Bézier curve is based on the relative position between the start of the curve (0%) and the end of the curve (100%):

```
Point on Bezier Curve =
  V start    * (1 - fPercent)³
+ V control 1 * 3 * fPercent * (1 - fPercent)²
+ V control 2  * 3 * fPercent² * (1 - fPercent)
+ V end      * fPercent³
```

The following example puts this formula to use.

KEYFRAME ANIMATION EXAMPLE

This example demonstrates a timed animation that moves a model CF-18 Hornet fighter jet on a fixed route. Two parts of the route are defined by straight lines and two parts of the route are defined by Bézier curves. The CF-18 fighter jet and route are shown in Figure 19-2.

FIGURE 19-2

CF-18 fighter jet animated on a timeline using keyframe animations

The code for this example starts with either the WinMGHBook or the Xbox360MGHBook project available in the download from this book's website.

A fixed period is specified for completing the combined sections. The total animation time needed to complete all combined routes is 11,200 milliseconds (11.2 seconds). At each pass through Update(), the algorithm checks to determine how far along the path the object should be at that specific time. The position of the CF-18 is projected using the keyframes, which store the fixed end points of the lines and points on the Bézier curves.

The first step is to store each route. Two Bézier curves are being used, and two lines are being used. The Bézier curve stores four control points:

```
private Vector3[] mv3BezA      = new Vector3[4]; // route 1
private Vector3[] mv3LineA     = new Vector3[2]; // route 2
private Vector3[] mv3BezB      = new Vector3[4]; // route 3
private Vector3[] mv3LineB     = new Vector3[2]; // route 4
```

This first routine will initialize the jet's route:

```
private void init_routes(){
    // advanced collision / keyframes
    const float BND = BOUNDARY;

    // 1st Bezier curve control points (1st route)
    mv3BezA[0] = new Vector3( BND + 5.0f, 0.4f, 5.0f);        // start
    mv3BezA[1] = new Vector3( BND + 5.0f, 2.4f, 3.0f * BND);// ctrl 1
    mv3BezA[2] = new Vector3(-BND - 5.0f, 4.4f, 3.0f * BND);// ctrl 2
    mv3BezA[3] = new Vector3(-BND - 5.0f, 5.4f, 5.0f);        // end

    // 1st line between Bezier curves  (2nd route)
    mv3LineA[0] = new Vector3(-BND - 5.0f, 5.4f, 5.0f);     // start
    mv3LineA[1] = new Vector3(-BND - 5.0f, 5.4f, -5.0f);    // end

    // 2nd Bezier curve control points (3rd route)
    mv3BezB[0] = new Vector3(-BND - 5.0f, 5.4f, -5.0f);      // start
    mv3BezB[1] = new Vector3(-BND - 5.0f, 4.4f, -3.0f * BND);// ctrl 1
    mv3BezB[2] = new Vector3( BND + 5.0f, 2.4f, -3.0f * BND);// ctrl 2
    mv3BezB[3] = new Vector3( BND + 5.0f, 0.4f, -5.0f);      // end

    // 2nd line between Bezier curves  (4th route)
    mv3LineB[0] = new Vector3(BND + 5.0f, 0.4f, -5.0f);    // start
    mv3LineB[1] = new Vector3(BND + 5.0f, 0.4f, 5.0f);     // end
}
```

You call the jet initialization routine from Initialize():

```
init_routes();
```

Next, you must add module declarations to initialize the time for the whole trip and each individual section of the trip:

```
private float[]  mfKeyFrameDuration    = new float[4];
private float    mfTripTime            = 0.0f;
private float    mfTotalTripTime       = 0.0f;
private const    int NUM_KEYFRAMES     = 4;
```

To initialize the timeline, you will provide five values. Each of the total times between keyframes is stored. Also, the total trip time is stored.

```
private void init_timeLine(){
    mfKeyFrameDuration[0] = 4.8f; // time to complete route 1
    mfKeyFrameDuration[1] = 0.8f; // time to complete route 2
    mfKeyFrameDuration[2] = 4.8f; // time to complete route 3
    mfKeyFrameDuration[3] = 0.8f; // time to complete route 4
    mfTotalTripTime       =11.2f; // total time for all keyframes
}
```

Call the time-initialization routine from Initialize():

```
init_timeLine();
```

The next step is to add module declarations for storing the Y rotation of the jet model. This will correct the jet so that it is always pointing in the correct direction:

```
Vector3 mv3CurrentPos, mv3PrevPos;
float   mfRotateY;
```

After the jet is pointing in the proper direction, your next hurdle to jump is keeping track of which route the jet is currently flying. Because we know how long each route will take, it's easy to check the time, and then figure out which route the jet is currently following. The get_route_number() function performs this check:

```
private int get_route_number(){
    float fTimeLapsed = 0.0f;

    // retrieve current leg of trip
    for (int i = 0; i < NUM_KEYFRAMES; i++){
        if (fTimeLapsed > mfTripTime)
```

```
        return i - 1;
      else
          fTimeLapsed += mfKeyFrameDuration[i];
    }
    return 3; // special case for last route
}
```

The next function uses the Bézier curve to figure out what part of the curve your object is on. Unlike the last function, which checked the time, this one is checking the physical location of the jet. For this example, we need two different ways of determining position; the first one checks the position on the Bézier curve:

```
private Vector3 get_position_on_curve(Vector3[] v3Bezier, float fPercent){
    return // returns position on curve based on percent of curve
    v3Bezier[0] * (1.0f - fPercent)*(1.0f-fPercent) * (1.0f-fPercent) +
    v3Bezier[1] * 3.0f * fPercent * (1.0f-fPercent) * (1.0f-fPercent) +
    v3Bezier[2] * 3.0f * fPercent * fPercent * (1.0f - fPercent) +
    v3Bezier[3] * fPercent * fPercent * fPercent;
}
```

The second position-checking function uses linear interpolation to figure out which part of a line the model jet is on:

```
private Vector3 get_position_on_line(Vector3[] v3Line, float fPercent){
    // returns position on line based on percent of line
    Vector3 v3Difference = v3Line[1] - v3Line[0];
    return v3Line[0] + fPercent * v3Difference;
}
```

The next function to add, update_keyframe_animation(), is the workhorse of this example. It uses all of the logic that you have added to update the animation. The function determines which part of the route the fighter jet is on and then uses the appropriate check to find out where it should be on that route:

```
private void update_keyframe_animation(GameTime gameTime){
    // update total trip time, use modulus to prevent variable overflow
    mfTripTime += (gameTime.ElapsedGameTime.Milliseconds / 1000.0f);
    mfTripTime = mfTripTime % mfTotalTripTime;

    // get the current route number from a total of four routes
    int iRouteNum = get_route_number();

    // find percentage of completion for current route
    // sum times for preceding keyframes
```

```
float fKeyFrameStartTime = 0.0f;
for (int i = 0; i < iRouteNum; i++)
    fKeyFrameStartTime += mfKeyFrameDuration[i];

// time spent during current route
float fTimeBetweenKeys = mfTripTime - fKeyFrameStartTime;

// percentage of current route completed
float fPercent = fTimeBetweenKeys / mfKeyFrameDuration[iRouteNum];

// get current X, Y, Z of object being animated
// find point on line or curve by passing in % completed
switch(iRouteNum){
case 0: // first curve
mv3CurrentPos = get_position_on_curve(mv3BezA, fPercent);
    break;
case 1: // first line
mv3CurrentPos = get_position_on_line(mv3LineA, fPercent);
    break;
case 2: // 2nd curve
mv3CurrentPos = get_position_on_curve(mv3BezB, fPercent);
    break;
case 3: // 2nd line
mv3CurrentPos = get_position_on_line(mv3LineB, fPercent);
    break;
}

// get rotation angle about Y based on change in X and Z speed
Vector3 v3Speed = mv3CurrentPos - mv3PrevPos;
mv3PrevPos      = mv3CurrentPos;
mfRotateY       =(float)Math.Atan2((float)v3Speed.X, (float)v3Speed.Z);
}
```

This update function obviously needs to be called from Update():

```
update_keyframe_animation(gameTime);
```

Next, you need to add the jet model to your program. To start the process of loading the fighter jet model, add these module declarations:

```
Model    mModJet;
Matrix[] matJetTransforms;
```

When you initialize the CF-18 model, make sure the cf18.x file is referenced in the Models folder within your project (with the matching cf18Color.jpg file). You can find these files in the Models folder in the book's download. Add this code to load and initialize the jet (this code is explained in Chapter 12, "3D Models"):

```
void init_cf18(){
    mModJet = content.Load<Model>(".\\Models\\cf18");
    matJetTransforms = new Matrix[mModJet.Bones.Count];
    mModJet.CopyAbsoluteBoneTransformsTo(matJetTransforms);
}
```

Next, add the jet initialization routine to Initialize():

```
init_cf18();
```

Now it's time to actually draw the jet model. Most of this code should be familiar to you—it has been used throughout this book. Lighting with the BasicEffect object is explained in Chapter 20, "Lighting."

```
private void draw_cf18(Model model){
    // 1: declare matrices
    Matrix matIdentity, matScale, matTransl, matRotX, matRotY;

    // 2: initialize matrices
    matIdentity = Matrix.Identity; // always start with identity matrix
    matTransl   = Matrix.CreateTranslation(mv3CurrentPos);
    matScale    = Matrix.CreateScale(0.1f, 0.1f, 0.1f);
    matRotX     = Matrix.CreateRotationX(0.0f);
    matRotY     = Matrix.CreateRotationY(mfRotateY);

    // 3: build cumulative world matrix using I.S.R.O.T. sequence
    // identity, scale, rotate, orbit(translate & rotate), translate
    mMatWorld = matIdentity * matScale * matRotX * matRotY * matTransl;

    foreach (ModelMesh mesh in model.Meshes){
        foreach (BasicEffect effect in mesh.Effects){
            effect.World=matJetTransforms[mesh.ParentBone.Index]*mMatWorld;
            effect.View = mMatView;
            effect.Projection = mMatProj;
            effect.EnableDefaultLighting();
            effect.SpecularColor = new Vector3(0.0f, 0.0f, 0.0f);
            effect.CommitChanges();
```

```
        }
        mesh.Draw();
    }
}
```

The final step to set up this example is to call draw_cf18() from Draw():

```
draw_cf18(mModJet);
```

When the program is run, it shows the jet model being interpolated over an 11.2-second interval. The first 0.8 seconds are spent on each straight line, and 4.8 seconds are spent on each Bézier curve. Interpolation is used to estimate where the jet should be at each frame. The CF-18 Hornet's path used is outlined back in Figure 19-2.

The keyframe animation created in this chapter is actually similar to a timeline animation you would create in Macromedia Flash or chUmbaLum sOft's MilkShape. As you can see, it's easy to implement a keyframe animation in code.

CHAPTER 19 REVIEW EXERCISES

1. Implement the step-by-step example demonstrated in this chapter.

2. Begin with the completed airplane example from Chapter 6, "Character Movement," and convert this solution so it uses three Bézier curves to move the airplane on a path in the X, Y, and Z planes.

CHAPTER 20

Lighting

A good lighting system is often a key differentiator between a high-quality game and an amateur game. Walk into any arcade and look at the games around you. Most likely, you will be more impressed with the games that use advanced lighting techniques. By adding interesting lighting—even in small amounts—you can excite your players' eyes with the details of your game.

This chapter shows you how to program the lighting inside your virtual worlds. Once you start using different lighting techniques, and adding multiple light sources to your games, you might be surprised by how much detail becomes visible. Even with subtle lighting, bumps, cracks, and depth that formerly went unnoticed will materialize.

When setting up your lights, it is strongly recommended that you add only one light at a time. This ensures that you know exactly how each new light affects your environment. Even when professional game artists light a scene, they will usually start by working with one main light to establish the right mood and ambience before adding other lights.

LIGHTING METHODS

There are many different ways to implement lighting. On the XNA platform, lighting must be applied using a shader. You can use XNA's BasicEffect shader, or you can write your own shader to implement customized lighting.

Most light-simulation models break the light into different components so that you can describe the source of the light and the reflective properties of the materials that are being lit. Source lights can range from the sun, to a fire, or even a light bulb. Materials being lit might be bright, shiny, or reflective—like a golden ore. In comparison, dull materials, such as unfinished wood or dark cloth, will reflect very little light.

Source Lights

Source lights generate light. This chapter presents two types of source light:

> **Directional light**   An example of directional light is the sun. This type of light source has no position, does not fade, is infinite, and has a direction.

> **Point light**   An example of point light is a light bulb. Point light has a range, a position, and it shines in all directions.

Reflective Lighting Properties of Materials

Reflective lighting properties define how light radiates from and around the materials being lit. Reflective lighting properties are just as important as source lights because they define the shininess, color, and brightness of the materials being lit. The three common types of reflective light properties are ambient, diffuse, and specular.

Ambient Light

Ambient light is a background light that has no source. The ambience is created by light bouncing off surrounding objects in all directions. The ambient property defines how background light colors and brightens materials in a scene. Here are some points to keep in mind:

> Ambient light is scattered background light and is everywhere in a scene.

> Ambient light has no direction.

Diffuse Light

Diffuse light defines how a source light colors and brightens materials in its path. Diffuse light increases as the angle between the light and surface normal decreases.

Specular Light

The specular property defines a material's shininess, gloss, or highlights. Specular light reflected from a surface depends on the viewer's angle to the surface and the light's angle to the surface. Glass, water, metal, and some plastics have high specular levels. Earth, concrete, and dull-colored materials have lower specular levels. Here are some points to keep in mind:

> Specular light is like a highlight that makes an object shiny.

> Specular light is used for simulating shiny, plastic, glossy, or metallic objects.

Reflective Normals

As described in Chapter 13, "Vectors," a *normal* is a directional vector that is perpendicular to a surface. When lighting is implemented, a normal vector is used to calculate the intensity of the light reflected from the surface. Each normal is drawn at right angles to the surface being rendered.

When rendering complex shapes using primitive objects, you will need to calculate the normal and store it with each vertex. Refer to Chapter 13 for details on how to calculate normals. Most models already store the normal data with each vertex used to build the model. These normal vectors are used to reflect light when a light source shines on them. When you are implementing lighting with a vertex shader, more normals will offer higher definition lighting. You will definitely want to use more vertices for your vertex shader–based lighting; otherwise, the effect will fall flat. To increase performance, when using large numbers of vertices, you should consider using an index buffer for rendering primitive objects with vertex shader–based lighting.

IMPLEMENTING DIRECTIONAL LIGHTING USING XNA'S BASICEFFECT CLASS

As mentioned in Chapter 4, "Shaders," XNA includes the BasicEffect class to access and implement built-in shader effects. This class exposes methods for setting shader properties to assist in implementing directional lighting. In Chapter 12, "3D Models," the BasicEffect class is used to implement default lighting for the models. It is a fuss-free way of getting decent lighting quickly.

BasicEffect Default Lighting

The easiest way to implement lighting with the BasicEffect class is to use the EnableDefaultLighting() method, which automatically sets directional lighting for you:

```
void EnableDefaultLighting();
```

When implementing either default lighting or custom lighting with the BasicEffect class, you must set the LightingEnabled property to true:

```
public bool                 LightingEnabled { get; set; }
```

You can get and set global lighting properties with the following methods:

```
public Vector3              AmbientLightColor { get; set; }
public Vector3              DiffuseColor { get; set; }
public Vector3              SpecularColor { get; set; }
public float                SpecularPower { get; set; }
```

Default lighting turns on three directional lights, which you can choose to disable or alter as needed. You don't actually need to use the default lighting. Instead, you can enable each directional light and customize it as you choose. Each directional light has an Enabled, Direction, DiffuseColor, and SpecularColor property that you can get or set:

```
bool    DirectionalLight0.Enabled
Vector3 DirectionalLight0.Direction
```

```
Vector3 DirectionalLight0.DiffuseColor
Vector3 DirectionalLight0.SpecularColor

bool    DirectionalLight1.Enabled
Vector3 DirectionalLight1.Direction
Vector3 DirectionalLight1.DiffuseColor
Vector3 DirectionalLight1.SpecularColor

bool    DirectionalLight2.Enabled
Vector3 DirectionalLight2.Direction
Vector3 DirectionalLight2.DiffuseColor
Vector3 DirectionalLight2.SpecularColor
```

XNA's default lighting option is a great way to quickly generate decent-looking directional light.

Directional lighting under the BasicEffect class is especially effective for lighting 3D models because it is easy to set up. For this case, the BasicEffect class implements lighting through the vertex shader. When the vertex data is sent to the pixel shader, it is interpolated between vertices. The definition of the light is enhanced with more vertices, so you may want to consider reducing the storage requirements by using an index buffer when drawing primitive objects.

Directional Lighting Example

This example implements directional lighting with XNA's BasicEffect class. Because the BasicEffect class implements vertex lighting, more vertices are needed for smoother application of light across the object surface or higher definition of light. Higher definition light is especially noticeable for specular lighting.

Because many vertices for storing surface normals are needed to enhance the lighting when the BasicEffect shader is used, this example uses our friend the index buffer. This demonstration starts with the solution from Chapter 9, "Index Buffers," which already has an index buffer set up. Surface normals are needed in the example. Figure 20-1 shows a before (left) and after (right) look at how directional lighting from this demonstration will change the look of the environment.

The subtle effect directional lighting has on detail makes it exciting to use. Most of the time, directional lighting is implemented during a daytime setting, so there will already be a high level of ambience and diffuse lighting around to brighten the area. With the BasicEffect class, the specular light increases the brightness of the primitive surface face.

Once you have the original index buffer solution from Chapter 9 open, you may notice that the PositionColorTexture type was used to store the vertex data. This needs to change because normal data is also required to enable lighting. A few minor

FIGURE 20-1

Before and after directional lighting

changes are needed. To implement lighting with a vertex that stores normal data, you must add a new VertexDeclaration to the top of the game class:

```
private VertexDeclaration mVertNTex;
```

The vertex declaration must be initialized when the program begins. This can be done by adding the statement to initialize it with a VertexPositionNormalTexture vertex type in Initialize():

```
mVertNTex = new VertexDeclaration(gfx.GraphicsDevice,
        VertexPositionNormalTexture.VertexElements);
```

We almost have what we need. To change the vertex type, inside init_dynamic_vb() replace the instruction that sets the color property with an instruction to store the normal. The vertices stored in this method are used to draw a ground surface, so a suitable normal vector is X = 0.0f, Y = 1.0f, and Z = 0.0f:

```
mVertGrid[iCol + iRow * NUM_COLS].Normal
= new Vector3(0.0f, 1.0f, 0.0f);
```

The vertex type declaration, mVertGrid, must also be replaced with a new definition that stores the normal:

```
private VertexPositionNormalTexture[] mVertGrid;  // store vertices
```

To complete the change to enable normal data storage, inside init_dynamic_vb() replace each of the references to VertexPositionColorTexture with the following:

```
VertexPositionNormalTexture
```

A higher number of vertices will improve the definition of the lighting. You can easily increase the total vertices by adjusting the definitions for the row and column totals, which define the vertices used to build the indexed surface. To ensure you have a suitable number of vertices to display the light for this demonstration, replace the current row and column definitions with these modified declarations:

```
const int NUM_COLS = 20;
const int NUM_ROWS = 20;
```

Now that a set of vertices is in place to enable high-definition lighting, changes can be made to implement the lighting using XNA's built-in BasicEffect shader. A reference to it is needed in the game class:

```
BasicEffect mBE;
```

To set up the BasicEffect object to apply lighting to a textured primitive, you must set the TextureEnabled and LightingEnabled properties to true. In this example, a fairly high level of ambient lighting is set, and the specular power is set to a noticeable level. Only one directional light is enabled, and the diffuse and specular color properties are set. The RGB color properties, for each type of light, range between 0 and 1. The direction is normalized to ensure consistent direction on the X, Y, and Z planes. Finally, the directional light is set to shine downward on the Y axis (–1) and inward on the Z axis (+1).

```
private void init_basic_effect(){
    mBE = new BasicEffect(gfx.GraphicsDevice, null);
    mBE.TextureEnabled     = true;  // needed if objects are textured
    mBE.LightingEnabled    = true;  // must be on for lighting effect
    mBE.SpecularPower      = 5.0f;  // highlights
    mBE.AmbientLightColor = new Vector3(0.6f,0.6f,0.5f);// background light
    mBE.DirectionalLight0.Enabled = true;               // turn on light 0
    // set diffuse and specular colors - RGB parameters range from 0 to 1
    mBE.DirectionalLight0.DiffuseColor  = (new Vector3(0.2f, 0.2f, 0.2f));
    mBE.DirectionalLight0.SpecularColor = (new Vector3(0.5f, 0.5f, 0.37f));
    mBE.DirectionalLight0.Direction                     // set normalized
     = Vector3.Normalize(new Vector3(0.0f,-1.0f, 1.0f));// direction
}
```

To initialize the BasicEffect properties when the program begins, you call init_basic_effect() from Initialize():

```
init_basic_effect();
```

The same indexed set of vertices is used to draw two surfaces. For convenience, identifiers are added to the game class to distinguish between the two surfaces:

```
private const int FLOOR = 0;
private const int WALL0 = 1;
```

You need two Texture2D objects to store and apply the floor and wall images. To do this, add these object declarations at the top of your game class:

```
private Texture2D mTexFloor;
private Texture2D mTexWall;
```

Of course, be sure to add the corresponding Stonefloor.tga and Brickwall.tga files (available from the Images folder in the download from this book's website) to your source folder so they can be loaded when the program runs. When these images are referenced in your project, you will be able to load them when the following load instructions are placed inside the LoadGraphicsContent() method:

```
mTexWall  = content.Load<Texture2D>(".\\Images\\Brickwall");
mTexFloor = content.Load<Texture2D>(".\\Images\\Stonefloor");
```

Next is the code to draw the grid. Most of the code is used to set up the transformation to move each surface into place. The Texture property for the BasicEffect object is set to the appropriate Texture2D object if either the floor or wall is being drawn. The World, View, and Projection matrices are set to position the surfaces properly in the camera's view. The view also provides the BasicEffect class with information on the viewer's Look direction, which will help implement specular lighting. Once these states have been set, the CommitChanges() method is used to finalize the change in the shader. The GraphicsDevice's VertexDeclaration property is set with the mVertNTex variable to assign it the VertexPositionTextureNormal format for data retrieval and rendering. All drawing performed by the BasicEffect shader is done between the Begin() and End() for each pass. Replace the existing version of draw_grid() with this revision to render the stone wall and ground texture surfaces:

```
private void draw_grid(int iObject){
    // 1: declare matrices
    Matrix matIdentity, matTransl, matRotX, matScale, matRotY;

    // 2: initialize matrices
```

```
matIdentity = Matrix.Identity; // always start with identity matrix
matScale    = Matrix.CreateScale(0.8f, 0.8f, 0.8f);
matRotY     = Matrix.CreateRotationY(0.0f);
matRotX     = Matrix.CreateRotationX(0.0f);
matTransl   = Matrix.CreateTranslation(0.0f, -3.6f, 0.0f);

// create two walls with normals that face the user
if (iObject == WALL0){
    matRotX     = Matrix.CreateRotationX(-(float)Math.PI / 2.0f);
    matTransl   = Matrix.CreateTranslation(0.0f, 9.20f, 12.8f);
    mBE.Texture = mTexWall;
}
else
    mBE.Texture = mTexFloor;// set ground image

// 3: build cumulative world matrix using I.S.R.O.T. sequence
// identity, scale, rotate, orbit(translate & rotate), translate
mMatWorld = matIdentity * matScale * matRotX * matRotY * matTransl;



// 4: pass wvp matrices to shader and commit changes
mBE.World       = mMatWorld;
mBE.Projection  = mMatProj;
mBE.View        = mMatView;
mBE.CommitChanges();

// 5: draw object - select vertex type, primitive type, index, and draw
gfx.GraphicsDevice.VertexDeclaration = mVertNTex;
gfx.GraphicsDevice.Vertices[0].SetSource(mVB, 0,
    VertexPositionNormalTexture.SizeInBytes);
gfx.GraphicsDevice.Indices = mIB;

mBE.Begin();

foreach (EffectPass pass in mBE.CurrentTechnique.Passes){
    pass.Begin();

    gfx.GraphicsDevice.Vertices[0].SetSource(mVB, 0,
        VertexPositionNormalTexture.SizeInBytes);
    // draw grid one row at a time
    for (int z = 0; z < NUM_ROWS - 1; z++){
        gfx.GraphicsDevice.DrawIndexedPrimitives(
```

```
            PrimitiveType.TriangleStrip,// primitive type
            z * NUM_COLS,                  // start point in vertex buffer
            0,                             // vertex buffer offset
            NUM_COLS * NUM_ROWS,           // total verts in vertex buffer
            0,                             // index buffer offset
            2 * (NUM_COLS - 1));           // index buffer end
        }
        pass.End();
    }
    mBE.End();
}
```

To draw the textured wall and floor surfaces using the same vertex and index buffer, replace the existing draw_grid() instruction with these two:

```
draw_grid(WALL0);
draw_grid(FLOOR);
```

When you run this program, you will notice how the walls are brightened by the light. Try experimenting with the normal values and direction values and notice their effect on the brightness level. Also, try changing the ambient RGB color values to 1.0f. Notice that other lights no longer have an effect as long as ambience is at full strength. Increase the specular value to 50.0f and notice how the highlights on the ground and wall radiate.

IMPLEMENTING POINT LIGHT USING THE PHONG REFLECTION MODEL

Once you have directional lighting working, you may want more lighting effects to differentiate a constant source of sunlight from lighting that has a position and range. Scenes that take place outside, during the day, may be fine with directional light. Scenes that are located indoors, or that take place at night, are going to need a different type of light. Point light offers a dramatic way to reveal the details of your 3D world by creating a sphere of light that can brighten the surrounding area. Point light is used to radiate light from a light bulb, fire, torch, or lantern.

When building point light, we use the Phong reflection model to describe the relationship between ambient, diffuse, and reflective light. The model is actually very simple. It was authored by Bui Tuong Phong in 1973. The simplicity and effectiveness of the Phong reflection model has made it a popular method for computer-generated lighting simulations even today. Phong's reflection model states that the shade value for each surface point equals

Ambient $_{Color}$ * Ambient $_{Intensity}$

  + Diffuse $_{Color}$ * Diffuse $_{Intensity}$ * N.L

  + Specular $_{Color}$ * Specular $_{Intensity}$ * $(R.V)^{\alpha}$

where

L = Light direction
V = Viewpoint vector
N = Surface normal
R = Reflection vector = 2 * (N.L) * N – L
α = An exponential factor for specular light that varies according to the user

Figure 20-2 illustrates how the Phong reflection model implements light, normal, view, and reflection vectors to predict values for ambient, diffuse, and reflective light.

The angle θ decreases as the view vector and reflection vector converge. As θ decreases, cos θ increases and the specular or shiny reflection increases. The specular light is brightest when the view direction is exactly opposite to the reflection vector.

As α decreases, the diffuse light increases. In other words, the directional reflection is brightest when the light shines in a direction directly opposite to the normal vector.

 If you need to understand the math in more detail, or you need a refresher on dot products and vector math, consider reviewing Chapter 13, "Vectors."

FIGURE 20-2

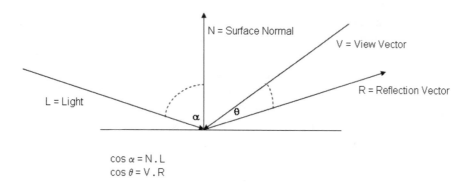

Lighting vectors used in the Phong reflection model

Calculating Point Light

Because point light shines in all directions, when you are calculating the diffuse component for each pixel, or vertex, the light direction vector can be calculated by subtracting the surface position from the point light position. The dot product of the light direction and surface normal gives the cosine of the angle between them. As the angle becomes smaller, in more direct light, the cosine approaches 1—which yields a light with full intensity. Therefore, the brightest light appears on the portion of the surface that is closest to the light; from there the light fades outward. The result is a great-looking globe of light in the center, with the light fading away from the center. Figure 20-3 shows the relationship between the light position and normal vector. The portion of the surface that is closest to the point light is the brightest, and the light fades outward as the angle between the light vector and surface normal increases.

FIGURE 20-3

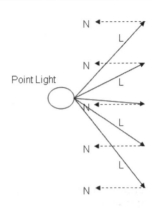

The dot product L.N is strongest at the center and fades as it moves away from the center.

Point Light in the Pixel Shader Example

The next example demonstrates a point light implementation in the pixel shader. It shows how to add a point light that moves with your camera as you travel through the world. If you wanted, you could easily set the position of this light to a constant value to simulate a stationary indoor light bulb. When you complete this example, a constant directionless light will illuminate your way. You can imagine using this sort of effect for a player's torch. If you wanted, this code could be modified to add a flicker to the light source to simulate a torch, a candle, a lantern, or a fire.

When the lighting calculations are performed in the pixel shader, the shading is automatically interpolated between pixels to show a gorgeously smooth, shiny light in the 3D world. Bear in mind that the processing demands of performing pixel-shading operations are expensive, so this effect needs to be used sparingly. However, it is attractive, and you can use it to liven up the parts of your game that you want noticed. After this demonstration of point light in the pixel shader, we'll view another example that shows how to perform the same calculations from the vertex shader when you feel the need for speed. Vertex shader–based lighting is not as attractive as lighting from the pixel shader, but it still delivers a punch.

The pixel shader–based point light does not actually need many vertices to produce high-definition light. This is because the pixel shader interpolates lighting between pixels. Even so, this example begins with the solution from the previous example, which uses an index buffer that offers potential for using large sets of vertices. You could actually skip the index buffer for pixel shader–based light. However, when this same example is converted to implement lighting from the vertex shader, you will want a larger number of vertices to produce high-definition lighting, so the index buffer is being used.

This example begins with the solution from the previous example. The shader code is contained in the PointLighPS.fx file, which can be found in the Shaders folder at the book's website. To try this illuminating example, add the PointLightPS.fx file to the Shaders folder in your project. All of the shader code in the PointLighPSt.fx file will be presented here in sequential order so that you can see how the point light is generated.

Point Light Example: The Shader Code

The globals section of the shader declares values that are accessed by the effect parameters in the game application. The global values allow you to send in different values for the camera and transformation matrices, textures, point light color, and point light intensity:

```
float4x4    gfxWVP;
float4x4    gfxMatWorld;
float4       gf4LightPos;
float4       gf4Color;
float        gfLightIntensity;
Texture      gfxTexture;
```

Because the lighting is going to be applied to an image, the texture effect parameter and sampler will also be included. A texture sampler, like the one used in Chapter 7, "Texturing Your Game World," defines how to filter your images:

```
sampler textureSampler = sampler_state
{
    Texture   = (gfxTexture);
    Minfilter = LINEAR;
    Magfilter = LINEAR;
    Mipfilter = LINEAR;
};
```

The input struct for the vertex shader allows you to retrieve and manipulate the position, normal, and texture data for each vertex:

```
struct VS_INPUT{
    float4 f4Pos        : POSITION0;
    float3 f3Norm       : NORMAL0;
```

```
    float2 f2UV            : TEXCOORD0;
};
```

The output struct from the vertex shader gives you control over the data that you send to the pixel shader. The position, *f4Pos*, is computed by multiplying the vertex by the WVP matrix so it can be viewed properly by the camera. However, the position is also expressed as *f3Pos*, which is the normalized product of the vertex position multiplied by the cumulative transformation matrix. *f3Pos* will be used in the pixel shader to compute the light direction vector for the point light. The normal, *f3Norm*, is also transformed and normalized, so it too can be used in the pixel shader to compute the dot product between the light vector, L, and the normal vector, N. Additional texture semantics allow you to pass your calculated data to the pixel shader from the vertex shader.

```
struct VS_OUTPUT{
    float4 f4Pos           : POSITION;   // position for view & cam
    float3 f3Pos           : TEXCOORD0;  // transformed position
    float2 f2Tex           : TEXCOORD1;  // uv data
    float3 f3Norm          : TEXCOORD2;  // normalized normal in world space
    float4 f4amb           : COLOR0;
};
```

In most cases, the pixel shader output is just a color for each pixel. By the time the output has been generated for each pixel, the pixel shader will have blended a shade of color against the texture. The color is altered by the light—hence the light is just a shade of color. The struct used for the pixel shader output only returns an RGBA color vector:

```
struct PS_OUTPUT{
    float4 color : COLOR;
};
```

The effect of ambience can easily be simulated by multiplying an RGBA color vector by an intensity coefficient. In your shader code, you can decide how much ambience you want to add. For this example, the ambient light intensity has been turned down to 0.1f to allow you to see the effect of the specular and diffuse point light:

```
// get background light
float4 get_ambient_light(){
    // ambient is just a color vector * intensity
    float4 f4Color       = (1.0f, 1.0f, 1.0f, 1.0f);
    float  fIntensity    = 0.1f;
    return f4Color * fIntensity;
}
```

A yellow specular light has been added to make the brick wall look as if it is covered with a bright finish. You can notice the yellow shine as you move closer to the wall.

If your object should have a glossy sheen—like a brand new Corvette—you will need a high level of specular light. Phong's reflection model calculates specular high-lights using the reflection vector and the view direction. The equation to generate the specular light is

$$\text{Specular Color} * \text{Specular Intensity} * (R.V)^{\alpha}$$

where $R = 2 * N.L * N - L$.

get_specular_light() implements this calculation to return an RGBA vector with color added to represent the specular light:

```
float4 get_specular_light(VS_OUTPUT IN){
    float4 f4Spec;

    // light and material properties for specular
    float4 fIntensity    = 0.2f;
    float4 f4Color       = { 1.0f, 1.0f, 0.0f, 1.0f };

    // already converted to world unit norm in shader
    float3 f3UnitNorm    = IN.f3Norm;                    // N

    float3 f3LightDir    = normalize(gf4LightPos - IN.f3Pos);
    float3 f3UnitLightDir = normalize(f3LightDir);      // L

    // (N.L) - dot product of surface normal and light direction
    float fcosA          = dot(f3UnitNorm, f3UnitLightDir);

    // R = 2 * (N.L) * N - L
    float3 v3Reflect = normalize(2 * fcosA * f3UnitNorm - f3UnitLightDir);

    // (R.V)^n specular reflection.
    float fSpec = pow(dot(v3Reflect, f3UnitLightDir), 2);

    f4Spec = f4Color * fIntensity  *  fSpec;
    return f4Spec;
}
```

The diffuse light is simply the dot product between the light direction vector and the object being lit. The dot product approaches 1 for full intensity with the direct-ness of the light to the surface. When this calculation is done in the pixel shader, the result is interpolated between pixels to produce a nice, smooth-looking light. As you move the camera closer to the wall, the light radiates brightly and fizzles outward from the point that is directly in front of the camera. Diffuse light is modeled by the following equation:

$$\text{Diffuse}_{Color} * \text{Diffuse}_{Intensity} * N.L$$

Because $N.L = \cos \alpha$, as the angle between the surface normal and light vector decreases, $\cos \alpha$ approaches 1 and diffuse light increases. Shining a light directly at a surface normal generates a brighter reflection than a light shone at an angle away from the normal vector. get_ptLght_diffuse() calculates the color added by the diffuse light:

```
float4 get_ptLght_diffuse(VS_OUTPUT IN){
    // unit direction of light vector L
    float3   LightDir = normalize(gf4LightPos - IN.f3Pos);

    // brightest angle between L and N = 0
    float    fDiffuse = dot(LightDir, IN.f3Norm);

    // point light diffuse * intensity and color
    return   fDiffuse * gfLightIntensity * gf4Color;
}
```

The point light vertex shader receives the vertex position, texture, and normal data. The position, *f4Pos*, is generated by multiplying the position by the WVP matrix so that each vertex can be seen properly by the camera. *f3Pos* is calculated by normalizing the product of the position and World matrix, so this unit vector can be used in the specular and diffuse lighting calculations. The normal vector is also transformed with the World matrix and is then normalized for the specular and diffuse calculations. Ambient light is uniform across the entire surface, so this calculation is performed in the vertex shader to save a little processing time:

```
void vertex_shader(in VS_INPUT IN, out VS_OUTPUT OUT){
    OUT.f4Pos       = mul(IN.f4Pos, gfxWVP);
    OUT.f3Pos       = mul(IN.f4Pos, gfxMatWorld);

    // unit normal in world coordinates
    OUT.f3Norm      = normalize(mul(IN.f3Norm, (float3x3)gfxMatWorld));
    OUT.f2Tex       = IN.f2UV;
    OUT.f4amb       = get_ambient_light();
}
```

The pixel shader combines the different lights together and blends them with the texture for each pixel. The sum of the ambient, specular, and diffuse light component vectors is equivalent to the combination of different lighting components in Phong's reflection model.

```
void pixel_shader(in VS_OUTPUT IN, out PS_OUTPUT OUT){
    float4 f4Diff= get_ptLght_diffuse(IN);
    float4 f4Spec= get_specular_light(IN);
    OUT.color    = tex2D(textureSampler,IN.f2Tex)*(IN.f4amb+f4Spec+f4Diff);
}
```

The technique is identical to others used before this chapter for compiling the vertex and pixel shaders and for calling them:

```
technique mytechnique{
    pass p0{
        // texture sampler initialized
        sampler[0] = (textureSampler);

        // declare and initialize vs
        vertexshader = compile vs_2_0 vertex_shader();

        // declare and initialize ps
        pixelshader = compile ps_2_0 pixel_shader();
    }
}
```

It is amazing that such a small amount of shader code can generate such a great lighting effect.

Point Light Example: The XNA Code

All of the shader code just described can be found in the PointLightPS.fx file in the Shaders folder in the download from this book's website. Be sure to add this file to your project in the Shaders folder.

To assist in setting the matrices for the shader, and to provide position data for the lighting calculations, the effect parameters *mfxPtLgt_World*, *mfxPtLgt_WVP*, and *mfxPtLgt_LightPos* are declared. A texture parameter, *mfxPtLgt_Tex*, allows you to set the image applied in the shader from the C# code. The parameter *mfxPtLgt_Intensity* lets you set the intensity of the diffuse point light at run time from the application, and *mfxPtLgt_Color* allows you to set the color of the light. Add these declarations to the game class module level so you can set these shader variables from your C# code:

```
private Effect mfxPtLgt;                  // point light shader
private EffectParameter mfxPtLgt_World;   // world matrix
```

```
private EffectParameter mfxPtLgt_WVP;        // wvp matrix
private EffectParameter mfxPtLgt_LightPos;   // light position
private EffectParameter mfxPtLgt_Intensity;  // pt light strength
private EffectParameter mfxPtLgt_Tex;        // texture
private EffectParameter mfxPtLgt_Color;      // color of pt light
```

To be able to use your shader, you must load and compile it when the program starts. Add code to set up the shader in Initialize():

```
mfxPtLgt = content.Load<Effect>(@"shaders\PointLightPS");
```

To set the data in the shader variables at run time, you must initialize the effect parameters to reference the correct shader variables when the program begins. To make this possible, assign the effect parameters to their corresponding shader variables from Initialize():

```
// declare lighting effect parameters
mfxPtLgt_WVP          = mfxPtLgt.Parameters["gfxWVP"];
mfxPtLgt_World        = mfxPtLgt.Parameters["gfxMatWorld"];
mfxPtLgt_LightPos     = mfxPtLgt.Parameters["gf4LightPos"];
mfxPtLgt_Intensity    = mfxPtLgt.Parameters["gfLightIntensity"];
mfxPtLgt_Tex          = mfxPtLgt.Parameters["gfxTexture"];
mfxPtLgt_Color        = mfxPtLgt.Parameters["gf4Color"];
```

Most of the code used to draw the primitive surface has been explained in previous chapters. This includes transforming the object and drawing the vertices using an index buffer reference. Also, the shader's effect parameters are used here to move the point light with the camera, to set the diffuse light intensity, and to set the texture value. In step 4 of the code, the global variables in the shader are assigned values for the WVP matrix and the World matrix. This combination allows you to generate light in the view space and then to render the objects based on the World matrix. Replace the existing version of draw_grid() with the following code to draw the surfaces with the point light shader:

```
private void draw_grid(int iObject){
    // 1: declare matrices
    Matrix matIdentity, matTransl, matRotX, matScale, matRotY;

    // 2: initialize matrices
    matIdentity = Matrix.Identity; // always start with identity matrix
    matTransl   = Matrix.CreateTranslation(0.0f, -3.6f, 0.0f);
    matScale    = Matrix.CreateScale(0.8f, 0.8f, 0.8f);
    matRotY     = Matrix.CreateRotationY(0.0f);
    matRotX     = Matrix.CreateRotationX(0.0f);
```

```
// create two walls with normals that face the user
if (iObject == WALL0){
    matRotX = Matrix.CreateRotationX(-(float)Math.PI / 2.0f);
    matTransl = Matrix.CreateTranslation(0.0f, 9.20f, 12.8f);
    mfxPtLgt_Tex.SetValue(mTexWall); // set wall image
}
else
    mfxPtLgt_Tex.SetValue(mTexFloor);// set ground image

// 3: build cumulative world matrix using I.S.R.O.T. sequence
// identity, scale, rotate, orbit(translate & rotate), translate
mMatWorld = matIdentity * matScale * matRotX * matRotY * matTransl;

// 4: pass world matrix to shader
mfxPtLgt_WVP.SetValue(mMatWorld * mMatView * mMatProj);    //cam view
mfxPtLgt_World.SetValue(mMatWorld);                        //transform
mfxPtLgt_LightPos.SetValue(new Vector4(cam.m_vPos, 1.0f)); //move light
mfxPtLgt_Intensity.SetValue(2.0f);                         //power
mfxPtLgt_Color.SetValue(new Vector4(1.0f,1.0f,1.0f,1.0f)); //lt color

mfxPtLgt.CommitChanges();

// 5: draw object - select vertex type, primitive type, index, and draw
gfx.GraphicsDevice.VertexDeclaration = mVertNTex;
gfx.GraphicsDevice.Vertices[0].SetSource(mVB, 0,
    VertexPositionNormalTexture.SizeInBytes);
gfx.GraphicsDevice.Indices = mIB;
gfx.GraphicsDevice.Vertices[0].SetSource(mVB, 0,
    VertexPositionNormalTexture.SizeInBytes);

    // draw grid one row at a time
    for (int z = 0; z < NUM_ROWS - 1; z++){
        gfx.GraphicsDevice.DrawIndexedPrimitives(
            PrimitiveType.TriangleStrip,// primitive
            z * NUM_COLS,               // start point in vertex
            0,                          // vertex buffer offset
            NUM_COLS * NUM_ROWS,        // total verts in vertex buffer
            0,                          // start point in index buffer
            2 * (NUM_COLS - 1));        // end point in index buffer
    }
}
```

The drawing routine needs to reference the PointLightPS.fx shader to apply the point light to the textures. Adding this code to Draw() will reference the PointLightPS.fx shader to apply point light to the objects you render with it. Be sure to comment out the original lines of code from the previous example that call draw_grid() so that only the new surfaces are drawn:

```
mfxPtLgt.Begin();
mfxPtLgt.Techniques[0].Passes[0].Begin();
    // draw objects
    draw_grid(FLOOR);
    draw_grid(WALL0);
    // end shader
mfxPtLgt.Techniques[0].Passes[0].End();
mfxPtLgt.End();
```

If you compile and run the project, you will see the point light traveling with the camera. Move closer to the wall, and the light reflected back will become brighter because the point light is closer to the wall surface.

Figure 20-4 shows the point light positioned above the center of the ground. The light is brightest directly beneath the light—hopefully this will help you see the point of point light!

FIGURE 20-4

Point light demo

Point Light in the Vertex Shader Example

You won't always be able to afford pixel-based lighting because it is expensive for the processor. Moving specular and diffuse lighting calculations into the vertex shader will drastically reduce the number of times these calculations need to be made each frame. The ambient, diffuse, and specular light can be combined in one color variable in the vertex shader, which can then be sent to the pixel shader so that the pixel shader doesn't have to generate it. When this color data is sent to the pixel shader, it is automatically interpolated between vertices. For this method to be effective, using more vertices provides more definition and smoother shading, so an index buffer is recommended for primitive surfaces.

This example begins with the solution from the previous example. You could follow the steps here to modify the shader to implement vertex shader–based point light, or you could just load and reference the PointLightVS.fx file in place of the PointLightPS.fx file in your project to implement it.

Once you have changed your shader reference, you will need to load the new shader from Initialize() when the program begins:

```
mfxPtLgt = content.Load<Effect>(@"shaders\PointLightVS");
```

With this change, less information needs to be passed to the pixel shader, so a new struct for the vertex shader output is added:

```
// vertex shader output
struct VS_OUTPUT2
{
    float4 f4Pos                    : POSITION0;
    float4 f4Col                    : COLOR;
    float2 textureCoordinate        : TEXCOORD0;
};
```

The revised version of the vertex shader uses the new struct to define the output. Note that the calculations for all lights are now performed in the vertex shader. The color variable that is sent to the pixel shader stores the sum of the ambient, diffuse, and specular lights. Replace the existing vertex shader with this revised version to process the lighting calculations before sending the output to the pixel shader:

```
void vertex_shader(in VS_INPUT IN, out VS_OUTPUT2 OUT){
    VS_OUTPUT tVS;
    tVS.f3Pos       = mul(IN.f4Pos, gfxMatWorld);   // transform
    tVS.f4Pos       = mul(IN.f4Pos, gfxWVP);        // relative to cam

    // unit normal in world coordinates
```

```
tVS.f3Norm       = normalize(mul(IN.f3Norm, (float3x3)gfxMatWorld));

tVS.f2Tex        = IN.f2UV;                    // get text coords

OUT.f4Pos            = tVS.f4Pos;              // output position
OUT.textureCoordinate = tVS.f2Tex;            // output texture

tVS.f4amb        = get_ambient_light();        // get ambient light
float4 f4Diff    = get_ptLght_diffuse(tVS);    // get diffuse light
float4 f4Spec    = get_specular_light(tVS);    // get spec light
OUT.f4Col        = (tVS.f4amb + f4Spec + f4Diff);// output color
}
```

A slight change is made in the pixel shader to receive the new vertex shader output, which already includes the combined ambient, diffuse, and specular light:

```
void pixel_shader(in VS_OUTPUT2 IN, out PS_OUTPUT OUT){
    OUT.color    = tex2D(textureSampler, IN.textureCoordinate)*(IN.f4Col);
}
```

To view a stationary point light, in your XNA code, set the position of the light to a constant value. (Or you could continue to move the light with your camera if you prefer.) You can make the position of the point light stationary by replacing the instruction that moves the light with the camera in draw_grid():

```
mfxPtLgt_LightPos.SetValue(new Vector4(0.0f, 0.0f, 0.0f, 1.0f));
```

When you run this version of the code, you will still see the point light. It will not be defined as much as the pixel shader point light, but you may notice a performance boost when running it.

A simple lighting system, such as a lone directional light or the sun, can add depth to your game and reveal the details in your environment. Point light can add intriguing details for nighttime or indoor settings. As you can see, the effect is quite brilliant.

CHAPTER 20 REVIEW EXERCISES

1. Complete the step-by-step examples presented in this chapter.

2. After completing the directional light demonstration using the BasicEffect object, try reducing the number of vertices that are stored in the vertex buffer by lowering the number of rows and columns to two each. Run the demo again (after this change has been made) and notice how the specular

detail diminishes. Then, increase the total number of vertices for rows and columns to 50 each. Notice how the specular lighting's effect improves with more vertices.

3. Using the directional light example, change the Y value of the normal in the vertex buffer from +1 to −1. Notice how everything turns black. Explain why this happens.

4. What is a useful intensity level for ambient light during daytime settings in the directional light demo? What is a useful intensity level for ambient light during evening settings in the directional light demo?

CHAPTER 21

Input Devices

EFFECTIVELY handling input is fundamental to every gamer's experience. Nowadays, this means that you need to support the keyboard, mouse, and Xbox 360 game controller, and possibly even a wireless racing wheel. The XNA Framework greatly simplifies this task. Specifically, the Microsoft.Xna.Framework.Input namespace enables the capture of button press and release events, mouse click events, and game controller button, thumbstick, DPad, and trigger events. You can even use the Input library to send rumbles to users' controllers to let them know when they have exploded.

You reference the input device–handling library in a GSE project with this namespace declaration:

```
using Microsoft.Xna.Framework.Input;
```

HANDLING KEYBOARD INPUT

The input library handles press and release events for all common keyboard keys. To view a full listing of key identifiers, type **Keys.** in the GSE Code window. This will open a drop-down menu that displays all identifiers available. These are the identifiers for common keyboard keys:

A to Z	Home	PageUp
Add	Insert	PrintScreen
CapsLock	Left	Right
D0 to D9	LeftAlt	RightAlt
Decimal	LeftControl	RightControl
Delete	LeftShift	RightShift
Divide	LeftWindows	RightWindows
Down	Multiply	Scroll
End	NumLock	Space
Enter	NumPad0 to	Subtract
Escape	NumPad9	Tab
F1 to F12	PageDown	Up
Help		

 **NOTE** D0 to D9 refer to the numbers at the top of the keyboard, whereas keys on the number pad use NumPad0 to NumPad9.

You will capture Key events using a KeyboardState object. At each frame, this object is updated by polling the keyboard with the GetState() method:

```
KeyboardState keyboardState = Keyboard.GetState();
```

Individual key events are distinguished with the IsKeyDown() method using a Keys identifier as a parameter:

```
bool KeyboardState.IsKeyDown(Keys Keys.Identifier);
```

HANDLING MOUSE INPUT

In many PC versions of major game titles, and even for the 3D graphics engine used in this book, the mouse can be used to control the player's direction. The Input namespace enables handling of mouse-based events. Mouse movements and click events are detected with a MouseState object. Every frame, the state of the mouse is refreshed with the GetState() method, which retrieves information about the cursor's position and the press state of the mouse buttons:

```
MouseState mouseState = Mouse.GetState();
```

With these continuous updates, the MouseState object's X and Y properties track the cursor's position in the game window:

```
int MouseState.X
int MouseState.Y
```

Press and release states of each mouse button are retrieved from the ButtonState property of each button. Most mice have a MouseState.LeftButton and MouseState.RightButton property, and some have a MouseState.MiddleButton property. The ButtonState attribute stores either a Pressed value, if the button is pressed, or a Released value, if it is not.

HANDLING CONTROLLER INPUT

In addition to the keyboard and mouse, the Input namespace also handles events for the game controller. The game controller itself provides several options to obtain user input through presses and shifts of the thumbstick, as well as presses to the DPad, buttons, left and right bumpers, and triggers. Figure 21-1 shows the name of each control.

Game Pad States

The GamePadState object for the controller allows you to check the state of each control on each game controller at every frame. Because it is possible to have up to four game controllers connected to your Xbox 360, the GamePadState object is often declared as an array with a size of four:

```
private GamePadState[] gamePadState = new GamePadState[4];
```

FIGURE 21-1

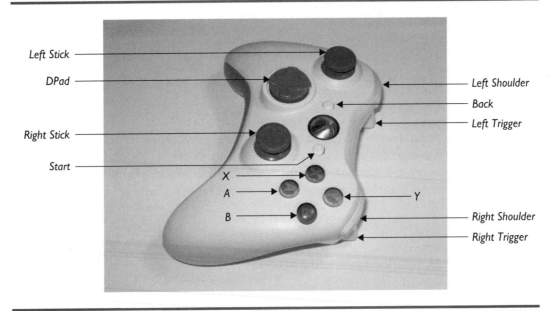

Left Stick

DPad

Right Stick

Start

X

A

B

Left Shoulder

Back

Left Trigger

Y

Right Shoulder

Right Trigger

Names of individual controls on the controller

NOTE Although the array has room for up to four controllers, if only one controller is connected, this controller will use the first object in the array; it is referenced with zero as the index.

At every frame, the states for each game pad are retrieved with the GetState() method and PlayerIndex attribute to identify the controller:

```
gamePadState[0] = GamePad.GetState(PlayerIndex.One);
gamePadState[1] = GamePad.GetState(PlayerIndex.Two);
gamePadState[2] = GamePad.GetState(PlayerIndex.Three);
gamePadState[3] = GamePad.GetState(PlayerIndex.Four);
```

Handling Pressed and Released States

Most of the controls on the game controller use a ButtonState.Pressed and a ButtonState.Released attribute to indicate whether or not the control is pressed. Here is a complete listing of controls that store either a Pressed or Released property.

Buttons.A	Buttons.Right Shoulder	DPad.Down
Buttons.B	Buttons.RightStick	DPad.Left
Buttons.Back	Buttons.Start	DPad.Right
Buttons.LeftShoulder	Buttons.X	DPad.Up
Buttons.LeftStick	Buttons.Y	

In *Soul Calibur*, certain button combinations allow Lizard Man to outwit the giant, Astaroth, with a powerful spring kick. In a more peaceful world, the right timing and button combination can ensure a better launch when gliding over the ocean in *Monkey Ball*.

Thumbsticks

Another way to enable user control is to use thumbsticks. They can be pushed up, down, and sideways to help with tasks such as controlling the player's view and guiding the direction of game characters. Each thumbstick stores a float to measure the deviation from its central resting position. The X and Y values range from –1 to +1, where 0 is the center position. These are the four possible thumbstick properties:

>) float ThumbSticks.Left.X

>) float ThumbSticks.Left.Y

>) float ThumbSticks.Right.X

>) float ThumbSticks.Right.Y

Triggers

You can enable intuitive features such as acceleration and rapid firing with the Xbox 360 controller triggers. On every controller there is one left and one right trigger. Each trigger returns a float that ranges from 0 (for released) to 1 (for fully pressed).

```
float   GamePadState.Triggers.Right
float   GamePadState.Triggers.Left
```

Adjusting the Input Device Responsiveness

The responsiveness needed for input controls can vary depending on the purpose of the control. The IsKeyDown() method and ButtonState.Pressed property can be used to check whether a key, mouse button, or controller's DPad, button, or thumbstick is pressed. Similarly, the Left and Right properties of a trigger and the X and Y properties of a thumbstick will return nonzero values when moved away from their default positions. Most of the time, an immediate response at every frame is useful for events such as rapid fire or speed control. In other situations, a delay may be needed to hold a result after the frame when the control is first pressed. For example, when a player is choosing a game character, selecting a map, changing weapons, or even entering a name through an input device, tens or even hundreds of true IsKeyDown() events or ButtonState.Pressed states are registered between the time that the user first presses the control and releases it. For cases like these, a delay is required to treat each series of IsKeyDown(), ButtonState.Pressed, thumbstick, or trigger results as one. The delay should be long enough to allow users to comfortably press and release the control when selecting or scrolling through a list of options.

The following code snippet shows one way to allow a player 0.2 seconds to press and release a key before the keypress is considered a distinctly separate event:

```
if(GameTime.TotalGameTime.TotalMilliseconds - mdblLastTpress > 200)
    // handle keypress as a new event
```

Adding a Rumble

The ability to make a controller rumble is a popular feature among gamers. Whether the player has crashed into a wall, been body-checked into the boards, or knocked unconscious by a rifle butt, sending a rumble through their controller will add to the effect. A rumble can be sent to the left and right sides of the game controller with the method SetVibration(). The vibration takes three parameters to identify the control and to set the strength of the rumble. The rumble strength is measured with a float that ranges from 0 to 1.

```
GamePad.SetVibration(int controllerNumber, float LRumble, float RRumble);
```

Input Example

This example demonstrates the handling of input from the keyboard, mouse, and game pad by drawing current information on their press, release, shift, and move states in the window. Figure 21-2 shows how the text in the PC window reports the states of the keys, mouse, and game controller. Text output that shows states for mouse, keyboard, and controller event handling will only be displayed on Windows. On the Xbox 360, when you run this code, only the control states for the Xbox 360 controller will be shown.

To begin with a project that has fonts enabled, this example uses the "Font Example: Displaying Text in the Game Window" solution from Chapter 11, "Score Tracking and Game Statistics." Some adjustments are required to prepare this solution to display the status of all input controls presented during this demonstration. The call to draw_ground() from the Draw() method should be disabled to clear the screen for drawing text only:

```
// draw_ground();
```

FIGURE 21-2

```
Score Tracking and Game Stats
Keyboard                                    Bumpers
              a:  released                     left shoulder:  released
              0:  released                    right shoulder:  released
    numberpad 0:  released
    t for toggle:  off                       DPad
                                                      right:  released
Mouse                                                  left:  released
   right button:  released                               up:  released
   left  button:  released                             down:  released
              x:  288
              y:  203                         Right stick
                                                     button:  released
Controller                                                x:  0
              0:  connected                               y:  0
              1:  not connected
              2:  not connected              Left stick
              3:  not connected                      button:  released
                                                          x:  0
Gamepad Button                                            y:  0
              a:  released
           back:  released                   Trigger
          start:  released                      left - rumble:  0
                                               right - rumble:  0
```

Input device states display

Also, because more data is being presented on the window in this example, to view all of the text output, you need to reduce the font size by replacing the class-level size definition:

```
const float MAGNIFY = 1.0f;
```

Handling Keyboard Input

Sometimes you will not have your game controller with you, or your intended audience may only have a keyboard and mouse as input devices. For this reason, when running your games on the PC, your code should always consider the keyboard as an alternative for user input.

To handle the input events, a reference to the Microsoft.Xna.Framework.Input namespace is required at the top of the Game1.cs file where the game class is located. For this case, the reference is already present, so you don't need to add it again.

```
using Microsoft.Xna.Framework.Input;
```

This first portion of the demonstration shows whether or not the 0 on the keyboard, the 0 on the number pad, and the A key are pressed. To store a user-friendly description of each key state, strings are declared for each key to later display the key's current press or release status in the game window:

```
private string mDpad0, m0key, mAkey;
```

To ensure accurate reporting of the input device status each frame, a function is required to poll the input device. In this routine, a KeyboardState object is refreshed with the GetState() method. Once the entire keyboard state has been updated, it is possible for you to check whether each key is pressed. If a key is pressed, the string that was defined earlier to display the key state for each key is set to Pressed. If the key is not pressed, the string retains a default value of Released. This value is set at the beginning of the algorithm. To implement this routine, you will add the UpdatePressEvents() method to your game class:

```
void UpdatePressEvents()
{
    KeyboardState kbState   = Keyboard.GetState();

    mDpad0 = m0key = mAkey = "released";   // refresh status each frame

    if (kbState.IsKeyDown(Keys.A))         // A pressed
        mAkey = "pressed";
    if (kbState.IsKeyDown(Keys.D0))        // 0 pressed
        m0key = "pressed";
    if (kbState.IsKeyDown(Keys.NumPad0))   // 0 on numberpad pressed
        mDpad0 = "pressed";
}
```

To ensure continuous updates to the KeyboardState object, UpdatePressEvents() is called from the Update() method at every frame:

```
UpdatePressEvents();
```

Now that you have implemented continuous tracking of the A, 0 (keyboard), and 0 (number pad) keys, their status can be reported in the game window. The display of each key's status is done in the Draw() method immediately before the base.Draw() instruction. The Draw() method first initializes the X and Y values within the title-safe region where new text is to be drawn. (The title-safe area has already been calculated in the code solution used to start this example and is explained in Chapter 11, "Score Tracking and Game Statistics.") Then the draw_string() method is called to show the text in the window. The draw_string() method accepts the string to be displayed and the X,Y coordinates where that string is to be displayed, along with the color of the text. To view the text output, you must place this code at the end of the Draw() method before the base.Draw() instruction. The instructions to draw to the window are encased in an #if…#endif series to prevent them from running on the Xbox, where only the controller will be handled:

```
int iX = (int)v2px0.X; // starting X position (title safe) on window
int iY = (int)v2px0.Y; // starting Y position (title safe) on window
#if !XBOX // text display for mouse and keyboard will only be on PC
// keyboard
draw_string("Keyboard           ", iX, iY += 20, Color.Black);
draw_string("             a:   " + mAkey, iX, iY += 20, Color.Black);
draw_string("             0:   " + m0key, iX, iY += 20, Color.Black);
draw_string("    numberpad 0:   " + mDpad0,iX, iY += 20, Color.Black);
```

Adding a Time Delay

The method you just implemented for displaying the press or release status of the A, 0 (keyboard), and 0 (number pad) keys treats each frame as a separate event. However, sometimes a player may use a button, control, or key to select an option. When the user presses a key, button, or control to select an option, several frames will pass before the user is able to release it. When handling a series of frames to process a combined press and release event, you can use a delay to ensure that the total frames needed to press and release the key are treated as one event.

To demonstrate the handling of a press and release event that occurs over several frames, you will add a delay to allow the user to toggle between On and Off settings whenever the T key is pressed. You will use a string to store the value of On or Off for display purposes. In addition to a string declaration, you should add two other variables for storing the game time and the time of the last keypress to the module level of the game class:

```
private string  mTkey = "off";
GameTime        mgameTime;
private double  mdblLastTpress = 0;
```

Every frame, you need to refresh the total game time to enable accurate tracking of time lapses between keypresses. An assignment to the *mgameTime* variable inside Update() refreshes the total game time value for use throughout the class. The total game time value can later be used to track the delay between key press and release events.

```
mgameTime = gameTime;
```

Once the total game time is tracked on a continuous basis and a variable for tracking time (since the last keypress) has been declared, it is possible for you to check and store the time lapse since the last keypress event. The code first checks if the key was pressed more than 0.2 seconds ago to ensure that the key was actually released before this keypress event. You need to add the following code to the end of the UpdatePressEvents() method where the KeyboardState is refreshed:

```
if (kbState.IsKeyDown(Keys.T) &&
    mgameTime.TotalGameTime.TotalMilliseconds - mdblLastTpress > 200)
{
    mdblLastTpress = mgameTime.TotalGameTime.TotalMilliseconds;

    if (mTkey == "off")
        mTkey = "on";
    else
        mTkey = "off";
}
```

You have already added the code required to enable a successful toggle, so the status of the toggle state can now be displayed in the window. Code to display the status of the On or Off setting belongs at the bottom of the Draw() method just before the base.Draw() instruction. Placing the code at the end of the Draw() method will ensure the Y position for the text output updates properly each frame on the PC.

```
draw_string("    t for toggle:   " + mTkey, iX, iY += 20, Color.Black);
draw_string(" ", iX, iY += 20, Color.Black);
```

If you were to run the program now (on the PC), you would be able to press and release the T key to switch back and forth between On and Off display settings in the window.

Handling Mouse Button and Move Events

At some point, you may want to handle mouse button events to enable features such as rapid fire when running your game on a PC. Handling the mouse move and button click events is even easier than handling keyboard events. To enable mouse event handling, you need a declaration for the MouseState object in the module declaration area of the game class. This has already been added to the base code, so you do not need to add it again for this example. You will notice code that handles all mouse input is enclosed using an #if…#endif condition to ensure that mouse-handling code is only executed on the PC. This check is necessary because the Xbox 360 does not include instructions to handle the mouse, and your code will not compile for the Xbox 360 without this condition:

```
#if !XBOX
    MouseState                          mMouse;
#endif
```

To show the left and right mouse button press or release states, you will display text output in the game window. A string declaration at the module level of the game class enables storage of mouse button press states; later, you can use these states to draw text to the window.

```
#if !XBOX
    private string mMouseL, mMouseR;
#endif
```

Every frame, the mouse state must be updated to refresh the button click values and the X and Y coordinates for the mouse. To ensure regular updates, check that the assignment of the mouse state is maintained in the Update() method. This code is already included in the base code, so you do not need to add it in again.

```
#if !XBOX
    mMouse = Mouse.GetState();
#endif
```

Now that the MouseState object is refreshed every frame, it is possible for you to update the string values that store the state of the left and right mouse buttons. This code checks if either button is pressed and updates the appropriate string accordingly. To perform the check for the left and right mouse buttons and store their states each frame, add this code to the UpdatePressEvents() method:

```
#if !XBOX
mMouseL = mMouseR = "released";
if (mMouse.LeftButton == ButtonState.Pressed)
    mMouseL = "pressed";
if (mMouse.RightButton == ButtonState.Pressed)
    mMouseR = "pressed";
#endif
```

To ensure the mouse information appears in the window on the PC at the proper position, add this code block to the end of the Draw() method. This will output the mouse button states on the PC window:

```
draw_string("Mouse                 "            , iX, iY += 20, Color.Black);
draw_string("    right button: " + mMouseR, iX, iY += 20, Color.Black);
draw_string("    left  button: " + mMouseL, iX, iY += 20, Color.Black);
```

Because the MouseState is already being updated each frame, you can add code to extract the X and Y coordinates of the cursor and convert them to string values for display in the game window:

```
draw_string("                    x:   " + mMouse.X.ToString(), iX, iY+= 20,
Color.Black);
draw_string("                    y:   " + mMouse.Y.ToString(), iX, iY+= 20,
Color.Black);
draw_string(" ", iX, iY += 20, Color.Black);
```

If you were to run the program now, the mouse coordinates would change as you moved the mouse. Pressing the mouse buttons would trigger the display of a Pressed listing on the game window.

Adding a Mouse Cursor

To further demonstrate mouse move events, you will add a cursor to show how mouse movements can be used to position the cursor in the game window.

By default, the cursor will not appear in the game window mainly because XNA is geared to run on the Xbox 360, where there is no cursor. To view the cursor on the PC, you have to create your own.

In the base code project used in this book, code is already in place to use the cursor and mouse to allow a player the ability to control direction. In the Initialize() method and in the changeView() methods are instructions to set the cursor position back to the middle of the window at each frame. Resetting the cursor position every frame allows the camera to measure the mouse deviation from the center of the window, which can then be used to adjust the view each frame. For this example, the SetCursorPos() instruction must be disabled in the Initialize() and changeView() methods; otherwise, you will not be able to move your mouse.

You will create the cursor using a sprite made from a mouse image. Declarations are required in the module declaration area to load and draw the cursor image as a sprite:

```
private SpriteBatch mSpriteCsr;
private Texture2D   mTex2DCsr;
```

You can now initialize the cursor and sprite objects when the program begins. To ensure proper setup when the program starts, add instructions to set the sprite and load the image in the Initialize() method:

```
mSpriteCsr = new SpriteBatch(this.gfx.GraphicsDevice);
```

To load the cursor image with the other images, place the cursor.dds file in the Images folder for your project. You can find this cursor in the Images folder of the download from this book's website. Add the reference to the cursor file in the Solution Explorer so

the ContentManager object can find it. Then, inside LoadGraphicsContent(), place your code to load the image when the program begins:

```
mTex2DCsr = content.Load<Texture2D>(".\\Images\\cursor");
```

Once the cursor image and sprite object have been defined and loaded, drawing the cursor as a sprite is easy. You will extract the X and Y coordinates of the mouse from the MouseState object. Adding the draw_cursor() method to your game class will display the cursor wherever the mouse is directed over the window:

```
void draw_cursor()
{
#if !XBOX
    mSpriteCsr.Begin(SpriteBlendMode.AlphaBlend);

    mSpriteCsr.Draw(
        mTex2DCsr,
        // X, Y position on window and pixel W&H area used on window
        new Rectangle(mMouse.X, mMouse.Y, 9, 15),
        // starting X&Y pixels in image and pixel W&H used in image
        new Rectangle(0, 0, 9, 15),
        Color.White);

    mSpriteCsr.End();
#endif
}
```

The cursor display needs to be triggered from the Draw() method to show the cursor on the window:

```
draw_cursor();
```

At this point, you have handled the keyboard and mouse. This portion of the example concludes the instructions that are to be executed only on the PC, so you can end them with an #endif statement so they will not execute on the Xbox 360:

```
#endif
```

To see the states for the keyboard and mouse and to see the cursor move as you move the mouse, compile and run your project.

Handling the Controller

Now that keyboard and mouse handling have been demonstrated, we will shift focus to the game controller. Many people find the game controller better suited to gaming than a keyboard and mouse. Therefore, it's important for Windows games to support both options in case the game player has a controller plugged into their PC.

It is possible to have up to four controllers attached to the machine, so the controller object is usually declared as a four-element array. Adding this instruction to the module declaration area allows access to the GamePadState object for each controller throughout the program. This instruction is already included in the base code:

```
private GamePadState[]  mGamePadState  =  new GamePadState[4];
```

Before handling game controller states, you first need to determine whether the game controller is actually connected. String variables, declared in the module declaration area, allow you to store and display the connected status of the controllers within the game window:

```
private string mgp0connect, mgp1connect, mgp2connect, mgp3connect;
```

All controller states, including the IsConnected property, are retrieved by calling the GetState() method for each controller. This code is already implemented in the base code in the UpdateGamePad() method:

```
mGamePadState[0]  = GamePad.GetState(PlayerIndex.One);
mGamePadState[1]  = GamePad.GetState(PlayerIndex.Two);
mGamePadState[2]  = GamePad.GetState(PlayerIndex.Three);
mGamePadState[3]  = GamePad.GetState(PlayerIndex.Four);
```

After you check whether a controller is connected, the "connected" or "not connected" status is stored in a string. The default value is "not connected," but if the game pad's IsConnected property is true, a "connected" value is stored in this string variable. Adding this code block, after the game controller's states are retrieved in Update(), will ensure that you accurately record the controller's connection state for each frame:

```
mgp0connect = mgp1connect = mgp2connect = mgp3connect = "not connected";
if (mGamePadState[0].IsConnected == true)
    mgp0connect = "connected";
if (mGamePadState[1].IsConnected == true)
    mgp1connect = "connected";
if (mGamePadState[2].IsConnected == true)
    mgp2connect = "connected";
if (mGamePadState[3].IsConnected == true)
    mgp3connect = "connected";
```

Now that the controller's connection status is updated every frame, this information can be displayed in the game window. Adding the following lines of code to Draw() will display the status that has been stored in the string variables in the game window:

```
draw_string("Controller          "                , iX, iY +=20, Color.Black);
draw_string("              0:  " + mgp0connect, iX, iY +=20, Color.Black);
draw_string("              1:  " + mgp1connect, iX, iY +=20, Color.Black);
draw_string("              2:  " + mgp2connect, iX, iY +=20, Color.Black);
draw_string("              3:  " + mgp3connect, iX, iY +=20, Color.Black);
draw_string(" ",                                  iX, iY +=20, Color.Black);
```

If you run the program at this point, the connection states for each of the four controllers in the array will appear. The listing will show a "connected" or "not connected" value in the game window.

Game Pad Buttons

The process of checking whether buttons on the game controller are pressed is similar to checking whether the mouse buttons or keyboard keys are pressed. For this portion of the example, during each update, checks will be made to determine whether the A, Back, and Start buttons on the game controller are selected. Similar to the keyboard and mouse button examples, you will use string variables to store either a Pressed or Released value. Adding string variable declarations at the module level will enable more than one method in the class to access these values:

```
private string gpA, gpBack, gpStart;
```

After the game controller state has been updated, the status of the game controller buttons is checked inside the Update() method. If a Pressed state is found for A, Back, or Start, the value Pressed is stored in the corresponding string variable:

```
gpA = gpBack = gpStart = "released";
if (mGamePadState[0].Buttons.A == ButtonState.Pressed)
    gpA = "pressed";
if (mGamePadState[0].Buttons.Back == ButtonState.Pressed)
    gpBack = "pressed";
if (mGamePadState[0].Buttons.Start == ButtonState.Pressed)
    gpStart = "pressed";
```

The results from the button state test can now be drawn to the window using the values stored in the string variables. These instructions for displaying the text must be called at the end of the Draw() method but before the base.Draw() instruction:

```
draw_string("Gamepad Button    ", iX, iY += 20, Color.Black);
draw_string("              a:  " + gpA,    iX, iY += 20, Color.Black);
draw_string("           back:  " + gpBack, iX, iY += 20, Color.Black);
draw_string("          start:  " + gpStart,iX, iY += 20, Color.Black);
draw_string("               ",            iX, iY += 20, Color.Black);
```

When you run this version of the code, it will show the Pressed or Released status of the A, Back, and Start buttons on the game controller.

Left Shoulder and Right Shoulder (Bumpers)

Shoulders (or *bumpers)* are another form of button that return a Pressed or Released state. Declaring these variables in the module declaration area allows you to store the status of the shoulder buttons:

```
private string mLShoulder, mRShoulder;
```

Inside Update(), checks can be made to determine whether a shoulder button is pressed. The status is assigned accordingly.

```
mLShoulder = mRShoulder = "released";
if (mGamePadState[0].Buttons.LeftShoulder == ButtonState.Pressed)
    mLShoulder = "pressed";
if (mGamePadState[0].Buttons.RightShoulder== ButtonState.Pressed)
    mRShoulder = "pressed";
```

Once the shoulder states have been evaluated and stored in a string, the results can be shown in the game window. But first, you will use some extra code at the end of the Draw() method to position the new text listings in a second column that follows:

```
iX = Window.ClientBounds.Width / 2 +100; iY = (int)v2px0.Y; // title safe
```

You should also add the shoulder state display instructions to the end of the Draw() method so that the shoulder states appear in the window:

```
draw_string("Bumpers              ", iX, iY += 20, Color.Black);
draw_string("   left shoulder:    " + mLShoulder, iX, iY += 20, Color.Black);
draw_string("   right shoulder:   " + mRShoulder, iX, iY += 20, Color.Black);
draw_string("                     ",               iX, iY += 20, Color.Black);
```

When the program is run, you will see the Pressed or Released status of your bumpers.

DPad

The DPad control is somewhat unique in that it has Right, Left, Up, and Down attributes. Each attribute has its own Pressed or Released state; it is possible to have two of the DPad's attributes return a Pressed result if the game player presses a corner of the DPad. A module-level string declaration enables the display of the status on the window each frame:

```
private string mDpadL, mDpadR, mDpadU, mDpadD;
```

To ensure the DPad press states are checked every frame, the ButtonState.Pressed property for the DPad is checked after the GamePadState is retrieved for the controller in the Update() method:

```
mDpadL = mDpadR = mDpadU = mDpadD = "released";
if (mGamePadState[0].DPad.Right == ButtonState.Pressed)
    mDpadR = "pressed";
if (mGamePadState[0].DPad.Left == ButtonState.Pressed)
    mDpadL = "pressed";
if (mGamePadState[0].DPad.Up == ButtonState.Pressed)
    mDpadU = "pressed";
if (mGamePadState[0].DPad.Down == ButtonState.Pressed)
    mDpadD= "pressed";
```

Now the status of the Right, Left, Up, and Down buttons on the DPad can be displayed on the window by adding instructions to output the text:

```
draw_string("DPad                 "           ,iX, iY +=20, Color.Black);
draw_string("            right:  " + mDpadR,iX, iY +=20, Color.Black);
draw_string("             left:  " + mDpadL,iX, iY +=20, Color.Black);
draw_string("               up:  " + mDpadU,iX, iY +=20, Color.Black);
draw_string("             down:  " + mDpadD,iX, iY +=20, Color.Black);
draw_string("                 ",           iX, iY +=20, Color.Black);
```

When you run this program, the output will show the Pressed or Released status for the DPad's Left, Right, Up, and Down attributes.

Left Stick and Right Stick

To track the left and right thumbsticks' Pressed and Released states, you should follows steps similar to those used for tracking the DPad states. However, the thumbsticks don't just track their Pressed and Released states; each thumbstick also tracks an X and Y value to gauge the distance from its center resting position. Declaring string variables at the module level will enable the storage of press and shift states in string format; this allows you to display the states in the game window:

```
private string mLstick, mRstick, mLstickX, mRstickX, mRstickY, mLstickY;
```

Inside the Update() method, after the status for each game controller has been updated, the press status of each stick can be checked and stored:

```
mLstick = mRstick = "released";
if (mGamePadState[0].Buttons.LeftStick == ButtonState.Pressed)
```

```
      mLstick = "pressed";
if (mGamePadState[0].Buttons.RightStick == ButtonState.Pressed)
      mRstick = "pressed";
```

To track the positions of the left and right thumbsticks, you need to add some more code in the Update() method. This code returns the floating-point attributes for the X and Y values of each stick. The float values in this code are converted to strings using the ToString() method so that they can be stored in a string value for display in the window:

```
mRstickX = mGamePadState[0].ThumbSticks.Right.X.ToString();
mRstickY = mGamePadState[0].ThumbSticks.Right.Y.ToString();
mLstickX = mGamePadState[0].ThumbSticks.Left.X.ToString();
mLstickY = mGamePadState[0].ThumbSticks.Left.Y.ToString();
```

Once the results for the thumbstick press and shift states are stored as string values, they can be displayed as text output in the window. To enable the output, add these statements to the end of the Draw() method:

```
// right stick
draw_string("Right stick        "              , iX, iY += 20, Color.Black);
draw_string("          button:  " + mRstick , iX, iY += 20, Color.Black);
draw_string("               x:  " + mRstickX, iX, iY += 20, Color.Black);
draw_string("               y:  " + mRstickY, iX, iY += 20, Color.Black);
draw_string("                   ",              iX, iY += 20, Color.Black);
// left stick
draw_string("Left stick         "              , iX, iY += 20, Color.Black);
draw_string("          button:  " + mLstick , iX, iY += 20, Color.Black);
draw_string("               x:  " + mLstickX, iX, iY += 20, Color.Black);
draw_string("               y:  " + mLstickY, iX, iY += 20, Color.Black);
draw_string("                   ",              iX, iY += 20, Color.Black);
```

When you run this version of the input example, you will see the press and shift states for the left and right thumbsticks displayed in the game window. Each thumbstick shows one Pressed or Released state. Also, each thumbstick lists floating-point values for its X and Y positions. These positions are relative to the thumbstick's resting position at the center of the control.

Left Trigger and Right Trigger

Triggers provide yet another unique way of obtaining user input. Each left and right trigger stores a float value that ranges between 0 and 1 to indicate how far the trigger is pulled. When the trigger is released, the value returned is 0. When the trigger is fully squeezed, the trigger returns a value of 1.

To show these floating-point values in the window, you will convert them to string format. These string declarations belong at the module level to ensure they can be updated and used throughout the game class:

```
private string mTriggerL, mTriggerR;
```

The status of triggers can be updated and stored in the strings just declared—after the game pad status is retrieved in the Update() method:

```
mTriggerL = mGamePadState[0].Triggers.Left.ToString();
mTriggerR = mGamePadState[0].Triggers.Right.ToString();
```

Once the trigger states have been gathered and converted to string output, the output can be shown as text in the game window. To do this, add the following code to the end of the Draw() method:

```
draw_string("Trigger               "           , iX, iY += 20, Color.Black);
draw_string("   left - rumble:  " + mTriggerL, iX, iY += 20, Color.Black);
draw_string("   right - rumble:  " + mTriggerR, iX, iY += 20, Color.Black);
```

When you run the program now, it shows changing floating-point values for the triggers as each is pulled and released. The floating-point values shown range between 0 (for fully released) and 1 (for fully pressed).

Setting the Rumble

A rumble can be added to this example with one instruction, SetVibration(). The vibration takes three parameters: the controller identifier (which in this case is the zero index), the strength of the rumble on the left side of the controller, and the strength of the rumble on the right side of the controller. The strength of the rumble ranges between 0 and 1. Add this instruction to the end of the Update() method to send rumbles to the left and right sides of the controller whenever a trigger is squeezed:

```
GamePad.SetVibration(0, mGamePadState[0].Triggers.Left,
mGamePadState[0].Triggers.Right);
```

You will notice if you run this code on the PC that the cursor appears underneath the text in the right column. This is because the cursor is drawn before the text is displayed, so it is layered underneath. If you move the call to draw_cursor() so that it is the last instruction to draw an item in the Draw() method, the cursor will appear properly over the text.

Finally, as explained in Chapter 11, "Score Tracking and Game Statistics," when you render SpriteBatch objects, the RenderState settings are reconfigured. These settings must be manually restored. Here are instructions to restore the GraphicsDevice after you finish drawing the cursor and fonts inside the Draw() method:

```
gfx.GraphicsDevice.SamplerStates[0].AddressU = TextureAddressMode.Wrap;
gfx.GraphicsDevice.SamplerStates[0].AddressV = TextureAddressMode.Wrap;
gfx.GraphicsDevice.RenderState.CullMode = CullMode.None;//see both sides
gfx.GraphicsDevice.RenderState.DepthBufferEnable = true;//re-enable 3D on Z
gfx.GraphicsDevice.RenderState.AlphaBlendEnable= false;//no transparency
gfx.GraphicsDevice.RenderState.AlphaTestEnable = false;//per pixel testing
// re-enable tiling
gfx.GraphicsDevice.SamplerStates[0].AddressU = TextureAddressMode.Wrap;
gfx.GraphicsDevice.SamplerStates[0].AddressV = TextureAddressMode.Wrap;
```

When you run the program now, your display shows the output shown back in Figure 21-2. You can also run this code on the Xbox 360 for similar output; however, the mouse event handling will be disabled.

After enabling keyboard, mouse, and game pad input you literally will have placed control of your game engine in the hands of your players. Your world is now their oyster.

CHAPTER 21 REVIEW EXERCISES

1. Try the step-by-step examples provided in this chapter.

2. If you run the solution from Exercise 1, when you left-click the mouse, the word "Pressed" appears in the window. Add a time delay so you can toggle between displaying Pressed and Released states in the game window. (A similar time delay exists that enables you to toggle between On and Off states when pressing the letter T.)

3. In the "Collision Detection Using Lines and Spheres" solution from Chapter 16, "Collision Detection," make your game pad rumble every time the camera collides with something.

CHAPTER 22

Content Pipeline Processors

UNTIL now, the media you have used for the examples in this book has been in formats supported by the XNA content pipeline. Using predefined content types in XNA allows for easy deployment on your PC or Xbox 360. For example, the XNA framework offers built-in methods for loading and accessing Texture2D, XACT (audio), XML, Effect (shaders), Autodesk FBX (model), and X (model) objects. This chapter shows how to extend the content pipeline to load files not defined in the XNA framework.

Aside from allowing you to load any graphics or data file on the PC and Xbox 360, custom content processors also enable faster game start-up times. A custom content pipeline processor will read the bulk data from your media files, process it, and then store it in intermediate form. This compiled binary intermediate data is stored in an .xnb file.

The content processor tracks changes to your media and to the content-processing code itself. If any changes are detected, when you build your game, the content processor reloads the bulk data from your media files and recompiles it. Otherwise, if no changes are detected, the content processor reads in the compiled data from the .xnb file that stores it. Being able to read preprocessed data can be a big timesaver when large compressed media files are loaded at game launch.

For the *Quake II* model loader (used in Chapter 23, "Animated Models"), setting up the model for XNA deployment requires loading the bulk data, organizing the faces in the polygon from the indexed information stored in the file, and generating the normal vectors to enable lighting. This processing time can add unwanted delays to your game launch. However, if you use a custom content processor to decompress and organize your .md2 data in an intermediate format during the first run, your game will not read from the *.md2 file again. Instead, your game will read the intermediate data from your compiled .xnb file during any consecutive run. The initial data processing is only performed when either the original media file changes or the processor code is modified. In short, you will notice an improvement to your load times when using the content processor.

The content processor can only be built on the Windows system. However, when it is built on Windows, GSE compiles it into a DLL. With this DLL referenced in your PC or Xbox 360 projects, you can import your media through the custom content pipeline.

CONTENT PROCESSORS

The content processor loads your external media and locates existing processor components. All custom processors must derive from the ContentProcessor base class in a manner similar to the following:

```
public class MyCustomContentProcessor : ContentProcessor<Tinput,Toutput>
{}
```

Tinput and Toutput are the user-defined input and output classes you create to input your bulk data and output your compiled data in the format you require.

ContentImporter

The ContentImporter class is defined with an Import method to read unprocessed data from your original media file. The class declaration is preceded with the ContentImporter attribute to list the file extension(s) associated with this loader and the processor used to convert it to a compiled format. Additional extensions, separated by commas, can be added to the string.

```
[ContentImporter(string fileExt, DefaultProcessor = string processorName)]
public class MyContentImporter : ContentImporter<MyTerrain>{
    public override MyCustomContent Import(String filename,
                                    ContentImporterContext context){}
}
```

Inside the Import method, the file is opened and can be read with a System.IO.File method or through the MemoryStream and BinaryReader objects. Using these objects, you can read text- and binary-based formats. After the reading, the data is structured according to your own custom data-storage class. You define how you want the data organized and how you want it exported to the .xnb file.

ContentTypeWriter

The ContentTypeWriter class assists in writing your intermediary data as binary output to the .xnb file. Output is done from the Write() method override. The GetRuntimeType() method retrieves the assembly for the data type you have defined. The GetRuntimeReader() reader method retrieves the assembly and loader.

```
[ContentTypeWriter]
public class MyContentWriter : ContentTypeWriter<MyCustomContent>{
    protected override void Write(ContentWriter   wr,
                                    MyCustomContent output){}
    public override string GetRuntimeType(TargetPlatform targetPlatform)
    {}
    public override string GetRuntimeReader(TargetPlatform targetPlatform)
    {}
}
```

ContentTypeReader

The ContentTypeReader loads the binary data you stored in the .xnb file. Most of the methods available to load the data with the ContentTypeReader object are inherited from the BinaryReader class. The ContentTypeReader loads your data and returns an initialized instance of your custom data class.

```
public class TerrReader : ContentTypeReader<MyCustomContent>{
    protected override MyCustomContent Read(ContentReader input,
```

```
                                    MyCustomContent existingInstance){}
}
```

When the Read() method override is finished importing your managed data, it returns this data in the format you defined in your storage class. This data is then made available to your game project.

CUSTOM CONTENT PROCESSOR EXAMPLE

This example demonstrates how to create a custom content processor for loading a height map from a .raw image. The solution from this example serves as the terrain loader used in Chapter 25, "Terrain with Height Detection." XNA does not provide a code library for loading .raw images, so you need an alternate way to load them. You can get away with BinaryReader methods to load them on Windows. On the Xbox 360, the BinaryReader methods will find your .raw files if you place your media resources in the debug folder when deploying your solution. However, to handle these files more gracefully, you should create a custom processor to load them through the content pipeline.

The .raw image stores an array of bytes. When it is used as a height map, each pixel stores height information between 0 and 255. For this example, not much processing is required because the data is basically ready to use as is. However, to demonstrate how the data can be modified when stored in intermediate form, a user-defined "hello" message is added into the compiled .xnb file. The extra item shows how you can use the processor to extend your data for more complex media formats. When reading from more complex media files, you may encounter situations when you need to modify your bulk data before storing it.

This example begins with the WinMGHBook project available in the BaseCode folder of the download from this book's website. For this example, you must use the Windows project to build a Windows game library because you obviously cannot do this on the Xbox 360.

Building a Custom Content Processor in Windows

In order to compile the content processor into a DLL that can be used either on Windows or the Xbox 360, you must add a separate Windows Game Library project to your solution from the Solution Explorer. To add it, right-click the solution name and choose Add | New Project. When prompted in the *Add New Project* dialog, select the *Windows Game Library* icon and enter the name. For this example, the name TerrImporter will be used. This name will be automatically given to your library's namespace shell (that is, generated in code), and the name will also be given to the DLL generated when compiling the library. Also, your importer class, which you will create in this library, should use this name to ensure your game project can find it through the content pipeline.

Once your new library project has been added, you will be able to see it as a separate project in the Solution Explorer. In the Class1.cs file that is generated for your Windows Game Library project, the references to the following content pipeline and system input/output namespaces are required to read, customize, compile, and write your data:

```
using Microsoft.Xna.Framework.Content.Pipeline;
using Microsoft.Xna.Framework.Content.Pipeline.Serialization.Compiler;
using System.IO;
```

Both your MGHBook project and your TerrImporter projects must reference the Microsoft.Xna.Framework.Content.Pipeline components. To do this, from the Solution Explorer right-click each project and choose *Add Reference*. In the *Add Reference* dialog that appears, select Microsoft.Xna.Framework.Content.Pipeline to add it.

Your MGHBook project also needs to reference the TerrImporter project to build the library. This can be added by right-clicking the MGHBook project in the Solution Explorer and choosing *Add Reference*. In the *Add Reference* dialog, click the *Projects* tab, where you can select the TerrImporter project to add it.

Your custom data class is designed by you to modify and store your data as you require. For this example, the user-defined class MyTerrain is added to receive your bulk data, process it, and store it in an intermediate format that is more accessible for your program. You can add methods to perform operations on your data, you can add constructor methods, and you can even add extra data that isn't included in the original media file. This class will be referenced throughout your content processor to store and retrieve your data, so it must be made public:

```
public class MyTerrain              // class to generate, store, and
{                                   // access compiled data

    public int miLabelSize;         // # of chars in label - this
    public char[] mchLabel;         // label isn't needed but shows
                                    // you can add any data you want

    public int miSize;              // tells reader terrain byte size
    public byte[] mByteHeightMap;   // and stores height information

    public MyTerrain(byte[] bytes){
                                    // constructor for compiled data
        mByteHeightMap = bytes;     // used during bulk data import
        miSize        = mByteHeightMap.Length;
        createLabel();
    }
```

```
    public MyTerrain(byte[] bytes, char[] label){
                                    // alternate
        mByteHeightMap = bytes;         // constructor for
        miSize = mByteHeightMap.Length;// reader of
        mchLabel = label;               // compiled data
        miLabelSize = mchLabel.Length;
    }


    public void createLabel(){ // example of a method you might
                            // use to alter or add data that
        mchLabel = new char[5];// differs from original media
        mchLabel[0] = 'H'; mchLabel[1] = 'e'; mchLabel[2] = 'l';
        mchLabel[3] = 'l'; mchLabel[4] = 'o';
        miLabelSize = 5;
    }
}
```

Next, add the content processor class to provide the foundation for the read and write components:

```
// gets existing processor components
[ContentProcessor] // <tinput, toutput>


// ContentProcessor provides a base for developing custom processor
// components
// all processors must derive from this class
public class TerrProcessor : ContentProcessor<MyTerrain, MyTerrain>
{   // contentProcessorContext
    // provides access to methods for converting
    // member data and triggering nested builds
    public override MyTerrain Process(MyTerrain input,
                            ContentProcessorContext context){
        return new MyTerrain(input.mByteHeightMap);
    }
}
```

Extending the ContentImporter class enables the overridden Import method to read your data from the original media file. The ContentImporter attribute precedes the ContentImporter class definition to list the file extensions that can use this importer.

For this example, the System.IO.File method ReadAllBytes() is used to read in the bytes from the .raw image. However, if you were reading text input instead, this could be read with the File method's ReadAllText() method. You can also load your data with MemoryStream and BinaryReader objects to read data in specific chunks to handle integers, floats, and other data types. If you want to see how other data types are read, the custom content processor used in Chapter 23, "Animated Models," has code that shows how to do this.

Once the data is read, it is passed to your custom data class. This data initializes a custom data object that organizes the data as you need it. The data object is then returned to your processor so it can be written in a compiled binary format to an .xnb file:

```
// stores information about importer, file extension, and caching
[ContentImporter(".raw", DefaultProcessor = "TerrProcessor")]

// ContentImporter reads original data from original media file
public class TerrImporter : ContentImporter<MyTerrain>{
    // reads original data from binary or text based files
    public override MyTerrain Import(String filename,
                                     ContentImporterContext context){
        byte[] bytes      = File.ReadAllBytes(filename);
        MyTerrain terrain = new MyTerrain(bytes);
        return terrain;    // returns compiled data object
    }
}
```

Adding the extended ContentTypeWriter class to your Windows game library allows you to output your compiled binary custom data to an .xnb file. The Write() method receives your integer, float, byte, char, string, and other data types and writes them in binary format to the file. When you write your data, you have to write it in the sequence you want to retrieve it. The writer/reader combination uses a "first in first out" sequence for your data storage and access:

```
// identify the type writer
[ContentTypeWriter]

// ContentTypeWriter provides methods for converting to binary format
// provides methods for compilation, state tracking, header creation
public class TerrWriter : ContentTypeWriter<MyTerrain>{
    protected override void Write(ContentWriter cw, MyTerrain value){
        cw.Write(value.miLabelSize);   // writes compiled data
        cw.Write(value.mchLabel);      // in binary format to *.xnb file
        cw.Write(value.miSize);
        cw.Write(value.mByteHeightMap);
    }

    public override string GetRuntimeType(TargetPlatform targetPlatform){
```

```
            return typeof(MyTerrain).AssemblyQualifiedName;
    }


    // Version info. Reader qualifier uses namespace id.
    public override string GetRuntimeReader(TargetPlatform targetPlatform){
        return "TerrImporter.TerrReader, TerrImporter, Version=1.0,
                Culture=neutral";
    }
}
```

The content reader reads the compiled data from the .xnb file. The ContentReader
is derived from the BinaryReader class and exposes similar methods for retrieving
data in the chunks you need, such as integers, floats, chars, and so on. Once the data
is read, an object of your custom data class is initialized. This custom data object is
then made available to your XNA game project:

```
public class TerrReader : ContentTypeReader<MyTerrain>{
    protected override MyTerrain Read(ContentReader cr,
                                      MyTerrain existingInstance){
        int    labelSize    = cr.ReadInt32(); // read label info
        char[] mylabel      = new char[labelSize];
        mylabel             = cr.ReadChars(labelSize);
        int terrainSz       = cr.ReadInt32(); // read terrain info
        MyTerrain myTerrain = new MyTerrain(cr.ReadBytes(terrainSz),
                                            mylabel);

        return myTerrain;
    }
}
```

Once you have added your Windows game library to your project, you must compile your projects to build the content processor DLL. Building your project generates a TerrImporter.dll file. You can find it in the Debug directory (for example,
MGHBook\bin\x86\Debug).

Referencing the DLL assembly exposes the custom content importer and processor
to the game class. To reference this assembly, right-click the game project's References
folder in the Solution Explorer and choose *Add Reference*. On the *Browse* tab on the
Add Reference dialog, navigate to this DLL to select it and click *OK*. You will now see
the TerrImporter reference listed with your other project references (see Figure 22-1).

You must also reference this new DLL in your Content Pipeline properties to make
it available to your ContentManager. To do this, right-click the project name,
MGHBook, and choose *Properties*. In the gray panel that appears, click *Content
Pipeline* on the left. Under the XNA Framework Content Pipeline Assemblies label,
click *Add* to browse to the TerrImporter.dll file and select it. Figure 22-2 shows the
Content Pipeline property reference in your game project.

FIGURE 22-1

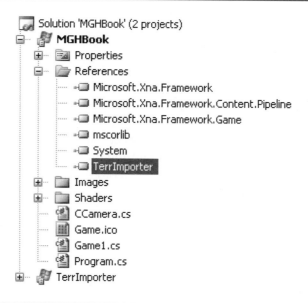

Game project reference to TerrImporter.dll

Wherever you wish to use your custom data type, the new namespace for your Windows game library must be referenced in your original game project:

```
using TerrImporter;
```

FIGURE 22-2

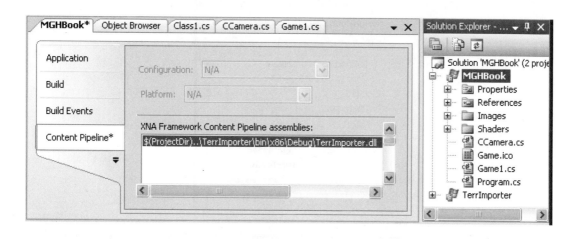

Game project content pipeline reference to TerrImporter.dll

Next, your heightMap.raw file must be referenced in the Images folder for your game project. You can get this file from the Images directory in the download for this book's website.

Once the heightMap.raw file is referenced, you can set its properties to use your custom content processor to load it. To assign the custom content processor to read the file, right-click heightMap in the Solution Explorer and select *Properties*. Under the *Build Action* property drop-down, select Content. Under XNA Framework Content Attribute, select True. The ContentImporter attribute should be set to TerrImporter, and the ContentProcessor attribute should be set to TerrProcessor. Figure 22-3 shows the content pipeline property settings for the heightMap.raw file.

Finally, in your game code, you should add the instruction to load your .raw data using the content pipeline. You can load this content when the program begins, so it is called from the Initialize() method:

```
MyTerrain terrain = content.Load<MyTerrain>(".\\Images\\heightMap");
```

FIGURE 22-3

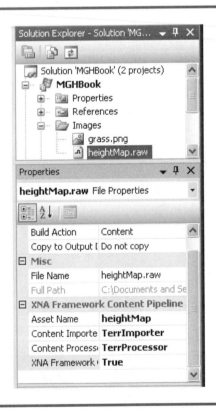

This media file's properties reference the content importer and processor.

To prove the content processor is working, you can print some of the data retrieved by the MyTerrain object to the Output panel. The Output panel can be accessed on the tab beside the Error List in GSE when the program is running. Add the following code to Initialize() after the call to content.Load():

```
for (int i = 0; i < terrain.miLabelSize; i++)
    System.Diagnostics.Trace.Write(terrain.mchLabel[i]);
System.Diagnostics.Trace.WriteLine("");
System.Diagnostics.Trace.Write("Total terrain bytes: ");
System.Diagnostics.Trace.WriteLine(terrain.miSize);
System.Diagnostics.Trace.Write("heightMap element 26315 = ");
System.Diagnostics.Trace.WriteLine(terrain.mByteHeightMap[26315]);
```

If everything is successful, your data will appear in GSE's output panel at the bottom of your project as follows:

```
Hello
Total terrain bytes: 263169
heightMap element 26315 = 15
```

When you run your game project, the Windows game library is compiled before your XNA game project. The implication from this is you will have limited ability to use debugging tools such as stepping and tracing in your game library. Outside the ContentTypeReader class, breakpoints and tracing are not available. However, you can obtain useful debug information by checking the data object that is returned to your game project by the custom content processor.

Implementing Your Custom Content Processor on the Xbox 360

To implement your custom content processor on the Xbox 360, you cannot add a Windows Game Library project to an Xbox 360 project. However, you can add this custom processor component by referencing the TerrImporter.dll file built in your Windows project. You can find the DLL in the MGHBook\bin\x86\Debug directory. To reference it from your Xbox 360 project, copy this file over to your Xbox 360 project folder. Next, right-click the References folder in the Solution Explorer and select *Add Reference*. On the *Browse* tab, navigate to TerrImporter.dll and select it. Refer back to Figure 22-1, which shows a similar reference to this DLL from the Windows project. Then, right-click the Xbox 360 project name in the Solution Explorer and select *Properties*. Choose *Content Pipeline* in the gray panel on the left and then click the *Add* button to navigate to TerrImporter.dll and select it. The resulting Xbox 360 project content pipeline reference should be similar to the one shown back in Figure 22-2 for the Windows project.

The namespace must be referenced in the file where your game class is located:

```
using TerrImporter;
```

When the heightMap.raw file is referenced in the Solution Explorer, right-click it and select *Properties* to ensure that Build Action is set to Content. The XNA Framework Content property must be set to True, and then you set the content importer and processor to use TerrImporter and TerrProcessor, respectively. When this is done, you will be able to use the content pipeline to load data from a .raw file to initialize your MyTerrain object. Figure 22-3 shows the same properties for the heightMap.raw in the Windows project.

Try the step-by-step example in this chapter to create the custom content processor. Then test it and deploy it on the Xbox 360 to get a better understanding of how it works. You'll have many project references and component dependencies to learn about and digest when studying custom content processors. To avoid the pitfalls of incorrect naming and referencing—until you become more familiar with the content processors—you may find it helpful to start with a working solution like the one from this chapter. Then you can modify it incrementally to turn it into a processor that suits your needs. After doing this a few times, you will be ready to create your own from scratch.

CHAPTER 22 REVIEW EXERCISES

1. Follow the step-by-step exercise in this chapter to create the custom content processor and run it on Windows and the Xbox 360.

2. After running the solution on Windows, navigate to the folder where the heightMap.xnb file is located and look at the timestamp. This file is located in the directory WinMGHBookBaseCode\MGHBook\bin\x86\Debug\Images. You'll notice that the file is not updated as long as you do not change the media file or alter the content processor code. This shows that the content processor tracks changes made to the media file and processor code and only updates the compiled binary data when changes are detected.

3. Create your own custom content processor to read the string "ABC" from a text file and store it in your user-defined class. You may start with the solution from this chapter, but when you finish, rename all processor components and call your namespace for the processor ABCimporter. Make sure it works on both Windows and the Xbox 360.

Animated Models

WE are sure you will agree that animated models are among the most exciting features of any game. This chapter presents several options for creating and loading pre-animated 3D models in your code. Unfortunately, XNA does not currently ship with a library that automatically animates 3D models, so you have to find a loader that you can integrate into your code or you have to write your own animated model loader. As an alternative, we provide a model loader that loads and displays animated *Quake II* models, which are stored in the .md2 model format.

Of course, you can use MilkShape to create and export your animated models to .md2 format. However, if you are using a different model loader for other 3D model formats, you may still be able to create your model in MilkShape and then export it to your desired format. Alternatively, if you developed your 3D model in another 3D model tool, you may be able to import it into MilkShape, animate it, and then export it to a *Quake II* model format or other format, as needed.

Whatever method you use to develop your models, make sure you test the load and display of your 3D models from your XNA code. It is worth the time to ensure your models load and animate properly in your loader before you invest heavily in creating and animating them.

THE QUAKE II FORMAT

This chapter does not fully explain how the animated *Quake II* model source code works. However, a brief overview of the .md2 format is presented, and if you need to study it more, all of the *Quake II* model loader code is available with this book for you to view and modify. This chapter explains how you can add this MD2 class to play your animations, change animations, play sequences of animations, or pause and resume your animations.

The MD2 format was developed by id Software, and it was first introduced as part of id Software's *Quake II*. id Software has since released the source code for their *Quake II* game engine to the public under the GNU General Public License. Since then, the *Quake II* model format has become popular with game coders because it is reliable for animations, it is easy to implement, and decent low-cost tools are available to create models.

The *Quake II* format implements animation entirely through keyframe animations. The model's vertices are positioned at each keyframe. During the animation, the vertices are projected according to their relative position on the timeline between the closest keyframes.

When creating *Quake II* models in a modeling tool such as MilkShape, you attach the groups of vertices (known as *meshes*) to bones. These bones are connected by a series of joints to create the skeleton. The bones can be moved and rotated at different frames in the timeline to create keyframes. The attached meshes move with the bones when you create the animation. The joints keep the bones together to ensure your meshes move properly within the skeletal system for the model. When you export the model and keyframes to the .md2 format, the bones are thrown out and you are left with a header file that describes the model's vertex data, the texture or skin information, and the information about the keyframe animations.

Unlike other model formats, *Quake II* models do not use the skeletal hierarchy or skin weights that are assigned during the model-creation process. This absence of information can lead to unrealistic crinkling of skin around model joints. However, you can avoid this crinkling (or minimize it) with careful planning while designing your model. Up close your *Quake II* model skins may appear to be a bit wobbly or watery due to their keyframe animation, but this defect isn't noticeable from most distances.

Quake II models cannot use more than 4,096 triangles. However, this limitation is reasonable because you can still generate decent-looking models with this polygon count.

A Closer Look at the .md2 Data

This section provides a brief overview of how the .md2 file is loaded and how it enables your animated models.

The *Quake II* data is stored in binary format in a manner that permits for some compression of the vertex and frame data. To help you unravel this data, the start of the file contains a header that describes the file type, the texture properties, the vertex properties, the total number of vertices, the total number of frames, and binary offsets in the file (to access details about the vertices and animation frames). Here is the standard .md2 header:

```
struct md2{  int fileFormatVersion; // file type which must equal 844121161
  int version;              // file format version which must be 8
  int skinWidth;            // texture width
  int skinHeight;           // texture height
  int frameSize;            // bytes per frame
  int numSkins;             // total skins used
  int numVertices;          // total vertices per frame
  int numUVs;               // total texture UV's
  int numTris;              // number of triangle coordinates
  int numglCommands;        // number of glCommands
  int numFrames;            // number of keyframes
  int ofsSkins;             // binary offset to skin data
  int ofsUV;                // offset to texture UV data
  int ofsTriangle;          // offset to triangle list data
  int ofsFrames;            // offset to frame data
  int ofsglcmds;            // offset to OpenGL command data
  int ofsEnd;               // offset to end of file
};
```

Each vertex in every frame is indexed. The indexes are ordered in a sequence of triangle lists. When the file is loaded, the indices are used to generate a list of vertex coordinates. The coordinates are then used to build a series of triangle lists. For efficiency, you could use the glCommands data to rewrite your model-loading and animation code to render your models using triangle strips or triangle fans.

As you would expect, it is possible to store more than one animation with the *Quake II* format. For example, your model may have a running, jumping, taunting, saluting, crouching, and idling animation. You will want to be able to switch between these animations on demand. To access this information, use the .md2 header, which contains the offset to the frame descriptions. The frame descriptions can be read in using a binary read at the offset. All frame descriptions are located together sequentially from the starting frame to the very last frame. Each frame description includes an animation name and a frame number.

To determine the starting and ending frames for each individual animation, you must parse each frame description so you can match the animation names. Once you have a series of matching animation names, you can store the starting and ending frame numbers in this series. When you want to play the animation on demand, you can set the frame number to the starting frame in the animation series. When the animation reaches the last frame in this animation, you can start the animation over again or you can switch to another animation.

During the animation sequence, the vertices are projected on the timeline between the keyframes used in the animation. The normal vectors must also be interpolated in this manner.

Textures with .md2 Format

For the actual *Quake II* game, *Quake II* models use .pcx files for textures. However, the .pcx format is not supported in XNA's content pipeline. A way to get around this limitation is to use an image-editing program such as GIMP to load your *.pcx skins and save them to *.tga format, which is supported in the content pipeline. You can then use the *.tga files to texture your *Quake II* models. Although it is possible to have more than one texture for a *Quake II* model, the *Quake II* model loader provided with this chapter only handles one texture or skin.

NOTE When you build your *Quake II* models, be sure to use only one skin. The code used in this chapter can only handle one skin.

ANIMATING MODELS IN MILKSHAPE

To show you how to create an animated model using MilkShape, this example demonstrates how to create an animated lamp that pivots left and right and also performs a bowing animation (see Figure 23-1).

FIGURE 23-1

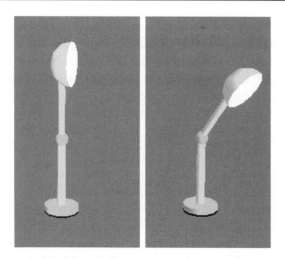

Separate pivoting and bowing animations

Creating the Quake II Model

Before you can create an animation, you first need to create a model. You can create your own model, use the one that is provided with the book, or search online for one to use.

Creating the Meshes

Your first task is to create two separate meshes for the top and bottom portions of a lamp, similar to the ones shown on the left side of Figure 23-2. For a refresher on how to use MilkShape to create meshes like these, review Chapter 12, "3D Models."

FIGURE 23-2

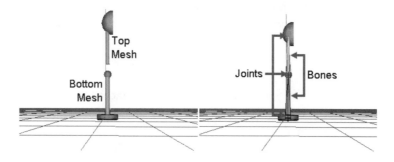

Two model pieces on the left; three joints and two bones for animating on the right

 To enable smooth animations, be sure to position your model at the origin.

Once you have created your meshes, you need to position them together so they appear as one lamp. However, to enable the animation, you must ensure that the meshes remain as two separate groups. If your model uses more than two mesh groups, you will need to merge them so you end up with a top mesh group and a bottom mesh group. Merging can be performed on the *Groups* tab using the *Regroup* button. (Merging groups is also explained in Chapter 12.)

Creating the Skeleton

Once you have the top and bottom mesh groups in position, you must add three joints to create pivot points for the animation. The end result is shown in the diagram on the right in Figure 23-2.

Joints can be added in MilkShape from the *Model* tab. While the *Joint* button is selected, click into the viewport to add a joint where the cursor is placed. To enable proper mesh positioning with the bones (when animating your lamp model), you must add each of the three joints in sequence from the bottom to the top. The first joint is placed at the base of the lamp. After the first joint is set, whenever a new joint is added, a bone is automatically generated between the new joint and the joint that was previously added.

To enable use of the bones as guides for the mesh animations, you must attach the meshes to the bones. The bottom mesh will be attached to the bottom bone. You can select the bottom bone by clicking the joint listed at the top on the *Joints* tab, then select the bottom mesh. When doing this, choose the *Select* button on the *Groups* tab to ensure the bottom mesh is the only mesh group highlighted in red. When the bottom mesh group is highlighted in red and the bottom joint is also highlighted in red, click the *Assign* button on the *Joints* tab to assign the bottom mesh to the bottom bone. Figure 23-3 shows the viewport and *Joints* tab where the bottom mesh has been assigned to the lower bone.

Next, you must repeat this process to assign the top mesh to the top bone. To select the top bone, click the middle joint, which is *joint2*, to highlight it in red. Then select the top mesh in the viewport on the *Groups* tab and ensure that is the only one highlighted in red. Once both the top joint and top mesh are selected, click the *Assign* button on the *Joints* tab to attach the upper mesh to the upper bone.

 To ensure you have the correct mesh attached to the correct bone, you can select the joint on the *Joints* tab and click the *SelAssigned* button to highlight the mesh that is attached.

FIGURE 23-3

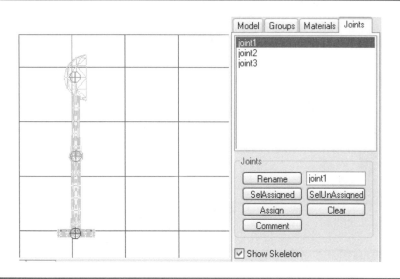

Attaching the bottom mesh to the bottom bone

Creating the Pivoting Animation

Now that you have attached the meshes to the skeleton, you can create your animation. For this example, you will create two separate animations. The first animation is a pivot animation where the lamp turns back and forth from left to right. This animation runs between frames 1 and 29. The second animation is a bowing animation where the lamp bows downward and then returns to the original upright position. This second animation runs from frames 30 to 50. Thankfully, to generate all 50 frames, you don't need to reposition the model each frame. You only need to set keyframes for the animation, and MilkShape will project the model at all frames in between.

To create the animation, you must select the *Anim* button in the lower-right corner of the MilkShape window. Note that if the *Anim* button is not selected, the meshes will not move with the bones. The current frame number is entered in the bottom-left text box just under the right panel. The last frame number for the entire animation series is in the text box next to it on the right. You also need a viewport projection that shows the model from a perspective that allows you to easily move or rotate the model when creating your keyframe. Figure 23-4 shows the first keyframe at frame number 1. The two numbers in the text boxes at the bottom indicate the current frame (on the left) and the total combined frames for all animations (on the right).

FIGURE 23-4

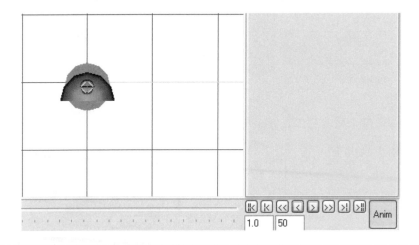

Setup for the first frame

A top view is used for easy access to permit rotations for the top of the lamp. The middle joint is selected so only the top bone and mesh will move or rotate when you are positioning the model. The middle joint is selected from the *Joints* tab. Once the joint is selected, on the *Models* tab you can rotate the bone and attached mesh when the *Rotate* button is selected. You can also move the bone and attached mesh when the *Move* button is selected. When the lamp is in position to start the animation, you can set the keyframe from the Animate menu by selecting Set Keyframe.

To create the next keyframe, change the frame number in the left text box from 1 to 8. You can do this by clicking in the text box and entering **8** with your keyboard. Then, while the middle joint is still selected, and while the *Rotate* button on the *Models* tab is selected, rotate the lamp 90 degrees in a clockwise direction about the Y axis. When you have done this, you can set a new keyframe by selecting Set Keyframe from the Animate menu.

To create the next keyframe in this animation, change the keyframe number in the text box to **15**. While the middle joint is selected and while the *Rotate* button on the *Models* tab is selected, rotate the upper portion of the lamp so it faces toward the middle again. Once the lamp faces the middle, select Set Keyframe from the Animate menu to set the keyframe. Next, enter **22** as the frame number in the left text box at the lower left of the MilkShape window. Rotate the lamp 90 degrees about the Y axis so it faces toward the right, and set a keyframe there.

To complete the animation, enter **29** in the frame text box and then rotate the upper portion of the lamp 90 degrees so it returns to the starting position where it faces the middle. Set the keyframe at frame 29 to complete the first animation. Figure 23-5 shows how the lamp is positioned for each keyframe at frames 1, 8, 15, 22, and 29.

FIGURE 23-5

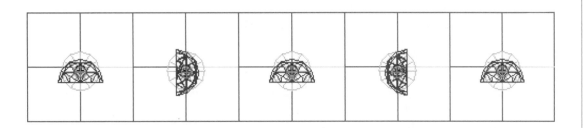

Top view of keyframes set at frames 1, 8, 15, 22, and 29

You can view your animation in MilkShape by setting the starting frame to 1 and the ending frame at 29 in the text boxes at the bottom of the MilkShape window. Then, while the *Anim* button is selected, click the > button (shown back in Figure 23-4). If your animation is set properly, you will see the upper portion of the lamp pivoting back and forth from left to right.

Creating the Bowing Animation

The bowing animation runs from frame number 30 to frame number 50. You will need to use a side view to create the keyframes for this animation. Figure 23-6 shows how to position the lamp for frames 30, 35, 40, 45, and 50 when creating keyframes for this animation.

Previewing Your Animation

When the keyframes have been set, you can preview your animation by clicking the > button in MilkShape while the *Anim* button is pressed. When you are satisfied that the animation looks the way it is intended, you can export your model.

FIGURE 23-6

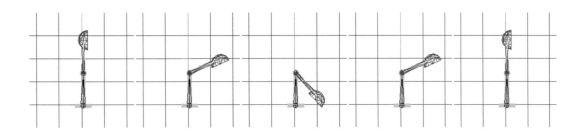

Side view of keyframes set at frames 30, 35, 40, 45, and 50

Exporting to Quake II .md2 Format

The XNA *Quake II* file loader included with this chapter requires that you export to *Quake II* MD2 format if you want to animate your model with this code. However, you can export to another model format from MilkShape in case you have a different type of loader. When exporting to the *Quake II* MD2 format, you must place an md2.qc file in the same directory where you export your model. The md2.qc file is used to help build the .md2 file. It contains information about the model name, the skin name, and skin pixel dimensions. It also contains the different animation names and their starting and ending frames. The md2.qc file is actually just a text file that you can edit in Notepad. You will have to edit this file or create one to list information about the image you use for your lamp and to document the frames used for the pivoting and bowing animations. If the md2.qc file is not present when you are exporting from MilkShape, you will receive an error. For this example, here are the required contents for the md2.qc file:

```
// Sample MD2 config, copy into export directory
$modelname lamp.md2
$origin 0.0 0.0 0.0

// skins
$skinwidth 128
$skinheight 128
$skin lamp.bmp

// sequences
$sequence pivot 1 29
$sequence bowing 30 50
```

When your md2.qc file has been created, place it in the same folder where your model's texture is located. You can now export your MD2 model to that directory by selecting File | Export | Quake 2 MD2. Save this file as lamp.md2.

Loading Your Quake II Model in Code

This code demonstration shows you how to load your *Quake II* model in code. It loads the lamp you created and animates it with the pivoting and bowing animations.

The example begins with either the WinMGHBook project or the Xbox360MGHBook project, which can be found in the BaseCode folder in the download available from this book's website. You will also need the MD2.cs source file from this directory. Of course, the MD2.cs file must be referenced in your game project from the Solution Explorer. Also, MD2.cs uses a content processor to load the *Quake II* model. This content processor is implemented in MD2Importer.dll, which you can obtain from the BaseCode folder as well.

For either the PC or the Xbox, the content processor must be included in your project references. In Chapter 22, "Content Pipeline Processors," you added a content processor DLL to your references by right-clicking your game project and choosing Add Reference. The steps to reference your *Quake II* loader are similar. From the *Add Reference* dialog, you select the *Browse* tab, navigate to the MD2Importer.dll file, and click *OK* to load it into your project references.

A reference to this library is also required in your project properties for content processing. Right-click the project in the Solution Explorer and choose Properties to add it. In the gray panel that appears, click *Content Pipeline* and then click *Add*. In the *Add XNA Framework Content Pipeline Assembly* dialog that appears, navigate to the MD2Importer.dll file and click *Open* to reference this library.

If you want to view or edit the code for this MD2Importer, the Windows solution for this example includes the game library project. When you first run this project (or if you modify the MD2Importer code), a new MD2Importer.dll file will be generated in a path similar to MD2Importer\bin\x86\Debug.

When your base code is ready, you will have to reference your model and the accompanying texture in your project. Add your lamp.md2 model to the Models folder in the Solution Explorer. The lamp.bmp texture needs to be placed in the Images folder in the Solution Explorer. With your *Quake II* model files in your project, you need to ensure that your lamp.md2 model uses the content pipeline. To be sure, click the .md2 file in the Solution Explorer to view this file's properties in the property browser. The Build Action property must be set to Content. The XNA Framework Content property must be set to True. The Content Importer property needs to be set to MD2Importer, and the Content Processor property must be set to md2Processor. If you do not see these properties or you are unable to set them, review your steps to ensure MD2Importer.dll has been referenced properly in your project. Figure 23-7 shows the properties for the lamp model when it has been referenced properly in the Solution Explorer (i.e., to use the content pipeline).

FIGURE 23-7

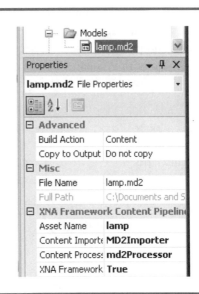

Model properties

Next, your Game1.cs file has to reference the MD2 class to access it, so you must include the namespace for this class:

```
using quakeMD2;
```

To create an object to use this class for loading and animating your *Quake II* models, a class-level object is required:

```
private MD2 md2;
```

The pivoting and bowing animations will be identified with a class-level enumeration. Declaring the enumeration at the top of the game class permits the use of these identifiers throughout the game class:

```
public enum meAnim
{    pivot,       bow     }
```

The model setup when the program starts is simple. The md2 object must be initialized. Then, the model can be loaded from the folder where the source is located. The *Quake II* model's texture, lamp.bmp, can be loaded with the ContentManager object as long as the image is referenced in the Solution Explorer. Also, when the model is initialized, the speed is set. The method setAnimSpeed(), with a parameter equal to 5.0f, sets the animation rate to a similar playback speed that you experienced when testing your animation in MilkShape. However, you can slow your animation down or speed it up with this method if you need to. To start animating the model when the game begins, the instruction setAnimSequence() plays two animations in succession. The first parameter sets the animation to play once only. The second parameter sets the second animation to play in a continuous loop when the first animation ends. Add this code to Initialize() to set up your model, load it, and play the bowing and pivoting animations:

```
md2 = new MD2();
md2.loadModel(gfx.GraphicsDevice, ".\\Models\\lamp",
                            ".\\Images\\lamp", content);
md2.setAnimSpeed(5.0f); // 5.0f is the default speed
md2.setAnimSequence((int)meAnim.bow, (int)meAnim.pivot);
```

XNA's BasicEffect class is used to render the model because it offers an easy implementation of lighting. To use it, declare an instance at the top of the game class:

```
BasicEffect mBE;
```

To prepare the mBE shader when the program launches, and to avoid costly cycles used when initializing the BasicEffect object, this object should only be created once when the program begins. With this in mind, the mBE object is set in Initialize():

```
mBE = new BasicEffect(gfx.GraphicsDevice, null);
```

Directional lighting only needs to be set once—unless your world has more than one sun. The lighting settings used here are explained in more detail in Chapter 20,

"Lighting." To provide a method that can be used by all objects that use BasicEffect's lighting and to enable the texturing when rendering objects with this shader, add the setBasicEffect() method to the game class:

```
public void setBasicEffect(){
    // set up lighting
    mBE.LightingEnabled              = true;
    mBE.DirectionalLight0.Enabled    = true;
    mBE.AmbientLightColor            = new Vector3(0.8f, 0.8f, 0.8f);
    mBE.DirectionalLight0.DiffuseColor = new Vector3(1.0f, 1.0f,  1.0f);
    mBE.DirectionalLight0.Direction  = Vector3.Normalize(
                                         new Vector3(0.0f, -0.3f, 1.0f));
    mBE.DirectionalLight0.SpecularColor= new Vector3(0.2f, 0.2f, 0.2f);
    mBE.SpecularPower                = 0.01f;
    mBE.TextureEnabled               = true;
}
```

To initialize the BasicEffect shader's properties when the program begins, call setBasicEffect() from the Initialize() method:

```
setBasicEffect();
```

A suitable VertexDeclaration that permits lighting, with XNA's BasicEffect class, is required. This variable is needed throughout the game class, so a declaration is needed at the top of it:

```
private VertexDeclaration  mVertPosNormTex;
```

The VertexDeclaration object is initialized when the application starts, so it can be used when drawing the first frame. To enable this setup, add the following code to the Initialize() method:

```
mVertPosNormTex = new VertexDeclaration(gfx.GraphicsDevice,
              VertexPositionNormalTexture.VertexElements);
```

Every frame, the .md2 model vertices must be updated with a time-scaled interpolation between frames. Adding the updateModel() instruction to the Update() method allows the MD2 class to take care of this interpolation to enable a smooth animation:

```
md2.updateModel(gfx.GraphicsDevice, gameTime);
```

The code used to draw the model is similar to code you have used to draw your .x or .fbx 3D models. A notable difference here is you must reference the model's vertex buffer when setting the data source. Also, this code is designed to use triangle lists when drawing the *Quake II* model, so you must specify this primitive type while rendering it.

The total number of triangles drawn is obtained from the model object while it is being rendered. Add the drawMD2model() method to your game class to draw your model:

```
void drawMD2model(){
    // 1: declare matrices
    Matrix matScale, matTranslation, matRotateY, matWorld;

    // 2: initialize matrices
    matScale       = Matrix.CreateScale(0.2f, 0.2f, 0.2f);
    matTranslation = Matrix.CreateTranslation(0.0f, -0.9f, 4.0f);
    matRotateY     = Matrix.CreateRotationY((float)Math.PI);

    // 3: build cumulative world matrix using I.S.R.O.T. sequence
    // identity, scale, rotate, orbit(translate & rotate), translate
    matWorld = Matrix.Identity * matScale * matRotateY * matTranslation;

    // 4: set shader matrices, and texture
    mBE.Begin();
    mBE.World      = matWorld;
    mBE.View       = mMatView;
    mBE.Projection = mMatProj;
    mBE.Texture    = md2.getTexture();
    mBE.CommitChanges();

    // 5: draw object - select vertex type, data source, # of primitives
    gfx.GraphicsDevice.VertexDeclaration = mVertPosNormTex;

    foreach (EffectPass pass in mBE.CurrentTechnique.Passes){
        pass.Begin();
        // get the data and draw it
        gfx.GraphicsDevice.Vertices[0].SetSource(
            md2.vertexBuffer, 0, VertexPositionNormalTexture.SizeInBytes);
        gfx.GraphicsDevice.DrawPrimitives(
            PrimitiveType.TriangleList, 0, md2.getNumTriangles());
        pass.End();
    }
    mBE.End();
}
```

As with all objects that are rendered, the instructions to draw the *Quake II* model are triggered from the Draw() method:

```
drawMD2model();
```

When you run the code, you will see your lamp performing the bowing animation followed by a continuous pivot back and forth from right to left. You may find that you need to scale your model and rotate it, depending on the scale and orientation used when creating the model.

Loading and Controlling Quake II Models in Code

The last demonstration showed you how to create your own *Quake II* model and animate it in code. This is definitely a useful exercise; however, *Quake II* models have the power to perform far more interesting animations than the one you just created. This next demonstration shows a more interesting animated model to demonstrate how to use the MD2 class to play animations on demand, switch animations, and pause or resume animations. This demonstration loads a model called Zarlag, which is stored in the tris.md2 file. The Zarlag.tga image is used for the skin. You can download this model and skin from the Models folder in the book's download.

The Zarlag model was created by Phillip T. Wheeler. Thank you very much, Phillip, for a great model.

Zarlag has many interesting animations, and this example shows you how to use the MD2 class to switch between them. Figure 23-8 shows Zarlag in the heat of battle.

This example begins with the solution code from the previous example. To be able to handle all of Zarlag's animations, replace the existing enumeration with the following revision, which provides friendly identifiers for all of Zarlag's animations. These enumerated values will be referenced later so you can play Zarlag's animations on demand:

```
public enum meAnim{
stand,    run,     attack,    pain1,
pain2,    pain3,   jump,      flip,
salute,   taunt,   wave,      point,
crstand,  crwalk,  crattack,  crpain,
crdeath,  death1,  death2,    death3

}
```

To load Zarlag instead of the lamp model, replace the loadModel() instruction inside Initialize() with this version. Also, make sure you place the tris.md2 file in the Model's folder and reference the Zarlag.tga image from the Solution Explorer.

```
md2.loadModel(gfx.GraphicsDevice, ".\\Models\\tris",
".\\Images\\Zarlag", content);
```

To begin with a standing animation, inside Initialize() replace the SetAnimSequence() call to start the bowing and pivoting animations with the following instruction, which sets a standing animation:

```
md2.setAnim((int)meAnim.stand);
```

FIGURE 23-8

Zarlag on the move

When drawing the animation, you need to position, rotate, and scale Zarlag differently from the lamp. Replace the scaling, translation, and rotation calculations in drawMD2model() with these revisions so Zarlag faces the viewer and appears to be standing on the ground when the program begins:

```
matScale        = Matrix.CreateScale(0.02f, 0.02f, 0.02f);
matTranslation  = Matrix.CreateTranslation(0.0f, -0.4f, 3.0f);
matRotateY      = Matrix.CreateRotationY((float)Math.PI / 2.0f);
```

The MD2 class has a few different methods to allow you to play an animation on demand, play an animation sequence for two animations, and to pause and resume an animation. These commands will be triggered by press events. To ensure that multiple animations are triggered in one press event, which can last over several frames, these variables are added to track the time of the last press event to ensure enough time passes before triggering the animation again:

```
private double mdblAnimDelay, mdblRunDelay, mdblJumpDelay = 0;
```

The first animation handler allows you to advance through the list of the *Quake II* model's animations by pressing either the SPACEBAR or the left thumbstick on the game pad. The MD2 class's advanceAnimation() scrolls through the list of animations. Add this code block to the Update() method to allow your users to view all animations for the *Quake II* file:

```
if (gameTime.TotalGameTime.TotalMilliseconds - mdblAnimDelay > 200)
{
    mdblAnimDelay = gameTime.TotalGameTime.TotalMilliseconds;
    if (kbState.IsKeyDown(Keys.Space) ||
        GamePad.GetState(PlayerIndex.One).Buttons.LeftStick
        == ButtonState.Pressed){
        md2.advanceAnimation();
    }
}
```

This next animation handler triggers the running animation if either the A key is pressed or the right trigger on the game pad is pulled. This code is added to the Update() method to catch these press events and start Zarlag running:

```
if (gameTime.TotalGameTime.TotalMilliseconds - mdblRunDelay > 100)
{
    mdblRunDelay = gameTime.TotalGameTime.TotalMilliseconds;

    // start running animation if it isn't already playing
    if ((kbState.IsKeyDown(Keys.A)
        || GamePad.GetState(PlayerIndex.One).Triggers.Right > 0.0f)
        && !md2.isPlaying((int)meAnim.run)){
        md2.setAnim((int)meAnim.run);
    }
}
```

This next code block triggers a one-time jump followed by a running loop when either the J key or right thumbstick is pressed. Add this code to the Update() method to enable this feature:

```
if (gameTime.TotalGameTime.TotalMilliseconds - mdblJumpDelay > 100)
{
    mdblJumpDelay = gameTime.TotalGameTime.TotalMilliseconds;

    // start jump animation if it isn't already playing
    if ((kbState.IsKeyDown(Keys.J) ||
        GamePad.GetState(PlayerIndex.One).Buttons.RightStick
        == ButtonState.Pressed )
        && !md2.isPlaying((int)meAnim.jump)){
        md2.setAnimSequence((int)meAnim.jump, (int)meAnim.run);
    }
}
```

You may also pause your animation when the P key or B button is pressed. You can resume it when the R key or the A button is pressed. Add the following code block to Update() to handle these pause and resume events:

```
if (kbState.IsKeyDown(Keys.P) ||
GamePad.GetState(PlayerIndex.One).Buttons.B == ButtonState.Pressed ){
    md2.Pause();
}
else if (kbState.IsKeyDown(Keys.R) ||
GamePad.GetState(PlayerIndex.One).Buttons.A == ButtonState.Pressed){
    md2.Resume();
}
```

Try running your program now. The model should first appear standing idle. You can make it run by pulling the right trigger or by pressing the SPACEBAR. You can advance it through all animations by pressing the left thumbstick or the SPACEBAR. Press the A key or pull the right trigger to start the running animation. A one-time jump followed by a running animation can be called when either the J key or right thumbstick is pressed. You can pause and resume animations with either the P and R keys or the B and A buttons on the game pad.

Loading the Quake II Weapon

Quake II weapons are usually separate from the actual character model. Separate weapons enable you to switch between holding a rifle, plasma gun, rocket launcher, or other artillery to fit the occasion. These weapons are animated to match the character's animation. As the model runs, jumps, crouches, or falls in pain, the weapon moves with the model's arms and hands. In the unfortunate event of death, the weapon may fall from the character's hands.

To add the weapon, the weapon.md2 file must be referenced from the Models folder and the weaponSkin.tga file must be referenced from the Images folder. These files can be found in the Models folder from the book's download.

To enable use of the MD2 class for a weapon object in addition to the *Quake II* character, some changes are needed. Identifiers at the top of the game class distinguish between the two separate models.

```
const int CHARACTER = 0;
const int WEAPON    = 1;
```

Also in the game class, a new instance of the MD2 class is needed, so this object must be declared at the module level:

```
private MD2 md2Weapon;
```

The weapon and texture are loaded when the game begins, so place the code to load them inside Initialize():

```
md2Weapon = new MD2();
md2Weapon.loadModel(gfx.GraphicsDevice,
        ".\\Models\\weapon", ".\\Images\\weaponSkin", content);
md2Weapon.setAnimSpeed(5.0f);
md2Weapon.setAnim((int)meAnim.stand);
```

Note the animation speed, 5.0f, and the starting animation are set to match the starting speed and starting animation for Zarlag. This ensures that the weapon will animate properly with the character.

Each frame, the weapon animation must be updated. This can be done from the Update() method with the instruction

```
md2Weapon.updateModel(gfx.GraphicsDevice, gameTime);
```

Inside the Update() method, five conditions were implemented above to handle user input for changing the character's animation to the next animation, setting a specific animation, setting an animation sequence, and pausing and resuming animations. To ensure the weapon also moves properly with these animation changes, the following five instructions must be included with their respective conditions in the Update() method:

```
md2Weapon.advanceAnimation();
md2Weapon.setAnim((int)meAnim.run);
md2Weapon.setAnimSequence((int)meAnim.jump, (int)meAnim.run);
md2Weapon.Pause();
md2Weapon.Resume();
```

Some minor changes are also needed in the drawMD2model() method. It needs to be able to handle an identifier for the model so it knows which one to draw. Replace the header with this revision that includes a parameter to identify the model:

```
void drawMD2model(int iModel)
```

Next, inside the drawMD2model() method, some additional changes are required to ensure Zarlag and the weapon are textured with the correct skin. A check is needed to determine which model is being drawn before skinning it. Replace the code that textures Zarlag with this code block:

```
if(iModel == WEAPON)
    mBE.Texture = md2Weapon.getTexture();
else
    mBE.Texture = md2.getTexture();
```

Then, inside the drawMD2Model() method, when setting the data source and drawing primitive surfaces from it, a check is needed to make sure the correct set of vertices and the correct number of triangles are used. Replace the existing code that selects the vertices and draws the primitive surface with this version:

```
if (iModel == WEAPON){
    gfx.GraphicsDevice.Vertices[0].SetSource(
    md2Weapon.vertexBuffer, 0, VertexPositionNormalTexture.SizeInBytes);
    gfx.GraphicsDevice.DrawPrimitives(
        PrimitiveType.TriangleList, 0, md2Weapon.getNumTriangles());
}
else{
    gfx.GraphicsDevice.Vertices[0].SetSource(
    md2.vertexBuffer, 0, VertexPositionNormalTexture.SizeInBytes);
    gfx.GraphicsDevice.DrawPrimitives(
        PrimitiveType.TriangleList, 0, md2.getNumTriangles());
}
```

Lastly, to draw your character model and weapon with the identifier parameter, replace the existing instruction inside draw with this change:

```
drawMD2model(CHARACTER);
drawMD2model(WEAPON);
```

When you run the code now and change the animations, Zarlag and the weapon will animate together.

This chapter has shown how easy it is to create your own animated models. You may build your models in other modeling tools and then load them in MilkShape to animate them and/or convert them to .md2 format. If you have a loader for a different model format, you can still use MilkShape to create 3D models for it. Whatever method you use to create and load your 3D models, just make sure they load and animate properly in code before investing a lot of time building them.

The demonstration for Zarlag shows how powerful and diverse the *Quake II* format is for enabling animations. Combining pre-animated models with the techniques discussed in Chapter 6, "Character Movement," and Chapter 19, "Keyframe Animations," opens up all kinds of possibilities to unleash lifelike creatures in your 3D game play.

CHAPTER 23 REVIEW EXERCISES

1. Follow the step-by-step exercises in this chapter to create your own animated model and load it in code.

2. Create a model that animates with four bones or more and has three or more animations. Load this model and at least one other model in your game project. Code it so you have the ability to view all animations for each model loaded. Use the setAnimSequence() sequence at least once to trigger an animation and follow it with another looping animation.

CHAPTER 21

Adding Audio to Your Game

AUDIO

effects not only raise the appeal of a game, you can also use them to challenge players to make judgments based on sound. This chapter shows you how to add audio to your game and create audio depth.

With 3D audio enabled, you can actually tell where things are just by their sounds. For example, if you heard distant footsteps in your right ear, but could not see anybody walking, you would know that somebody is walking behind you off to the right. If you were to turn 180 degrees, you would see the person walking and the sound would be louder in your left ear. Your game will offer far more appeal and vibrancy with sounds throughout the environment—and with music to match.

ABOUT XACT

XNA audio is created using the Cross-Platform Audio Creation Tool (XACT). The XACT audio studio is intended to simplify the process of managing your audio files and sound cues. You can use it to organize wave files and to set their playback properties. XACT is installed as part of XNA Game Studio Express, so you don't need to worry about downloading or installing it.

Currently, WAV (wave) files are the only audio format supported in XNA. If you want to play back other formats—such as MP3—you should search the Audio/XACT forums to read up on the latest conversion utilities you can use to convert other audio formats to WAV files.

PROGRAMMING XNA AUDIO

To implement XNA audio, you must (at least) use these five main objects:

❱ XACT audio project file

❱ Audio engine

❱ Global settings

❱ Wave banks

❱ Sound banks

XACT Audio Project File

The XACT audio project file is the file created from XACT—also known as the *XACT authoring tool*. The XACT project file has an .xap extension. This file stores the wave file references, sound cue instances, and their playback settings. The .xap file extension is useful for deployment on both Windows and on the Xbox 360.

You don't need to reference this file in the code you write. However, when the .xap file is referenced in your XNA game project (from the Solution Explorer), your game project will automatically generate a global settings file, a wave bank file, and a sound bank file for you to regulate audio playback according to your audio project settings.

You could export the global settings, wave bank, and sound bank files separately from the audio authoring tool and then reference them manually in your project. However, to simplify referencing and loading your audio files in both your Windows and Xbox 360 game projects, referencing the .xap file in your project is recommended. When you reference the .xap file in your game project, it also provides a relative file path reference to the wave files used in your project.

Audio Engine

The AudioEngine object instantiates and manipulates core sound objects for playing game audio. This object is initialized with a set of properties loaded from a global settings file generated from the XACT authoring tool. As mentioned earlier, if you reference the .xap project file in the Solution Explorer, the global settings file will automatically be generated in your project at run time. Even though you cannot physically see the global settings file in the same folder as your .xap file, you can load it in code as long as the directory path is the same as your project file, as shown here:

```
AudioEngine audioEngine = new
AudioEngine(".\\Audio Project File Folder\\GlobalSettings.xgs");
```

Once you have initialized the sound engine in your code, it is then used to initialize the WaveBank and the SoundBank. As with the global settings file, these files will not be physically present in the audio folder when you use the .xap project file to generate them. However, they, too, can be loaded from the same directory in your project as your *.xap project file:

```
WaveBank waveBank    = new
WaveBank( audioEngine, "".\\Audio Project File Folder\\Wave Bank.xwb");
SoundBank soundBank  = new
SoundBank(audioEngine, "".\\Audio Project File Folder\\Sound Bank.xsb");
```

When you are loading your audio project, engine, wave bank, and sound bank files in this manner, your files will need to be in the same directory path (relative to the location where your .xap project file is saved).

Global Settings

Global settings are the definitions for the audio controls created by the sound designer. You use this file to initialize the sound engine.

Wave Banks

A *wave bank* is a collection of wave files loaded and packaged in an .xwb file.

Sound Banks

A *sound bank* is a collection of instructions and cues for the wave files to regulate how the sounds are played in your program.

Cues

You can use *cues* to trigger audio playback from the sound bank. Cues may contain a list of sounds to play in a specific sequence when an event is triggered, or they may provide a list of sounds that can be selected randomly for playback.

Categories

Categories are used to group sound banks with similar properties. You might consider categorizing sounds by how they are played back. For example, sounds with volumes that need to be adjusted together or sounds that need to be paused and resumed at the same time can be grouped in the same category.

Playback Methods

You have the option of using two methods for audio playback. The first involves using the SoundBank's GetCue() method to retrieve the sound instance and then the Play() method to play it:

```
cue = soundBank.GetCue(String cueName);
cue.Play();
```

This method is useful if you need to set the volume, or pause or resume the sound. However, if you are constantly using the GetCue() method, playing your sound, and disposing of the cue, you will hear the sound cutting out during playback. If you know you will be using these cues later, you can avoid this problem by placing your idle cues on a stack.

Another method that can be used to play your audio is the SoundBank's PlayCue() method. This method is useful for playing sounds in quick succession, such as the sound of a rapid-firing machine gun:

```
PlayCue(String cueName);
```

With this method, there is no disposal of the cue. This helps to avoid disruptions to the audio that can be caused by the garbage collection that happens when cues are disposed.

Programming 3D Audio

3D audio scales the volume of your sound sources and positions them in each speaker. The volume and position properties for each sound are derived from the listener's relative distance and orientation to the sound source. The listener object is defined by the AudioListener class. This object governs what you hear and how you hear it.

Normally, there is only one listener in a game, and it moves and changes direction with the camera. Moving this listener object with the camera allows you to update the position and orientation of each sound as the viewer travels through the world.

The AudioEmitter class stores the sound source's position, speed, and orientation. An AudioEmitter object is required for each sound source.

Both the listener and emitter objects store the following four vectors:

```
Vector3  Forward;    // direction
Vector3  Speed;      // direction and magnitude
Vector3  Position;
Vector3  Up;         // uprightness
```

The vectors are updated for the listener and all emitters every frame. Then the calculations to position the sound and scale the volume for each are applied with the method Apply3D():

```
void Cue.Apply3D(AudioListner listener, AudioEmitter emitter);
```

Because the cue is used to apply 3D audio, GetCue() must be used to retrieve the cue for playback.

XACT Authoring Tool

The XACT audio authoring tool provides a sound designer studio that allows you to create wave banks, add sound banks, and edit their properties for controlling how they are played from within your code.

The authoring tool is feature rich, and you may be pleased to discover how much you can customize your audio beyond the standard settings. You can use the audio authoring tool to randomize how sounds are played back, add reverb, randomize the sound volume, and implement great audio effects such as a Doppler effect.

XACT AUTHORING TOOL EXAMPLE

This demonstration shows how to use the audio authoring tool to generate an .xap project file that stores references for your wave files and their playback properties. Later on, you will reference this project file in your XNA project to regulate the playback of the wave files within your game.

The project uses four wave files: an introduction, a drumbeat, a crow, and a bell. The audio files for this project can be found in the Audio folder in the download from the book's website.

Later, in your code, you will reference these files so that the introduction plays when the game starts, the drumbeat starts playing in a loop after the introduction, the crow caws twice every two seconds, and the bell plays whenever you left-click the mouse or pull the right trigger.

Launching the XACT Authoring Tool

Next, launch the XACT authoring tool, which can be found in the Start menu under Programs | Microsoft XNA Game Studio Express | Tools | Microsoft Cross-Platform Audio Creation Tool (XACT). The authoring tool will appear as shown in Figure 24-1.

Creating a Wave Bank

To load a wave file, click the Wave Banks menu and then choose New Wave Bank.

You can now add wave files to your wave bank. Start by adding the intro.wav file. Click the Wave Banks menu and choose Insert Wave File(s). When the *Open* dialog launches, select the intro.wav file. Your wave file now appears in the Wave Bank panel (see Figure 24-2).

FIGURE 24-1

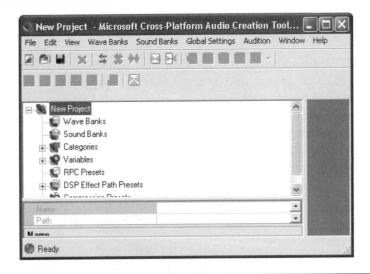

XACT authoring tool

FIGURE 24-2

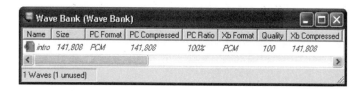

Wave file appears in the Wave Bank panel

Adding a Sound Bank

Next, you need a sound bank so you can customize properties that determine how the wave file will be played. The sound bank consists of two parts—a sound bank name and a cue name. To add a sound bank, select the Sound Banks menu and then click New Sound Bank.

You then need to create a cue that your code will use to trigger playback. This can be done by left-clicking the wave file in the Wave Bank panel and dragging it down, with the left mouse button pressed, into the lower panel of the Sound Bank panel. Your wave file instance should now appear in both the upper and lower sections of the Sound Bank panel (see Figure 24-3).

Repeating the Steps for the Drum, Crow, and Bell

For this part of the example, you repeat the steps you just completed for the intro.wav file for the drum.wav, crow.wav, and bell.wav files. When you are finished, these files will appear in wave bank, sound bank, and sound bank cue panels, as shown in Figure 24-4.

FIGURE 24-3

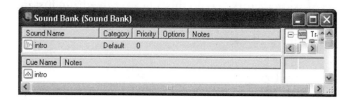

Sound bank name and cue

FIGURE 24-4

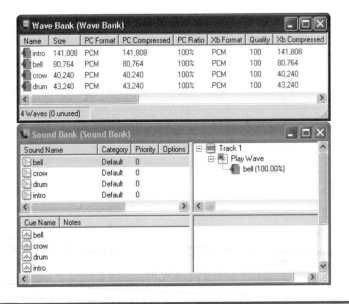

Wave bank, sound bank, and cues

Setting the Category Property for the Drum

Sometimes you will want to group your sound banks by category. Having sounds that fulfill a similar role under the same category simplifies your ability to control how the sounds are played back in your code. Some code instructions can be applied once to an entire category rather than individually for each sound in the category.

For this example, you need a different category for the drum; this will enable the drum to be paused and resumed separately in your code. The intro, bell, and crow have been assigned to the Default category. When the volume is set in code for the Default category, both the intro and bell sounds are affected. The drum will be assigned to the Music category. To do this, click on the drum instance in the top sound bank panel and then select *Music* under the *Category* setting in the lower-left property panel (see Figure 24-5).

Creating an Infinite Loop

The drum is meant to play in an infinite loop, so the playback repeats every time the track finishes. To enable the loop, select the drum sound bank and highlight *Play Wave* in the tree view in the top-right panel of the XACT authoring tool.

FIGURE 24-5

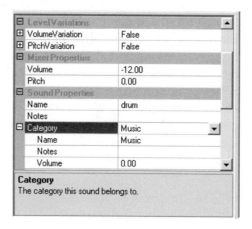

Setting the Category property for the drum file

Once you have highlighted *Play Wave* for the drum's sound bank, you can set the LoopEvent in the property view panel at the bottom left of the XACT authoring tool. Selecting the *Infinite* property in the *LoopEvent* drop-down menu enables the infinite loop for the drum sound (see Figure 24-6).

FIGURE 24-6

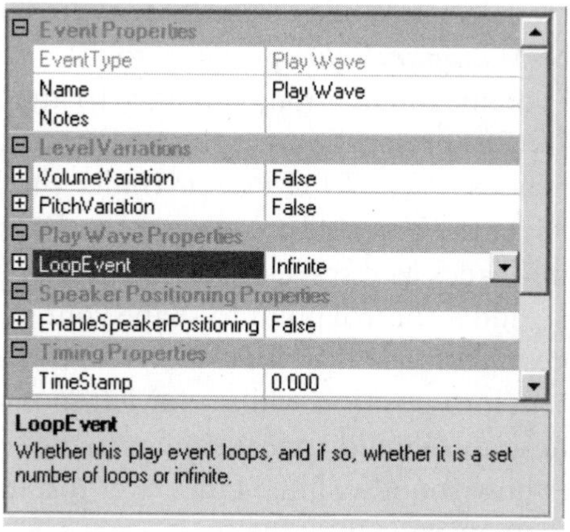

Adding an infinite loop

Adding a Finite Loop

The crow wave file only plays one caw. This example requires the caw sound to play twice every time it is played, so the sound is heard as "caw, caw." Creating a loop that repeats a specific number of times is called a *finite loop*. You can add the "caw, caw" sound by creating a finite loop with one repeat. To set the finite loop, select the crow wave file in the sound bank and then highlight *Play Wave* in the tree view.

Highlighting the *Play Wave* property button in the tree view at the top-right of the XNA authoring tool will display the Play Wave Properties panel at the bottom left. In the Play Wave Properties panel, expand the *LoopEvent* attribute. Select *Finite* in the *LoopEvent* drop-down. You can then expand the LoopEvent drop-down where you can enter 1 for the LoopCount property.

Testing Your Audio

Now that the sound banks have been created and properties have been assigned to them, you can test their playback with the XACT Auditioning Utility. This tool allows you to hear how they will sound when played from your game. Launch the XACT Auditioning Utility by navigating from the Start menu to Programs | Microsoft XNA Game Studio Express | Tools. A command prompt window will appear with the message "Waiting for the XACT authoring tool to connect...." When you want to test a sound bank, select it, right-click *Play Wave* in the right panel, and choose *Play Sound*.

Enabling Volume Attenuation

Audio attenuation refers to how the volume changes as the sound source travels toward and away from the listener. First, you must adjust the maximum distance value for the cue. To do this, in the left panel of the XACT project, expand *Cue Instance* and click *Distance* to select it. While Distance is selected, in the Properties panel that appears, change the *MaximumValue* property to 50.

Next, to enable volume attenuation, you have to attach the sound to a Runtime Parameter Control (RPC) preset. To create an RPC preset, right-click *RPC Presets* in the left panel and choose *New RPC Preset*. Under the Parameter column choose *Sound : Volume*. Under the Variable column choose *Distance*. The line that appears shows how the sound fades as it travels away from the listener. Two control points define the graph. To add a control point to shape your graph, click the *Runtime Parameter Control* preset dialog and choose *Add*. You can then left-click these control points and drag them into position while your left mouse button is pressed. When you are finished, the graph should appear similar to the one in Figure 24-7. This volume level simulates how sound volume fades over distance.

To associate this attenuation with the crow, right-click your new RPC preset that appears in the left panel and choose *Attach/Detach Sounds*. When prompted, choose Sound Bank crow and click *Attach*. Click *OK* when you are finished.

FIGURE 24-7

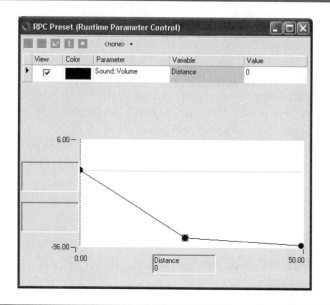

Runtime Parameter Control settings to adjust volume with distance

The crow should now be listed as one of the attached sounds in the properties display for the AttachedSounds property under the RPC preset. The crow's sound volume will now adjust according to the increase or decrease in distance between it and the listener. Figure 24-8 shows the new RPC Preset with the crow's sound attached.

FIGURE 24-8

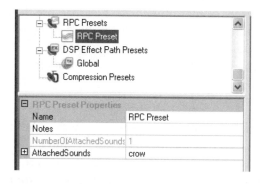

RPC Preset with crow's sound attached

Saving Your Audio Project

Now your wave banks and sound banks are prepared to play your sounds as required for this example. The next step requires that you save your XACT project. The .xap project file that is generated is used by your XNA game project to set the playback properties for your wave files. To generate the .xap project file, under the XACT authoring tool's File menu, select Save Project As. In the *Save Project As* dialog, browse to the directory where you want to export your project.

For the code portion of the example that follows, the .xap project file needs to be saved to the folder where the wave files are located; this ensures the project file's directory has the same relative path as the wave files. Enter the name **audioProject** in the *File Name* text area and click the *Save* button. This action generates an audioProject.xap file that stores your project and includes your wave bank, sound bank, and sound bank cue settings. Also, be sure to keep this .xap file in case you want to edit your XACT authoring tool project later.

MUSIC AND CROWS AUDIO EXAMPLE

The code portion of this demonstration takes the .xap project file you have created, and the accompanying wave files, and loads them for playback in your game project. After you add this code, you will be able to hear the introduction when the game begins. When the introduction ends, a drumbeat will play in an infinite loop. Also, a bell will ring whenever you pull the right game controller trigger or left-click the mouse, and a crow will fly back and forth in your world, cawing twice every two seconds. The crow's volume will be adjusted according to the flying crow's distance relative to the location of the camera. With this implementation, the crow will sound louder when it is close to your camera, and the sound will fade as the crow flies away.

You can start this example with either the WinMGHBook project or the Xbox360MGHBook project, found in the BaseCode folder in the download from the book's website. You can use the intro.wav, crow.wav, drum.wav, and bell.wav files in the Audio folder in the book's download. You may use the audioProject.xap file you created, or you can find a copy in the Audio folder. To reference these files in your project, add an Audio folder to your solution, add each of the .xap and wave files to it, and then reference each file within the Audio folder from the Solution Explorer.

Adding a Flying Crow

For this first portion of code, you create a crow that flies back and forth in the 3D world. You draw the crow using a model wing and a model crow. Altogether, the model crow consists of the crow.fbx, wing.fbx, and crow.bmp files. The two .fbx files must be referenced in your game project. You can find these files in the Models folder in the book's download.

Two model objects and matrices for storing their meshes are needed in the game class to store, transform, and draw the model:

```
Model      mModCrow;    Model      mModWing;
Matrix[]   matWing;     Matrix[]   matCrow;
```

You will use the same draw routine to draw the crow model's body and wings. To ensure the correct transformations are applied to each part of the crow, identifiers for each item are defined in the game class:

```
const int CROWMODEL = 0;   const int WING1 = 1;   const int WING2 = 2;
```

You must initialize the crow and wing models and their bone transformation matrices when the game begins. You can add this code to the game class to load and initialize them:

```
void initialize_crow_model(){
    mModCrow = content.Load<Model>(".\\Models\\crow");
    matCrow = new Matrix[mModCrow.Bones.Count];
    mModCrow.CopyAbsoluteBoneTransformsTo(matCrow);

    mModWing = content.Load<Model>(".\\Models\\wing");
    matWing = new Matrix[mModWing.Bones.Count];
    mModWing.CopyAbsoluteBoneTransformsTo(matWing);
}
```

To ensure the crow models are set up properly when the program begins, add the call statement for init_crow_model() to the Initialize() method in your game class:

```
initialize_crow_model();
```

The crow is going to be animated, so it translates back and forth on the Z axis. To perform this animation, you use variables to store the crow's current position and previous position, the crow's direction on Z, and the speed of the crow. These corresponding class-level declarations are needed at the top of your game class:

```
private Vector3 mv3CrowPos   = new Vector3(0.0f, 0.6f, 3.0f);// curr pos
private bool     mbCrowIncZ  = true;                         // inc on Z
private float    mfSpeedCrow = 0.001f;                       // speed on Z
```

To animate the crow's wings, you need additional variables to track the wing rotation angle about the Z axis, the speed of rotation, and the upward or downward direction. Adding these declarations to the module declarations area of your game class will assist you with the wing animation:

```
private float              mfWingRotation   = 0.0f;
private float              mfWingSpeed      = 0.0035f;
private bool               mbWingIncrease   = true;
```

This next method, update_crow(), allows you to update the crow each frame so it translates back and forth in your world along the Z axis while flapping both wings.

A check is made to determine if the crow has reached the front or back edge of the world on the Z axis. If it reaches the edge of the world, the crow's direction is reversed and its position is then incremented.

Another check is made to determine if the wing rotation has reached the upper maximum or lower minimum to simulate a wing flapping animation. If the wing's angle about the X axis is reached, the flapping direction is reversed accordingly. The wing's rotation about the Z axis is incremented by an amount that is consistent with the upward or downward motion of the wing.

Adding the update_crow_animation() method ensures that the position and angle of the crow's body and wings are updated each frame for a smooth animation:

```
private void update_crow_animation(){
    // time between frames
    float fTime = this.TargetElapsedTime.Milliseconds;

    // check if crow flies past boundary and reverse direction
    if (mv3CrowPos.Z > BOUNDARY && mbCrowIncZ == true ||
        mv3CrowPos.Z < -BOUNDARY && mbCrowIncZ == false){
        mbCrowIncZ        = !mbCrowIncZ;
        mfSpeedCrow       = -mfSpeedCrow;
    }
    mv3CrowPos.Z += fTime * mfSpeedCrow; // move crow on Z

    // check if wing tips rise above max or fall below min
    if (mfWingRotation > (float)Math.PI/9.0f && mbWingIncrease == true ||
        mfWingRotation < -(float)Math.PI/9.0f && mbWingIncrease == false){
        mbWingIncrease   = !mbWingIncrease;
        mfWingSpeed      = -mfWingSpeed;
    }
    mfWingRotation       += fTime * mfWingSpeed; // rotate crow's wings
}
```

The code for updating the crow's angle and position is triggered from the Update() method with a call to the update_crow_animation() method:

```
update_crow_animation();
```

You use the same method to draw the crow's body and wings. For each case, adjustments are made to customize the rotations to ensure the pieces of the crow are animated properly together. The routine for drawing the models is similar to other drawing routines used previously in this book. Add draw_crow() to render each separate piece of the crow:

```
void draw_crow(Model model, int iModel, GameTime gameTime)
{
    foreach (ModelMesh mesh in model.Meshes){
        // 1: declare matrices
        Matrix matIdentity,matScale,matTransl,matYRot,matZRot,matWorld;

        // 2: initialize matrices
        matIdentity = Matrix.Identity; // always start with identity matrix
        matTransl = Matrix.CreateTranslation(mv3CrowPos);

        // set Y rotation based on crow's direction on Z
        float rot = 0.0f;
        if (mbCrowIncZ) // if crow's Z value is increasing
            rot = ((float)Math.PI);

        matYRot   = Matrix.CreateRotationY(rot);
        matScale = Matrix.CreateScale(0.09f, 0.09f, 0.09f);
        matZRot   = Matrix.CreateRotationZ(0.0f);

        // create the wing flap rotation for both wings
        switch (iModel){
            case WING1:
                matZRot = Matrix.CreateRotationZ(mfWingRotation); break;
            case WING2:
                matZRot = Matrix.CreateRotationZ((float)Math.PI -
                mfWingRotation); break;
        }

        // 3: build cumulative world matrix using I.S.R.O.T. sequence
        // identity, scale, rotate, orbit(translate & rotate), translate
        matWorld = matIdentity * matScale * matZRot * matYRot * matTransl;

        foreach (BasicEffect effect in mesh.Effects){
            // 4: pass wvp to shader
            if (iModel == CROWMODEL)
```

```
            effect.World = matCrow[mesh.ParentBone.Index] * matWorld;
        else
            effect.World = matWing[mesh.ParentBone.Index] * matWorld;
        effect.View = mMatView;
        effect.Projection = mMatProj;

        // 4b: set lighting
        effect.EnableDefaultLighting();
        effect.CommitChanges();
    }
    // 5: draw object
    mesh.Draw();
    }
}
```

To draw the crow's body and wings, you call draw_crow() separately with the correct model and identifier as parameters from the Draw() method:

```
draw_crow(mModCrow, CROWMODEL, gameTime);
draw_crow(mModWing, WING1, gameTime);
draw_crow(mModWing, WING2, gameTime);
```

When you compile and run the program, you will see the crow flying back and forth in your 3D world.

Adding Audio to Your Game Class

At this point, the wave files are referenced in your project and are located in the Audio folder with your .xap project file. Also, the crow model flies back and forth when you run it. This next section discusses how to add the code to play the audio.

To enable audio in the code project, a reference is required at the top of your Game1.cs file to include the XACT audio library. This reference has already been added to the base code project:

```
using Microsoft.Xna.Framework.Audio;
```

Some additional preparation in code is needed to store the different components of your audio system. As mentioned earlier, the project file will be referenced in the project and will generate the global settings file, the wave bank, and the sound bank. Module-level declarations for loading and storing the sound engine, wave bank, and sound bank files will make these objects available for loading and playing your audio files throughout your game class:

```
// set up sound objects
private static AudioEngine   mSndEngine;
private static WaveBank      mWaveBank;
private static SoundBank     mSoundBank;
```

Your global settings, wave bank, and sound bank can now be loaded from the Initialize() method when the program begins. The file path specified leads to the same directory where your audioProject.xap project file is located. Even though these files are not physically present when your project is not running, the directory references are needed:

```
mSndEngine   = new AudioEngine(".\\Audio\\audioProject.xgs");
mWaveBank    = new WaveBank(mSndEngine, ".\\Audio\\Wave Bank.xwb");
mSoundBank   = new SoundBank(mSndEngine, ".\\Audio\\Sound Bank.xsb");
```

To ensure that your audio files unload when the program ends, add some code to dispose of them when the user exits from the program. deleteAudio() will remove your sound bank, wave bank, and engine from memory when the application is shut down:

```
void deleteAudio(){
    mSoundBank.Dispose();
    mWaveBank.Dispose();
    mSndEngine.Dispose();
}
```

To ensure deleteAudio() is called when the game ends, inside Update(), just before this.Exit(), add a call statement to dispose of the audio:

```
{   deleteAudio();
    this.Exit();    }
```

The introduction sound plays once at the start of the program. When the introduction finishes, a background drumbeat starts up and repeats for the rest of the game. Before the drumbeat begins, the introduction Cue object's IsPlaying attribute is used to determine if the introduction is still playing. When the introduction ends, a Boolean flag, mbIntroOver, is set to true. To assist in playing the drum sound only after the introduction has finished, these variable declarations are added to the module declarations of the game class:

```
private static bool    mbIntroOver = false; // play intro one time only
private static Cue      mCueIntro, mCueDrum;
```

Reader-friendly identifiers for the sounds will help you track which sounds are playing from your game class. Defining them in the module-level declaration area of your game class will enable their use throughout the class:

```
private const int            NUM_SOUNDS  = 4;
private const int            INTRO       = 0;
private const int            DRUM        = 1;
private const int            CROWAUDIO   = 2;
private const int            BELL        = 3;
```

When the game begins, after the audio files have been initialized, one of the first tasks required is to set the volumes for the different categories and to start playing the introduction.

You cannot set the volume for an individual sound bank. However, you can set the volume for a group of sounds in the same category. For this case, the introduction and bell are in the Default category, so their volumes are set with the same instruction. The drum's volume also needs to be set. However, you have assigned the drum to the Music category, so you must assign the drum's volume separately.

Adding the setup_audio_playback() method to your game class will set the volumes for the introduction, bell, and drum sounds. It also starts the playback of the introduction sound:

```
void setup_audio_playback(){
    mSndEngine.GetCategory("Default").SetVolume(1); // intro, bell
    mSndEngine.GetCategory("Music").SetVolume(1);    // drum
    play_sound("intro", INTRO);                      // play intro at start
}
```

To ensure the playback for the introduction, drum, and bell are set up when the program begins, setup_audio_playback() is called from Initialize():

```
setup_audio_playback();
```

At every frame, you must update the sound engine. If you omit this update, it may seem for many frames that your audio is working. However, Microsoft warns that without continuous updates, the sound engine will inevitably crash.

Before you actually update the sound engine, an additional check is made to ensure that the sound engine exists. You use the sound engine's IsDisposed property for this check. Trying to update the sound engine when it has been disposed will cause a program crash. To implement the sound engine update, add the following code to the Update() method:

```
if (!mSndEngine.IsDisposed)
    mSndEngine.Update();
```

As mentioned earlier, there are two methods for playing sound. play_sound() uses the GetCue() method to retrieve the sound and play it with the Play() method. This playback routine is useful for the introduction and drum sounds because they are either played once or played in a continuous loop during the game. The GetCue() / Play() combination also offers the ability to pause and resume audio play. Adding the play_sound() routine to the game class provides a mechanism for playing the introduction and drum audio:

```
void play_sound(string strCueName, int iEmit){
    if (!mSoundBank.IsDisposed){
        Cue cue = mSoundBank.GetCue(strCueName);
        // handle case where intro plays once at beginning
        if (strCueName == "intro")
            mCueIntro = cue;
        // be able to pause and resume drum
        else if (strCueName == "drum")
            mCueDrum = cue;
        cue.Play();
    }
}
```

To enable proper timing for pausing and resuming the drum, and to enable better timing for the playback of the bell, add module declarations for variables to store the time lapse from the first press event that triggers each sound:

```
private double mdblDrumDelay;
private double mdblBellDelay;
```

This next method handles sound events for starting the drum after the introduction finishes, for pausing and resuming the drum, and for ringing the bell.

Before anything is done in this routine, a check is made to ensure the audio engine and sound bank actually exist. Failing to check whether these objects exist will cause the program to crash if the sound banks or cues are used after the audio engine or sound banks have been disposed.

The drum is started only after the introduction finishes. When the program begins, a check is made each frame to determine whether the introduction is playing. When the introduction's IsPlaying attribute is false, the drumbeat is started and a Boolean flag is set so that this condition is never entered again during the game.

When you're coding the routine for toggling between the drum's paused and resumed states, a check is made to ensure there is a time delay of 0.25 seconds before the pause or resume state can be changed. This delay allows the user enough time to release the P key or the A button before their state is toggled again.

The code used to ring the bell implements a delay between rings to allow each bell sound to play completely before it rings again. The PlayCue() method is used to play the bell audio because it is a rapid-fire sound that is played during a right trigger event or a left-mouse-click event. The PlayCue() method is not prone to disruptions to the audio, which can be caused by garbage collection that occurs with the GetCue() and Dispose() methods. The PlayCue() method requires that the cue be stored in memory for as long as the audio is needed during the game.

```
void handleSoundEvents(GameTime gameTime)
{
    KeyboardState kbState = Keyboard.GetState();

    // ensure the engine and sound bank exist before using them
    if (!mSndEngine.IsDisposed && !mSoundBank.IsDisposed){
    // play drum loop as soon as intro is finished
    if (mbIntroOver == false){
        if (mCueIntro.IsPlaying == false){
            mbIntroOver = true; // ensure that drum loop starts once only
            play_sound("drum", DRUM);
        }
    }
    // if P key or A button pressed toggle drum on and off
    if ((kbState.IsKeyDown(Keys.P) |
        GamePad.GetState(PlayerIndex.One).Buttons.A == ButtonState.Pressed)
        // 1/4 s delay between press event allows sound to play till end
        && gameTime.TotalGameTime.TotalMilliseconds - mdblDrumDelay > 250){
        // track time that drum is played
        mdblDrumDelay = gameTime.TotalGameTime.TotalMilliseconds;

        // toggle between pausing and playing drum
        if (mCueDrum.IsPlaying && !mCueDrum.IsPaused)
            mSndEngine.GetCategory("Music").Pause();  // pause drum
        else if (mCueDrum.IsPaused)
            mSndEngine.GetCategory("Music").Resume(); // play drum
    }
    // play bell when user left-clicks mouse or pulls right trigger
    if (// 1.0 s delay between press event allows sound to play till end
        ((gameTime.TotalGameTime.TotalMilliseconds-mdblBellDelay)>1000.0f)
     && (
            #if !XBOX // mouse events only apply on windows
                mMouse.LeftButton == ButtonState.Pressed |
            #endif
```

```
          GamePad.GetState(PlayerIndex.One).Triggers.Right != 0.0f)
    ){  // track game time that bell is played
        mdblBellDelay = gameTime.TotalGameTime.TotalMilliseconds;
        mSoundBank.PlayCue("bell");
    }
  }
}
```

handleSoundEvents() is called from Update() to ensure the bell and drum playback are handled every frame:

```
handleSoundEvents(gameTime);
```

Adding 3D Audio

The last sound played in this demonstration is the crow. This sound uses 3D audio to give it depth. The 3D audio positions the sound in your speakers according to the distance and orientation between the camera and sound source.

Two game class–level objects are required for 3D audio to calculate the proper volume for each speaker. The AudioListener stores the position, speed, and orientation of the viewer, which is usually defined at the camera. The AudioEmitter stores the position and orientation of the object that makes the noise (which is the crow in this case).

```
AudioListener    mListener    = new AudioListener();
AudioEmitter     mEmitterCrow = new AudioEmitter();
```

As mentioned previously, GetCue() must be used to retrieve the cue before playback when you're using 3D audio. However, after every queue is played, it is automatically disposed and removed later through garbage collection. When cues are frequently disposed and regenerated, this causes unwanted static in your audio during playback. To avoid this problem, you will place a helper class just inside the game class to store the cue for reuse and to track the sound emitter attached to it:

```
private class Audio3DCue{
    public Cue cue;
    public AudioEmitter emitter;
}
```

With this helper class in place, a module-level list and stack are declared to track the active sound cues and to store inactive cues:

```
List<Audio3DCue>  mActiveCueList= new List<Audio3DCue>();
Stack<Audio3DCue> mCueStack     = new Stack<Audio3DCue>();
```

Because the camera speed and crow speeds are used to update the listener and help it perform the 3D audio calculations, variables are needed at the module level to store the previous position for determining the magnitude of change in distance:

```
private Vector3 mv3PrevCamPos, mv3CrowPosOld;
```

The previous camera and crow positions can be assigned at the start of the Update() method before the current positions are reassigned. Later you can use these values to calculate the speed of the camera and crow:

```
mv3PrevCamPos = cam.m_vPos; mv3CrowPosOld = mv3CrowPos;
```

updateAudioListener() is added to the game class to update the listener position and orientation vectors:

```
void updateAudioListener(){
    Vector3 v3Look  = cam.m_vView - cam.m_vPos;
    Vector3 v3speed = cam.m_vPos  - mv3PrevCamPos;

    v3Look.Normalize();
    mListener.Position    = cam.m_vPos;
    mListener.Forward     = v3Look;
    mListener.Up          = cam.m_vUp;
    mListener.Velocity    = v3speed;
}
```

You will use these listener vectors to later position the audio in the speaker.

For this demonstration, you will update the emitter vectors just before the calculation that positions the sound in the speaker. In the game class, the Apply3DAudio method first updates the crow's position, speed, and orientation vectors. Then it calls the Cue object's Apply3D() method. Apply3D() uses the listener and emitter data to set the volume and position for the crow's sound:

```
private void Apply3DAudio(Audio3DCue cue3D)
{
    Vector3 v3Speed = mv3CrowPos - mv3CrowPosOld;

    mEmitterCrow.Position = mv3CrowPos;
    mEmitterCrow.Up       = new Vector3(0.0f, 1.0f, 0.0f);
    mEmitterCrow.Velocity = v3Speed;
    v3Speed.Normalize();
    mEmitterCrow.Forward  = v3Speed;
```

```
if (   !cue3D.cue.IsDisposed && !mSoundBank.IsDisposed
       && !mSndEngine.IsDisposed)
       cue3D.cue.Apply3D(mListener, mEmitterCrow);
}
```

The updateAudioEmitters() method calls the Apply3DAudio method after managing the existing cues. If a cue has stopped playing, updateAudioEmitter() disposes of it and pushes the cue instance on the stack for reuse later to prevent unwanted garbage collection. The cue is no longer active, so it is removed from the active cue list. Otherwise, if the cue is playing, it is retrieved from the active cue list and Apply3DAudio() is called to perform the 3D audio calculations:

```
void updateAudioEmitters(){
    for(int i = 0; i<mActiveCueList.Count; i++){

        Audio3DCue audio3Dcue = mActiveCueList[i];

        if (!audio3Dcue.cue.IsDisposed && audio3Dcue.cue.IsStopped){
            audio3Dcue.cue.Dispose();    // dispose when stops playing
            mCueStack.Push(audio3Dcue); // store Audio3DCue for reuse
            mActiveCueList.RemoveAt(i); // remove inactive cue from list
        }
        else
            Apply3DAudio(audio3Dcue);    // cue playing so update 3D
    }
}
```

The emitter and listener objects must be updated each frame so they are called from the end of the Update() method:

```
updateAudioListener();
updateAudioEmitters();
```

play3DAudio() is placed in the game class either to retrieve an available cue from the stack (if it exists) or to create one if it does not exist. Once the cue is ready, Apply3DAudio() is called to calculate the volume and sound position in each speaker. After these calculations have been performed, the cue is played and the active cue is added to the active cue list. Add play3DAudio to your game class to implement this routine:

```
public Cue play3DAudio(string strCueName)
{
    Audio3DCue audio3Dcue;
```

```
        if (mCueStack.Count > 0)      // reuse cue if any on stack
            audio3Dcue      = mCueStack.Pop();
        else                           // otherwise create new one
            audio3Dcue      = new Audio3DCue();

        // store current cue and emitter
        audio3Dcue.cue     = mSoundBank.GetCue(strCueName);
        audio3Dcue.emitter = mEmitterCrow;

        Apply3DAudio(audio3Dcue);        // set pos and orientation
        audio3Dcue.cue.Play();           // play it
        mActiveCueList.Add(audio3Dcue);  // store in active audio list

        return audio3Dcue.cue;
}
```

The crow's sound was set in the XACT authoring tool to repeat once every time it is played. The result is you hear the sound twice in succession—"caw, caw." You will use a timer to play the crow's cawing every two seconds. In the module declarations section of your game class, a declaration for the time of the previous frame will assist in tracking the time lapse between caws:

```
private double mDblPreviousCrowTime;
```

A timer like the one that was first used in Chapter 10, "Combining Images for Better Visual Effects," enables playback of the crow audio every two seconds:

```
bool crowTimer(GameTime gameTime)
{
    bool bNewInterval;
    double dblMS = (double)gameTime.TotalGameTime.TotalMilliseconds;
    double dblCurrentFrame = dblMS % 2000;

    if (dblCurrentFrame >= mDblPreviousCrowTime) // interval incomplete
        bNewInterval = false;
    else                                          // interval complete
        bNewInterval = true;

    mDblPreviousCrowTime = dblCurrentFrame;
    return bNewInterval;
}
```

As long as the sound engine has not been disposed, the timer triggers the crow's audio playback event every two seconds at the end of the Update() method. Add the following code to verify the sound engine and to check for the timer event before playing the crow audio:

```
if (!mSndEngine.IsDisposed && crowTimer(gameTime) == true)
    play3DAudio("crow");
```

When you run the program, the game will begin with the introduction sound. When the introduction is finished, the drumbeat starts. You have the option to pause or resume the drumbeat by pressing P on the keyboard or the A button on the game pad. A bell sound can be triggered by left-clicking the mouse or pulling the right trigger of the game controller. The crow can still be heard in each speaker—according to the listener's position and angle relative to the crow.

This demonstration has shown how to create several different types of sound. You can employ the same logic used in the demonstration to create most other types of audio you would need in a game. Scenarios covered include rapid-fire sounds, background music, looping noises, and audio that must be updated based on the relative distance between your camera and the sound emitter. We are sure you will notice how much more enjoyable your games are when you add audio.

CHAPTER 24 REVIEW EXERCISES

1. Implement the step-by-step example in this chapter to create your own XACT audio project file. Then load your audio and play it from code.

2. Using the solution for the arcing projectiles example from Chapter 17, "Ballistics," add in audio to handle a launch sound and a 3D audio–enabled explosion sound when the rocket hits the ground.

3. Using the solution for "Adding a Car as a Third-person Object" from Chapter 12, "3D Models," add a looping noise that repeats to create a continuous engine sound whenever the car moves forward or backward.

CHAPTER 25

Terrain with Height Detection

WHEN

playing *Halo*, did you ever stop to appreciate the beautiful scenery as you ran toward the Blood Gulch caves after picking up the rocket launcher? It may be tough to take time to enjoy the moment when you have to watch out for players who might suddenly appear from behind a big grassy hill, but this does not mean that gamers will not appreciate the effort you devote to the terrain in your games.

This chapter shows you how to create rolling fields, with height detection. This way, you not only see this impressive terrain, but your camera will adjust to rise above the ground as you travel up or down the hilly landscape. The same logic can be used to implement height detection for other objects in your game. The terrain in this chapter is generated using a type of topographical map called a *height map*. Figure 25-1 shows a grassy landscape similar to the one that will be created in this chapter. As you travel over the hills, the camera rises or falls according to the height of the ground.

HEIGHT MAPS

A *height map* is an image that stores information in each pixel about terrain elevation. Using a height map to create terrain is popular because it is easy for designers to generate landscapes with an image-editing tool, and it is easy to convert this information to implement height detection in a 3D environment. The demonstration used in this chapter shows how to create and implement a height map using an 8-bit .raw grayscale image. Each pixel in the .raw image stores information about the elevation—in a range between 0 and 255. This information is read into an array when the program begins; the height data in each pixel can then be accessed with the pixel row and column number. When this technique is applied in a 3D environment, the ground is divided up into the same number of rows and columns as the image. When positioning the camera or other objects, you calculate the elevation by determining the row and column position of the object and then passing this information to the height map array to retrieve the elevation for the corresponding cell on the landscape.

FIGURE 25-1

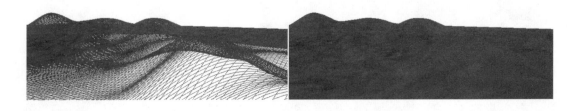

Terrain drawn from elevation data that is contained in a height map

CREATING A HEIGHT MAP USING TERRAGEN

This demonstration shows you how to create a height map using Planetside's Terragen. Terragen does an excellent job in creating realistic terrain. If you configured the landscape before making your skybox (as shown in Chapter 8, "Adding Skies and Horizons to Your Levels"), you can use it to create terrain that matches your skybox.

Creating the Height Map

Terragen offers many different ways to create a height map. You can select a pattern for creating the terrain randomly or you can sculpt it on your own. This demonstration shows you how to sculpt it so you can have more control over the hills and fields you generate. You can download a trial version of Terragen from www.planetside.co.uk/terragen/. Once you have installed the application, you can launch it by selecting Terragen from the Start menu. This will open the Terragen window. To create the terrain, select *Landscape* from the *View* menu.

Adjusting the Height Map Size

With the noncommercial edition of Terragen, you can choose from several preset sizes for your height map. The size 513×513 will be used for this demonstration because it offers enough pixels to draw smooth hills. However, the size is not so large that it will impact performance on your PC or Xbox 360. To adjust the size, click the *Size* button in the *Landscape* dialog. Then select 513 in the *Landscape Settings* dialog that appears. Note that later in this demonstration you will create a 512×512 texture, which will be applied to the ground surface. Terragen's 513×513 pixel dimensions do not need to match the dimensions of the texture as long as the proportions of the width compared to the height are the same.

Starting with Level Ground

To clear the terrain so you can start with a flat surface, in the *Landscape* dialog select the *Modify* button. Then, in the *Terrain Modification* dialog that appears, click *Clear / Flatten*. After returning to the *Landscape* dialog, you will notice the height map preview area is black; this means the ground is level (that is, no area on it has been elevated).

Adding Hills to Your Terrain

To start adding hills to your terrain, from the *Landscape* dialog, select *View / Sculpt*. Select the *Basic Sculpting* tool in the top-left corner of the *View / Sculpt* dialog and then left-click the mouse and drag in the dialog to add terrain. Right-clicking the mouse and dragging in the dialog lowers the terrain. Elevated areas will be lighter—bright white indicates high elevation and black indicates ground level. Figure 25-2 shows two clusters of hills that have been created from left-clicking the mouse and dragging in the *View / Sculpt* dialog.

When you return to the *Landscape* dialog, the changes you have made to the terrain will appear on the left.

Adjusting the Color

You can also adjust the color of the landscape from the *Landscape* dialog. This color has no effect on your height map, but it will affect the texture you will generate to cover it. In the *Landscape* dialog, high-light *Surface Map* and then click *Edit*. In the *Surface Layer* dialog that appears, click *Color* on the *Base Surface* tab. The *Surface Color* dialog will open and you can adjust the red, green, and blue settings to establish a general color for your terrain. To look more realistic, the color will not be uniform across the terrain but it will use the general value you set. The color will also be affected by shadows from the sun, elevation, and other factors—if you choose these in your project settings. When you are satisfied with the general colors, click *OK* to exit from the *Surface Color* dialog. Then close the *Surface Layer* dialog to return back to the *Landscape* dialog.

Exporting Your Height Map

Your height map is now ready for export. You can export the height map from the *Landscape* dialog by clicking the *Export* button. In the *Terrain Export* dialog, select the *Export Method* drop-down and choose *Raw 8 bits,* which is the format needed for the code demonstration. Then click *Select a File and Save*. When prompted, in the *Export Heightfield* dialog, after navigating to the folder where you want to save your height map, enter the name **heightMap.raw** and click *Save*. This action will export your height map. Now you can create the texture to match the height map. Keep the *Landscape* dialog open to have the height map settings available when you generate the texture.

Creating the Terrain Texture to Match the Height Map

As you may have figured out already, the height map is separate from the texture. You do not have to use Terragen to create your terrain texture. If you want, you can use the tiled grass texture included with the base project for your terrain texture. However, you might consider using Terragen to generate this texture for several reasons. Terragen generates the terrain in a manner that considers many environmental factors, including the following:

FIGURE 25-2

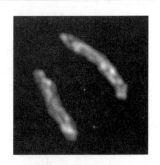

Two clusters of hills created in the View / Sculpt dialog

❯ Blending of images

❯ Shadows based on cloud cover, sunlight, and change in elevation

❯ Snow, rock, and grass cover quantity, density, and color

❯ Elevation

When creating the texture for the terrain, you will use the same camera settings from Chapter 8, "Adding Skies and Horizons to Your Levels." This will ensure the terrain can be viewed from the same perspective as your original skybox. Figure 25-3 shows the *Rendering Control* dialog settings used to generate the terrain image. Terragen will automatically adjust some of the properties as others are set, so you may not be able to replicate these properties exactly. However, you need to ensure the *Pitch (Y)* value for the camera orientation is set to –90 so the camera points at the ground when the texture is rendered.

The camera settings applied for the terrain are summarized in Table 25-1.

FIGURE 25-3

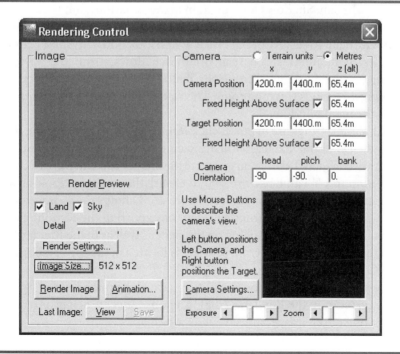

Settings for generating the terrain texture

TABLE 25-1

	X	Y	Z
Camera Position	4200m	4400m	65.4m
Target Position	4200m	4400m	65.4m
Camera Orientation	−90	−90	0

Camera Settings for Terrain Creation

Also, as in Chapter 8, "Adding Skies and Horizons to Your Levels," the *Zoom / Magnification* property is set to 1 to ensure the image is scaled properly when it is rendered by Terragen. This setting can be adjusted in the *Camera Settings* dialog. You can navigate there by clicking the *Camera Settings* button in the *Rendering Control* dialog. Note that the *Detail* slider is at a maximum setting in the *Rendering Control* dialog; this ensures the highest quality. Lastly, the texture size is set to 512×512, which matches the size used to create the skybox images you created earlier in the book.

At this point, you will make an additional adjustment to reduce the shadows caused by the sun. Shadows look great in many situations, but they will look odd for the current project because they create a large dark area over the ground, which makes it difficult to see. Also, this effect would look odd in the absence of a surrounding series of mountains. To turn off the shadows, from the *View* menu select *Lighting*. In the *Lighting Conditions* dialog that appears, deselect *Terrain Casts Shadows and Clouds Cast Shadows*. Then close the *Lighting Conditions* dialog to return to the main window.

When these settings are in place, click *Render Preview* to check the color, randomness, and view of the image. If you are seeing sky, it is probably because the camera orientation changed. Before you generate the image, you will have to change the camera orientation's Y value back to −90 to ensure the camera is looking at the ground when generating the terrain texture. Figure 25-4 shows the *Rendering Control* and *Landscape* dialogs with settings suitable for exporting the terrain. The height map preview is in the *Landscape* dialog on the right as well as in the *Rendering Control* dialog in the lower left. The terrain preview is located in the top-left corner of the *Rendering Control* dialog.

Once your texture setup looks right, you can export the texture by selecting *Render Image*. Next, in the *Rendering* dialog, choose *Save*. When prompted, you can enter the name of the image and save it as a bitmap.

FIGURE 25-4

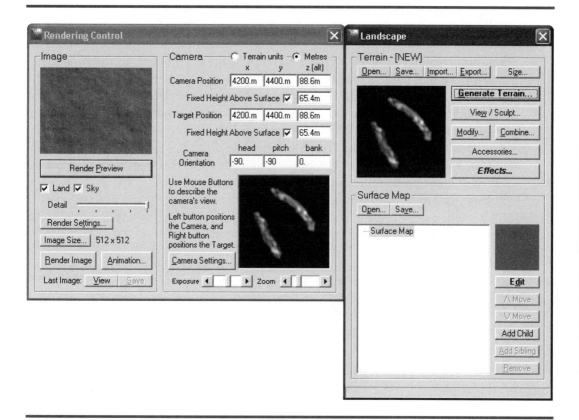

Texture preview on the left and height map preview on the right

HEIGHT MAP CODE EXAMPLE

Now that you have created a height map and accompanying texture, you can load them in code. When you run your code, the height map appears and your camera travels above it. Because many vertices are used to render the height map, an index buffer is used to reference them to reduce the storage requirements. This code example begins with the solution from the first example in Chapter 9, "Index Buffers." The solution already has code to render a set of vertices using an indexed buffer.

Once you have obtained the solution for Chapter 9 from the Solutions folder in the download from the book's website, you must also reference the custom content processor you generated in Chapter 22, "Content Pipeline Processors." To access your custom content processor, copy the TerrImporter.dll library file you built for your solution in Chapter 22 to your current project folder. You may obtain a copy of the TerrImporter.dll file from the solution for Chapter 22 in the Solutions folder from the download. The TerrImporter.dll file needs to be referenced in your project in two different places. To add the first reference, right-click the project name in the Solution Explorer and select *Add Reference* in the drop-down. In the *Add Reference* dialog that launches, select the *Browse* tab and navigate to TerrImporter.dll. Selecting this file will add the first reference. Next, to add the content pipeline reference so you can load your .raw file using the ContentManager class, right-click your project name in the Solution Explorer and choose *Properties*. In the gray panel that appears, click *Content Pipeline* in the lower-left corner. Then click the *Add* button and navigate to the TerrImporter.dll file. Selecting the file and choosing *Open* will enable your custom content processor.

Next, you must include the TerrImporter's namespace at the top of the Game1.cs file so your game class can access the terrain importer's load methods and objects:

```
using TerrImporter;
```

The NUM_ROWS declaration stores the number of "height" pixels for the image, and the NUM_COLS declaration stores the number of "width" pixels for the image. If the dimensions of the .raw file were to change, then the row and column declarations must change accordingly. The terrain grid used will be split into a total number of cells equivalent to NUM_ROWS * NUM_COLS. To ensure the dimensions fit the height map, replace the existing row and column definitions with these:

```
const int NUM_COLS = 513;
const int NUM_ROWS = 513;
```

Module-level variables are required in the game class to store the height map and texture:

```
MyTerrain  myterrain;
Texture2D  mTexTerrain;
```

Now that the reference to your custom terrain importer has been added, you can use it to load your heightMap.raw file. The heightMap.raw file can be obtained from the Images folder in the download available from the book's website. Alternatively, you can use the heightMap.raw file you just created in Terragen. Either way, the heightMap.raw file must be referenced from the Images folder in the Solution Explorer. If your terrain importer is referenced in the project correctly, when you select the heightMap.raw file in the Solution Explorer, you will see it can be loaded using the ContentManager in the *Properties* panel that appears. If not, select *Content* for the *Build Action*. Then in the XNA Framework content area of the *Properties* panel, choose *True*. This will allow you to select TerrImporter as the content importer and TerrProcessor as the content processor.

To ensure the height map is loaded when the program begins, load it from the Initialize() method. Because the height map data is needed to initialize the vertex buffer, load it before the call to init_dynamic_vb():

```
myterrain = content.Load<MyTerrain>(".\\Images\\heightMap");
```

The terrain texture you created in Terragen must be loaded and referenced from the Images folder for your project so it can be loaded with the ContentManager. Inside LoadGraphicsContent(), the terrain texture can then be loaded with the following instruction:

```
mTexTerrain = content.Load<Texture2D>(".\\Images\\Terrain");
```

When the world is rendered in this example, it is divided into rows and columns that match the width and height pixel dimensions of the .raw file. The row and column values for the world are passed to the get_height() method, which uses these coordinates to retrieve the corresponding height from the height map array.

If the camera, or any other object that uses this height-detection routine, travels beyond the outer limits of the world, the height value is taken from the closest cell in the world that has height detection.

The height stored in the .raw file can range between 0 and 255. These values must be scaled through division to be sized properly for your 3D world. You may adjust the scaling to expand or shrink the size of your hills.

Add get_height() to your game class to initialize your terrain when the program begins, and also to return height information to objects that use height detection at run time:

```
float get_height(int iRow, int iCol){
    // if camera not over terrain
    // then use closest pixel on height map for height data
    if (iRow >= NUM_ROWS)
        iRow = NUM_ROWS - 1;
    if (iCol >= NUM_COLS)
        iCol = NUM_COLS - 1;

    // image data is loaded starting with the bottom right pixel
    // to retrieve the corresponding value in the array the equation is:
    // row * NUM_COLS + ( NUM_COLS - col - 1)
    float f_height;
    f_height = myterrain.mByteHeightMap[iRow * NUM_COLS
                            + (NUM_COLS - iCol - 1)];
```

```
        // scale hills. 0 to 255 is too big for our world
        const float HEIGHT_SCALE = 0.0024f;
        f_height *= HEIGHT_SCALE;

        return f_height;
}
```

When the program begins, while the vertex buffer is initialized inside init_dynamic_vb(), the height information from the height map is used. Replace the existing assignment for the Y coordinate inside init_dynamic_vb() with this revision:

```
fy = get_height(iRow, iCol);
```

getCellPosition() returns the camera's X and Z cell positions relative to the terrain grid. For example, if the camera is located in the middle of the cell at row 10 and column 12, a value of 10.5 is returned for Z and 12.5 is returned for X.

In the original base code, the ground boundary spans from –BOUNDARY to +BOUNDARY. However, the terrain grid cells are all positive. To simplify the calculation when we express the camera's position relative to the terrain grid, temporary values for the ground are shifted on X and Z as if the ground starts at 0, 0 and increases along X and Z. The calculation to generate the X and Z cell positions becomes the following:

$$X = (camera.x + BOUNDARY) / CellWidth;$$
$$Y = (camera.y + BOUNDARY) / CellHeight;$$

When the camera is no longer above the terrain, the closest row and column on the terrain grid are returned.

Add getCellPosition() to your game class to return the height for each cell of the terrain grid. This will assist with setting up the terrain and with implementing the height detection:

```
Vector3 getCellPosition(){
    // total grid row cells = total rows - 1
    // same for column cells
    float fNumRowCells    = (float)NUM_ROWS - 1.0f;
    float fNumColumnCells = (float)NUM_COLS - 1.0f;

    float fCellWidth  = 2.0f * BOUNDARY / fNumColumnCells;
    float fCellHeight = 2.0f * BOUNDARY / fNumRowCells;
```

```
// calculate X and Z
float fPosX = (cam.m_vPos.X + BOUNDARY) / fCellWidth;
float fPosZ = (cam.m_vPos.Z + BOUNDARY) / fCellHeight;

// if camera off grid where there is no height map
// use the closest position on grid
if (cam.m_vPos.X > BOUNDARY)
    fPosX = 2.0f * BOUNDARY / fCellWidth;
else if (cam.m_vPos.X < -BOUNDARY)
    fPosX = 0.0f;
if (cam.m_vPos.Z > BOUNDARY)
    fPosZ = 2.0f * BOUNDARY / fCellHeight;
else if (cam.m_vPos.Z < -BOUNDARY)
    fPosZ = 0.0f;
return new Vector3(fPosX, 0.0f, fPosZ);
}
```

When a change in height is detected, the camera's position and view are incremented. To calculate this increment, the camera's position over the terrain grid is determined using getCellPosition(). Usually the camera's position is somewhere inside the cell rather than exactly at the start of a row and column. If the height of the camera was only incremented every time the cell changed, the camera's ride over the terrain would be a rough one because it would be forced to jump from elevation to elevation whenever entering another cell. To provide a smoother ride over the terrain, linear interpolation is used to calculate height inside the cell; this is based on the heights of the surrounding cell corners. The values used in the linear interpolation are based on the three closest corners of the cell. To determine the three closest corners, the cell is divided in half (i.e., into two triangles). If the offset between the cell rows is less than 1 minus the offset between cell columns, the corners of the bottom triangle are used. Otherwise, the corners of the top triangle are used in the linear interpolation to estimate the height within the cell. In pseudo-code, the condition looks like this:

```
if (dz < 1.0f - dx)
        // lower right triangle
else
        // upper left triangle
```

Figure 25-5 shows how each cell is divided to determine which corners should be considered in the linear interpolation. It also gives the equations used to project the height of the camera.

FIGURE 25-5

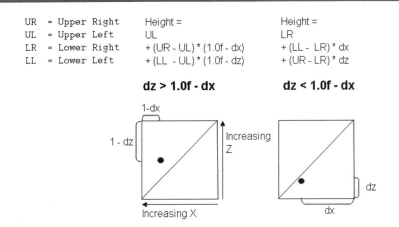

```
UR  = Upper Right      Height =                Height =
UL  = Upper Left       UL                      LR
LR  = Lower Right      + (UR - UL) * (1.0f - dx)   + (LL - LR) * dx
LL  = Lower Left       + (LL - UL) * (1.0f - dz)   + (UR - LR) * dz
```

dz > 1.0f - dx   **dz < 1.0f - dx**

Height based on linear interpolation of the three closest cell corners

Add set_camera_height() to adjust how the camera view and position are incremented with this change in height:

```
void set_camera_height(){
    Vector3 v3Pos = getCellPosition();
    float fPosX = v3Pos.X;
    float fPosZ = v3Pos.Z;

    // cast values to get closest cell row and column
    int iRow = (int)fPosZ;
    int iCol = (int)fPosX;

    // prevent variable overflow at edge of map
    if (iRow >= (int)NUM_ROWS - 1.0f)
        iRow = (int)(NUM_ROWS - 2.0f);

    // create two triangles to make a rectangle based on grid cell points
    float fLR, fLL, fUL, fUR; // lower L, lower R, upper R, upper L

    fLR = mVertGrid[iRow * NUM_COLS + iCol].Position.Y;
    fLL = mVertGrid[iRow * NUM_COLS + iCol + 1].Position.Y;
    fUR = mVertGrid[(iRow + 1) * NUM_COLS + iCol].Position.Y;
    fUL = mVertGrid[(iRow + 1) * NUM_COLS + iCol + 1].Position.Y;
```

```
// get offset between cam position and row start and column start
float dx = fPosX - iCol;
float dz = fPosZ - iRow;

float fHeight;
// determine which half the camera is in and use three closest cell
// corners to project the height with linear interpolation

// lower right triangle
if (dz < 1.0f - dx)
    fHeight = fLR + (fLL - fLR)*dx + (fUR - fLR)*dz;
// upper left triangle
else
    fHeight = fUL + (fUR - fUL)*(1.0f - dx) + (fLL - fUL)*(1.0f - dz);

// get height difference and adjust view and position by change in Y
float f_HeightDiff;
f_HeightDiff  = fHeight + 0.3f - cam.m_vPos.Y;
cam.m_vView.Y += f_HeightDiff;
cam.m_vPos.Y  += f_HeightDiff;
}
```

The updates to the camera height belong at the end of the set_view_matrix() method where the camera view and position are adjusted:

```
set_camera_height();
```

The method that draws the terrain, draw_grid(), must be modified to draw solid terrain. The parameter for the primitive type in DrawIndexedPrimitives() must be changed from a LineStrip to a TriangleStrip:

```
PrimitiveType.TriangleStrip
```

Also, the new texture created in Terragen should be referenced in draw_grid(). Add an instruction to apply the terrain texture before the changes are committed to texture the terrain surface:

```
mfxTexture.SetValue(mTexTerrain);
```

When you run the program, your hills will appear, and as you move over them the camera will rise and fall with their elevation. As you can see, this impressive effect was created with very little effort. If you like the textures generated by the noncommercial version of Terragen, you should consider purchasing a license so you have the ability to create even larger image sizes and you can access more features.

CHAPTER 25 REVIEW EXERCISES

1. Implement the step-by-step demonstration discussed in this chapter.

2. Create your own height map. Load it into your application. To add detail, apply multitexturing to the terrain.

CHAPTER 26

Multiplayer Gaming

WE'RE sure you can appreciate the difference between playing video games against the computer and against your friends. Whether you're knocking baseballs over their heads, swerving in front of them to maintain a lead, or volleying rockets at them, it's all good. Most people have a lot more fun playing against an unpredictable human opponent who puts up a tough fight and trash talks while doing it.

Until now, the examples in this book have been geared for single-player games. You can easily change this by converting your base code to enable a multiplayer environment—where up to four people at a time can take the controls in a split-screen game. This type of environment is exactly what you would expect in a 3D first-person shooter game or a racing game.

You could actually split the screen into more than four sections, but the controller limit is four. You might want additional dimensions, though, if you were to show different views of the world. For example, maybe you want to create a radar screen with an aerial view of your entire world in addition to the main viewer for navigation. The split-screen technique offers many useful possibilities for dividing up the graphics that are rendered in your window.

For XNA projects, the split-screen technique is currently the only supported method for creating a multiplayer game. At the time of writing, XNA does not support networked games. You may be able to find a way to enable online networking for your PC-based games. Even so, a networked solution for your PC-based XNA games is not supported, and it may be potentially unsafe for your computer.

The code changes required to enable a split-screen game are surprisingly simple. The Viewport class makes it easy to split your screen. And if your camera is carefully designed, like it is in this book, you can easily create separate instances to give each additional player control over her own viewport.

VIEWPORT

A *viewport* is a section of the window that you use to draw a scene from a specific view. As you'll see, using the Viewport class to split the screen is actually very simple. The Viewport class is used to create a viewport object:

```
Viewport viewport = new Viewport();
```

Each viewport object has several properties to set the position and area covered in the game window. Each section of the window is assigned values for the starting top-left pixel, the width and height in pixels, and the depth for clipping:

```
int        viewport.X        // top left pixel X coordinate
int        viewport.Y        // top left pixel Y coordinate
int        viewport.Width    // width in pixels
```

```
int        viewport.Height    // height in pixels
float      viewport.MinDepth  // minimum depth of clip volume (usually 0)
float      viewport.MaxDepth  // maximum depth of clip volume (usually 1)
```

The bulk of the code changes needed to convert to a multiplayer game are in handling a separate instance of the camera for each player. However, even this task is relatively simple.

When your multiplayer games are rendered on the Xbox 360, your viewports may be truncated on the televisions where they are played. It is possible that up to 20% of the screen will be truncated. This issue can be addressed by implementing a routine to create margins that equal 10% of the window height at the top and bottom and 10% of the window width for the left and right. An example of how to do this is presented in the demonstration later in this chapter.

CREATING SEPARATE CAMERAS FOR EACH PLAYER

To give each user the ability to navigate through the world, a separate camera instance is required for each player. The camera instance gives the players the ability to change their position and view within the 3D world.

Adjusting the View

For the graphics engine used in this book, whenever a player moves the mouse or shifts the right thumbstick, he changes his view. In other words, his position in the world stays the same but his Look direction changes as his view target changes. A separate view is needed for each player in the game. For example, in a racing game you might need to focus your camera to watch the contours of a hairpin turn so you don't crash. Your friend might need to watch out for an oil slick to maintain control of the car, and yet another player might be focused on the finish line.

When you assign a separate viewport for each player, every object that is drawn in the viewport must be rendered according to that player's view. Even the base code, which draws nothing but ground, must draw the ground once for each viewport according to the viewport owner's Look direction.

To handle this need for separate views, you can store the View matrix in an array with a separate instance for each viewport owner. The example presented later in this chapter shows how to implement multiple views to accompany the separate viewports.

Adjusting the Projection

The Projection matrix transforms vector coordinates into clip space (a cone that the viewer sees through). If the viewport size changes, you must also adjust the projection to match. If you do not resize the perspective's aspect ratio properly, you could end up with a camera that displays everything in a bloated manner—as if the scene was either viewed through a fish-eye lens or in a house of mirrors. A properly defined aspect ratio parameter (width/height) in the Projection matrix will correct this.

The Projection matrix is defined with the following syntax:

```
// parameters are field of view, aspect ratio w/h, near clip, far clip
Matrix proj = Matrix.CreatePerspectiveFieldOfView(
          float fov, float aspect, float nearClip, float farClip)
```

If you divide the window into top and bottom viewports, the aspect ratio becomes this:

```
Window.ClientBounds.Width / (Window.ClientBounds.Height/2)
```

HANDLING THE USER INPUT

It is possible to have up to four game controllers, so you could write code to handle up to four different players and split the screen accordingly at run time. For the PC, you can even use the mouse and keyboard as one of these inputs. Handling the different controllers is easy with the GamePadState class because each controller is referenced by a separate instance of the class. The states for each control on the game pad can be obtained using the getNewState() method for each player's game pad.

SPLIT-SCREEN CODE EXAMPLE

This example demonstrates multiplayer 3D gaming in a split-screen environment. Two aliens will be rendered and controlled in two separate viewports. Each player has her own viewport and is given control of one alien's spaceship, which moves with her camera as she travels. Figure 26-1 shows a split-screen for two players. Each player can control her view and position inside the viewport and ultimately travel within the world independently of the other player.

A multiplayer racing game or first-person shooter game uses the same code foundation, so converting the logic to suit a different type of 3D multiplayer game is a simple task. Converting this logic to handle more than two players is straightforward.

When you run this code on the Xbox 360, you will be able to handle two players, each with her own controller. When the code is run on the PC, you can handle either two controllers, or one controller and a mouse/keyboard combination. If you run this code on the PC with only a mouse and keyboard, you will be able to control one of the viewports, but the other viewport will be disabled until a controller is connected.

This example begins with either the WinMGHBook or Xbox360MGHBook project, which can be found in the BaseCode folder in the download available from this book's website.

FIGURE 26-1

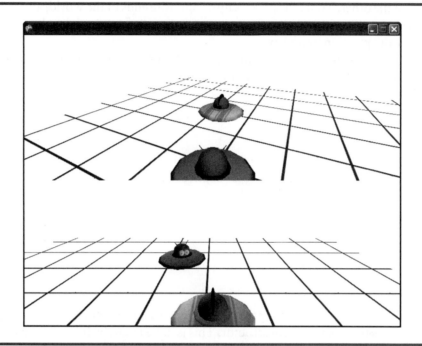

Two viewports for a two-player game. Each player controls her view of the world and can travel independently.

To enable a two-player game, and to identify each player, you declare the NUMPLAYERS, ALIEN1, and ALIEN2 definitions at the top of the game class:

```
const int NUMPLAYERS    = 2;
const int ALIEN1        = 0;    const int ALIEN2 = 1;
```

Also, to enable an independent view for each player, an array of view matrices is used to replace the existing View matrix at the start of the game class:

```
private Matrix[] mMatView = new  Matrix[NUMPLAYERS];
```

To give each player control to move through the 3D environment, and to allow them to view it independently, you declare an array with two separate instances for the camera. Use this revision to replace the existing camera object declaration:

```
private CCamera[]    cam = new CCamera[NUMPLAYERS];
```

When you're initializing each camera, the starting position and view position for each person needs to be different. Otherwise, with just a default position and view, when the game begins, the players would all be positioned in the same place, one on top of the other. To set the players up at opposite ends of the world, and to have them looking at their opponent, each instance of the camera is initialized with parameters to set the position and view.

An override to the camera constructor allows you to set the position and view of the camera when it is initialized for each player:

```
public CCamera(Vector3 v3Pos, Vector3 v3View)
{
    mfTimeLapse = 0;

    // set up view and position for each player
    m_vPos  = v3Pos;
    m_vView = v3View;

    // each player is upright
    m_vUp   = new Vector3(0.0f, 1.0f, 0.0f);
}
```

To initialize the camera for the players, you pass their individual starting positions and views to the camera constructor. This is done from the Initialize() method (in the game class) at the program start:

```
Vector3 v3Pos, v3View;
v3Pos  = new Vector3( 0.5f, 0.0f,  BOUNDARY - 0.5f);
v3View = new Vector3( 0.5f, 0.0f,  BOUNDARY - 1.0f);
cam[0] = new CCamera(v3Pos, v3View);

v3Pos  = new Vector3(-0.5f, 0.0f, -BOUNDARY + 0.5f);
v3View = new Vector3(-0.5f, 0.0f, -BOUNDARY + 1.0f);
cam[1] = new CCamera(v3Pos, v3View);
```

As mentioned earlier in this chapter, because both viewport heights are half the actual window height, the aspect ratio parameter in the Projection matrix must be adjusted. The aspect ratio for the projection becomes (width/(height/2)). To apply this to the Projection matrix, replace the code that initializes the Projection matrix in set_proj_matrix() with this revision:

```
// define what our lens sees
// parameters are field of view, aspect ratio, near clip, far clip
mMatProj = Matrix.CreatePerspectiveFieldOfView(
(float)Math.PI / 4.0f,
```

Multiplayer Gaming

```
(float)Window.ClientBounds.Width/((float)Window.ClientBounds.Height/2.0f),
0.005f, 1000.0f);
```

The changeView(), move(), strafe(), and draw_ground() methods inside the game class need to be modified so they can be used for each player. As a result, their headers must be adjusted to accept the player number, as follows:

```
Vector2   changeView(GameTime gameTime, int iPlayer)
float     move(int iPlayer)
float     strafe(int iPlayer)
void      draw_ground(int iPlayer)
```

The game pad is currently hard-coded to default to the first player with an index of 0. For this example, you require a more dynamic way to handle controller input. To fix this, in the changeView(), move(), and strafe() methods, replace each instance of mGamePadState[0] with an array instance that uses the player number as the index:

```
mGamePadState[iPlayer]
```

Also, to ensure that code for the mouse is executed on the PC when only one or zero controllers are connected, replace the else statement in changeView() with the following:

```
else if(iPlayer != 0)
```

The code inside set_view_matrix() must also change to handle each player's view. Each player is assigned her own view, so she can look out at the world in any direction she chooses. Replace set_view_matrix() with this new version to update the view for more than one player:

```
void set_view_matrix(GameTime gameTime)
{
    Vector2 v2View = new Vector2();

    for (int i = 0; i < NUMPLAYERS; i++){
        v2View       = changeView(gameTime, i);
        cam[i].changeView(v2View.X, v2View.Y);
        mMatView[i] = Matrix.CreateLookAt(
                    cam[i].m_vPos, cam[i].m_vView, cam[i].m_vUp);
    }
}
```

The code that sets the WorldViewProjection matrix inside draw_ground() must also be adjusted according to the player's view. This adjustment sets the WorldViewProjection matrix so it is drawn according to each viewport owner's view:

```
mfxTex_WVP.SetValue(mMatWorld * mMatView[iPlayer] * mMatProj);
```

Because each player has a separate instance of the camera, each camera must be updated separately; this gives the players the ability to travel independently in the game world. To enable this, inside Update(), replace the code that handles the time tracking, forward movement, backward movement, and strafing with this revision to update these values for each player:

```
for (int i = 0; i < NUMPLAYERS; i++)
{
    cam[i].set_frame_interval(gameTime);
    cam[i].move(move(i));
    cam[i].strafe(strafe(i));
}
```

When multiple viewports are used, each one is rendered separately. In effect, the same scene is drawn more than once. With careful planning, the same methods can be used for drawing your primitive objects and models. Add the drawScene() method to draw all objects in each viewport according to the view and perspective of each player:

```
void drawScene(int iPlayer)
{
    // clear screen, set background, start drawing
    gfx.GraphicsDevice.Clear(Color.CornflowerBlue);

    // begin shader - TexturedShader.fx
    mfxTex.Begin(SaveStateMode.SaveState);
    mfxTex.Techniques[0].Passes[0].Begin();

        // draw objects
        draw_ground(iPlayer);

    // end shader - TexturedShader.fx
    mfxTex.Techniques[0].Passes[0].End();
    mfxTex.End();
}
```

When the viewports are being drawn (while your code is run on the Xbox 360), it is possible that the full window may not be visible—it may fall outside the title-safe region. On some televisions, this nonvisible range may be as high as 20%. To adjust for this possibility, the starting top-left pixel that is used as the viewport should allow for this potential difference. Add the getTopViewport() and getBottomViewport() methods to calculate the starting top-left pixel for each viewport in this demonstration:

```
Vector2 getTopViewport()
{
    Vector2 v2px = new Vector2(0, 0);      // PC shows all pixels

    #if XBOX                               // if code run on Xbox 360
        const float kPercent = 0.2f;       // nonvisible region is 20%
        float fMargin = kPercent / 2;      // only draw inside margins
        v2px.X = (float)(fMargin * Window.ClientBounds.Width);
        v2px.Y = (float)(fMargin * Window.ClientBounds.Height);
    #endif

    return v2px;
}


Vector2 getBottomViewport(Vector2 v2TopLeft)
{
    // adjust render target starting Y pixel for PC and Xbox 360
    float fPercent = 0.5f;
    v2TopLeft.Y += ((float)Window.ClientBounds.Height * fPercent);
    return v2TopLeft;
}
```

In a multiplayer game, the Draw() method must trigger rendering of the entire scene for each viewport. Before drawing each viewport, you must set the top-left pixel where the viewport begins, the height and width properties for each viewport, and the clip minimum and maximum. If the clip minimum and maximum values are not set between 0 and 1, your 3D models may not appear with the proper depth.

Replace the existing Draw() method with this version to iterate through the rendering routine for each player and draw all objects in each viewport:

```
protected override void Draw(GameTime gameTime)
{
    Viewport viewport                     = new Viewport();
    gfx.GraphicsDevice.RenderState.CullMode = CullMode.None;

    Vector2 v2 = new Vector2(0.0f);

    for (int i = 0; i < NUMPLAYERS; i++){
        // get starting top left pixel for viewport
```

```
    if(i==0)                    // player1 is top view
        v2 = getTopViewport();
    else                        // player2 is bottom view
        v2 = getBottomViewport(v2);

    // assign viewport properties
    viewport.X        = (int)v2.X;                    // top left pixel X
    viewport.Y        = (int)v2.Y;                    // top left pixel Y
    viewport.Width    = Window.ClientBounds.Width;    // pixel width
    viewport.Height   = Window.ClientBounds.Height/2;// pixel height
    viewport.MinDepth = 0.0f;                         // set depth between
    viewport.MaxDepth = 1.0f;                         // 0 & 1 or 3D
                                                      // models won't
                                                      // look right

    // set the viewport for the graphics device
    gfx.GraphicsDevice.Viewport = viewport;
    drawScene(i);
  }
  base.Draw(gameTime);
}
```

If you ran the project now, you would see two viewports. Remember that this code can serve as a base for any multiplayer game.

To make this demonstration more interesting, two aliens will be added. Each player will be given control of an alien, which will be used as a third-person character. The alien will move with the camera. This not only allows each player to control her own spaceship, but also enables her to view the movements of her opponent in her own viewport.

For this example, you can use the alien models in the Models folder in the book's download. To do this, obtain the alien1.fbx, alien2.fbx, and spaceA.bmp files from the Models folder. Create a Models folder in your project and reference the .fbx files from the Solution Explorer.

To load these models and to control their transformations, declarations for the model objects and their bone transformation matrices are required at the top of the game class:

```
Model     mModAlien1;
Model     mModAlien2;
Matrix[]  mMatAlien1;
Matrix[]  mMatAlien2;
```

The code used to load these two models and their accompanying transformation matrices is contained in the init_aliens() method. To initialize the models, add this method to your game class:

```
void init_aliens()
{
    mModAlien1          = content.Load<Model>(".\\Models\\alien1");
    mMatAlien1          = new Matrix[mModAlien1.Bones.Count];
    mModAlien1.CopyAbsoluteBoneTransformsTo(mMatAlien1);

    mModAlien2          = content.Load<Model>(".\\Models\\alien2");
    mMatAlien2          = new Matrix[mModAlien2.Bones.Count];
    mModAlien2.CopyAbsoluteBoneTransformsTo(mMatAlien2);
}
```

To load the aliens when the program begins, add the call statement init_aliens() to the Initialize() method:

```
init_aliens();
```

For this two-player game, one alien and its spaceship are controlled by each player. Each alien's spaceship moves with the player's camera. To rotate the alien about the Y axis, so it always points in the direction it is traveling, use the following method to calculate the angle of direction based on the camera's Look direction:

```
float getRotationAngle(Vector3 v3View, Vector3 v3Pos)
{
    Vector3 v3Look = v3View - v3Pos;
    return (float)Math.Atan2((double)v3Look.X, (double)v3Look.Z);
}
```

To save on code, the same method is used to draw both aliens. When these items are rendered in a viewport, this method is called once for each model. This process is repeated for each player. For this example, alien1's position and angle of orientation is based on player1's camera. Alien2's position and orientation is based on player2's camera. The view is adjusted for each player. The rest of the routine is identical to the routines you have already used in this book for drawing models.

```
void drawAliens(Model model, int iModel, int iPlayer)
{
    float fYrotation = 0.0f;
```

```
foreach (ModelMesh mesh in model.Meshes){
    // 1: declare matrices
    Matrix matWorld,matIdent,matScale,matRotY,matTransl,matTransOrb;

    // 2: initialize matrices
    matIdent    = Matrix.Identity;
    matScale    = Matrix.CreateScale(0.5f, 0.5f, 0.5f);
    matTransl   = Matrix.CreateTranslation(Vector3.Zero);
    matRotY     = Matrix.CreateRotationY((float)Math.PI);
    matTransOrb = Matrix.CreateTranslation(0.0f, 0.0f, 1.0f);
    switch (iModel){
    case ALIEN1:
        matTransl   = Matrix.CreateTranslation(
                    cam[ALIEN1].m_vPos.X,-0.7f,cam[ALIEN1].m_vPos.Z);
        fYrotation = getRotationAngle(cam[ALIEN1].m_vView,
                    cam[ALIEN1].m_vPos);
        break;
    case ALIEN2:
        matTransl   = Matrix.CreateTranslation(
                    cam[ALIEN2].m_vPos.X,  -0.7f,
                    cam[ALIEN2].m_vPos.Z);
        fYrotation = getRotationAngle(cam[ALIEN2].m_vView,
                    cam[ALIEN2].m_vPos);
        break;
    }
    matRotY = Matrix.CreateRotationY(fYrotation);

    // 3: build cumulative world matrix using I.S.R.O.T. sequence
    // identity, scale, rotate, orbit(translate & rotate), translate
    matWorld = matIdent * matScale * matTransOrb * matRotY * matTransl;

    foreach (BasicEffect effect in mesh.Effects){
        // 4: pass wvp to shader
        effect.View = mMatView[iPlayer];
        switch (iModel){
            case ALIEN1:
                effect.World =
                mMatAlien1[mesh.ParentBone.Index]*matWorld;
                break;
            case ALIEN2:
```

```
                effect.World =
                mMatAlien2[mesh.ParentBone.Index]*matWorld;
                break;
        }
        effect.Projection = mMatProj;

        // 4b: set lighting
        effect.EnableDefaultLighting(); effect.CommitChanges();
    }
    // 5: draw object
    mesh.Draw();
    }
}
```

To draw each model, add these call statements to the end of the drawScene() method:

```
// draw 3D models
drawAliens(mModAlien2, ALIEN2, iPlayer);
drawAliens(mModAlien1, ALIEN1, iPlayer);
```

When you run this version of the code, each of the two players can control the movement of her alien separately. In addition, she can view her world and travel independently of the other player.

Being able to shift the view up and down might be useful for a first-person shooter game, but it doesn't look right for this setup. Inside set_view_matrix(), you can prevent the camera from bobbing up and down by modifying the change to the Y view so it is always zero:

```
cam[i].changeView(v2View.X, 0.0f);
```

Finally, to allow each player to see her spaceship out in front of the camera, you can add a tilt to the Y view so the camera looks downward. Inside the new camera constructor, add code to adjust the Y view:

```
m_vView.Y = -0.2f;
```

When you run the code now, each player will be able to control her view of the world. This example was kept simple, but you can apply this logic for different types of games, such as first-person shooter, racing, role-playing, or adventure games.

CHAPTER 26 REVIEW EXERCISES

1. Implement the step-by-step demonstration presented in this chapter.

2. Create a three-person viewport window. The first two viewports should split the top half of the window, and the third viewport should be located in the bottom half of the window. The user input should be handled in a way to permit up to three controllers. If the code is run on the PC, and fewer than three controllers are detected, the mouse and keyboard should be enabled for the third player. You will need to create a separate Projection matrix to permit proper viewing from each viewport.

Index

3D models
    introduction to, 164
    See also animated models, 3D;
        animation (*various*); car model, 3D;
        windmill model, 3D

A

ACT. *See* XNA Cross-Platform Audio
    Creation Tool (XACT)
animated models, 3D
    introduction to, 366
    .md2 data, overview of, 367–368
    Quake II format, discussion of,
        366–367
    See also 3D models; lamp model,
        animated; MilkShape; *Quake II*;
        Zarlag model

animation, basics of
    direction, calculating, 76–80
    identity matrix (for transforming
        objects), 66
    Math.Atan function, 77–78, 87
    Math.Atan2 function, 78–79, 87–88
    matrix logic (and World matrix),
        65–66
    moving-object orientation (using
        vectors), 79–80
    Right Hand Rule, 64–65
    rotation/translation matrices, 67
    scaling matrix (size), 67
    transformations, types of, 64
    trigonometric equations for, 76, 77
    See also animation examples, specific
        topics (e.g., ballistics; matrices;
        primitive objects; rotation/revolution;
        vectors; etc.)